MW00634850

2023

BARRON'S
THE TRUSTED NAME IN TEST PREP

AP®
Microeconomics/
Macroeconomics
PREMIUM

Elia Kacapyr, Ph.D,

James Redelsheimer, M.A, and

Frank Musgrave, Ph.D.

Dedication

To Carly, Grant, and Abby.
–JR

Acknowledgment

We would like to thank Jennifer Goodenough, our editor, for her wonderful guidance, patience, skill, and many hours of outstanding work in bringing this revised edition to publication.

Published by Kaplan North America, LLC d/b/a Barron's Educational Series
1515 West Cypress Creek Road
Fort Lauderdale, FL 33309
www.barronseduc.com

ISBN: 978-1-5062-9181-9

10 9 8 7 6 5 4 3 2 1

Kaplan North America, LLC d/b/a Barron's Educational Series print books are available at special quantity discounts to use for sales promotions, employee premiums, or educational purposes. For more information or to purchase books, please call the Simon & Schuster special sales department at 866-506-1949.

About the Authors

James Redelsheimer has over 20 years' experience teaching AP Economics at Armstrong High School in Plymouth, Minnesota. James is a Master Teacher with the Minnesota Council on Economics Education (MCEE) and is a Next Gen Personal Finance Teacher Fellow. He has been awarded the 3M Economics Educator Excellence Award and the Thrivent Financial Leadership Award from the Minnesota Council on Economic Education. He has been a guest lecturer in the economics department at Batumi State University in The Republic of Georgia and has taught Macroeconomics for Educators at The University of Minnesota. James has received travel grants and fellowships to visit and learn about the economies of Japan, China, Korea, Germany, Turkey, and Costa Rica.

Elia Kacapyr is a professor of economics at Ithaca College. He holds a B.A. in economics from the University of Maryland. His Ph.D. is from the Andrew Young School of Policy Studies at Georgia State University. Elia's fields are macroeconomic theory and econometrics. He has published numerous scholarly articles and three books, including *A Guide to Basic Econometric Techniques*.

Table of Contents

MICROECONOMICS

MACROECONOMICS

Visit Barron's Online Learning Hub for more full-length practice tests and vocabulary.

How to Use This Book

This book offers a comprehensive review of each of the 6 units and 4 big ideas aligned with the College Board's learning objectives for Microeconomics and Macroeconomics. Each section of the book is designed to prepare you for both exams by beginning with breaking down the disciplines and basics of economics.

Review and Practice

The book is broken down into two main parts: Microeconomics and then Macroeconomics, where specific content is explained by unit and by big idea. Following each chapter are practice questions that highlight specific content within that chapter. Both multiple-choice and free-response questions include stimuli, such as graphs and tables that aid with more difficult questions. All questions include fully answered explanations.

Practice Tests

Within the first section of the book, the Introduction, there is an opportunity to check your strengths and weaknesses by taking pretests for both AP Microeconomics and AP Macroeconomics. From there you have the opportunity to develop a solid study plan based on your results. At the end of each section, there are full-length practice tests for each course where you will find comprehensive answer explanations for all questions.

Online Practice

There are two full-length online practice exams—one for Microeconomics and one for Macroeconomics. You may take these exams in practice (untimed) mode or in timed mode. All questions include answer explanations. Also available as an online resource are helpful terms and their definitions by chapter for both Microeconomics and Macroeconomics. Use this book along with the Barron's Learning Hub for this additional resource.

For Students

This review book highlights the key topics in each of the 6 units for both AP Microeconomics and AP Macroeconomics. It explains them by giving content examples and offering hundreds of graph examples and tables to aid in understanding the most difficult of those topics. How you use the book depends on how your school offers the course. Nevertheless, by answering the review questions at the end of each chapter and by taking the practice tests, you will have an indication of how well you will do on the actual exams. Good luck!

For Teachers

Suggest to your students that they use this book along with other classroom resources to help them prepare for one exam or both exams.

Introduction

1

The AP Tests in Microeconomics and Macroeconomics

Learning Objectives

In this chapter, you will learn:
- → Where to find Micro and Macro
- → Multiple-choice questions
- → Answering strategies
- → Free-response questions

Introduction

Economics is a fascinating and enlightening subject that provides students with valuable insights to help understand the world and analyze complex issues while also helping one make better decisions and make the most of life. That being said, your most immediate concern is not likely solving global issues but preparing for the Advanced Placement (AP) Economics exam. Whether you are feeling extremely confident or in serious need of help preparing for the AP Economics exam, you have already made a wise economic decision by using this very book right now to prepare for the AP Economics exam. Like the tens of thousands of students around the world preparing for AP Economics exams this year (over 200,000 AP Economics exams are taken around the world every year), you may be feeling a bit overwhelmed by the extensive content in Economics, or thinking, "Where do I even begin to start studying?" Rest assured that in using this book, you have turned to a fantastic resource to study for the AP exam. This book will help you learn the essential content in a clear and concise format. It highlights the important material to know based on a careful analysis of past AP Economics exams and provides tips for success on either the AP Macroeconomics exam, AP Microeconomics exam, or both. It is clearly organized and written to help you focus on what you will actually be tested on and will prepare you for success for the AP Economics exam. In this book, you will find countless ways to practice for the AP exam and your class, including a pretest, a full-practice exam, practice multiple-choice and free-response questions at the end of every chapter, and a key graphs to know section. Every question in the book comes with a detailed explanation.

Microeconomics, Macroeconomics, or Both?

To make sure you are efficient with your review, let's make sure you are in the correct section of the book. Some students take both the AP Microeconomics and AP Macroeconomics tests, but others may just take one of these. Please see Table 1.1 for the correct chapters to focus on for your specific test(s). Following this chapter there are two 50-question multiple-choice pretests for both Micro and Macro. All questions come with complete answer explanations with the location in the book of the concept so you can review areas of weakness. At the end of the assessment you can also calculate your number correct and see a chart estimating what your AP exam score might be at this point. *Note:* The basic economics section is the same for both AP Microeconomics and Macroeconomics, so all students should study Chapters 1–4.

Table 1.1 What Chapters Should You Study?

Micro	Macro
Chapters 2–11, with a pretest, a full practice exam, key graphs summary, and practice questions at the end of each chapter	Chapters 2–4 and 12–19, with a pretest, a full practice exam, key graphs summary, and practice questions at the end of each chapter

The Tests: What Topics Will You See?

The College Board is very specific about what information will appear on the exams. For instance, an entire 55–70 percent of the AP Microeconomics exam is made up of the nature and function of product markets! Spending time studying product markets is obviously a smart decision. Table 1.2 shows the approximate percentage of the multiple-choice questions that will come from each content area, as stated by the College Board. For example, you can be assured that, as 55–70 percent of the AP Microeconomics exam is the nature and function of product markets, anywhere from 33 to 42 of the 60 multiple-choice questions on the exam will come from this content area. For more specific details about the exam topics, see Table 1.2. You will find the entire AP Microeconomics and Macroeconomics course outline on the College Board's website.

Table 1.2 Micro and Macro Exam Topics and Approximate Percentages (Multiple-Choice)

Micro	Macro
1. Basic Economics Concepts (12–15%) 2. Supply and Demand (20–25%) 3. Production, Cost, and the Perfect Competition Model (22–25%) 4. Imperfect Competition (15–22%) 5. Factor Markets (10–13%) 6. Market Failure and the Role of Government (8–13%)	1. Basic Economic Concepts (5–10%) 2. Economic Indicators and the Business Cycle (12–17%) 3. National Income and Price Determination (17–27%) 4. Financial Sector (18–23%) 5. Long-Run Consequences of Stabilization Policies (20–30%) 6. Open Economy–International Trade and Finance (10–13%)

On both AP Economics exams, two-thirds of your test grade comes from the multiple-choice section; the other third comes from the free-response questions (FRQs), with one long and two short questions (Table 1.3). More details and strategies for the multiple-choice and free-response questions are given later in this chapter.

Table 1.3 Exam Breakdown: Both Microeconomics and Macroeconomics

Section	Questions	Allotted Time
1. Multiple-choice questions (66.7% of final score)	60	70 minutes
2. Free-response questions (33.3% of final score)	1 long, 2 short FRQs	60 minutes

You may also be wondering what percent of questions one needs to answer correctly for a 4 or 5 on the exam. The AP Economics exam has a significant curve on it. In fact, only a handful of the 200,000-plus students who take the Economics exam every year get a perfect score! (If you do beat the odds and get a perfect score, you, your principal, and your teacher will receive a personalized letter of congratulations from the College Board on your achievement.) So now that we know that well over 99 percent of students will get at least one question wrong, you can see Table 1.4 for the minimum correct percent of correct answers you need to earn for different AP scores (1–5). Keep in mind that the averages may change slightly from year to year due to different test questions being used and variations in student performance.

**Table 1.4 Percent Correct Needed
on Exam for Different AP Scores:
Both Microeconomics and Macroeconomics**

AP Score	Minimum Correct Points Earned on Exam (%)
5	80
4	60
3	50
2	33
1	0

Multiple-Choice Questions

The first part of the AP Economics exam is the multiple-choice section. In this section, students are given 70 minutes to complete 60 questions. Each multiple-choice question works out to be 1.1 percent of your final AP exam grade, so every question is important. Even though students today have grown up in a era of standardized testing and have taken no shortage of multiple-choice tests, it's a good idea to refresh your skills or learn some new ideas in this section (some of which are directly relevant to the AP Economics exam). Here are some tips and suggestions:

1. **YOU'VE GOT 60 PROBLEMS, SO MAKE SURE RUNNING OUT OF TIME ISN'T ONE MORE.** Of the 60 questions, don't allow yourself to become stuck on or obsessed with one or two questions. Most students run out of time not because of the overall difficulty level but because of spending too much time on too few questions. If you don't know the answer, star it, and return to it later. The time limit works out to be around 70 seconds per question, yet no one question is worth more points than others. Of the two sections of the test, the multiple-choice part is the one that you must be most mindful of the time.

2. **WHEN IN DOUBT, GRAPH IT OUT.** You will definitely be required to draw graphs in the free-response section, but doing so can be very helpful in the multiple-choice section as well. A brief graph drawn in the margins can easily lead to the correct answers. For example, let's look at the following sample question:

   Which of the following changes in the demand for and the supply for widgets will definitely result in a decrease for both the equilibrium price and quantity of widgets?

	Supply	Demand
(A)	Increase	Increase
(B)	Increase	No change
(C)	No change	Decrease
(D)	Decrease	Increase
(E)	Decrease	Decrease

Trying to visualize all of those options can seem overwhelming; however, a well-prepared student could do a quick sketch of these supply and demand graphs. Graphing it out can easily clarify the correct answer. Even economic experts are fond of drawing out graphs to be sure of an answer. By the time a student has drawn option C, he or she will have identified the correct answer and can move on to the next question.

3. **NO QUESTION LEFT BEHIND.** Answer every question. There is no penalty for incorrect answers, only points for right ones. So if you have no clue about the answer, guess anyway. Each question will have five choices, and you at least have a 20 percent chance at getting it right.

4. **ABSOLUTELY NOT THE RIGHT CHOICE.** Be careful when dealing with a question that uses absolutes. Anytime a possible answer uses absolute words such as *always, never, rarely,* and *none,* that choice is usually not the correct one.

5. **STAY POSITIVE, BUT RECOGNIZE THE NEGATIVES.** Make sure to read every word of the question carefully. A common way test writers employ negatives is found in this sample question:

   The long-run growth rate of an economy will be increased by an increase in all of the following **except**

   (A) capital stock.
   (B) labor supply.
   (C) real interest rate.
   (D) rate of technological change.
   (E) spending on education and training.

   A student could possibly miss the word *except* at the end of the question and just put answer A, which would be correct if there was no *except*, and miss the correct answer, C. Another similar technique to confuse students is "which of the following is NOT . . ."

6. **DON'T BE INTIMIDATED BY A QUESTION'S LOOKS.** Some questions can look overwhelmingly difficult, but when approached correctly, they are usually less intimidating than their looks. Here is a sample of a question that can initially appear very difficult:

   An opportunity cost is entailed in which of the following situations?

   I. A student decides to attend college full-time.
   II. A family uses its $20,000 savings to purchase an automobile.
   III. A farmer decides to grow more wheat and less corn.

   (A) I only
   (B) II only
   (C) III only
   (D) I and III only
   (E) I, II, and III

Consider questions of this nature to be merely glorified true/false questions. Walk through all of the options, and cross out the false ones. In this case, all three are true, making E the correct answer. Here is another sample of a question type that can appear intimidating:

<u>**Economic Data (Millions of People)**</u>

Population	150
Labor force	100
Unemployed	10
Part-time workers	5

Based on the economic figures in the table above, what is the unemployment rate?

(A) 0%

(B) 5%

(C) 10%

(D) 15%

(E) 33%

Just because there are four different options under economic data does not mean all of them need to be calculated. In this case, a student should recognize that the unemployment rate is calculated by dividing the number of unemployed by the labor force. Hence, you can ignore two of the four options under economic figures, and a simple calculation gives you the correct answer, C.

Free-Response Questions

After the multiple-choice section and a short break, you move on to the free-response questions. This 60-minute section makes up one-third of your AP score. This section is comprised of one long question, worth about 16 percent of your final AP score, and two short questions, each worth about 8 percent. Try to use no more than 25 minutes for the long question and 12.5 minutes for each of the two short questions. Past students report that they are more likely to run out of time on the multiple-choice section as opposed to the free-response questions, so be sure to double-check all of your answers in the free-response section. Here are some general tips for success on both the AP Microeconomics and the AP Macroeconomics free-response questions.

1. **YOU GET SECOND CHANCES.** They don't come only in life but also on the AP Economics exam. A very important thing to know about the free-response questions is that even if you answer the first part of a question incorrectly, it is still possible to earn "consistency" points on other parts of the question related to the initial incorrect answer. To give you an example from a question similar to one on a recent AP Microeconomics exam, let's look at the monopoly graph in Figure 1.1. Students were asked to begin by identifying the profit-maximizing quantity for the monopolist. From there, students were asked to identify the price, total revenue, and total cost of production; all of these answers are based on the profit-maximizing quantity chosen at the beginning. If a student chooses the wrong quantity, technically all of the following answers will be wrong as well. However, if a student incorrectly identifies the wrong quantity of 25 (the correct answer is a quantity of 15 and a price of 40), he/she missed that point but is still eligible to get the other questions correct! The other answers are now based on the incorrect quantity of 25, which would result in different price, cost, and revenue answers that could be counted as correct. Despite this initial incorrect answer, several consistency points could be earned.

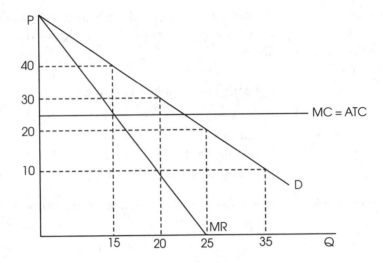

Figure 1.1 Free-Response Example: Sample Monopoly Graph

Here is another example of how students can earn consistency points despite a wrong answer, this time from the AP Macroeconomics exam: The question reads "*Interest rates increase in the United States relative to Japan. Based on this change, what will happen to the value of the U.S. dollar vs. the Japanese yen, and exports from the U.S. to Japan? Explain.*" The correct answer is that the demand for the U.S. dollar would increase, making the U.S. dollar appreciate in value vs. the yen. As the U.S. dollar appreciates vs. the yen, exports to Japan decrease, because U.S. goods are now relatively more expensive for the Japanese. However, if a student incorrectly claims the U.S. dollar depreciates, one point is taken off, but not all is lost. The student can still earn a consistency point by stating that exports to Japan would increase, based on the initial wrong answer of a depreciated U.S. dollar.

2. **MIND YOUR Ps AND Qs.** Always completely label your graphs. You are guaranteed to have to draw graphs on the free-response section, and you will get several points on the test for labeling your graphs correctly. At a minimum, this means putting the correct label on the *x*- and *y*-axes and all your curves. Also, be sure to show with an arrow when the curve shifts, and clearly identify any changes in price or quantity. For example, if the demand curve increases, leading to an increase in price, you could label the first curve D_1 and the new curve D_2, just like the graphs you will see in this book. The same goes for price and quantity, or any other item you are asked to label. Also, the graders of AP tests may take off points for not drawing dotted lines to the *x*- and *y*-axes to show price and quantity; be sure to do this. To be sure of how to correctly label a graph, see any graph in this book.

3. **SAVE THE FIVE-PARAGRAPH ESSAY FOR ANOTHER AP EXAM.** Being verbose, or using far more words than are required, is a common mistake students make. If a question asks you to identify a price or quantity, all that is required is to list the answer, (e.g., price of $5, quantity of 20). The amount of writing required for full credit on a question is actually quite minimal. See more information on what is required for a correct answer in item 5 below.

4. **A WELL-DRAWN GRAPH IS WORTH A THOUSAND WORDS.** OK, maybe not a thousand words, but it is worth a few points on the AP exam. AP graders are looking for specific labels and information when grading your exam, and a well-drawn, neat graph with correct shifts can clearly display your understanding of content. There are just a few graphs to memorize and know. Draw them neatly and clearly, and show your shifts. This will lead to success on the test.

5. **EXPLAIN? IDENTIFY? DRAW? SHOW?—WHAT ARE GRADERS LOOKING FOR?** Speaking from our vast experience as AP exam graders, you would be surprised at how many students know the content yet lose points because they either don't fully read the question or misunderstand what the question is asking.

Students should pay careful attention to understanding what the question is actually asking. Here are a few common phrases that often confuse students and an explanation of what is expected for full credit when asked.

- *Show your work.* Do exactly what it says here. For example, if you are asked to calculate profit on the AP Microeconomics exam and show your work, don't just say that total revenue minus total cost equals profit, which is $100. This will not suffice for credit (write out that $150 – $50 = $100). Plug in all the numbers, and show all of your work.

- *Explain.* You may not always be asked for an explanation, but be sure to give one if asked. Even if you have the correct answer, no point will be given if the explanation is missing. This is when you should write a whole sentence or two. Here is an example question: "*What happens to economic growth if real interest rates decrease? Explain.*" You will not receive full credit by merely stating that economic growth will increase because interest rates decreased. A correct answer for full credit would say: "*Economic growth will increase, because lower real interest rates will lead to increased investment and capital formation.*" Explain your whole line of reasoning, such as this answer does. **Note:** If the question does not ask you to explain, it's not required for credit.

- *Identify or determine.* When you see these words, graders are expecting a straightforward answer that requires little writing. The question may ask you to identify the price, quantity, or profit.

- *Draw or show.* This is when graders are looking for a graph or a change on a graph. A question using these words may look like this: "*Draw a correctly labeled loanable-funds graph, and show how an increase in government borrowing affects the real interest rate on the graph.*" Here a student should label all axes and curves, and clearly show all shifts with arrows.

- *Calculate.* When a question asks you to calculate, it is asking you for a specific number, not just an area on a graph. Let's assume a correct calculation is $3 \times 100 = 300$. If you set up the problem correctly but mistakenly write the wrong answer, you may still get credit! For example, if you write $3 \times 100 = 400$, you will likely still receive credit by setting up the problem correctly with 3×100.

Here are a few other tips and reminders going into the AP Economics exam's free-response section:

- Be sure to practice free-response questions in this book. The questions in this book have been carefully developed to be similar to what you can expect to see on the actual exam.

- Be neat and organized. AP Economics graders are looking for specific words, numbers, or labels on a graph, and clear, legible answers will help your cause. Also, clearly label the question number you are answering. If you are answering question 2(ii), label it as such before your answer.

- Memorize the various graph labels and curves. You will get several points just by labeling your graphs correctly. There are only a few graphs to know for both the Microeconomics and Macroeconomics exams. Know them well.

- Don't repeat the question in your answer.

- Write your answers in the correct designated answer section. AP graders are instructed not to grade answers written in the wrong section. You would be surprised how many times students lose points for writing their answers or drawing graphs in the wrong section of the answer booklet. The location of the test booklet designated for answers is clearly labeled, but always double-check.

Here are some tips that are specific to either the Microeconomics or Macroeconomics free-response questions.

Microeconomics Free-Response

- Know the four market structures. The long free-response question frequently asks students about one of these three market structures: perfect competition, monopoly, and monopolistic competition. The fourth, oligopoly, has been frequently asked about in one of the short questions, applying game theory.

- The other two short questions can come from a wide range of topics from the course outline. Common past topics for these questions in recent years have included labor markets, externalities, accounting vs. economic profit, utility maximization, elasticity, natural monopolies, price ceilings/floors, tax incidence, and allocative and productive efficiency. Please note that any topic from the course outline could potentially be asked in this section.

Macroeconomics Free-Response

- Know the Big 5 graphs. When you have to draw a graph, most likely it will be one of the Big 5. They are aggregate supply and demand, the Phillips curve, the money market, the loanable funds market, and the foreign exchange market.
- Of the Big 5, the one that almost always appears is the aggregate supply and demand graph.
- Question number 1 (the long one) almost always starts by asking students to draw an economy either at full employment, in a recession, or with inflation using the aggregate supply and demand model. It then moves on by asking for an appropriate monetary or fiscal policy for the situation. It will usually ask students to draw a second graph as well, likely the Phillips curve, the loanable funds market, or the money market.
- The other two short questions can come from a wide range of topics from the course outline. Common past topics for these questions in recent years have included comparative advantage and terms of trade, nominal vs. real interest rates, the foreign exchange market, banking money expansion using the money multiplier, gross domestic product, price indexes, and the balance of payments. Please note that any topic from the course outline could potentially be asked in this section.

Table 1.5 Supplies

Items to Bring to the Exam
■ No. 2 pencils (for multiple-choice answers)
■ Black or dark-blue ballpoint pens (for free-response answers)
■ Four-function calculator

Practice, Practice, Practice

Now that you have all the information and strategies for the exams in AP Economics, be sure to use them whenever you do the practice exercises at the end of each chapter, the practice exams in the book, and, of course, when you take the actual tests. Don't forget to review the many helpful Microeconomics and Macroeconomics terms available online to help with your studying.

Microeconomics Pretest

Answer each question or complete each statement with the correct letter. To get a true assessment of your strengths and weaknesses, do not look up any hints or answers. At the end of the assessment, calculate your number correct out of 50 and you will see a chart estimating what your AP exam score might be at this point.

1. Which of the following would NOT be considered a characteristic of a market or capitalistic economy but that of a command or communist economy?

   (A) Protection of private property
   (B) Negative externalities
   (C) The price system to allocate resources
   (D) Competition among firms
   (E) Centralized decision making

   Use this graph for question 2.

   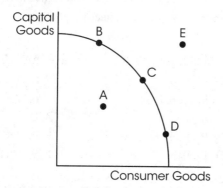

2. In the graph above, which movement would show a movement from inefficiency to efficiency?

   (A) B to C
   (B) C to B
   (C) C to E
   (D) A to C
   (E) C to A

3. According to the law of comparative advantage, the U.S. should specialize production in _____ and Germany should specialize production in _____.

   (A) peanuts; neither good
   (B) peanuts; oranges
   (C) oranges; oranges
   (D) oranges; peanuts
   (E) oranges; neither good

Tons of peanuts and oranges produced in a day:		
	Peanuts	Oranges
U.S.	20	60
Germany	10	20

4. The table shows the quantity of chocolate candy bars consumed and the total utility. In eating which candy bar would the consumer begin to experience diminishing marginal utility?

Number of Candy Bars Consumed	Total Utility
1	5
2	12
3	20
4	26
5	30
6	32

   (A) 1st
   (B) 2nd
   (C) 3rd
   (D) 4th
   (E) 5th

5. Assume Ahmed spends all his income on two goods: pizza and video games. The current cost of pizza is $6 and of video games is $20, and at his consumption level the marginal utility from eating pizza is 18 and from playing video games is 40. In order to maximize his utility, Ahmed should

   (A) consume more pizza and buy fewer video games.
   (B) buy more video games and consume less pizza.
   (C) consume more of both.
   (D) consume less of both.
   (E) keep consumption at his current level.

6. Assume a friend offers to give you a "free" ticket to a local professional baseball team's game that night. You decide to attend the game. The game takes five hours and costs you $15 for transportation. If you had not attended the game, you would have worked 5 hours at your part-time job for $8 an hour. What is the opportunity cost to you of attending the game?

   (A) $0
   (B) $23
   (C) $40
   (D) $55
   (E) $65

7. Which of the following would shift the demand curve for avocados to the right?

   (A) A decrease in the price of a complementary good for avocados
   (B) An increase in productivity of avocado farmers
   (C) A decrease in the price of avocados
   (D) A decrease in the price of a substitute for avocados
   (E) The imposition of a price floor in the avocado market

Use the following graph for questions 8 and 9.

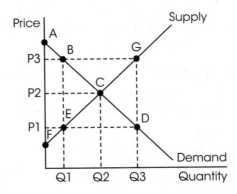

8. Assume the perfectly competitive market shown above is in equilibrium, but then the government adds a price ceiling at P_1. With the price ceiling in effect, please choose the correct area of the consumer surplus and deadweight loss.

Consumer Surplus	Deadweight Loss
(A) P_2, A, B	E, C, D
(B) P_1, A, B, E	E, B, C
(C) A, C, F	A, D, P_1
(D) P_1, P_3, B, E	E, B, D
(E) P_1, E, F	P_1, P_3, B, E

9. Assume the perfectly competitive market shown above is in equilibrium, but then the government adds a price floor at P_3. With the price floor in effect, please choose the correct area of the consumer surplus and deadweight loss.

Consumer Surplus	Deadweight Loss
(A) F, A, C	B, C, G
(B) P_2, A, C	E, C, D
(C) P_3, A, B	E, B, C
(D) A, B, E, F	E, B, D
(E) P_1, P_3, B, E	E, B, C

10. If the supply of good X decreases and this leads to an increase in both the price and quantity for good Y, which of the following is true?

(A) Good Y is a substitute for good X.
(B) Good Y is a complement of good X.
(C) Good Y is an inferior good.
(D) Good Y is a normal good.
(E) Good X is independent of good Y.

Please use this graph for question 11.

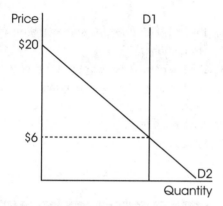

11. According to the graph, what combination below best describes the elasticity of demand curves D1 and D2 at a price of $6?

	Demand Curve D1	**Demand Curve D2**
(A)	Perfectly elastic	Perfectly elastic
(B)	Relatively elastic	Relatively elastic
(C)	Perfectly elastic	Perfectly inelastic
(D)	Relatively inelastic	Relatively elastic
(E)	Perfectly inelastic	Relatively inelastic

12. SPAM (meat in a can) is considered an inferior good and grapes are a normal good. If consumers' income decreases, what would an economist predict to happen to the price and quantity of these two goods?

	SPAM		Grapes	
	Price	**Quantity**	**Price**	**Quantity**
(A)	Unchanged	Increase	Decrease	Decrease
(B)	Increase	Increase	Decrease	Decrease
(C)	Decrease	Increase	Unchanged	Increase
(D)	Decrease	Decrease	Unchanged	Increase
(E)	Increase	Increase	Increase	Increase

Use the following graph for question 13.

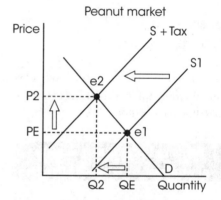

13. The graph shows a market in equilibrium at P_E and Q_E. Then the government imposes an excise tax on peanuts, with supply shifting to the left at P_2, Q_2. What will happen to each of the following after the imposition of the sales tax?

	Producer Surplus	**Consumer Surplus**	**Total Surplus**
(A)	Increase	Increase	Increase
(B)	Decrease	Decrease	Decrease
(C)	Increase	Decrease	Increase
(D)	Decrease	Increase	Increase
(E)	Decrease	Increase	Decrease

14. If a 10% increase in the price of a good leads to a 5% decrease in the quantity demanded of that good, demand is

    (A) perfectly elastic.
    (B) relatively elastic.
    (C) unit elastic.
    (D) relatively inelastic.
    (E) perfectly inelastic.

15. Assume the elasticity of demand for fidget spinners is 4. A 20 percent decrease in the price causes the quantity demanded for fidget spinners to increase by

    (A) 5%.
    (B) 20%.
    (C) 40%.
    (D) 80%.
    (E) 160%.

16. This table shows the total production of widgets with different numbers of workers used. Which of the following is true?

Number of workers	Total widgets produced per day
1	5
2	15
3	26
4	34
5	40
6	45

    (A) Marginal product is greatest at 6 workers.
    (B) Diminishing marginal returns begin with the 2nd worker.
    (C) At 6 workers, both marginal and total product equal 45.
    (D) The firm should hire 6 workers to maximize profit.
    (E) Diminishing marginal returns begin with the 4th worker.

17. This graph best depicts which of the following concepts?

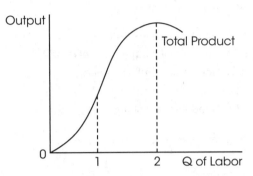

    (A) The law of diminishing marginal returns in production
    (B) The law of increasing opportunity cost
    (C) The law of diminishing marginal utility in consumption
    (D) Absolute advantage
    (E) Economies of scale

Use this chart for questions 18 and 19.

Output	Total Cost
0	5
1	20
2	30
3	38
4	50
5	65
6	85

18. What is the marginal cost of producing the 5th unit of output?

    (A) 5
    (B) 10
    (C) 13
    (D) 15
    (E) 20

19. What is the total variable cost of producing the 4th unit of output?

    (A) 5
    (B) 12
    (C) 12.5
    (D) 45
    (E) 50

20. If a company has an average total cost of $100 and a marginal cost of $90 at the 4th unit of output, then which of the following must be true?

    (A) The average total cost of producing the 3rd unit is less than $100.
    (B) The average total cost of producing the 3rd unit is more than $100.
    (C) The average fixed cost curve is increasing as production moves from 3 to 4 units.
    (D) The average variable cost of producing the 4th unit is more than $100.
    (E) The marginal cost curve has intersected the average total cost curve before the 4th unit.

21. Fields' Flour Corporation can produce 500 units of output a day employing 40 workers and 10 robots. Which of the following combinations correctly shows constant returns to scale?

	Workers	Robots	Units of Output
(A)	20	10	250
(B)	40	5	250
(C)	80	20	1,000
(D)	80	10	1,000
(E)	80	40	1,000

22. This graph shows a perfectly competitive market. Which of the following statements are true at the firm's profit-maximizing level of output?

    I. The firm is incurring economic losses.
    II. The firm is earning economic profits.
    III. The firm is earning a normal profit.
    IV. Price is greater than ATC.
    V. Firms will exit the industry.

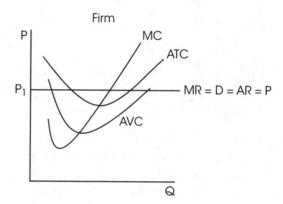

    (A) I and II
    (B) I, III, and V
    (C) II and IV
    (D) I, II, and IV
    (E) I, III, and V

23. If a firm is experiencing diseconomies of scale, which of the following is correct?

    (A) Long-run average total costs are increasing as output increases.
    (B) Long-run average total costs are decreasing as output increases.
    (C) Firms will enter the industry if firms are experiencing diseconomies of scale.
    (D) The firm is incurring economic losses.
    (E) Long-run average total costs remain constant as output increases.

24. Jacob was a corporate lawyer, who quit his job to open a yoga studio. His income as a lawyer was $100,000, and he earned $60,000 as a yoga studio entrepreneur. He also took $10,000 of his savings out of his bank savings account to invest in his business, where he was earning 10% interest. What is Jacob's economic profit from his yoga studio?

    (A) −$41,000
    (B) −$40,000
    (C) $40,000
    (D) $60,000
    (E) $70,000

25. Why do perfectly competitive firms earn zero economic profit in the long run?

    (A) Perfectly competitive firms have lower costs than other market structures.
    (B) Perfectly competitive firms have more technological innovation than other market structures.
    (C) Perfectly competitive firms have higher start-up costs than other market structures.
    (D) It is difficult for other firms to enter and exit a perfectly competitive industry.
    (E) It is easy for other firms to enter and exit a perfectly competitive industry.

26. At a production level of zero, ABC Corporation has a total cost of $10. The marginal cost of producing the first unit is $40, and the marginal cost of producing the second unit is $20. What is the total average cost of producing two units?

    (A) $15
    (B) $20
    (C) $35
    (D) $60
    (E) $70

27. Which of the following is NOT a characteristic of a perfectly competitive firm?

    (A) It should shut down if price is less than average variable cost where marginal revenue = marginal cost.
    (B) In long-run equilibrium, it is allocatively efficient but not productively efficient.
    (C) It is a price taker.
    (D) Demand, marginal revenue, and average revenue are all equal.
    (E) There are low barriers to entry into the market.

28. In which of the following market structures are mutual interdependence and game theory used to describe how firms relate to one another?

    (A) Oligopoly
    (B) Monopoly
    (C) Monopolistic competition
    (D) Perfect competition
    (E) Both monopoly and oligopoly

29. In a monopoly that practices perfect price discrimination, which of the following is correct regarding the demand curve, marginal revenue curve, and consumer surplus?

    (A) Demand > marginal revenue and consumer surplus is negative.
    (B) Demand > marginal revenue and consumer surplus is positive.
    (C) Demand > marginal revenue and consumer surplus is zero.
    (D) Demand = marginal revenue and consumer surplus is positive.
    (E) Demand = marginal revenue and consumer surplus is zero.

Use this graph for questions 30, 31, and 32.

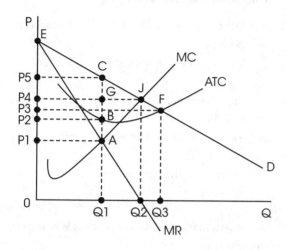

30. Assume the monopoly in the graph is producing at the profit-maximizing level of output. Choose the correct combinations of price, quantity, and deadweight loss.

Price and Quantity	Consumer Surplus	Deadweight Loss
(A) P_4, Q_2	P_4, E, J	A, G, J
(B) P_4, Q_2	G, C, J	A, G, J
(C) P_5, Q_1	P_5, E, C	G, C, J
(D) P_5, Q_1	P_5, E, C	A, C, F
(E) P_3, Q_3	P_3, E, F	A, C, F

31. Assume the monopoly in the graph is producing at the point where it maximizes total revenue. Choose the correct combinations of price, quantity, and deadweight loss.

Price and Quantity	Consumer Surplus
(A) P_3, Q_3	P_3, E, J
(B) P_3, Q_3	G, C, J
(C) P_4, Q_2	P_5, E, C
(D) P_4, Q_2	P_4, P_5, C, G
(E) P_4, Q_2	P_4, E, J

32. Assume the monopoly in the graph is producing at the profit-maximizing level of output. What is the area of economic profit?

(A) P_4, G, B, P_2
(B) 0, P_5, C, Q_1
(C) P_2, P_5, C, B
(D) P_1, P_5, C, A
(E) P_2, E, C, B

33. Which of the following is true for monopolistically competitive firms in long-run equilibrium?

(A) They are price takers.
(B) Their demand curves are equal to the marginal revenue curves.
(C) There are positive economic profits
(D) There are high barriers for firms to enter the market.
(E) They sell similar but differentiated products.

Use the game theory matrix here for questions 34 and 35.

		Kevin's Kicks	
		High	Low
Tommy's Tennies	High	$50, $45	$40, $50
	Low	$35, $35	$30, $20

34. In a small town there are only two shoe sellers, Tommy's Tennies and Kevin's Kicks. They are both trying to decide whether to price high or low. The first number in each box refers to the daily profit for Tommy's Tennies, and the second number refers to Kevin's daily profit. Based on the numbers in the game theory matrix, which of the following is true?

(A) Pricing high is a dominant strategy for Tommy's Tennies.
(B) Pricing high is a dominant strategy for Kevin's Kicks.
(C) Pricing low is a dominant strategy for Tommy's Tennies.
(D) Pricing low is a dominant strategy for Kevin's Kicks.
(E) Neither firm has a dominant strategy.

35. In a small town there are only two shoe sellers, Tommy's Tennies and Kevin's Kicks. They are both trying to decide whether to price high or low and know all the information in the payoff matrix. The first number in each box refers to the daily profit for Tommy's Tennies, and the second number refers to Kevin's daily profit. Based on the numbers in the game theory matrix, what is the Nash equilibrium?

Tommy's Tennies	**Kevin's Kicks**
(A) High	High
(B) High	Low
(C) Low	Low
(D) Low	High
(E) There is no Nash equilibrium.	

36. Which of the following correctly describes monopolistically competitive firms in long-run equilibrium? (D = demand, MR = marginal revenue, MC = marginal cost, ATC = average total cost.)

    (A) MR = MC, P > ATC, D > MR
    (B) MR > MC, P = ATC, D = MR
    (C) MR = MC, P < ATC, D < MR
    (D) MR < MC, P = ATC, D > MR
    (E) MR = MC, P = ATC, D > MR

37. If the regulators of a natural monopoly mandate the price to be set where price = average total cost, what best describes this situation?

    (A) The firm is pricing at the socially optimal price.
    (B) The firm is pricing at the fair-return price.
    (C) The firm is pricing at the unregulated price.
    (D) The firm is producing an output level where MR = MC.
    (E) The firm is realizing economic profits.

38. Why do most governments in market economies enforce antitrust laws?

    (A) To ensure oligopolies don't have monopoly power
    (B) To prevent too much competition in an industry
    (C) To ensure natural monopolies price at the socially optimal level of output
    (D) To ensure oligopolies reach a Nash equilibrium
    (E) To prevent price ceilings from being imposed on a market

39. A worker's marginal revenue product is best described as

    (A) the total revenue a firm makes when selling a product.
    (B) the change to a firm's revenue when employing an additional worker.
    (C) the change to a firm's profit when employing an additional worker.
    (D) the total amount of a firm's labor costs.
    (E) the change in resource cost divided by total revenue.

40. Assume a perfectly competitive labor market is initially in equilibrium with a downsloping demand curve and an upsloping supply curve. If the government then sets a binding minimum wage, which of the following is correct?

    (A) There would be a shortage in the labor market.
    (B) The quantity of labor supplied would be greater than the quantity of labor demanded.
    (C) The number of workers hired would remain the same.
    (D) The number or workers hired would increase.
    (E) The market would remain in equilibrium regardless of the wage paid.

Use this chart for question 41.

Number of Workers	Bushels of Apples
1	15
2	32
3	38
4	43
5	45
6	46

41. Assuming both perfectly competitive labor and product markets, if a bushel of apples sells for $10 and each hired worker costs $20, how many workers should be hired to maximize profits?

(A) 2
(B) 3
(C) 4
(D) 5
(E) 6

42. Assume a firm producing computer screens uses only two inputs in the production process, labor and robots. The price of a robot is $100 per unit, and labor is $20 per unit. At current output levels, the robot's marginal product is 1,000 and labor's is 100. In order to lower total production costs, how should the firm change its use of labor and robots?

Labor	Robots
(A) Increase	Decrease
(B) Increase	Increase
(C) Decrease	Decrease
(D) Decrease	Increase
(E) No change	Increase

Use this graph for question 43.

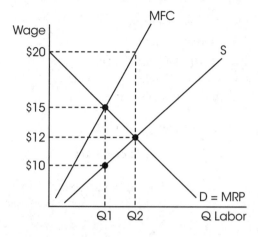

43. According to this labor market graph, what is the quantity and wage paid for both a monopsony and a perfectly competitive labor market?

	Perfectly Competitive Market	Monopsony
(A)	Q_2, $12	Q_1, $10
(B)	Q_2, $20	Q_1, $15
(C)	Q_1, $15	Q_1, $20
(D)	Q_1, $20	Q_1, $12
(E)	Q_2, $12	Q_1, $20

44. This table shows the total product for a perfectly competitive firm. If the product sells for $10, what is the marginal revenue product for the 4th worker hired?

Number of Workers	Total Product
1	10
2	30
3	44
4	54
5	60
6	64

(A) $10
(B) $27
(C) $40
(D) $54
(E) $100

45. Which of the following is the best example of a pure public good?

    (A) National defense
    (B) Internet service
    (C) Garbage pick-up services
    (D) A publicly funded sports stadium
    (E) The U.S. Postal Service

Use this graph for question 46.

Flu Shot Market

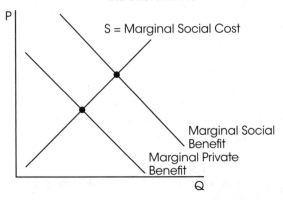

46. Which of the following is true based on the graph?

    (A) Producers should have a per-unit tax imposed to allow for production at the socially optimal output level.
    (B) The marginal private benefit is greater than the marginal social benefit at the free-market output level.
    (C) Producers should be given a per-unit subsidy to allow for production at the socially optimal output level.
    (D) There are no externalities present at the free-market quantity.
    (E) At the socially optimal quantity, marginal private benefit is greater than the marginal social benefit.

Use this graph for question 47.

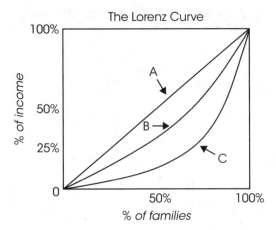

47. Which of the following is true based on this graph, where lines A, B, and C each represent a country?

    (A) Country A has more income inequality than B or C.
    (B) Country B has more income inequality than A or C.
    (C) Country C has more income inequality than A or B.
    (D) Countries A, B, and C all have an equal amount of income inequality.
    (E) Country A has income inequality but less than B and C.

48. Clearing lakes and waterways of pollution will result in increased efficiency if

    (A) the marginal social cost is greater than the marginal social benefit.
    (B) the marginal social benefit is greater than the marginal social cost.
    (C) the marginal social cost is positive.
    (D) the marginal external benefit is less than the marginal social cost.
    (E) companies that pollute are given a per-unit subsidy.

49. If residents of a city oppose a new highway being built through local neighborhoods, what economic concept best describes their opposition?

   (A) Free-rider problem
   (B) Economic rent
   (C) Private goods
   (D) Monopolies
   (E) Externalities

50. Of the following, which is the best representation of a positive externality?

   (A) Enjoying the beauty of a neighbor's meticulously cared for flowers
   (B) Using high-speed Internet access
   (C) Paying for a ticket to a sporting event
   (D) Being disturbed from a neighbor's loud music
   (E) Getting a car ride from a friend

Pretest AP Score Estimate

When you have finished, calculate the number correct out of 50 and compare it to the chart for a rough estimate of what your AP exam score might be at this point.

AP Microeconomics Score Estimator	
Pretest Score	**AP Score**
40–50	5
33–39	4
25–32	3
17–24	2
0–16	1

Study Guide for the Pretest

Note the questions you missed. Each correct response is followed by the chapter and section that covers the material for answering the question correctly. Concentrate your efforts on these chapters.

Each correct response has an explanation. If you do not understand the explanation, it means you have significant review work in that chapter before you are ready for the exam.

Answer Explanations

1. **(E)** (Chapter 3) A command economy is reliant on central planners to make decisions about production and prices. Market economies rely on prices to allocate resources, the protection of private property, and competition.

2. **(D)** (Chapter 2) Producing anywhere on the production possibilities curve is considered efficient. Inside the curve is inefficient, and you cannot get outside the curve to point E with current resources, only with future economic growth.

3. **(D)** (Chapter 2, Comparative Advantage) Nations should export the good in which they hold the comparative advantage. Comparative advantage means having the lower opportunity cost in production. As this is an output problem, to calculate the opportunity cost of the U.S. of producing peanuts, take the U.S. oranges number (60) and put it over the peanuts number (20). This makes 60/20, or a per-unit opportunity cost of 3 oranges given up when a peanut is produced.

	Peanuts	Oranges
U.S.	20	60
Germany	10	20

Calculation of Opportunity Costs

U.S.

Opportunity cost of making a unit of peanuts = 60/20 = 3 oranges

Opportunity cost of making a unit of oranges = 20/60 = 1/3 peanuts

Germany

Opportunity cost of making a unit of peanuts = 20/10 = 2 oranges

Opportunity cost of making a unit of oranges = 10/20 = 1/2 peanuts

Germany has the comparative advantage in peanuts: the per-unit opportunity cost is 2 oranges for Germany vs. 3 oranges for the U.S..

The U.S. has the comparative advantage in oranges: the per-unit opportunity cost is 1/2 peanuts for Germany vs. 1/3 peanuts for the U.S..

Therefore, the U.S. should produce oranges and Germany peanuts.

4. **(D)** (Chapter 2, Marginal Analysis and Consumer Choice) Here marginal utility is calculated as the change in total utility. As you can see in the added marginal utility column, it starts to decrease when eating the 4th candy bar as it falls from 8 to 6. Up until this time, it was increasing.

Number of Candy Bars Consumed	Total Utility	Marginal Utility
1	5	5
2	12	7
3	20	8
4	26	6
5	30	4
6	32	2

5. **(A)** (Chapter 5, Marginal Analysis and Consumer Choice) The utility-maximization formula is $MU_X/P_X = MU_Y/P_Y$. Here it's $18/\$6 \neq 40/\$20$, as 3 pizzas > 2 video games. His marginal utility per dollar spent is higher for pizza than video games. Therefore, to maximize his utility, he should buy more pizza and fewer games. Diminishing marginal utility sets in as more pizza is consumed and the numbers will eventually equal out.

6. **(D)** (Chapter 2, Opportunity Cost) When calculating the opportunity cost, you need to consider both the explicit cost (cab fare, $15) plus the implicit cost ($40 of lost wages) for the total opportunity cost of $55.

7. **(A)** (Chapter 4, Demand) The demand increases for a good when the price of a good's complement decreases. For example, if salsa and avocados are complements, when salsa goes down in price the demand shifts right for avocados. C is incorrect as this is a change in quantity demanded, not demand. A change in quantity demanded is just a price change in the market with a move along a fixed demand curve.

8. **(B)** (Chapter 5, Price Ceiling) The binding price ceiling puts the price at P_1. At this price there is a shortage, as buyers want to buy a quantity of Q_3, but sellers are only going to offer Q_1 for sale at P_1, so this is the quantity sold. The consumer surplus will be P_1, A, B, E, which are all left of Q_1. The deadweight loss used to be both consumer and producer surpluses at the previous equilibrium, but the loss is now E, C, B.

9. **(C)** (Chapter 5, Price Floor) The binding price floor puts the price at P_3. At this price there is a surplus, as sellers want to offer Q_3 for sale, but buyers are going to consume less at a higher price, so the quantity sold in the market is now Q_1. So, the consumer surplus shrinks to P_3, A, B, which are all left of Q_1. The deadweight loss used to be both consumer and producer surpluses at the previous equilibrium, but the loss is now E, C, B.

10. **(A)** (Chapter 4, Demand) As the supply of good X decreases, the price would increase, and the quantity sold would decrease. This results in an increase in demand for good Y, which means X and Y are substitute goods. People want to buy more of Y as X increases in price.

11. **(E)** (Chapter 5, Elasticity of Demand) A vertical curve like D_1 is perfectly inelastic. Consumers will buy the same quantity regardless of a change in price. For a downsloping curve with a 45-degree angle like D_2, the lower half of the curve is the relatively inelastic portion. The upper half is the relatively elastic portion, and the midpoint of the curve is unit elastic.

12. **(B)** (Chapter 5, Normal vs. Inferior Goods) With an inferior good, there's an indirect relationship between income and demand. When income falls, demand increases and shifts right, thus increasing price and quantity. With a normal good, there's a direct relationship between income and demand. As income falls, the demand decreases and shifts left for a normal good, decreasing price and quantity.

13. **(B)** (Chapter 5, Taxation) When the tax is imposed, the supply curve shifts left by the amount of the tax. This creates a new higher price at P_2, reducing consumer surplus. Sellers receive a higher price but must pay the sales tax to the government and sell less quantity, so their after-tax revenue is less, decreasing producer surplus. Thus, total surplus also decreases.

14. **(D)** (Chapter 5, Elasticity of Demand) To calculate the elasticity of demand, use the elasticity of demand formula: $0.05/0.1 = 0.5$. As this is less than 1, demand is relatively inelastic.

$$\frac{\%\Delta \text{ Quantity Demanded}}{\%\Delta \text{ Price}}$$

Elasticity Coefficient Value

Type of Elasticity	Elasticity Value
Relatively Elastic	> 1
Perfectly Elastic	∞ (infinity)
Relatively Inelastic	< 1
Perfectly Inelastic	$= 0$
Unit Elastic	$= 1$

15. **(D)** (Chapter 5, Elasticity of Demand) Take the elasticity of demand $\times$ the percentage change in price. $4 \times 20 = 80\%$.

16. **(E)** (Chapter 6, Diminishing Marginal Returns) The change in total produced is the marginal product. You can see in the table with adding marginal product that marginal product begins to decline with the 4th worker. Production declines due to the law of diminishing marginal returns: as more workers are added to fixed resources, production eventually declines. Answer D is incorrect as there's not enough information given here to determine the profit-maximizing number of workers.

Number of Workers	Total Widgets Produced per Day	Marginal Product
1	5	5
2	15	10
3	26	11
4	34	8
5	40	6
6	44	4

17. **(A)** (Chapter 6, The Production Function) The graph shows the production function where initially each worker contributes more marginal product, then marginal product increases at a decreasing rate, and eventually turns negative and more and more workers are added to fixed resources (machines, factories, etc.). This phenomenon is known as the law of diminishing marginal returns.

18. **(D)** (Chapter 6, Marginal Cost) Marginal cost is the change in total cost, so as the total cost of producing 4 is 50 and 5 is 65, $65 - 50 = 15$.

19. **(D)** (Chapter 6, Production Costs) Anytime there is a cost of production with zero output, that is a fixed cost, which is 5. As costs rise with increased output, these are variable costs. Total variable cost = total cost − fixed cost. At an output level of 4, $50 - 5 = 45$.

20. **(B)** (Chapter 6, Average and Marginal Costs) If the marginal cost (MC) curve is less than the average total cost (ATC) curve, the ATC curve must be decreasing in slope as output increases. Conversely, as output decreases from 4 to 3, ATC increases. The MC curve always intersects the ATC curve at its minimum point.

21. **(C)** (Chapter 6, Economies of Scale) Constant returns to scale occurs when output changes at exactly the same proportion as the change in inputs. Answer C shows both inputs and outputs increasing by 100%.

22. **(C)** (Chapter 7, Perfect Competition) At the profit-maximizing level of output of MR = MC, the firm is earning economic profits as P > ATC.

23. **(A)** (Chapter 6, Long-Run Costs) With diseconomies of scale, long-run average total costs increase as output increases. If there are economies of scale, long-run average total costs decrease as output increases, and with constant returns to scale, long-run average total costs remain the same as output increases.

24. **(A)** (Chapter 6, Economic Profit) Economic profit considers one's opportunity cost, unlike accounting profit. Accounting profit is always greater than economic profit as there's always an opportunity cost. The accounting profit from the yoga studio is $60,000, but he could have earned $100,000 as a lawyer and earned $1,000 in interest, for a total opportunity cost of $101,000. So, the $60,000 is accounting profit, but an economic loss of −$41,000 occurs.

25. **(E)** (Chapter 7, Perfect Competition) In a perfectly competitive market, firms can easily enter and exit an industry. If there's economic profits in an industry, firms will enter until economic profits disappear. If there's economic losses in an industry, firms will leave, causing remaining firms to eventually break even in the long run.

26. **(C)** (Chapter 6, Average Total Cost) Average total cost (ATC) is total cost (TC) divided by quantity. (Anytime you must find an average, just divide the total by quantity). The $10 at zero units of output is a fixed cost, and the total of the two units' marginal cost is total variable cost (TVC), which is $60. TC = TFC + TVC, so $10 + $60 = $70. ATC = TC/Q, so $70/2 = $35.

27. **(B)** (Chapter 7, Perfect Competition) In long-run equilibrium, perfectly competitive firms are both allocatively and productively efficient.

28. **(A)** (Chapter 9, Oligopoly) Game theory strategy and mutual interdependence are key characteristics of an oligopoly.

29. **(E)** (Chapter 8, Monopoly) If a monopoly practices perfect price discrimination, D = MR and there is no consumer surplus. Consumers pay the highest price they are willing to pay.

30. **(D)** (Chapter 8, Monopoly) The profit-maximizing output level is where MR = MC, so quantity is Q_1. From Q_1 head straight up to the demand curve and over to the price, P_5. Consumer surplus is the area above the price, below the demand curve, and left of quantity. See the chapter for visuals of a deadweight loss.

31. **(E)** (Chapter 8, Monopoly) Total revenue is at its maximum when marginal revenue (MR) = zero. MR hits zero at Q_2, and the price taken from the demand curve is P_4. Consumer surplus is the area above the price, below the demand curve, and left of quantity.

32. **(C)** (Chapter 8, Monopoly) Economic profit = P − ATC × Q. At the profit-maximizing price and quantity (MR = MC) of P_5, Q_1, the area is from point C on the demand curve down to B on the ATC, and left of the quantity, Q_1.

33. **(E)** (Chapter 9, Monopolistic Competition) Monopolistically competitive firms sell differentiated, but similar, products compared to their competitors.

34. **(A)** (Chapter 9, Oligopoly) A dominant strategy is when a player has a best choice regardless of what the other player chooses. If Tommy's Tennies goes high, he has a profit of $50 if Kevin goes high and $40 if Kevin goes low. If Tommy goes low, his profits are only $40 if Kevin goes high and $30 if Kevin goes low. So high is Tommy's best option regardless of what Kevin does. Kevin does not have a dominant strategy.

35. **(B)** (Chapter 9, Oligopoly) A Nash equilibrium is where each player chooses the best action for them given the actions of the other player. Tommy's Tennies' dominant strategy is to go high. Kevin's Kicks doesn't have a dominant strategy but knows Tommy will go with his dominant strategy, high. Kevin will get $45 if he goes high but $50 if he goes low, which is his best option when Tommy goes high. So, the Nash equilibrium is circled with Tommy high and Kevin low.

Kevin's Kicks

		High	Low
Tommy's Tennies	High	$50, $45	$40, $50
	Low	$35, $35	$30, $20

36. **(E)** (Chapter 9, Monopolistic Competition) In long-run equilibrium, a monopolistically competitive firm like firms in all market structures produces where MR = MC to maximize profits. Here P > MC, and there's zero economic profits as P = ATC.

37. **(B)** (Chapter 9, Monopolistic Competition) When a natural monopoly prices where P = ATC, it's the fair-return price, with zero economic profits. P = MC is socially optimal pricing, and MR = MC is the unregulated price.

38. **(A)** (Chapter 9, Oligopoly) The purpose of antitrust law is to prevent oligopolies from becoming a monopoly or acting like one.

39. **(B)** (Chapter 10, Marginal Revenue Product) Marginal revenue product (MRP) is the addition to a firm's revenue when an additional input (worker) is employed. It's calculated as follows:

$$MRP = \frac{\Delta \text{ in Total Revenue}}{\Delta \text{ in Resource Quantity}} \text{ or } MP * P$$

40. **(B)** (Chapter 10, Minimum Wage) A binding minimum wage in a perfectly competitive labor market with a downsloping demand curve and an upsloping supply curve would lead to a surplus and fewer workers hired.

41. **(D)** (Chapter 10, Marginal Factor Cost [MFC] and Marginal Revenue Product [MRP]) A firm maximizes profits where MRP = MFC. Based on a wage of $20 and a price of $10 per bushel, you can see these calculated in the two new columns added to the chart in the question. A firm will continue to hire labor where MRP > MFC up until they are equal. MFC = change in resource cost/quantity. MRP = marginal product × price.

Number of Workers	Bushels of Apples	MFC	MRP
1	15	$20	$150
2	32	$20	$170
3	38	$20	$60
4	43	$20	$50
5	45	$20	$20
6	46	$20	$10

42. **(D)** (Chapter 10, Least-Cost Rule) Using the least-cost rule formula, you can see that the MP/P of labor ($100/\$20 = 5$) is less than the MP/P for robots ($1,000/\$100 = 10$). The firm should then use more robots and less labor. Eventually, as production increases, diminishing returns set in and the numbers will equal out.

$$\frac{MP_L}{P_L} = \frac{MP_K}{P_K}$$

43. **(A)** (Chapter 10, Monopsony) A monopsony produces at the output level where MRP = MRC but pays a wage from the supply curve, which is Q_1 and $10. A perfectly competitive market is where supply and demand (MRP) meet, or Q_2, and $12.

44. **(E)** (Chapter 10, Marginal Revenue Product [MRP]) In a perfectly competitive market, the MRP = P $\times$ MP. The marginal product of the 4th worker is 10. $10 \times \$10 = \$100$.

45. **(A)** (Chapter 11, Public Goods) A pure public good is nonrival and nonexcludable. The benefits of national defense do not exclude others, and everyone can benefit.

46. **(C)** (Chapter 11, Externalities) The socially optimal quantity is where marginal social cost (MSC) = marginal social benefit (MSB). The free-market quantity where marginal private benefit (MPB) = MSC is less than the socially optimal quantity, so there should be a per-unit subsidy the size of the marginal external benefit (distance between the MPB and MSB curves) to increase production.

47. **(C)** (Chapter 11, Lorenz Curve) The lines with bigger curves (or the bigger banana shape) have more income inequality. Line A at 45 degrees shows perfect income equality.

48. **(B)** (Chapter 11, Externalities) If society values the marginal social benefit of clean water more than the marginal social cost, efforts to improve water quality will lead to increased efficiency.

49. **(E)** (Chapter 11, Externalities) The highway will have spillover effects (such as noise, pollution) on others who may not use or benefit from the highway. This is a negative externality.

50. **(A)** (Chapter 11, Externalities) Spillover benefits that occur to others not involved in a transaction is a positive externality, such as enjoying a neighbor's flowers.

Macroeconomics Pretest

Answer each question or complete each statement with the correct letter. To get a true assessment of your strengths and weaknesses, do not look up any hints or answers. At the end of the assessment, calculate your number correct out of 50 and you will see a chart estimating what your AP exam score might be at this point.

1. Economics is the study of

    (A) business.
    (B) government regulation.
    (C) central planning.
    (D) how societies manage their scarce resources.
    (E) society, politics, and government combined.

2. If buyers bid up the price of a good in a capitalist economy, then

    (A) sellers will try to bring more of it to market.
    (B) sellers will bring less to market, anticipating less demand at the higher price.
    (C) fewer resources will be devoted to its production.
    (D) they must not want it.
    (E) its price will eventually fall back to normal.

3. If a capitalist society demands more coffee, then the relative price of coffee will

    (A) decrease.
    (B) increase.
    (C) not necessarily change.
    (D) remain unchanged.
    (E) change indeterminately.

4. Which of the following shifts the production possibilities frontier inward?

    (A) Exports
    (B) Imports
    (C) A large wildfire that destroys timber, homes, and factories
    (D) Rising prices
    (E) An increase in the number of unemployed people

5. ____ has the absolute advantage in guns, and ____ has the absolute advantage in butter.

    (A) Cuba; Spain
    (B) Cuba; Cuba
    (C) Spain; Cuba
    (D) Spain; Spain
    (E) Spain; neither country

Labor hours needed to produce a unit of:

	Guns	Butter
Spain	5	10
Cuba	20	20

6. According to the law of comparative advantage, Cuba should export ____ and import ____ .

    (A) butter; neither good
    (B) butter; guns
    (C) guns; cloth
    (D) guns; guns
    (E) guns; neither good

Labor hours needed to produce a unit of:

	Guns	Butter
Spain	5	10
Cuba	20	20

7. Which of the following events has no effect on GDP this year?

    (A) You buy a 1957 Chevy from a friend.
    (B) The Department of Transportation repaves a road.
    (C) Your friends make a music CD that does not sell any copies.
    (D) A college buys computers.
    (E) You buy a bottle of domestic wine.

8. GDP in year 1 is

   (A) $100.
   (B) $200.
   (C) $300.
   (D) $400.
   (E) $500.

Year	Price of Waffles	Quantity of Waffles	Price of Pancakes	Quantity of Pancakes
1	$2.00	100	$1.00	100
2	$2.00	120	$2.00	150

9. Assume the base year is year 1. Real GDP in year 1 is

   (A) $100.
   (B) $200.
   (C) $300.
   (D) $400.
   (E) $500.

Year	Price of Waffles	Quantity of Waffles	Price of Pancakes	Quantity of Pancakes
1	$2.00	100	$1.00	100
2	$2.00	120	$2.00	150

10. The unemployment rate is

    (A) 5.5 percent.
    (B) 10 percent.
    (C) 12.5 percent.
    (D) 14.3 percent.
    (E) 80 percent.

Adult Population	Number of Employed	Number of Unemployed
2,000	1,800	200

11. If the consumer price index was 100 in the base year and 107 in the following year, then the inflation rate was

    (A) negative 10.7 percent.
    (B) 1.07 percent.
    (C) 7 percent.
    (D) 10.7 percent.
    (E) 107 percent.

12. Rising prices are a problem because

    (A) households are encouraged to save more.
    (B) incomes generally do not rise with prices.
    (C) the economy could run out of money.
    (D) borrowers have to repay loans with more dollars.
    (E) money in household savings accounts can now buy fewer goods and services.

13. A business cycle trough is immediately followed by the

    (A) expansion.
    (B) peak.
    (C) inflexion.
    (D) nadir.
    (E) contraction.

14. If people save more for retirement, holding all else constant, then the immediate effect is the

    (A) aggregate demand curve shifts right.
    (B) aggregate demand curve shifts left.
    (C) short- and long-run aggregate supply curves shift right.
    (D) short- and long-run aggregate supply curves shift left.
    (E) short-run aggregate supply curve shifts left.

15. Which of the following shifts the aggregate demand curve to the right?

    (A) An increase in the price level
    (B) A decrease in the price level
    (C) An increase in income taxes
    (D) A decrease in income taxes
    (E) An increase in the cost of borrowing

16. If the economy is at A and there is a decrease in aggregate demand, in the short run the economy

    (A) stays at A.
    (B) moves to B.
    (C) moves to C.
    (D) moves to D.
    (E) experiences an increase in output.

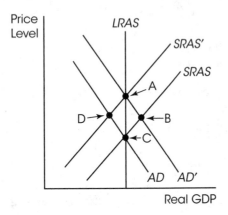

17. What can cause the economy to move from B to A?

    (A) An increase in the money supply
    (B) A decrease in the money supply
    (C) An increase in the nominal wage rate
    (D) A decrease in government spending
    (E) An increase in immigration from abroad

18. Which of the following shifts the short-run aggregate supply curve to the right?

    (A) A fire that destroys a huge timber stand
    (B) A technological advance in production methods
    (C) A fire wipes out much of the plant and equipment in the economy
    (D) Prices are expected to increase in the near future
    (E) A decrease in income taxes

19. Which of the following shifts the long-run aggregate supply curve to the right?

    (A) An increase in government spending on military equipment
    (B) An increase in the labor force
    (C) A decrease in unemployment
    (D) A decrease in the money supply
    (E) An increase in the money supply

20. In the short run, what will happen to the equilibrium price level and the equilibrium quantity of output if short-run aggregate supply increases?

    (A) The equilibrium price level increases while the equilibrium quantity of output decreases.
    (B) The equilibrium price level decreases while the equilibrium quantity of output increases.
    (C) The equilibrium price level and quantity of output increase.
    (D) The equilibrium price level and quantity of output decrease.
    (E) The equilibrium price level and the equilibrium quantity of output remain unchanged.

21. In the short run, what will happen to the equilibrium price level and equilibrium real GDP if the federal government decreases spending?

    (A) The equilibrium price level increases while equilibrium real GDP decreases.
    (B) The equilibrium price level decreases while equilibrium real GDP increases.
    (C) The equilibrium price level and equilibrium real GDP increase.
    (D) The equilibrium price level decreases and equilibrium real GDP is unchanged.
    (E) The equilibrium price level and equilibrium real GDP remain unchanged.

22. Imagine an economy on its production possibilities frontier. In the long run, what will happen to the equilibrium price level and equilibrium real GDP if the federal government decreases spending?

    (A) The equilibrium price level increases while equilibrium real GDP decreases.
    (B) The equilibrium price level decreases while equilibrium real GDP increases.
    (C) The equilibrium price level and equilibrium real GDP increase.
    (D) The equilibrium price level decreases and equilibrium real GDP is unchanged.
    (E) The equilibrium price level and equilibrium real GDP remain unchanged.

23. Assuming the MPC = 0.80 and considering only the multiplier effect, if government spending increases by $40 billion, then national income can potentially increase by

    (A) $2 billion.
    (B) $8 billion.
    (C) $20 billion.
    (D) $80 billion.
    (E) $200 billion.

24. Assuming the MPC = 0.80 and considering only the multiplier effect, if government taxation increases by $40 billion, then national income can potentially _____ by _____ .

    (A) increase; $2 billion
    (B) decrease; $20 billion
    (C) increase; $200 billion
    (D) decrease; $8 billion
    (E) decrease; $160 billion

25. If the economy is currently in short-run equilibrium at point B and policy makers do nothing, then long-run equilibrium eventually will be achieved at point

    (A) A.
    (B) B.
    (C) C.
    (D) D.
    (E) E.

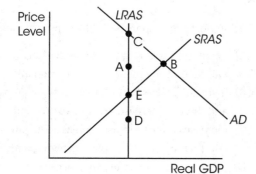

26. If the economy is currently in short-run equilibrium at point E, then an increase in aggregate demand moves the economy to ____ in the short run and ____ in the long run.

    (A) D; E
    (B) A; E
    (C) B; E
    (D) B; C
    (E) A; C

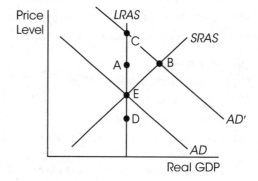

27. The appropriate fiscal policy to remedy a recession calls for

    (A) the federal government to run a deficit.
    (B) the federal government to run a surplus.
    (C) increased taxes and government spending.
    (D) decreased government spending and taxes.
    (E) increased taxes and reduced government spending.

28. One drawback of using fiscal policy to remedy a recession is that

    (A) unemployment will rise.
    (B) taxes will have to be raised.
    (C) the equilibrium price level will rise.
    (D) government spending on important programs will have to be cut.
    (E) equilibrium output will fall.

29. During recessions, automatic stabilizers make government expenditures

    (A) and tax collections fall.
    (B) and tax collections rise.
    (C) rise and tax collections fall.
    (D) fall and tax collections rise.
    (E) stable.

30. The nominal interest rate is 6 percent, and the inflation rate is 2 percent. What is the implied real interest rate?

    (A) Negative 4 percent
    (B) 3 percent
    (C) 4 percent
    (D) 8 percent
    (E) 12 percent

31. With a net worth of $2 million, Jim is wealthier than Tim, whose net worth is $1 million. These figures show that money can be used as a

    (A) store of value.
    (B) medium of exchange.
    (C) unit of account.
    (D) means of deferred payment.
    (E) way to avoid a double coincidence of wants.

32. Which of the following is included in M1?

    (A) Currency in a bank's vault
    (B) Credit cards
    (C) Small time deposits
    (D) Money market mutual funds
    (E) Deposits in savings accounts

33. If the reserve requirement is 2 percent, then the money multiplier is

    (A) 5.
    (B) 5 percent.
    (C) 50.
    (D) 50 percent.
    (E) one-half.

34. According to the quantity equation, if P = 2, Q = 6, and M = 4, then V =

    (A) 1.3.
    (B) 2.
    (C) 3.
    (D) 4.
    (E) 12.

35. An increase in the supply of money moves the economy from point D to point ____ . The equilibrium nominal interest rate ____ .

    (A) A; decreases
    (B) C; decreases
    (C) C; increases
    (D) B; increases
    (E) B; decreases

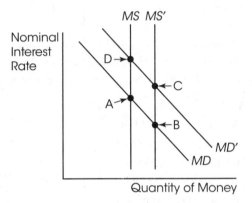

36. If the discount rate is lowered, banks

    (A) borrow more from the Fed so bank reserves increase.
    (B) borrow less from the Fed so bank reserves increase.
    (C) borrow more from the Fed so bank reserves decrease.
    (D) borrow less from the Fed so bank reserves decrease.
    (E) conduct open market purchases.

37. In the short run, a decrease in the supply of money

    (A) decreases interest rates, decreases borrowing, and thereby decreases aggregate demand.
    (B) increases interest rates, increases borrowing, and thereby increases aggregate demand.
    (C) increases interest rates, decreases borrowing, and thereby decreases aggregate demand.
    (D) decreases interest rates, increases borrowing, and thereby increases aggregate demand.
    (E) decreases interest rates, increases borrowing, and thereby decreases aggregate demand.

38. Open market operations are when the Fed buys or sells

    (A) loans to banks.
    (B) Federal Reserve Notes to banks.
    (C) Federal Reserve Notes to the public.
    (D) Federal Reserve Notes to the U.S. Treasury.
    (E) U.S. Treasury securities in the secondary market.

39. If the federal funds rate is above the Fed's target and banks hold limited reserves, the Fed should

    (A) buy bonds to increase the money supply.
    (B) buy bonds to decrease the money supply.
    (C) sell bonds to increase the money supply.
    (D) sell bonds to decrease the money supply.
    (E) raise the reserve requirement to decrease the money supply.

40. If the demand for loanable funds increases, then the equilibrium real interest rate

    (A) increases but the equilibrium quantity of funds remains unchanged.
    (B) increases and the equilibrium quantity of funds increases.
    (C) increases and the equilibrium quantity of funds decreases.
    (D) decreases and the equilibrium quantity of funds decreases.
    (E) decreases and the equilibrium quantity of funds increases.

41. An increase in the money supply _____ the price level in the short run and _____ it in the long run.

    (A) increases; decreases
    (B) increases; increases
    (C) decreases; decreases
    (D) decreases; increases
    (E) increases; does not affect

42. What is the appropriate monetary policy to move the economy from point A to point B?

    (A) Increase in tax collections
    (B) Decrease in tax collections
    (C) Increase the federal funds rate
    (D) Increase the money supply
    (E) Increase the discount rate

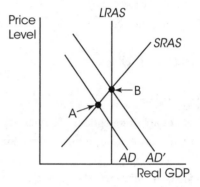

43. Monetary and fiscal policy

    (A) are not used in command economies.
    (B) are not used in capitalist economies.
    (C) affect only long-run aggregate supply.
    (D) are less effective in an open economy.
    (E) shift the long- and short-run aggregate supply curves.

44. To reduce the inflation rate

    (A) the federal government should deficit spend.
    (B) taxes should be reduced.
    (C) government spending should be increased.
    (D) long- and short-run aggregate supply should be shifted left.
    (E) the growth rates of M1 and M2 should be decreased.

45. A reduction in the income tax rate shifts the aggregate demand curve to the

    (A) right, and the economy slides up the Phillips curve.
    (B) left, and the economy slides down the Phillips curve.
    (C) right, and the economy slides down the Phillips curve.
    (D) left, and the economy slides up the Phillips curve.
    (E) left, but the Phillips curve is unaffected.

46. In the long run

    (A) prices are independent of the money supply.
    (B) prices move in the opposite direction as the money supply.
    (C) the GDP deflator is independent of the money supply.
    (D) inflation is always the result of shortages.
    (E) inflation rates parallel money supply growth rates.

47. The federal _____ is the amount the U.S. government owes to all its creditors. The federal _____ is the amount by which federal spending exceeds federal tax revenues in any given year.

    (A) budget; account
    (B) account; budget
    (C) deficit; debt
    (D) debt; deficit
    (E) deficit; excess

48. Which of the following correctly explains the crowding-out effect?

    (A) A decrease in the federal deficit decreases interest rates and so increases investment spending.
    (B) A decrease in the federal deficit increases interest rates and so decreases investment spending.
    (C) An increase in the federal deficit increases interest rates and so decreases investment spending.
    (D) An increase in the federal deficit decreases interest rates and so decreases investment spending.
    (E) An increase in the federal deficit increases the interest rate and employment.

49. An increase in ____ promotes economic growth.

    (A) the price level
    (B) the real interest rate
    (C) the nominal interest rate
    (D) the labor force
    (E) consumer spending

50. Economic growth is most likely to be promoted by an increase in

    (A) the price level.
    (B) the real interest rate.
    (C) government spending on higher education.
    (D) the money supply.
    (E) consumer spending.

Pretest AP Score Estimate

When you have finished, calculate the number correct out of 50 and compare it to the chart estimating what your AP exam score might be at this point.

AP Macroeconomics	
Pretest Score	**AP Score**
40–50	5
33–39	4
25–32	3
17–24	2
0–16	1

Study Guide for the Pretest

Note the questions you answer incorrectly. Each correct response is followed by the chapter and section that covers the material for answering the question correctly. Concentrate your efforts on these chapters and sections.

Each correct response has an explanation. If you do not understand the explanation, it means you have significant review work in that chapter before you are ready for the exam.

Answer Explanations

1. **(C)** (Chapter 2, What Is Economics?) Addressing scarcity is a central theme in the discipline of economics.

2. **(A)** (Chapter 3, Capitalism) In a capitalist economy, sellers respond to the profit motive and supply more of a good when its price increases.

3. **(B)** (Chapter 3, Capitalism) In a capitalist economy, an increase in the demand for a good causes the price to increase. This, in turn, causes more resources to be devoted to the production of that good.

4. **(C)** (Chapter 2, Production Possibilities Frontier) The production possibilities frontier reflects the economy's production potential. When resources are destroyed, the economy has less productive potential.

5. **(D)** (Chapter 2, Comparative Advantage) It takes Spain 5 hours to make a gun, while Cuba takes 20 hours. Spain is more efficient in gun production. It takes Spain 10 hours to make a unit of butter, while Cuba takes 20 hours. Spain is more efficient in butter production.

6. **(B)** (Chapter 2, Comparative Advantage) Nations should export the good in which they hold the comparative advantage. Comparative advantage means having the lower opportunity cost in production.

Labor hours needed to produce a unit of:		
	Guns	Butter
Spain	5	10
Cuba	20	20

Calculation of Opportunity Costs

Spain

Opportunity cost of guns $= 5/10 = 1/2$ butter

Opportunity cost of butter $= 20/10 = 2$ guns

Cuba

Opportunity cost of guns $= 20/20 = 1$ butter

Opportunity cost of butter $= 20/20 = 1$ gun

Spain has the comparative advantage in guns: 1/2 butter versus 1 butter.

Cuba has the comparative advantage in butter: 1 gun versus 2 guns.

Therefore, Cuba should export butter and import guns.

7. **(A)** (Chapter 12, Gross Domestic Product) Secondhand sales do not count in current GDP. The Chevy was included in 1957 GDP.

8. **(C)** (Chapter 12, Gross Domestic Product) Year 1 GDP = $2.00 × 100 + $1.00 × 100 = $300.

Year	Price of Waffles	Quantity of Waffles	Price of Pancakes	Quantity of Pancakes
2019	$2.00	100	$1.00	100
2020	$2.00	120	$2.00	150

9. **(C)** (Chapter 12, Real GDP) Year 1 Real GDP = $2.00 × 100 + $1.00 × 100 = $300. Real GDP is calculated using the prices in the base year and the quantities in the current year. In this case, year 1 is the base year and the current year, so real and nominal GDP both equal $300.

10. **(B)** (Chapter 13, Unemployment) The unemployment rate is the number unemployed divided by the labor force. The labor force is equal to the number employed plus the number unemployed.

Adult Population	Number of Employed	Number of Unemployed
2,000	1,800	200

$$\text{Unemployment Rate} = \frac{\text{Number of unemployed}}{\text{Labor force}} \times 100 = \frac{200}{2,000} = \frac{1}{10} = 0.1 = 10 \text{ percent}$$

11. **(C)** (Chapter 13, Inflation) The inflation rate is the percentage change in the consumer price index. When the CPI goes to 107 from 100, the percentage change is:

$$\text{Inflation rate} = \frac{107 - 100}{100} = \frac{7}{100} = 0.07 = 7\%$$

12. **(E)** (Chapter 16, Aggregate Demand) Incomes rise with inflation, but deposits in savings accounts do not. A savings account with $100,000 can buy less and less as prices rise.

13. **(A)** (Chapter 16, Business Cycles) The phases of the business cycle in order are expansion, peak, contraction, and trough.

14. **(B)** (Chapter 16, Aggregate Demand) More saving means less consumer spending. Therefore, aggregate demand decreases.

15. **(D)** (Chapter 16, Aggregate Demand) A decrease in income taxes means more disposable income for households to spend.

16. **(D)** (Chapter 16, Using the AS/AD Model) The aggregate demand curve shifts to the left, and the new short-run equilibrium is at D.

17. **(C)** (Chapter 16, Short-Run Aggregate Supply) An increase in resource prices, especially the price of labor, causes the short-run aggregate supply curve to shift to the left.

18. **(B)** (Chapter 16, Short-Run Aggregate Supply) A technological advance means more supply is possible in the short run and in the long run.

19. **(B)** (Chapter 16, Short-Run Aggregate Supply) An increase in the labor force means the economy has more resources and more supply potential. Both long- and short-run aggregate supply curves shift to the right.

20. **(B)** (Chapter 16, Using the AS/AD Model) After the short-run aggregate supply curve shifts right, the equilibrium moves to E_2 from E_1. The price level is lower and real GDP is higher at E_2.

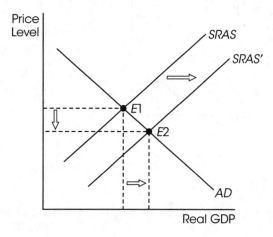

21. **(B)** (Chapter 16, Using the AS/AD Model) The aggregate demand curve shifts left. The equilibrium moves to E_2 from E_1. The price level is lower and real GDP is lower at E_2 compared to E_1.

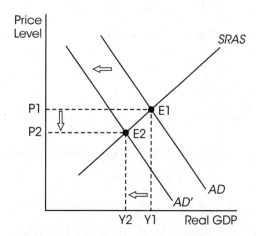

22. **(D)** (Chapter 16, Using the AS/AD Model) The decrease in government spending shifts aggregate demand to the left. The equilibrium moves to E_2 from E_1. This is a short-run equilibrium since all three curves are not crossing at E_2. The economy is producing at Y_1, below potential (Y_f) at E_2, so this is a recession. Unemployment will rise, and eventually the nominal wage rate will fall. Falling wages and other resource prices falling as well cause short-run aggregate supply to shift to the right. The equilibrium moves from E_2 to E_3. This is a long-run equilibrium since all three curves cross here. Comparing E_3 with E_1, the price level is lower but real GDP is unchanged.

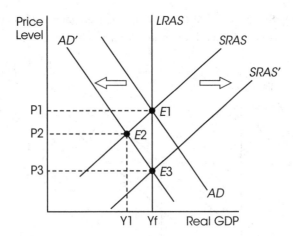

23. **(E)** (Chapter 18, Government Spending and Tax Multipliers) Calculate the government spending multiplier

$$\text{Multiplier} = \frac{1}{1 - \text{MPC}} = \frac{1}{1 - 0.8} = \frac{1}{0.2} = 5$$

Then, multiplier × change in government spending = potential change in national income

$$5 \times \$40 \text{ billion} = \$200 \text{ billion}$$

24. **(E)** (Chapter 18, Government Spending and Tax Multipliers) A tax increase decreases disposable income and therefore decreases national income. The amount of the decrease is calculated as follows:

Calculate the government spending multiplier

$$\text{Multiplier} = \frac{1}{1 - \text{MPC}} = \frac{1}{1 - 0.8} = \frac{1}{0.2} = 5$$

Then, multiplier × tax change × MPC = potential change in national income

$$5 \times \$40 \text{ billion} \times 0.8 =$$

$$5 \times \$32 \text{ billion} = \$160 \text{ billion}$$

25. **(C)** (Chapter 16, Using the AS/AD Model) At point B the economy is producing beyond its long-run potential. This is an inflationary gap. Resources are stressed, and labor is working overtime. This causes resource prices and wages to rise. Rising nominal wages and resource prices decrease short-run aggregate supply, shifting the short-run aggregate supply curve to the left. The new long-run equilibrium is at point C, where all three curves cross.

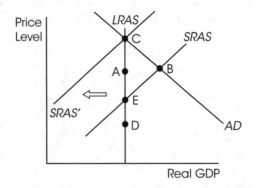

26. **(D)** (Chapter 16, Using the AS/AD Model) The increase in aggregate demand moves the economy from long-run equilibrium at point E to short-run equilibrium at point B. Here the economy is producing above its long-run potential (it's to the right of LRAS), and this strains resources. Unemployment is very low. Eventually, resource prices and nominal wages increase. This decreases short-run aggregate supply, shifting the short-run aggregate supply curve to the left. The new long-run equilibrium is at point C, where all three curves cross.

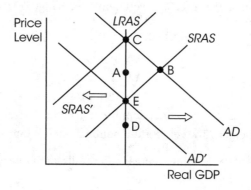

27. **(A)** (Chapter 18, Fiscal Policy in Theory) A federal deficit is achieved by increasing government spending and/or decreasing government tax collections. Both of those fiscal policies are appropriate during a recession because they increase aggregate demand.

28. **(C)** (Chapter 18, Fiscal Policy in Practice) The appropriate fiscal policy during a recession is to increase aggregate demand by increasing government spending and/or decreasing tax collections. The increase in aggregate demand causes the equilibrium price level to rise.

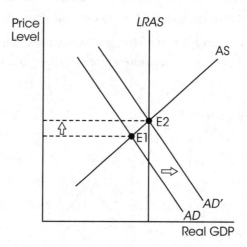

29. **(C)** (Chapter 18, Automatic Stabilizers) Spending on programs like unemployment insurance rise during recessions since more people qualify. Government tax collections fall during recessions because less income and profits translates into less tax revenue.

30. **(C)** (Chapter 15, The Loanable Funds Market) The real interest rate = nominal interest rate − the inflation rate

$$4 = 6 - 2$$

31. **(C)** (Chapter 14, Functions of Money) When dollar figures are used to measure or compare, money is functioning as a unit of account.

32. **(E)** (Chapter 14, M1, M2, and the Monetary Base) Deposits in savings accounts are included in M1 but not any of the other responses.

33. **(C)** (Chapter 14, Money Multiplier) The money multiplier is the reciprocal of the reserve requirement.

$$\text{The money multiplier} = \frac{1}{\text{reserve requirement}} = \frac{1}{0.02} = 50$$

34. **(C)** (Chapter 15, The Equation of Exchange) The equation of exchange is $M \times V = P \times Q$. Using algebra, the value of V can be determined:

$$M \times V = P \times Q$$
$$4 \times V = 2 \times 6$$
$$V = (2 \times 6)/4 = 3$$

35. **(B)** (Chapter 15, The Money Market) The money supply curve in the diagram shifts to the right. The equilibrium moves from point D to point C. The equilibrium nominal interest rate is lower at point C than at point B.

36. **(A)** (Chapter 14, Policy Tools of the Federal Reserve) A lower discount rate encourages banks to borrow more from the Fed. Those borrowings increase bank reserves.

37. **(C)** (Chapter 15, The Money Market) In the short run, a decrease in the money supply means less is available for borrowing. Interest rates increase, and that discourages borrowing. With less borrowing there is less spending by businesses and consumers.

38. **(E)** (Chapter 14, Policy Tools of the Federal Reserve) Open market operations are when the Fed buys or sells U.S. Treasury securities in the secondary market.

39. **(A)** (Chapter 14, Policy Tools of the Federal Reserve) When the Fed buys bonds in the secondary market, the sellers deposit the proceeds in the banking system. This increases bank reserves and the money supply. With more money in circulation, it can be borrowed at a lower interest rate.

40. **(B)** (Chapter 15, The Loanable Funds Market) An increase in the demand for loanable funds shifts the demand curve to the right. The new equilibrium interest rate (r_e') is higher, and the new equilibrium quantity of loanable funds (Q_e') is greater as well.

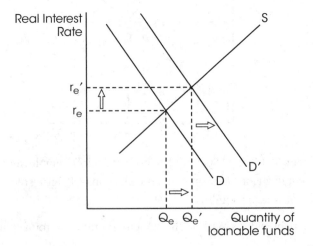

41. **(A)** (Chapter 16, Using the AS/AD Model) It does not matter if the short-run or long-run aggregate supply curve is used. An increase in the money supply increases aggregate demand and the price level. The diagrams show an increase in aggregate demand with short-run aggregate supply (SRAS) and long-run aggregate supply (LRAS) curves. In both diagrams, the price level increases.

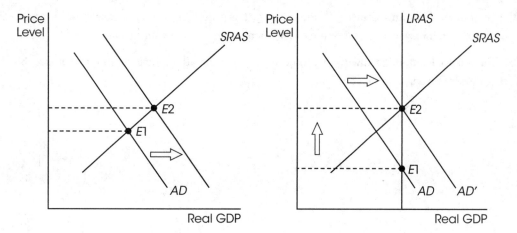

42. **(C)** (Chapter 17, Monetary Policy in Theory) The diagram shows an increase in aggregate demand. The monetary policy to achieve that is an increase in the money supply. Decreasing tax collections would have the same effect, but that is a fiscal policy.

43. **(D)** (Chapter 19, Monetary and Fiscal Policy in an Open Economy) The effects of monetary and fiscal policy get dispersed to other nations through international trade. Open economies feature international trade as opposed to closed economies.

44. **(E)** (Chapter 17, Monetary Policy in Theory) Reducing the growth rates of the money supply decreases aggregate demand. This takes pressure off rising prices.

45. **(A)** (Chapter 17, The Phillips Curve) Tax reductions increase income and promote spending. The increase in spending increases aggregate demand, shifting it to the right. More demand means less unemployment and a higher price level. Lower unemployment and higher prices is a point higher up on the Phillips curve.

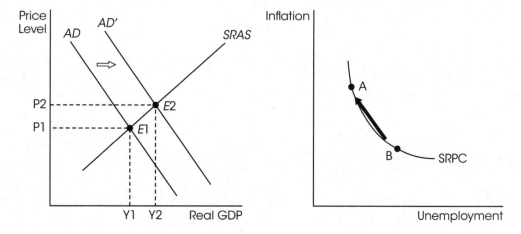

46. **(E)** (Chapter 15, The Equation of Exchange) The quantity theory of money predicts that the growth rate of the money supply and the inflation rate should be about the same in the long run. Studies bear this out as well.

47. **(D)** (Chapter 18, The Federal Debt and Deficits) This federal debt is the amount the U.S. government owes to all its creditors. The federal deficit is the amount by which federal spending exceeds federal tax revenues.

48. **(C)** (Chapter 18, Crowding Out) Crowding out is when the federal deficit drives interest rates higher. The higher rates reduce borrowing and spending by corporations and households.

49. **(D)** (Chapter 16, Economic Growth) Economic growth is promoted by an increase in resources or technological advances. An increase in the labor force is an increase in an important resource.

50. **(C)** (Chapter 16, Economic Growth) By promoting higher education, the government is improving the quality of an important resource—the labor force.

2

The Discipline of Economics

Learning Objectives

In this chapter, you will learn:

→ What is economics?

→ Macroeconomics vs. microeconomics

→ Positive vs. normative economics

→ Opportunity cost

→ Production possibilities frontier

→ Comparative advantage

What Is Economics?

Economics is a social science that studies how resources are used and is often concerned with how resources can be used to their fullest potential. Is it wise to use our resources to explore outer space or should we build low-income housing instead? Should old-growth forests be harvested for their superior wood or should they be preserved for their majesty and environmental benefits?

Consider the case of a student who has only 24 hours to spend each day. Some of this precious resource (time) must be spent on the necessities of life such as eating and sleeping. But of the hours remaining, how many should be devoted to studying? Socializing? Relaxing? Too much socializing and relaxing will not allow the student to live his or her life to its fullest potential. Neither will going overboard on the study time. One problem every student faces is just how much time should be allocated to each of the various activities that make for a full life. This is an economic problem, since the student must decide how the resource (time) will be used to its maximum potential.

The discipline of economics is not directly concerned with money or politics or the stock market; however, economic problems abound in each of these areas. People want to spend their money in the best way. Politicians want to make decisions to achieve the maximum benefit, and investors want the highest return from their savings. Anytime someone is trying to make the most out of what he has, we are in the realm of economics.

Notice that our resources are scarce compared to our unlimited wants. There must be some resources that are unlimited. Air? Water? Time? No, all resources have their limits. You might contend that your material wants are modest, but then don't you have friends and relatives you would like to help? Economics is about how we deploy our resources to deal with scarcity.

It is only natural for families, firms, and nations to strive for the best outcomes, given their endowments of resources. For that reason, every person and institution must grapple with economic problems every day.

Macroeconomics vs. Microeconomics

The discipline of economics is broken into two fields: macroeconomics and microeconomics. Macroeconomics involves economic problems encountered by the nation as a whole. For example, do we spend too many of our resources on national defense and not enough on education of our youth? If households are required to pay fewer taxes, will

 TIP

The general distinction between macroeconomics and microeconomics is that the former deals with the overall economy whereas the latter is concerned with particular individuals, firms, industries, or regions within the economy.

43

national savings be affected? Will prices rise or fall because of a tax cut? Will increasing the money supply increase production levels in the economy?

Microeconomics is concerned with the economic problems faced by individual units within the overall economy. Here the focus is on particular families, individuals, and firms. Some examples of microeconomic issues are: Does a particular family save enough to provide for its future needs? How will a tax break affect XYZ Corporation's output? If the Smiths win the lottery, how will their spending patterns change?

Positive vs. Normative Economics

The discipline of economics can be split in another way—positive and normative economics. Positive economics is based on the scientific method. That means hypotheses are formulated and tested. For instance, one theory holds that if a family's income increased, their spending will increase but not by as much as the increase in income. There are several ways that this theory could be tested. One way is to observe how a group of families behave when their income is increased. Another might be to survey lottery winners to see how they disposed of their winnings.

Normative economics involves value judgments. Someone may feel that resources are better spent exploring outer space than providing free breakfasts for elementary school children. If this is the person's opinion, not based on a scientific investigation of the matter, then we are in the realm of normative economics. Normative economics is economics based on the way someone believes things *ought* to be.

It may appear as if positive economics is a superior form of the discipline since it is grounded in the scientific method and normative economics is based on opinions. However, normative economics is a crucial part of the economics discipline. Any scientific study will require an experiment, and experiments can be designed to highlight a scientist's prejudices. Even if an economist can keep her biases out of a study, why did she choose this particular question to investigate? However much economists strive to be like biologists and physicists, there will always be a large normative aspect to economics. Some economists claim that the normative side of the economics discipline is the more interesting.

Resources

Economists, like most professionals, have special words and phrases that are used to describe concepts and ideas that occur frequently in their work. In order to understand economics, one must master the jargon. Familiar words and expressions can take on new meaning as economic jargon. The term "resource" is a case in point. To the layperson, a resource is something that can be used or drawn upon in a particular situation or endeavor. Economists do not dispute this definition and use the word "resource" to mean much the same thing. However, the economist gives the term a special, more particular definition. *A resource is anything that can be used to produce a good or service.* This definition is broad enough to cover such dissimilar things as farmland, crude oil, machinery, and even intellectual ability.

In macroeconomics every resource is classified into one of three categories: land, labor, or capital.

- **Land** does not only refer to the ground we walk on, but all natural resources. Therefore, resources such as farmland, crude oil, timber stands, oceans, and mineral deposits are all classified under the term "land."
- **Labor**, the second classification, encompasses all human attributes that are productive. Humans have the ability to perform a multitude of tasks, so there are many forms of this type of resource. Labor can be the person pounding nails at a construction site or the neurosurgeon in the operating room. Anytime anyone is performing a service, function, or task, it is the resource "labor" at work. The professor in the classroom is using his intellectual capability to provide a service, just as a professional basketball player uses her athletic ability to produce points. In both cases, humans are using their attributes to produce things society finds valuable.
- **Capital**, in the economic sense of the term, is productive equipment or machinery. Again, many disparate items can fit into this classification: factory buildings, forklifts, computers, and paper clips are a few examples.

Not all resources fit neatly into this classification scheme. Resources such as time, health, money, adventurousness, and the willingness to take risks would all be difficult to categorize. Some economists have added categories to the classification system so that hard-to-classify resources have a place of their own, but most economists stick with the jargon and maintain that the productive assets of an economy are land, labor, and capital.

Opportunity Cost

Opportunity cost is what must be sacrificed to obtain something. The concept of opportunity cost is quite general and ubiquitous in everyday life. When someone decides to spend two hours studying—obtaining wisdom or better grades—something must be sacrificed. For some individuals this might be two hours of watching TV; for others the opportunity cost of two hours of study time may be two hours of lost quality time with the family.

When someone decides to attend college, costs are always a consideration. Even if the money cost of tuition and books is not an issue for the student, the opportunity costs are. The opportunity costs of attending college will be different for each student, since each student sacrifices something different to attend. For most students, the opportunity cost of college is the work experience or leisure activities that must be foregone in order to be in college.

In the macroeconomic sphere, opportunity cost takes on a more specific meaning. If a nation decides to produce one more unit of product A, how many units of product B will have to be sacrificed? Producing another unit of product A will use up resources. Exactly how many units of product B could have been produced with those resources?

Table 2.1 shows various combinations of guns and butter that an economy could produce using all of its resources fully and efficiently. Using resources efficiently means that they are not used foolishly or wasted in the production process. Efficiency implies using resources to their maximum potential.

Table 2.1 Hypothetical Production Possibilities

Point	Guns	Butter
A	0	30
B	3	25
C	6	20
D	9	15
E	12	10
F	15	5
G	18	0

It may seem peculiar that this society produces only guns and butter. Guns can be thought of as all types of national defense, while butter represents consumer goods. The number of products in our example could be increased, but that would complicate the analysis unnecessarily.

Notice that each time the country portrayed in Table 2.1 produces three more guns, it must give up five pounds of butter. If it were decided to produce one more gun, then 1.67 pounds of butter would have to be sacrificed. Therefore, the opportunity cost of guns is 1.67 pounds of butter for this nation.

Conversely, if one more pound of butter were produced, society would have to forego the production of 0.6 guns. The opportunity cost of butter is 0.6 guns.

To calculate the opportunity cost of guns, divide the change in butter production by the change in gun production as you move from one line of Table 2.1 to the next.

$$\text{Opportunity Cost of Guns} = \frac{\text{Change in Butter Production}}{\text{Change in Gun Production}} = \frac{5}{3} = 1.67 \text{ Pounds Butter}$$

The opportunity cost of butter is the reciprocal of the opportunity cost of guns.

$$\text{Opportunity Cost of Butter} = \frac{\text{Change in Gun Production}}{\text{Change in Butter Production}} = \frac{3}{5} = 0.6 \text{ Guns}$$

The concept of opportunity cost illustrates the simple fact that some amount of one product must be given up when more of another product is desired.

Production Possibilities Frontier

The production possibilities frontier is the graphical portrayal of the information contained in Table 2.1. It shows the combinations of two goods that can be produced if the economy uses all of its resources fully and efficiently. Figure 2.1 is the production possibilities frontier that corresponds to Table 2.1. Points A through G are plotted with gun production measured on the vertical axis and butter production along the horizontal axis.

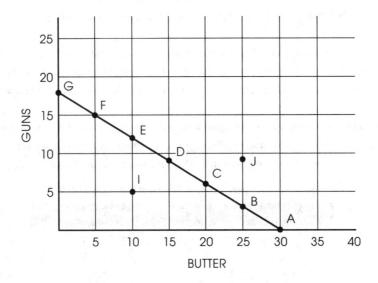

Figure 2.1 Production Possibilities Frontier

The economy has the option of producing any combination of guns and butter along the frontier. At Point B most of the economy's resources are devoted to butter production. Only three guns are produced. At Point F gun production is predominant. Still, the economy is using its resources fully and efficiently at both points. A normative analysis is required to determine which point is preferred. On efficiency grounds, all the points along the frontier are equal.

Points inside the frontier (Point I) are possible also. However, if the economy is operating at a point inside the frontier, resources are not being used fully or efficiently. Consider Point I, where 10 pounds of butter and five guns are being produced per year. By the definition of the production possibilities frontier, we know that when the economy produces 10 pounds of butter, 12 guns could be produced if resources were used fully and efficiently (Point E). Point I represents a combination of guns and butter that does not require full or efficient resource utilization. The economy could do better by producing some combination of the two goods that lies on the frontier.

Points outside the production possibilities frontier (Point J) are unobtainable. Point J represents a combination of 25 pounds of butter and nine guns per year. By the definition of the production possibilities frontier, we know that if 25 pounds of butter are produced, only three guns can be produced (Point B) if resources are used fully and efficiently. Therefore, points outside the frontier cannot be attained at this time.

Points outside the production possibilities frontier may be attained at some future date because the frontier may shift so that points like J lie along the new frontier. The frontier can also shift inward representing a change for the worse. Two factors cause the production possibilities frontier to shift:

1. changes in the amount of resources in the economy, and
2. changes in technology and productivity.

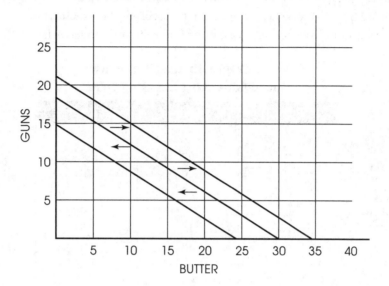

Figure 2.2 Shifts in the Production Possibilities Frontier

It stands to reason that if the economy obtains more resources, larger combinations of guns and butter could be produced. This would shift the frontier to the right as in Figure 2.2. Similarly, a technological advance that made a given amount of resources more productive would also shift the frontier to the right.

The amount of resources in a country can increase for a variety of reasons. The amount of labor could increase through population growth. New territories could be acquired, or existing land could be opened up for oil exploration or mining. The amount of capital could be increased by producing and putting in place more equipment and machinery.

The production possibilities frontier would shift to the left if the amount of resources were decreased or technology took a step backward. It is easy to imagine the amount of resources in an economy decreasing due to devastating weather, war, or a decline in population. But why take a technological step backward? However, economies sometimes do use less efficient production techniques because of government regulation or tradition.

Government regulations to ensure worker safety or protect the environment often force firms to use less efficient production techniques. Hopefully, the benefits of increased worker safety and a less polluted environment are worth the cost of lower output. By tradition, Amish farmers still use horses to plow their fields. When less efficient production techniques are adopted, the production possibilities frontier shifts to the left. Again, the costs of maintaining this tradition (less output) might be worth the benefits (a more wholesome life).

TIP

A decline in unemployment does not shift the production possibilities frontier. If unemployment exists, then the economy is operating inside the frontier. A decline in unemployment would move the economy to a point closer to or onto the frontier.

Law of Increasing Costs

The production possibilities frontier is not typically a straight line as in Figures 2.1 and 2.2. You may have noticed that each time gun production increases by three in Table 2.1, butter production decreases by five. The opportunity cost of gun production is $5/3 = 1.67$ pounds of butter between all points. In other words, opportunity cost is constant throughout Table 2.1. This gives rise to the straight-line production possibilities frontier.

However, there is a good reason why opportunity cost will not be constant in the real world. The law of increasing costs states that as more of a product is produced, the opportunity cost increases. Table 2.2 presents data that comply with the law of increasing costs. The opportunity cost of guns is $2/3 = 0.67$ pounds of butter between Points A and B, and rises to $3/3 = 1$ pound of butter between Points B and C. A quick check will show that the farther down Table 2.2 we go, the higher the opportunity cost of guns. The more guns we are initially producing, the more expensive it will be to produce one more gun in terms of butter production lost.

Table 2.2 Hypothetical Production Possibilities with Increasing Costs

Point	Guns	Butter
A	0	25
B	3	23
C	6	20
D	9	15
E	12	10
F	15	5
G	18	0

This holds true for butter production also. In this case, we move up Table 2.2 since more butter is produced as we go toward the top of the table. Between Points D and C, the opportunity cost of butter is $3/5 = 0.6$ guns, whereas the opportunity cost is $3/2 = 1.5$ guns between Points B and A. These numbers are in line with the law of increasing costs, which states that the more of a product that is initially being produced, the higher the opportunity cost will be to produce still more.

When the numbers in Table 2.2 are graphed to form the production possibilities frontier, the result is a line that is curved concave to the origin. This is shown in Figure 2.3. Concave-to-the-origin production possibilities frontiers are due to the law of increasing costs.

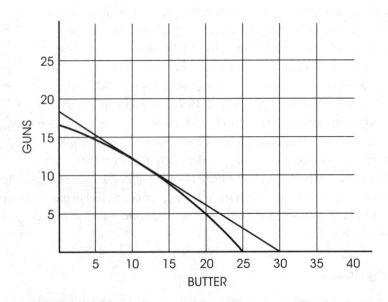

Figure 2.3 Concave to the Origin Production Possibilities Frontier

But what is the cause of the law of increasing costs? Why does it cost more (in terms of butter) to produce another gun when a lot of guns are already being produced? To see the answer to these questions, you must imagine the situation in an economy that is already producing a lot of guns. Most of the resources in the economy will be devoted to gun production, while only a few resources, such as farmers, cows, milking machines, and so forth, are engaged in butter production. Now, if that society wants to produce more guns, resources will have to be taken from butter production and used to produce guns. This means some farmers and cows will be employed in gun manufacture. (The cows could be used to turn mills that polish gun bores.) But farmers and cows are good at making butter and are not used in gun production, so when the resources are shifted from butter to gun production, not many more guns are produced, but a lot of butter must be sacrificed. In short, the opportunity cost of producing guns is high when gun production is already at a high level.

When gun production is low, the opportunity cost of increasing gun production is low. That is because most of society's resources are employed making butter. Imagine gunsmiths and gun-making equipment being used to make butter since they are not needed to make the small number of guns being produced. Now, when gun production is increased, the resources that are adept at making guns can be shifted off the farm and into gun production—not much butter will be lost, but many more guns are produced. The opportunity cost of guns is low when a low level of guns is being produced.

The law of increasing costs is due to the fact that some resources are more adept at the production of one good than another. When resources are forced to work in an industry where they are not proficient, they are less productive. Thus, the opportunity cost of producing a good becomes greater as more resources are forced into industries where they are not as productive. This causes the production possibilities frontier to be concave to the origin.

Comparative Advantage

A survey of economists undertaken in early 2018 indicates that 96 percent of them believed that restrictions to free trade, such as tariffs and quotas, reduce economic welfare for the country that imposes them. The basis for this widespread support of free trade is the law of comparative advantage.

The law of comparative advantage was delineated convincingly by David Ricardo in the early 1800s. The law is an important element in introductory micro- and macroeconomics courses. It is also an application of the concept of opportunity cost.

The law of comparative advantage advocates specialization for increased output. The idea that specialization can improve productivity impressed Adam Smith when he visited a pin factory in the 1700s. In his famous tome *The Wealth of Nations* he wrote about his observations:

> One man draws out the wire, another straights it, a third cuts it, a fourth points it, a fifth grinds it at the top for receiving the head; to make the head requires two or three distinct operations; to put it on is a peculiar business; to whiten the pins is another; it is even a trade by itself to put them into the paper; and the important business of pin making is, in this manner, divided into about eighteen distinct operations, . . .

Smith showed how the division of labor into specialized tasks could increase productivity and output. The law of comparative advantage shows that the notion of specialization for increased productivity and output applies to nations as well.

When David Ricardo wrote about the benefits of free trade, it was in opposition to the Corn Laws of England. The Corn Laws prohibited the importation of grains from outside England in order to protect domestic farmers. Ricardo, like 93 percent of today's economists, felt that the economic well-being of England suffered because of this restriction of trade.

To prove his point, Ricardo set up a scenario very similar to the one depicted in Table 2.3.

Table 2.3 A Hypothetical Example of Production Costs

Country	Labor Hours Needed to Produce a Unit of:	
	Wheat	Cloth
Portugal	10	20
England	20	60

The table shows how many hours of labor are required to produce one unit of wheat or cloth in Portugal and England. According to Table 2.3, Portugal can produce both products more efficiently than England. In Portugal, a unit of wheat can be produced with 10 hours of labor, while it requires 20 hours in England. One unit of cloth can be produced in Portugal with 20 hours of labor, while the corresponding number in England is 60.

Portugal is said to have the absolute advantage in the production of both wheat and cloth. Absolute advantage implies that the product can be produced more efficiently, that is, with fewer inputs. You might wonder why Portugal would want to trade with England at all, as England is an inefficient producer of both products. That was the genius of Ricardo's exposition—trade can be mutually advantageous to both countries even if one country has the absolute advantage in all products, because mutually advantageous trade is based on comparative advantage, not absolute advantage.

Comparative advantage means that a nation can produce the good with a lower opportunity cost. Consider the opportunity cost of wheat in Portugal. It takes 10 hours to produce a unit of wheat. If it was decided to produce another unit of wheat in Portugal, then half a unit of cloth would have to be given up since the labor would be pulled off cloth production and it takes 20 hours to produce a unit of cloth.

Opportunity cost, you will recall, is how much of one thing must be sacrificed in order to obtain a unit of something else. Here half a unit of cloth must be given up in order to obtain an extra unit of wheat. By similar reasoning, the opportunity cost of cloth in Portugal is two units of wheat. Table 2.4 outlines the calculations required to determine the opportunity costs of wheat and cloth in Portugal and England.

Portugal has the lower opportunity cost in cloth production (two units of wheat), and England has the lower opportunity cost in wheat production ($1/3$ unit of cloth). Portugal has the comparative advantage in cloth and England in wheat. Ricardo showed that if each country produced only the good in which it held a comparative advantage and traded for the other product, then both countries could consume more of both goods.

Table 2.4 Calculations of Opportunity Costs from Table 2.3

Portugal
Opportunity cost of wheat = 10/20 = 1/2 cloth
Opportunity cost of cloth = 20/10 = 2 wheat
England
Opportunity cost of wheat = 20/60 = 1/3 cloth
Opportunity cost of cloth = 60/20 = 3 wheat

You might convince yourself of this by assuming that each nation has 120 hours of labor to divide between the production of both goods. For instance, England could use 120 hours to produce a unit of cloth and three units of wheat; Portugal could produce five units of cloth and two units of wheat. Total cloth production by both countries would be six units, and total wheat production would be five units.

Table 2.5 Production of Wheat and Cloth in 120 Hours

In Isolation		Wheat	Cloth
	Portugal	2	5
	England	3	1
Total		5	6
Specialization		**Wheat**	**Cloth**
	Portugal	0	6
	England	6	0
Total		6	6
With Trade		**Wheat**	**Cloth**
	Portugal	2.5	5
	England	3.5	1

However, if Portugal devoted its entire 120 hours to cloth production, there would be six units produced and England could use 120 hours to make six units of wheat. This is specialization according to comparative advantage. Notice that total cloth production is six units as it was before specialization, but total wheat production is now six units, not five. The extra unit of wheat could be shared by the citizens of each country through specialization of production and trade. Essentially, Portugal and England are able to consume outside their production possibilities frontiers by trading according to comparative advantage.

In fact, we could determine what the terms of trade would have to be so that the extra unit of wheat would add to the welfare of at least one, if not both, countries. Suppose England offered to trade two units of wheat for two units of cloth. Portugal would not accept since she would be left with four units of cloth and the two units of wheat. In isolation she could have enjoyed five units of cloth and two units of wheat.

The terms of trade would have fallen somewhere between two units of wheat for one unit of cloth (which would leave Portugal no better off than in isolation) and three units of wheat for one unit of cloth (which would leave England no better off than in isolation). Let's say the two countries strike a deal to trade 2.5 units of wheat for one unit of cloth. Then both countries would consume 0.5 units more wheat than in isolation and the same amount of cloth. In other words, the countries would share the extra unit of wheat production that was gained by specialization according to comparative advantage and trade.

Notice that the terms of trade must fall between the opportunity costs of both countries. Portugal's opportunity cost of cloth from Table 2.4 is two wheat and England's is three wheat. So the terms of trade must lie between two and three wheat, for one unit of cloth. It amounts to the same thing to state the terms of trade as falling between $\frac{1}{2}$ and $\frac{1}{3}$ cloth for one unit of wheat.

The idea that trade is beneficial to all parties involved even when one party has an absolute advantage in everything has an analogy in microeconomics. Consider a lawyer who happens to be very fast and accurate at keying legal documents. It would still pay for the lawyer to hire a secretary to do the keying, even if the secretary is not as efficient. That is because the secretary has the comparative advantage (lower opportunity cost) in keying. If the lawyer does her own keying, the opportunity cost is the income that could have been earned writing law briefs.

SUMMARY

- Economics is about using resources wisely. When we focus on one individual or one household or one firm and analyze its use of resources, we are practicing *microeconomics*. When we study whether a nation is allocating its resources in an efficient manner, we are practicing *macroeconomics*.

- Both macroeconomics and microeconomics will require some normative analysis. That is, value judgments will have to be made at some point to answer most economic questions, but there is a tendency to be as positive as possible. Being positive means sticking to the scientific method of reaching conclusions and avoiding personal biases and opinions.

- Even if you have never studied economics before, you are well acquainted with it because everyone strives to make the most out of what they've got. Many people associate businesspeople or stocks and bonds with economics. That is correct because businesspeople are trying to make the most out of their company's resources, while stock and bond traders are trying to maximize their returns—but economics is so much more than that. Whenever a person, a firm, or a nation tries to make the most of its resources, it is practicing economics.

- Remember that the next time you have to decide between studying and watching TV. There's nothing wrong with watching TV. But you should realize that there is a cost to watching TV that goes beyond the cost of the electricity. The opportunity cost of watching TV is the study time you sacrifice. If you think it's worth it, then go for the TV, especially if you have a headache and wouldn't get much out of studying anyway. It's not just businesspeople and Wall Street players who make economic decisions.

- The idea that something must be sacrificed in order to pursue an alternative is captured in the concepts of opportunity cost and the production possibilities frontier. The law of increasing costs suggests that the production possibilities frontier will be bowed and concave to the origin as opposed to a straight line.

Multiple-Choice Review Questions

1. Economics is a social science that

    (A) is primarily concerned with money.
    (B) is primarily concerned with how resources are used.
    (C) relies solely on the scientific method for analysis.
    (D) is primarily concerned with maximizing spiritual well-being.
    (E) is purely normative.

2. Macroeconomics focuses on

    (A) government and its laws that affect commerce.
    (B) individuals and their resource use.
    (C) corporations and their production levels.
    (D) the resource use of the entire nation.
    (E) money.

3. Given the table below, what is the opportunity cost of wheat in France?

Country	Labor hours needed to produce a unit of:	
	Wheat	Cloth
France	5	10
England	20	60

    (A) ½ cloth
    (B) ½ wheat
    (C) 2 cloth
    (D) 2 wheat
    (E) ½ cloth

4. Given the table below, which statement is true?

Country	Labor hours needed to produce a unit of:	
	Wheat	Cloth
France	5	10
England	20	20

    (A) England has the absolute advantage in both products.
    (B) France should specialize in and export wheat while England should specialize in and export cloth.
    (C) France has the comparative advantage in cloth.
    (D) England has the comparative advantage in wheat.
    (E) France has the absolute advantage in wheat while England has the absolute advantage in cloth.

5. Which of the following statements is positive?

    (A) An economy that produces more butter than guns is better off than an economy that produces more guns than butter.
    (B) Nations should concentrate their resources on producing wholesome consumer goods as opposed to the weapons of war.
    (C) The production possibilities frontier is concave to the origin because of the law of increasing costs.
    (D) Nations ought to devote at least some of their resources to national defense.
    (E) Nations would do better by producing toward the middle of their production possibilities frontiers as opposed to the extreme points near the axes.

6. The primary focus of microeconomics is

    (A) families and how they make money.
    (B) firms and how they make profits.
    (C) individual units within the overall economy.
    (D) government.
    (E) small countries.

7. Economists use the term "capital" to mean

    (A) money.
    (B) plant and equipment.
    (C) where the central government is located.
    (D) the center of the economy.
    (E) a major idea.

8. What you give up to pursue another alternative is known as

    (A) capital.
    (B) land.
    (C) money cost.
    (D) the price of the product.
    (E) opportunity cost.

9. Given the following table (combinations that can be produced using resources fully and efficiently),

Apples	Oranges
0	20
7	10
14	0

    the opportunity cost of apples is

    (A) $10/7$ oranges.
    (B) $7/10$ oranges.
    (C) $10/7$ apples.
    (D) $7/10$ apples.
    (E) 70 percent.

10. Given the following table (combinations that can be produced using resources fully and efficiently),

Soup	Nuts
0	15
1	10
2	5

    the opportunity cost of soup is

    (A) 5 nuts.
    (B) 5 soup.
    (C) 20 percent.
    (D) 500 percent.
    (E) not constant.

11. Production possibilities frontiers are concave to the origin because

    (A) of inefficiencies in the economy.
    (B) of opportunity cost.
    (C) of the law of increasing costs.
    (D) of constant opportunity costs.
    (E) the extreme points are not as well established.

12. When opportunity cost is constant across all production levels, the production possibilities frontier is

    (A) concave to the origin.
    (B) convex to the origin.
    (C) undefined.
    (D) shifted.
    (E) a straight diagonal line sloping downward from left to right.

13. When an economy produces a combination of goods that lies on the production possibilities frontier,

    (A) resources are being used fully and efficiently.
    (B) prices are constant.
    (C) opportunity cost is constant.
    (D) resources will never be depleted.
    (E) prices will rise.

14. The law of increasing costs

   (A) does not apply to guns and butter.
   (B) is the result of resources not being perfectly adaptable between the production of two goods.
   (C) implies that prices will rise when the costs of making a good rise.
   (D) causes the production possibilities frontier to be a straight line.
   (E) implies that opportunity costs will rise as production levels fall.

15. Land refers to

   (A) all productive resources.
   (B) all natural resources.
   (C) farmland only.
   (D) real estate.
   (E) chattels.

Free-Response Review Questions

1. Someone claims that air is not a scarce resource since it is all around us. Classify air as land, labor, or capital and explain why it could be considered scarce.

2. In the space below, draw a production possibilities frontier that reflects constant opportunity costs between Good 1 and Good 2. Now suppose the economy's labor force grows larger. Draw the new production possibilities frontier.

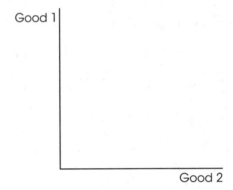

3. Explain why a nation that does not produce any good or service more efficiently can still be a valued trading partner.

Answer Explanations

1. **(B)** Economics encompasses many topics including money, science, spirituality, and normative opinions. However, the way resources are deployed to meet society's needs is its primary concern.

2. **(D)** Rather than individuals, firms, industries, or regions, macroeconomics focuses on how a nation deploys its resources.

3. **(A)** Since the table shows hours required to produce one unit of wheat and cloth, the opportunity cost of wheat in France is calculated by dividing hours to produce a unit of wheat by hours required to produce a unit of cloth. 5/10 = ½ cloth. If France wants another unit of wheat, it must give up a half of a unit of cloth.

4. **(B)** All four opportunity costs must be calculated to get the correct answer.

France	England
opportunity cost of wheat = 5/10 = ½ cloth	opportunity cost of wheat = 20/20 = 1 cloth
opportunity cost of cloth = 10/5 = 2 wheat	opportunity cost of cloth = 20/20 = 1 wheat

   France has the lower opportunity cost and therefore the comparative advantage in wheat. That implies France should specialize in, and export, wheat. England has the comparative advantage in cloth. That implies England should specialize in, and export, cloth.

5. **(C)** Only statement (C) does not involve a value judgment.

6. **(C)** Microeconomists study individual units be they a family, a firm, an industry, or a region.

7. **(B)** Economists use the term "capital" in a specific way. It refers to plant and equipment.

8. **(E)** This is one way to define opportunity cost.

9. **(A)** Since the table shows production amounts per some unspecified unit of time, the opportunity cost of apples is calculated by taking the change in orange production over the corresponding change in apple production. For instance, increasing orange production from 0 to 10 is an increase of 10. The corresponding change in apple production is 14 to 7, or 7. Now divide 10 by 7 to obtain the opportunity cost of one apple: 10/7 oranges.

10. **(A)** The opportunity cost of soup is 5 nuts $= \dfrac{\text{change in nut production}}{\text{change in soup production}} = \dfrac{5}{1} = 5$. Alternately, it is apparent from the table that every time an additional unit of soup is produced, 5 nuts are sacrificed.

11. **(C)** Production possibilities frontiers are bowed outward from the origin due to the law of increasing costs.

12. **(E)** Straight-line production possibilities frontiers can only result from constant opportunity costs along the entire range of production levels.

13. **(A)** No matter where on the production possibilities frontier the nation is producing, it is using its resources fully and efficiently.

14. **(B)** Opportunity costs rise as production levels increase solely because the resources that are required to produce one of the goods is not as effective in producing the other good.

15. **(B)** The term "land" has a particular meaning in economics. It refers to any and all natural resources.

Free-Response Review Answers

1. The atmosphere, or air, is best classified as land since economists use that term to mean all natural resources. Air may be abundant, but like all resources, it is scarce in the sense that it is not unlimited. Air may be free but that does not mean it has no value or is in unlimited supply. Certainly clean air can be hard to find and people pay to have it in some instances.

2.

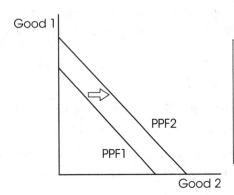

The production possibilities frontier is a straight line, not bowed, to reflect constant opportunity costs.

When the labor force expands, the economy has more resources. This shifts the production possibilities frontier outward.

3. The benefits from trade do not depend on producing more efficiently. The benefits from trade depend on comparative advantage, not absolute advantage. If a nation has the lower opportunity cost in production, then it holds the comparative advantage. If a nation exports the good in which it holds the comparative advantage and imports the other good, then both nations can consume more of both goods.

3

Economic Systems

| Learning Objectives

In this chapter, you will learn:

→   The fundamental economic questions
→   Economic systems
→   The circular flow diagram

The Fundamental Economic Questions

In every nation there are a variety of issues that demand attention: What can be done about poverty and unemployment? Pollution? The national debt? Inflation? And so on. Yet before these questions can be addressed—indeed, before these problems even crop up—there are some fundamental economic questions that each and every country will have to contend with.

Even Robinson Crusoe had to deal with economic issues on his deserted island. What resources were on hand to provide food and shelter? Was clothing necessary? Crusoe had to decide how to best employ his meager resources to ensure his survival. In the same manner, each nation must decide what is the best way to use the resources at its disposal.

Would it be wise for Crusoe to spend all his time keeping a signal fire burning and searching the horizon for a rescue ship? Or should the same wood that might be used in the signal fire be used to build a shelter? Should the United States use its resources to explore Mars or to build low-income housing? One of the most fundamental questions any economy will have to address, whether it is one man trapped on an island or a highly industrialized nation, is what should be produced given its resources.

In Cuba it is virtually impossible to get cosmetic surgery, while the United States devotes a significant amount of its resources to this. Part of the reason why this is so has to do with the fact that the United States has so many resources compared to Cuba, but another reason why Cuba spends hardly any resources on plastic surgery is because of the way the decision is made about what will be produced in Cuba.

Opportunity Costs

Before exploring further the differences in the way economic decisions are undertaken in Cuba versus in the United States, let us consider some other fundamental economic questions. Once it is decided to produce a certain set of goods and services, how much of each item should be produced? The concept of opportunity cost comes into play here. If it is decided to produce more than one item, then some amount of another item must be sacrificed.

Not only that, but many goods and services are related to one another. For instance, if it is decided to produce more wheat, this will require an increase in the production of tractors, seed, fertilizer, and other products needed to produce wheat. Considering opportunity costs and the fact that many products are related, the decision of how much to produce of each good and service becomes an extremely complex issue.

Who Gets What?

After having decided what and how much of each item is to be produced, there is still another basic question: Who is going to get how much of each good and service? In the United States, a medical doctor can obtain more and higher-quality goods and services than a schoolteacher. In Cuba doctors and teachers have roughly equal living standards. Certainly a person's income is important in determining how many goods and services can be obtained. But why do doctors receive so much more income than teachers in the United States and not in Cuba? The answer to that question involves how each economy responds to the basic economic issue of "who gets what?"

So there are two fundamental economic questions that any society will have to address:

1. How much, if any, of each good and service should be produced?
2. Who will get how much of each good and service?

In order to appreciate the complexity of these questions, imagine yourself shipwrecked on a desert island with 11 other people. It is possible to produce only a limited number of items with the resources on hand. The necessities of life will have to be produced: food, clothing, and shelter.

Should you attempt to build a boat large enough to take 12 people back to civilization? Or is a signal fire more logical? It would be possible to provide haircuts, and makeup could be manufactured, however crude. Exactly what should be produced?

If the production of cosmetics and haircuts is forsaken in order to produce more food, it will be necessary to produce more tools for working the land and harvesting the crops.

Who will get how much of each item produced? Should the doctor get more than the food production manager? Should the sick people get more or less than the others?

Now try to imagine coping with these questions when there are 350 million people and the array of goods and service encompasses everything from rubber bands to super computers. The organization of large economies is a mind-boggling task. How is it accomplished?

Economic Systems

There are three basic ways to address the economic questions that are imposed upon a society: (1) government commands, (2) capitalism, and (3) a blend of government commands and capitalism.

The Command Economy

A command economy is one in which the central government dictates what will or will not be produced. The government also stipulates how much of each item is to be produced and who is to get how many of the final products. Cuba and North Korea are examples of nations that rely heavily on the command system. The terms *communism* and *socialism* are sometimes used to describe economies that use central commands to address the fundamental economic questions.

Cosmetic surgery is not available in Cuba because the central government does not allow resources to be used on this service. Through the use of quotas and production plans, the Cuban government dictates how much of each good and service will be available. This is no simple task since thousands of items are produced.

Moreover, the production levels of the various goods and services must be coordinated so that if more sugar is to be produced, then more arable land, fertilizer, farm labor, and so on must be provided.

Finally, by setting the prices on almost all goods and services, and by setting the wage rates for almost all citizens, the Cuban government can dictate who gets what share of these products.

Setting prices and wages and stipulating how much of each item is to be produced for the whole economy are Herculean tasks. They are done with the help of computers by a large bureaucracy. Often, mistakes are made. The quota of sugar cannot be met because not enough tractors are available. Without sugar, the rum quota cannot be met.

On the other hand, the command system has some commendable features. Wages can be set so that there is no lower class. However, if everyone makes about the same income, incentives to work hard and develop new lines of business are discouraged. Still, the price of alcohol can be set high to curtail alcoholism, while the price of textbooks can be established artificially low to encourage education.

The Cuban economy is not a pure command economy. There is some experimentation with households and firms being allowed to sell their excess production in markets where prices are not fixed by the government. And there are many transactions between households that the government cannot control. Some products and a variety of services are provided in the "underground economy."

Capitalism

Capitalism has been defined by different writers in remarkably different ways. Some point to the importance of private property in capitalist economies, while others note the emphasis on risk-taking and entrepreneurial skills. The best definition of capitalism, however, is in regard to how the basic economic questions are addressed. Capitalism is an economic system where supply and demand determine prices. These prices coordinate the economy by resolving what and how much will be produced. Supply and demand will also determine a person's income and therefore how much of the production the person can obtain for his or her own use.

In this type of system, the government does not run the economy but, instead, attempts to create an environment where prices can be determined in free markets. Amazingly, these prices coordinate the economy.

In a capitalist economy, prices determine how much of each item will be produced. If consumers want more baggy, pleated pants instead of blue jeans, then the price of baggy, pleated pants increases and the price of jeans falls. Producers, with an eye on profit possibilities, then manufacture more baggy, pleated pants and fewer jeans. In fact, textile manufacturers who do not respond to the price changes could go out of business.

Consumers, not the government, determine how much of each item will be produced. They do this by purchasing the products they like. When consumers demand and purchase products, they are voting for those products. The prices of consumers' favorite products rise, and this sends a signal to suppliers to provide more of that product.

An individual's income determines how much of the production he can obtain and enjoy, but income is largely determined by the wages an individual receives. And the wage rate is just another price in the economy: the price of labor.

Notice that the government does not have to get involved in setting prices and wages in capitalist economies. Prices and wages are determined in free markets, and these prices serve to coordinate the economy and answer the basic economic questions. Prices govern the behavior of consumers and producers who seek to make the most out of their respective resources. Just the right goods and services are produced in just the right amounts. This is known as "allocative efficiency" in economic jargon.

Allocative Efficiency

A market is a mechanism that allows buyers and sellers to exchange a good or service. A free market is unfettered by interference from anyone not directly involved in the exchange. The hallmark of a capitalist economy is prices determined in free markets. Markets that are regulated by the government or any other agency are not truly free. By this definition, the market for beef in the United States is not free because it is regulated by several agencies including the U.S. Department of Agriculture. However, because Americans mostly want to buy inspected beef, we can argue about whether or not the market for inspected beef in America is truly free.

In the next chapter, we shall see in great detail how prices are determined in perfectly competitive markets—free markets with many buyers and sellers. The more perfectly competitive markets there are in an economy, the closer the economy is to perfect capitalism.

When the prices of products are determined in perfectly competitive markets, an amazing thing happens: The economy's fundamental problems are answered. Consider the question of how much of a particular good is to be produced. In the market for tulips, if the most any buyer is willing to pay is two cents per tulip, then none will be produced. But if buyers have a mania for tulips and are willing to pay a lot, then many will be produced, and the amount of resources devoted to tulip production will be vast.

The other fundamental question is: *Who will get how much of each good or service*? If our tulip-crazed society is capitalist, then competitive markets will answer this question as well. A person's income will determine how many tulips he gets, and those incomes are determined in competitive markets. Labor is another product, and if the most any buyer is willing to pay is two cents an hour, then little or no labor will be supplied. But if buyers (or shall we call them employers?) are willing to pay quite a bit for an expert in tulip production, then a lot of experts will step forward offering their labor services in this industry. Indeed, a lot of resources will be devoted to tulip production in this society, and those with agricultural skills or fertile land or greenhouses will be handsomely rewarded.

Not only does capitalism answer the fundamental economic questions, it does so in a decentralized way. No authority has to be on the lookout that enough tulips are produced. When buyers offer high prices, sellers respond to the profit motive and bring a bounty to market. But sellers are discouraged from bringing too much because in that case they would not be able to sell all their stock. They would begin to lower their asking price. The new lower price would caution others from entering the market as sellers, and current sellers would have less incentive to work overtime to bring so many tulips to market.

Capitalist societies respond very well to changes in the population's preferences. Imagine that tulips become passé and now people want roses. Buyers offer low prices for tulips and high prices for roses. Sellers respond to the profit motive by bringing fewer tulips to market and more roses. In this way, resources are switched from tulip production to rose production.

When all of the prices in an economy are determined in competitive markets, resources will be deployed in the optimal way to ensure the right products are made in just the right amounts to satisfy the buyers. This result is truly amazing since it is the result of decisions made by buyers and sellers across the economy in a decentralized way. No central planning is required. The only necessity is that people pursue their own self-interest.

This fascinating result of competitive markets is known as allocative efficiency. The mathematical proof that capitalism results in allocative efficiency is attributed to Léon Walras, but Adam Smith understood the concept well and put it in a very memorable way in 1776:

> *Every individual . . . neither intends to promote the public interest, nor knows how much he is promoting it . . . he intends only his own security; and by directing that industry in such a manner as its produce may be of the greatest value, he intends only his own gain, and he is in this, as in many other cases, led by an invisible hand to promote an end which was no part of his intention.*

> The Wealth of Nations, *Book IV, Chapter II, p. 758, para. 9.*

The fact that allocative efficiency follows from free markets leads some people to conclude that the government should not interfere in economic matters. Government intervention can only interfere with the working of the invisible hand. Once again, Adam Smith pointed out that there will always be a need for government. Who will ensure that markets are indeed competitive? Who will settle disputes between buyers and sellers? Who will protect people, their products, and their money while they are conducting market exchanges? In the next section, we explore why no economy can be purely capitalist.

The Mixed Economy

All of the countries in the world today use a blend of government commands and capitalism to address the fundamental economic questions that arise. In the United States, capitalism is emphasized, but government commands are used when free markets break down. For instance, society benefits when people pursue education beyond high school. The government promotes higher education by providing scholarships, grants, and loans. Private colleges have competition from state schools. Our government doesn't trust the production of higher education to the market. It gets involved and increases the equilibrium quantity of college degrees granted.

Similarly, there is no pure command economy on the planet; even Cuba and North Korea have some free markets. It is best to view the economies of the world on a spectrum with pure capitalism on the right and pure command economies on the left. The United States is closer to pure capitalism than France, and France is closer to pure capitalism than Cuba.

As we go forward, we will focus on the fundamental macroeconomic concepts of capitalist economies such as the United States where the decentralized decision making of the price system predominates.

> **TIP**
>
> There are several other instances where competitive markets break down. You will need to know these well only if you are taking the Microeconomics exam.

The Circular Flow Diagram

In capitalist economies, most of the resources are owned by individuals and households. The government and business enterprises will own some resources in such a system but not the lion's share. Moreover, since most of the large firms are owned by stockholders (individuals and households) and most government resources, such as Yosemite National Park, are considered to be jointly owned by everyone, it is fair to assume that all of the resources are owned by individuals and households.

The circular flow diagram portrayed in Figure 3.1 shows these resources (land, labor, and capital) flowing from households to firms. In return, households receive wages and profits. This exchange of resources for money is known as the *market for resources*.

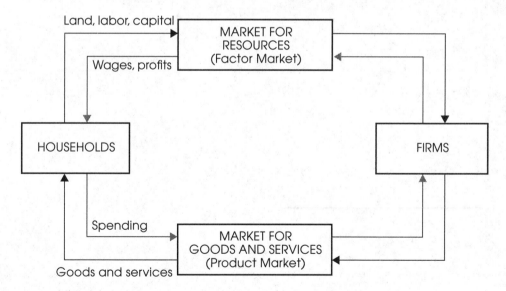

Figure 3.1 The Circular Flow Diagram

Households spend their wage and profit income to purchase the goods and services supplied by firms. This exchange of income for products is known as the *market for goods and services*.

The circular flow diagram shows how resources are used to produce goods and services and how these goods and services are distributed. Essentially, individuals and households sell their resources to firms that use the resources to produce goods and services. Individuals and households use the proceeds from the sale of their resources to purchase the output of the firms.

The circular flow diagram can be expanded to include the government and banks. There would be more boxes and more lines representing flows of money and products, but no matter how complicated or simple, the circular flow diagram shows how institutions in capitalist economies are tied together.

SUMMARY

Even if you drop out of society and go to live as a hermit on an isolated mountaintop, you will have to cope with the fundamental economic questions: What should be produced with the resources on hand and how much of each item should be produced? Hermits, however, do not have to deal with the other fundamental economic question: How much of the production should each member of society get?

- Government commands and capitalism are two general ways to address the fundamental economic questions. Each approach has its strengths and weaknesses. Basically, an economy organized by government commands can be more equitable while a market economy is more efficient.

- When supply and demand are allowed to determine prices in competitive markets, just the right amount of goods and services will be produced to satisfy society's wants. This is known as *allocative efficiency*. Resources are deployed in the production of the things society desires.

- No country in the world is purely capitalistic. Even in the United States the government does not allow free markets to determine all prices. Similarly, no nation is a pure command economy. Even Cuba has some free markets.

Multiple-Choice Review Questions

1. Which of the following is a fundamental economic question?

   (A) Who will get how much of each good and service?
   (B) Who should pay taxes?
   (C) Who will work?
   (D) Who will make the economic decisions?
   (E) Who will be allowed into the economy?

2. In a command economy

   (A) the market dictates the answers to the fundamental economic questions.
   (B) competition helps answer the fundamental economic questions.
   (C) state and local governments respond to the fundamental economic questions.
   (D) the central government dictates the answers to the fundamental economic questions.
   (E) laws are set up to answer the fundamental economic questions.

3. Market economies

   (A) rely on markets to coordinate economic activity.
   (B) rely on the government to address the fundamental economic questions.
   (C) rely on elected officials to make the most important economic decisions.
   (D) rely on courts to ensure people and firms get what they deserve.
   (E) are more equitable than command economies.

4. Prices in capitalist economies are

   (A) unfair.
   (B) determined in competitive markets.
   (C) determined, in most cases, by the federal government.
   (D) a reflection of our basic values.
   (E) a means to achieve equality.

5. If the market for corn is competitive, then

   (A) it is difficult for new suppliers to join in.
   (B) buyers will get all they want at a good price.
   (C) the market favors buyers.
   (D) the market is fair.
   (E) there must be many buyers and sellers.

6. Compared to a command economy, a capitalist economy emphasizes

   (A) equity.
   (B) planning.
   (C) efficiency.
   (D) centralization.
   (E) human rights.

7. Allocative efficiency

   (A) implies optimal resource deployment.
   (B) means no inferior products will be produced.
   (C) ensures the distribution of output is equitable.
   (D) can only occur in pure command economies.
   (E) defies the idea of the invisible hand.

8. Scarcity

   (A) implies nonoptimal resource deployment.
   (B) applies to some, but not all, resources.
   (C) is an issue in every economy.
   (D) exists in command economies only.
   (E) is eradicated by the invisible hand.

9. If buyers bid up the price of a good, then

   (A) sellers will try to bring more of it to market.
   (B) sellers will bring less to market anticipating less demand at the higher price.
   (C) fewer resources will be devoted to its production.
   (D) they must not want it.
   (E) its price will eventually fall back to normal.

10. If a capitalist society wants more coffee, then the relative price of coffee will

   (A) fall.
   (B) rise.
   (C) not necessarily change.
   (D) remain unchanged.
   (E) change indeterminantly.

11. If the relative price of coffee rises due to a change in tastes in a capitalist society, then

   (A) less coffee will be consumed.
   (B) more resources will be devoted to coffee production.
   (C) less tea will be consumed.
   (D) suppliers will bring less to market.
   (E) the price will eventually return to where it was prior to the change in tastes.

12. The invisible hand

   (A) works in command economies as well as capitalist economies.
   (B) works in capitalist societies.
   (C) is concerned with resource allocation when markets are regulated.
   (D) refers to regulation in command economies.
   (E) requires altruism.

13. In the market for resources in the circular flow diagram, households

   (A) get goods and services from firms.
   (B) send only labor to firms.
   (C) send only land and labor to firms.
   (D) send land, labor, and capital to firms.
   (E) send spending to firms.

14. In the market for goods and services in the circular flow diagram, households

   (A) get wages and profits from firms.
   (B) get goods and services from firms.
   (C) send only land and labor to firms.
   (D) send land, labor, and capital to firms.
   (E) send labor to firms.

15. Suppose we observe the price of a product rising and more of the product being bought and sold. This could be a result of

   (A) a decrease in the supply of the product.
   (B) an increase in the supply of the product.
   (C) an increase in demand for the product.
   (D) a decrease in demand for the product.
   (E) a shortage.

Free-Response Review Questions

1. What are the fundamental economic questions?

2. Contrast how the fundamental economic questions are addressed in command versus capitalist economies.

3. Cite the advantages and disadvantages of command economies.

Answer Explanations

1. **(A)** Any society will have to determine how all that is produced is distributed to its members.

2. **(D)** Command economies are characterized by centralized control.

3. **(A)** Market economies rely on supply and demand to determine prices in free markets.

4. **(B)** Capitalism needs competitive markets to function properly. Competitive markets feature many buyers and sellers and no outside interference.

5. **(E)** Markets with one or only a few sellers cannot be competitive. Similarly, markets with only one or a few buyers cannot be competitive.

6. **(C)** Competitive markets are ruthless in promoting efficiencies. Command economies have the potential to be more equitable.

7. **(A)** Allocative efficiency occurs when just the right products are produced in just the right amounts to satisfy society's demands. To achieve this, resources must be optimally deployed.

8. **(C)** Coping with scarcity is the essence of economics.

9. **(A)** A price increase induces sellers to bring more of the good to market.

10. **(B)** In a competitive market, if buyers demand more of a good, its price increases.

11. **(B)** If the price of a good increases, then sellers bring more to market. The only way to bring more to market is to devote more time, energy, and resources in order to increase supply.

12. **(B)** The invisible hand guides an economy to allocative efficiency when individuals do what is best for themselves in an environment of free markets.

13. **(D)** In the market for resources, households send resources (land, labor, and capital) to firms in return for payment in the form of wages and profits.

14. **(B)** In the market for goods and services, households receive goods and services from firms in return for payment.

15. **(C)** In a free market, if the demand for the good increases, then its price will rise. Sellers will bring more to market, and more ends up being bought and sold.

Free-Response Review Answers

1. There are two fundamental economic questions that any society will have to address:
    (1) How much, if any, of each good and service should be produced? and (2) Who will get how much of each good and service?

2. In command economies, the central government stipulates what and how much of most products will be produced. By setting prices and wages, the central government can also dictate how much of the production is allotted to each household. In short, the central government controls production and income in command economies.

    In capitalist economies, free markets coordinate output and income. Supply and demand, which depend upon the decentralized decision making of all consumers and producers, determine what and how much will be produced. Supply and demand also determine incomes and, therefore, who gets how much of each good and service.

3. One disadvantage of command economies is that there can be a lack of incentive to work hard to get ahead. Since the government decides one's income level, it may not pay to put one's nose to the grindstone—the government may reward you all the same, anyway. One advantage of command economies is that prices can be set to achieve social goals. For example, the price of textbooks could be set low to promote education. Another advantage of command economies is that incomes can be set more equitably than capitalist economies.

    Capitalist economies are typically more allocatively efficient than command economies; also, they do not require the large bureaucracy of command economies.

Demand and Supply: The Basics

Learning Objectives

In this chapter, you will learn:

→ Changes in demand and supply
→ Law of demand and law of supply
→ Equilibrium
→ Changes in quantity demanded and quantity supplied

Introduction

Economics is sometimes said to be "common sense made complicated." This description is somewhat true of the concepts of supply and demand, as all of us have experience buying and likely selling products. Supply and demand are fundamental to the study of economics, and understanding them is essential for performing well on both the AP Micro and Macro exams. At the heart of economics is the role of prices in decision making and in the allocation of scarce resources through supply and demand. By mastering the basics of supply and demand, essential concepts in AP Micro and Macro are understood much more easily. This chapter will cover the basics of supply and demand for you in detail, and with a little effort, it will be common sense made simple.

Demand and the Law of Demand

A market's **demand** shows the quantity of a product a consumer is willing and able to purchase at each and every price. The demand for a product is shown graphically as a demand curve (see Figure 4.1). The demand curve performs one important job, and that is showing the quantity consumers want to buy at every price. You likely already know that at higher prices, people tend to buy less of a product, and at lower prices, people buy more (common sense!). If so, then you also already know the **law of demand**, which states that when the price of a product increases, the quantity demanded decreases, and vice versa (*ceteris paribus*—"all other things remaining unchanged"). This relationship is shown in the downsloping demand curve shown in Figure 4.1. An easy way to remember the demand curve's slope is "DEmand DEclines."

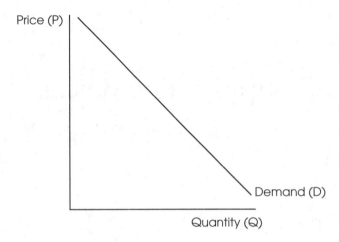

Figure 4.1 A Demand Curve

Reasons for the Law of Demand

There are three important reasons why people buy less of a good when the price increases and more when a price decreases, giving the demand curve its downward slope.

1. **THE INCOME EFFECT.** When prices fall, consumers can afford to buy more of a particular good or service. When prices rise, consumers' incomes will not buy as many goods and services, and the quantity people will buy of a product decreases. This is known as the income effect.
2. **THE SUBSTITUTION EFFECT.** When the price of a good increases, its price has also gone up relative to the prices of other goods, all else equal. If we assume apples and oranges are substitutes, an increase in the price of apples will lead consumers to purchase more oranges and fewer apples. This is known as the substitution effect and further reinforces the notion of a downward-sloping demand curve and the law of demand.
3. **DIMINISHING MARGINAL UTILITY.** As more units of the same product are consumed, the utility or satisfaction from each good decreases with each additional unit. As utility decreases, so does the price you are willing to pay; thus, the decrease in price as quantity demanded increases as shown on a demand curve.

Change in Quantity Demanded vs. Change in Demand

One of the most challenging concepts for students to understand is the difference between a change in quantity demanded and a change in demand. These two phrases have different meanings although they sound similar. When the market for a product only has a price change, there is not a shift in the demand curve but a movement along an existing curve. This is known as a change in the **quantity demanded.** As shown in Figure 4.2, as the price decreases from P_1 to P_2, the quantity demanded increases from Q_1 to Q_2. As price is the only variable that changes, this is just a change in the quantity people would buy at the new price (the quantity demanded), and no shift in the curve occurs. A change in price is just a movement along a fixed demand curve, a change in the quantity demanded.

> ### Useful Hint
>
> The only variable that leads to a change in quantity demanded (a movement along a fixed curve) is a change in price.

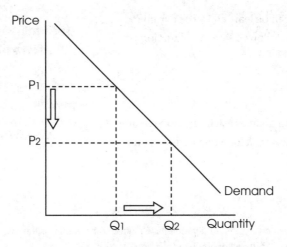

Figure 4.2 A Change in Quantity Demanded

Shifts of the Demand Curve: The Determinants of Demand

In addition to a price change affecting consumers' choices, what happens when consumers want to buy more or less of a product at the same price? These are not just price changes that result in a change in the quantity demanded but variables that cause consumers to buy more or less of a product at the same price. These are called the **determinants of demand** (also called shifters of demand). As shown in Figure 4.3, an increase in one of these determinants of demand would shift the demand curve to the right (D_1 to D_2), and a decrease would shift the curve to the left (D_1 to D_3).

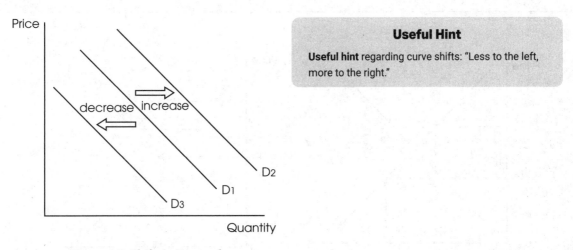

> ### Useful Hint
>
> **Useful hint** regarding curve shifts: "Less to the left, more to the right."

Figure 4.3 Shifts in Demand

The determinants of demand can be learned by the acronym SPICE shown in the box below, followed by an explanation of each with examples.

Substitute Goods

Two goods are substitutes when an increase in the price of one good results in an increase in demand for a related good, and vice versa.

**Determinants of Demand—SPICE
(Shifters of the Demand Curve)**

S—Substitute goods
P^2—Preferences or population
I—Income
C—Complementary goods
E—Expectations

Useful Hint

Price and demand for substitute goods have a direct relationship: if the price of one goes up, the demand for the other product goes up.

EXAMPLE

Assume consumers view apples and oranges as perfect substitutes. If the price of apples increases while the price of oranges remains constant, the quantity demanded of apples decreases, and consumers will now demand more oranges at each price, shifting the curve for oranges to the right (see Figures 4.4 and 4.5). (**Note:** the demand curve for apples will not shift; this is just a decrease in the quantity demanded, a movement along a fixed demand curve. The demand curve for oranges will increase and shift to the right.)

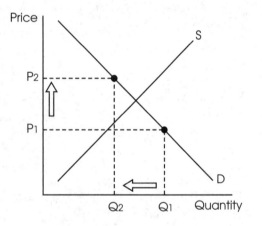

Figure 4.4 Market for Apples

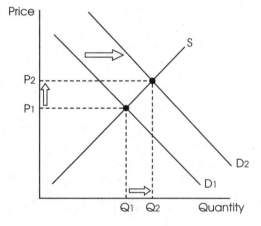

Figure 4.5 Market for Oranges

Preferences

Preferences refers to a consumer's tastes or preferences for a good or service. If people's preferences for a specific product increase, the demand curve will shift to the right.

> **EXAMPLE**
>
> A successful advertising campaign for a product by a celebrity increases the demand for a product, making consumers want to buy more at each price level (a shift from D1 to D2 in Figure 4.3). Other examples of preferences changing demand are the latest fads in fashion or a decline in popularity for out-of-date technology.

Population

Sometimes also referred to as the number of consumers in a market, population refers to the total number of buyers in a specific market. A bigger market will mean more demand.

> **EXAMPLE**
>
> If there is a huge baby boom in a country, there will be more demand for baby supplies. An increase in the number of people older than 65 would lead to more demand for retirement and nursing homes (both increasing demand D1 to D2 in Figure 4.3).

Income

When people have more income, they generally increase their demand for most products. Most goods are **normal goods**, where as income increases, the demand for a product increases. Some goods, however, are **inferior goods**, where an increase in income leads to a decrease in demand.

> **EXAMPLE**
>
> Some normal goods are steak and vacation homes. As consumers have more income, their demand would go up for these products (a shift from D1 to D2 in Figure 4.3). Or consider used cars or goods sold at thrift stores. As consumers' incomes increase, they may buy more new cars instead of used or shop for new clothing as opposed to secondhand clothes. In this case, used cars and thrift store clothes would be examples of inferior goods.

Complementary Goods

Goods that are purchased separately but are used together are known as complementary goods.

> **Useful Hint**
>
> The price and demand for complementary goods have an inverse relationship. If the price of one increases, the demand for the other complementary good decreases, and vice versa.

> **EXAMPLE**
>
> Consider the market for large cars and gasoline. If the price of gas rises significantly, consumers will find it more expensive to own a large, gas-guzzling car. The demand for large cars would decrease due to the increase in price for gas (a shift from D_1 to D_3 in Figure 4.3). Another example would be hot dogs and hot dog buns. If the price of hot dogs decreases, the quantity of hot dogs purchased would increase, and the demand for buns would increase, shifting the bun demand curve to the right (a shift from D_1 to D_2 in Figure 4.3).

Expectations

Consumers' expectations of future prices can have a large effect on current demand for a product. An expectation of higher prices in the future will cause an increase in current demand before the price increases.

EXAMPLE

If consumers expect prices of new houses to increase dramatically in the future, the present demand for new houses will increase, shifting demand to the right (a shift from D1 to D2 in Figure 4.3). If people feel that home prices will decrease significantly next year, that would decrease current demand for housing, as consumers will wait until next year (a shift from D1 to D3 in Figure 4.3).

Supply and the Law of Supply

Price changes send different signals to buyers and sellers. Buyers dislike high prices, but they are likely to make sellers happy. Since buyers and sellers feel differently about prices, the supply curve will have a different meaning and slope than the demand curve. A market's **supply** shows the quantity of a product a producer is willing and able to offer for sale at various prices. The supply for a product is shown graphically as a supply curve, as in Figure 4.6. The supply curve performs one important job, which is showing the quantity producers want to offer for sale at every price. The **law of supply** states that when the price of a product increases, the quantity supplied increases, *ceteris paribus*.

> **Useful Hint**
>
> An easy way to remember the positive slope of the supply curve is "Supply to the sky." Also, when drawing note the quantity axis and how it's increasing as it slopes upward.

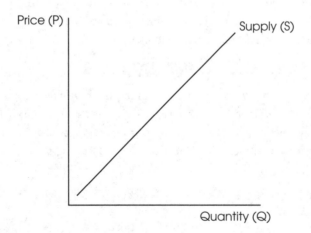

Figure 4.6 A Supply Curve

Reasons for the Law of Supply

When prices increase, sellers have greater opportunities for increasing their profits. This is one reason to explain why as prices rise, so does the quantity supplied. Also, as producers increase production, the cost of producing each additional unit generally increases as sellers face rising marginal costs of production. Hence, it takes a higher price for the product to induce producers to offer more for sale. Conversely, if the price falls for a product, there is less incentive or motivation to offer a product for sale and the quantity brought to market will decrease. As prices fall, firms find it harder to cover costs of production and earn smaller profits, so less is offered for sale.

Change in Quantity Supplied vs. Change in Supply

Similar to demand, there is also a distinction between a change in quantity supplied vs. a change in supply. When the market for a product only has a price change, there is not a shift in the supply curve but a move along an existing curve. This is known as a change in the **quantity supplied**. As shown in Figure 4.7, as the price increases from P_1 to P_2, the quantity supplied also increases from Q_1 to Q_2. Because price is the only variable that changes, this is only a change in the quantity supplied, and no shift in the curve occurs. There is a change in the quantity producers will offer for sale, but the curve does not shift. A change in price is just a movement along a fixed supply curve.

> **Useful Hint**
>
> The only variable that leads to a change in quantity supplied (a movement along a fixed curve) is a change in price.

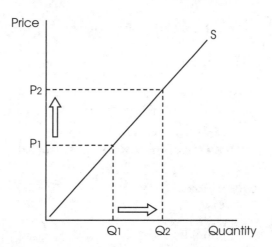

Figure 4.7 A Change in Quantity Supplied

Shifts of the Supply Curve: Determinants of Supply

There are many factors for producers that impact the amount of a good that will be offered for sale at each price. Just as with the demand curve, these are more than mere price changes. These factors that cause producers to offer more or less of a product for sale at the same prices are called the **determinants of supply** (also called shifters of supply). As shown in Figure 4.8, an increase in one of these determinants of supply would shift the supply curve to the right (S_1 to S_2), and a decrease would shift the curve to the left (S_1 to S_3).

> **Useful Hint**
>
> Students sometimes mistakenly shift an increase in supply to the left, as it looks like it is going up. However, an increase in supply shifts to the right, and a decrease to the left, just like demand shifts.

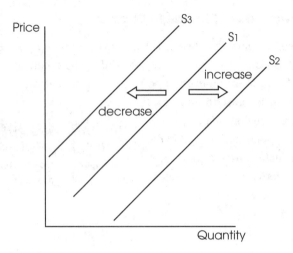

Figure 4.8 Shifts in Supply

The determinants of demand can be learned by the acronym ROTTEN shown on page 83, followed by an explanation of each with examples.

> ### Determinants of Supply—
> ### ROTTEN (Shifters of the Supply Curve)
> R—Resource costs and availability
> O—Other goods' prices
> T—Technology
> T—Taxes and subsidies
> E—Expectations
> N—Number of sellers

Resource Costs and Availability

When the cost of producing a product increases, the supply of a product decreases, and vice versa. A change in the cost of producing a product affects the supply of a good or service. Anytime one of the resources (land, labor, capital) used in production changes in price, supply changes. Note that labor is a resource and is usually the largest cost of running a business.

EXAMPLE

If the cost of fertilizer used in the production of corn increases, the supply of corn would decrease (shown by a shift from S1 to S3 in Figure 4.8). If labor costs decrease for smartphone producers, resource costs fall, and the supply of phones would increase (shown by a shift from S1 to S2 in Figure 4.8).

Other Goods' Prices

Sometimes a firm can easily switch between production of several different products. Profit-maximizing firms will choose to produce what gives them the most profit. The prices of these alternative products affect their supply of both.

> **EXAMPLE**
>
> A farmer who has a fixed amount of land is producing corn but can use his land to grow either corn or wheat. If the price of wheat increases significantly relative to corn, the farmer will switch from producing corn to producing wheat. The opportunity cost of producing corn increased, thus the switch to wheat. This would decrease the supply curve for corn and shift to the left (a shift from S1 to S3 in Figure 4.8).

Technology

New technology can decrease production costs and increase productivity that results in the supply curve shifting to the right.

> **EXAMPLE**
>
> Many automobile factories today use robots and other machines in the production process, increasing productivity and shifting the supply curve to the right. Several hundred years ago, the invention of the cotton gin drastically increased the supply of cotton (a shift from S1 to S2 in Figure 4.8).

Taxes and Subsidies

A **tax** on the production of a good will result in increased production costs, which will decrease supply. If a firm is fortunate enough to get a **subsidy**, a payment from the government to produce a product, profits increase at each price level that induce increased supply.

> **EXAMPLE**
>
> A farmer receives a subsidy for producing corn and now has an incentive or motivation to increase supply. Conversely, a cigarette producer may be taxed on each unit produced, thus increasing the cost of production and decreasing supply, shifting the supply curve to the left (a shift from S1 to S3 in Figure 4.8).

Expectations

Similar to buyers, sellers also include future price considerations into their actions in a market. If sellers think the price will increase in the future, they may hold back the amount offered for sale, decreasing current supply, with the ultimate goal of increasing profits in the future. The converse holds true if producers think the price of a good may fall. They would increase current production today, increasing supply, shifting the supply curve to the right.

> **EXAMPLE**
>
> A cotton farmer who thinks the prices will rise next year may not bring his current harvest to market, with the hope of selling for higher prices in the future. This would decrease the current supply curve for cotton (shown by a shift from S1 to S3 in Figure 4.8).

Number of Sellers

As more sellers and competition enter a market, the supply increases. While the extra competition may be difficult for sellers, the extra supply usually is good for consumers, who receive more choice and lower prices as the supply curve shifts to the right.

EXAMPLE

The opening of new pizza restaurants in a college town increases the supply of pizzas, shifting supply to the right. Students benefit from more choice and lower prices from the extra competition (a shift from S_1 to S_2 in Figure 4.8).

Market Equilibrium: Supply and Demand Together

A market's equilibrium price is the only price in a market where buyers want to buy the exact amount sellers want to sell (also known as the market-clearing price). There is no surplus or shortage. A **surplus** exists when the quantity supplied is greater than the quantity demanded, which is when price is above the equilibrium price. In a competitive market with a surplus, prices will eventually fall to the equilibrium price. A **shortage** is when the price below equilibrium and the quantity demanded is greater than the quantity supplied. Buyers want more products than are offered for sale. In a competitive market, prices will increase to the equilibrium price. Increases in the price reduce the shortage (buyers or consumers "bid" against one another, driving up the price until the surplus or shortage disappears).

Equilibrium—The Illustration (see Figure 4.9)

Equilibrium occurs at E (price = $5; quantity demanded and supplied = 300), the intersection of S and D (supply and demand), where the quantity demanded = quantity supplied. The characteristics of equilibrium (above) apply.

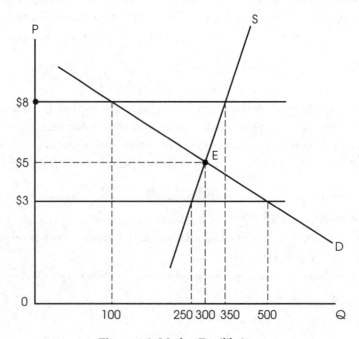

Figure 4.9 Market Equilibrium

Disequilibrium

If the price is $8, then there is disequilibrium since the quantity demanded at $8 would equal 100 and the quantity supplied would equal 350; therefore, there would be a surplus of 250. As the market (suppliers) reacts to the surplus, the price will drop until it equals $5 (equilibrium price) at which the market is "cleared" of the surplus. The converse holds, when the price is *below* the equilibrium, such as $3, when a shortage of 150 would develop. At $3, the quantity demanded exceeds the quantity supplied (500 > 250) and the consumers (buyers) would bid the price up until it reaches $5 (equilibrium price) and the market is cleared of any shortage.

Changes in Equilibrium

To solve a problem on supply and demand shifters, use the following steps:
1. **Is it supply or demand?** (Or both if it is a double shifter—watch out for those!) Knowing the acronyms for the determinants of demand (SPICE) and supply (ROTTEN) are necessary.
2. **Is it an increase (shift to the right) or decrease (shift to the left)?**
3. **Just shift it, noting your new equilibrium price and quantity.**

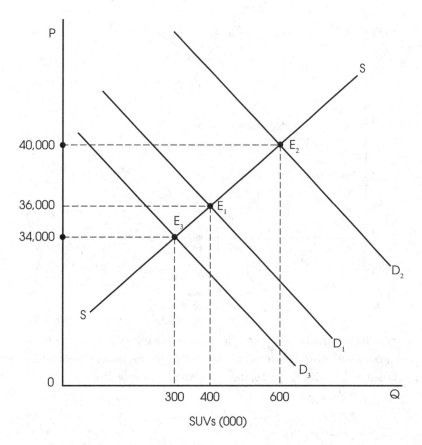

Figure 4.10 Market for SUVs: Equilibrium Changes

For example, if there is an increase in consumer preferences for SUVs, then the demand curve would shift (increase) from D_1 to D_2 (note the supply curve does not shift, but there is a change in the quantity supplied from 400,000 to 600,000). As illustrated above, the new equilibrium is at E_2 with the equilibrium price of $40,000 (up from $36,000) and the equilibrium quantity at 600,000 SUVs (up from 400,000 SUVs). This same kind of effect would occur if one of the other determinants of demand changed in the same direction.

Useful Hint

With supply constant, an increase in demand will cause an increase in equilibrium price and quantity. Conversely, a decrease in demand leads to a decrease in equilibrium price and quantity.

With supply again given at S, and with the expectation that the prices of SUVs will decrease very soon since the market is becoming saturated with new models from competitors, demand for SUVs will now decrease as potential buyers wait for a better deal. This is illustrated (in Figure 4.10) with a shift of D_1 to D_3 and a new equilibrium at E_3 (equilibrium price at $36,000, down from $36,000, and equilibrium quantity at 300,000, down from 400,000 SUVs).

We will now analyze shifts in supply with demand as the constant.

With demand constant, an increase in supply will lead to a decrease in equilibrium price and an increase in equilibrium quantity; conversely, a decrease in supply will lead to an increase in equilibrium price and a decrease in equilibrium quantity. Thus, if a producer of a particular form of steel faces increasing costs of coking coal (an input in steel production), he will decrease his supply of steel. This is illustrated in Figure 4.11.

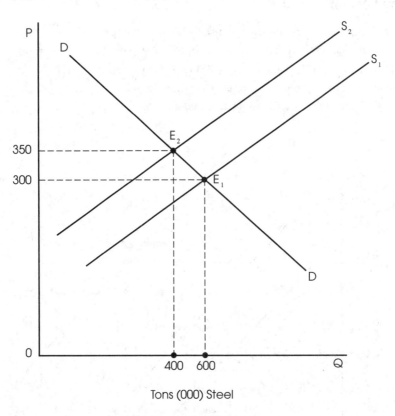

Tons (000) Steel

Figure 4.11 Steel Market

As a result of a supply shift (decrease) from S_1 to S_2, the equilibrium price increases to $350 a ton (from $300) and the equilibrium quantity decreases to 400,000 tons (from 600,000). Note the demand curve doesn't shift, but there is a change in the quantity demanded, a movement along a fixed demand curve.

Effects of Supply and Demand Shifts on Price and Quantity

See Figure 4.12 for a summary of how demand and supply shifts affect price and quantity. Note that on the curve that doesn't shift, there is a change in the quantity demanded or supplied, a movement along a fixed curve.

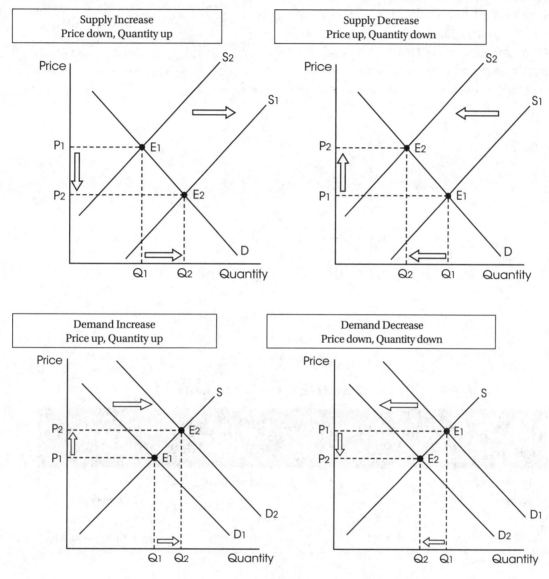

Figure 4.12

The Double-Shift Rule

The double-shift rule says that when there are simultaneous shifts in both demand and supply, either price or quantity will be indeterminate. For example, in Figure 4.13 demand increases while supply decreases, resulting in a price increase, while quantity is indeterminate. For the purposes of the AP Economics test, you will not know how far each curve shifts, leading to one of the two being indeterminate. See Table 4.1 for the double-shift possibilities on price and quantity.

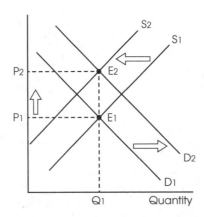

Figure 4.13

Table 4.1 Effects on Price and Quantity

Change in Demand	Change in Supply	Effect on Equilibrium Price	Effect on Equilibrium Quantity
Increase	Increase	Indeterminate	Increase
Decrease	Decrease	Indeterminate	Decrease
Increase	Decrease	Increase	Indeterminate
Decrease	Increase	Decrease	Indeterminate

SUMMARY

DEMAND

1. A market's **demand** curve shows the quantity of a product a consumer is willing and able to purchase at various prices.
2. If the price of a good changes, move along an existing demand curve for that good. A price change does not shift the curve. This is called a **change in quantity demanded**.
3. A nonprice change in demand, one of the determinants of demand (remember the SPICE shifters), shifts the demand curve. Shift to the right for an increase or left for a decrease. This is called a **change in demand**.
4. The **law of demand** states that when the price of a product increases, the quantity demanded decreases, and vice versa.
5. The demand curve is downward sloping due to the diminishing **marginal utility**, **income**, and **substitution effects**.

SUPPLY

1. A market's **supply** curve shows the quantity of a product a producer is willing and able to offer for sale at various prices.
2. If the price of a good changes, move along the existing supply curve of the good. A price change does not shift the curve. This is called a **change in quantity supplied**.
3. A nonprice change in supply, one of the determinants of supply (remember the ROTTEN shifters), shifts the supply curve. Shift to the right for an increase or left for a decrease. This is called a **change in supply**.
4. The **law of supply** states that when the price of a product increases, the quantity supplied increases and vice versa.
5. The supply curve is upward sloping because as the price of a good rises, producers will have a greater incentive to produce more.

EQUILIBRIUM

1. The steps for solving supply and demand problems are as follows: Is it the supply or demand curve affected? Is it an increase or a decrease? Just shift it!
2. The **equilibrium price** is the market-clearing price where the curves intersect. Here there is no surplus or shortage.
3. Only at this one price will the quantity demanded be equal to the quantity supplied. The quantity at this price is called the equilibrium quantity.
4. At any price above the equilibrium price, there is a surplus as quantity supplied is greater than quantity demanded. Competitive market forces will cause the price to decrease.
5. At any price below the equilibrium price, there is a shortage as quantity demanded is greater than the quantity supplied. Competitive market forces will cause the price to increase.

Multiple-Choice Review Questions

1. If the government subsidizes the production of corn,

   (A) the demand curve will shift to the left.
   (B) the demand curve will shift to the right.
   (C) the supply curve will shift to the left.
   (D) the supply curve will shift to the right.
   (E) the quantity supplied will increase along a fixed supply curve.

2. If consumers are advised that multigrain bread will substantially lessen the risk of cancer, which of the following will happen in the market for multigrain bread?

   (A) The demand curve will shift to the left, decreasing the price of multigrain bread.
   (B) The supply curve will shift to the left, increasing the price of multigrain bread.
   (C) The demand curve will shift to the right, increasing the price of multigrain bread.
   (D) The supply curve will shift to the right, decreasing the price of multigrain bread.
   (E) None of the above.

3. Assume the supply of bananas decreases due to rising costs of production while demand increases due to consumer preferences. What will happen to the new equilibrium price and quantity?

	Price	**Quantity**
(A)	Increase	Increase
(B)	Increase	Indeterminate
(C)	Decrease	Decrease
(D)	Decrease	Increase
(E)	Indeterminate	Increase

Use the figure below to answer questions 4 and 5.

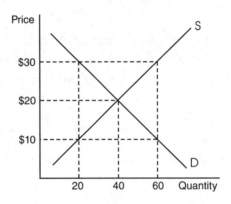

4. The figure shows the market for fidget spinners. Which of the following is true at $30?

   (A) There is a shortage of 60 fidget spinners.
   (B) There is a shortage of 40 fidget spinners.
   (C) There is a surplus of 60 fidget spinners.
   (D) There is a surplus of 40 fidget spinners.
   (E) The market is in equilibrium with no surplus or shortage.

5. Which of the following is true if the government sets a price ceiling at $30? (Note that the price ceiling is set above the equilibrium price.)

   (A) There is a shortage of 60 fidget spinners.
   (B) There is a shortage of 40 fidget spinners.
   (C) There is a surplus 60 fidget spinners.
   (D) There is a surplus of 40 fidget spinners.
   (E) The market is in equilibrium with no surplus or shortage.

6. Suppose that the demand for sugar does not change while at the same time the supply of sugar decreases. One result will be that there will be less sugar bought and sold in the market. How can this occur if there was no shift in demand?

   (A) It cannot occur without a shift in the demand curve.
   (B) There was a decrease in the quantity demanded as the market found a new (higher) equilibrium price.
   (C) The market was in disequilibrium.
   (D) The slope of the demand curve changed.
   (E) There was a decrease in the quantity supplied as the market found a new (higher) equilibrium price.

7. Which of the following would cause the demand for good X to decrease?

   (A) Producers of good X find that the cost of producing Y has increased dramatically.
   (B) The workers who produce good X receive a large increase in wages.
   (C) Goods X and Y are substitutes, and the government imposes a tax on good Y.
   (D) Good X is a normal good, and the government lowers income taxes by 10%.
   (E) Good X is an inferior good, and the government decreases income taxes
       by 15%.

8. What would happen to the market for avocados if a new study claims eating avocados improves heart health and the wages increase for workers who grow avocados?

	Demand	Supply	Price	Quantity
(A)	Increase	Increase	Increase	Increase
(B)	Decrease	Increase	Decrease	Indeterminate
(C)	Increase	Decrease	Increase	Indeterminate
(D)	Decrease	Increase	Indeterminate	Increase
(E)	Increase	Decrease	Increase	Increase

Free-Response Review Questions

1. For each of the following simultaneous changes in demand and in supply for a product, indicate the effect on equilibrium price *and* equilibrium quantity.

   (a) An increase in demand and an increase in supply

   (b) A decrease in demand and a decrease in supply

   (c) An increase in demand and a decrease in supply

2. Assume the market for leather baseball gloves is in equilibrium.

   (a) Draw a correctly labeled graph of the market for leather baseball gloves, labeling the price P_E and the quantity Q_E at equilibrium.

   (b) Now assume the price of leather increases and it is an input used to produce baseball gloves. Using a correctly labeled supply and demand graph, show how this event affects the new equilibrium price and quantity for baseball gloves, labeled P_2 and Q_2.

Answer Explanations

1. **(D)** A subsidy is a supply curve shifter and increases supply. It is a government payment to producers.

2. **(C)** Preferences is a demand shifter, and this would increase demand for bread, shifting the curve to the right and increasing price and quantity.

3. **(B)** The double-shift rule states that when both the demand and supply curves shift, either price or quantity will be indeterminate. Trick to solve: Draw both shifts independently and combine the results. The decrease in supply will increase P and decrease Q. The increase in demand will increase both P and Q. Combining those two results, P definitely increases, and Q is indeterminate.

4. **(D)** At the price of $30, head to the supply curve and down to the quantity supplied, which is 60, and then from the price of $30 to the demand curve and down to the quantity demanded, which is 20. $60 - 20 = 40$.

5. **(E)** A price ceiling is not effective or binding if placed above the equilibrium price, so it is irrelevant, and price is at the market equilibrium of $30.

6. **(B)** The supply curve decreases, leading to a higher price. At higher prices, quantity demanded decreases. There was a change in quantity demanded (a move along a fixed curve due to a price change) but not a change in demand (a shift in the curve).

7. **(E)** People buy more of an inferior good when their income decreases and less when income increases. The tax cut increases income, so demand decreases for inferior goods.

8. **(C)** As this is a double shifter, either P or Q will be indeterminate. Considered separately, the health study increases demand, increasing P and Q. Wages increasing is an increase in resource costs, decreasing the supply curve, increasing P, and decreasing Q. Combining those two shifts, price increases and Q is indeterminate.

Free-Response Review Answers

1. (a) An increase in demand and an increase in supply would result in an increase in equilibrium quantity; the effect on equilibrium price is indeterminate.

   (b) A decrease in demand and a decrease in supply will result in a decrease in equilibrium quantity, and the effect on equilibrium price is indeterminate.

   (c) An increase in demand and a decrease in supply would result in an increase in equilibrium price; the effect on equilibrium is indeterminate.

2. (a), (b) Resource costs are a determinant of supply. So as the costs of producing gloves increases, supply decreases and shifts to the left. This results in a decrease in equilibrium quantity and an increase in price, as shown in the figure below. Hint: Be sure to check that you have labeled price and quantity, the supply and demand curves, and the supply decreasing, as in Figure 4.9.

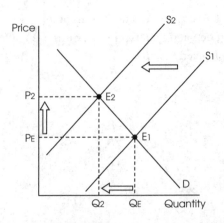

Microeconomics

BARRON'S ESSENTIAL 5

As you work toward achieving that 5 on your AP Microeconomics exam, here are five essentials that you **<u>MUST</u>** know above everything else:

Characteristics of the 4 market structures: You will be asked specific questions on these characteristics as well as questions about pricing, output, and the effects of government regulation. These questions may constitute 25 percent or more of the multiple-choice questions and more than 50 percent of the free-response questions.

- Know how to both correctly graph and interpret the following markets: perfect competition, monopoly, and monopolistic competition. Also, be sure to fully understand an oligopoly's game theory payoff matrix.

- Be sure to know how these markets differ on the degree of efficiency, price elasticity, barriers to entry, economic profits, availability of substitutes, the numbers of sellers, and the independence or interdependence (the latter as in game theory) in pricing strategy among sellers.

- Be sure to know how government regulation of monopolies affects prices, profits, and output.

Relationships of costs and production and their application to output and price decisions. Marginal analysis is central in this context.

- You should know the law of diminishing marginal returns, the relationships between average and marginal costs and product curves, and the distinctions between the long and short run.

- Pay attention to economies of scale, particularly in the adjustment from the short run to the long run in plant capacity.

- Be able to demonstrate the relationship of production to costs (e.g., the inverse relationship between the marginal cost and marginal product curves).

The applications of demand and supply to elasticity and consumer choice.

- You should know the concept of diminishing marginal utility and the utility-maximizing rule. You will be expected to find the utility-maximizing combination of two goods given the constraints.

- You should be able to explain the graph and calculate consumer and producer surpluses. Know the income and substitution effects of a downward-sloping demand curve.

- Know the concepts and the formulas for price, cross price, and income elasticity of demand.

The factor markets for resources used in production: land, labor, and capital.

- Be able to calculate the marginal factor (resource) cost and marginal revenue product.

- Know the profit-maximizing amount of resource employment, where marginal factor product = marginal revenue product.

- Understand and be able to apply the least-cost rule.

Understand how to graph the following 5 graphs, and practice drawing these before the AP exam: 1. Supply and demand (also with a price ceiling or floor added). 2. Perfectly competitive product market side-by-side graphs (the market and firm). 3. Monopoly and monopolistic competition (very similar graphs, only slight differences). 4. Perfectly competitive labor markets side-by-side graphs (labor market and firm). 5. Externalities, both positive and negative.

5

Elasticity, Taxation, and Consumer Choice

Learning Objectives

In this chapter, you will learn:

- → Price elasticity of demand and of supply
- → Income elasticity of demand
- → Cross-price elasticity of demand
- → Impact of taxes on consumers and suppliers
- → Trade, tariffs, and quotas

Introduction

The law of demand states that consumers will buy more of a product when the price falls and less when the price increases. In the real world, however, people may still buy a product when the price of a product increases. How much more or less will people buy with price changes? For business owners, deciding on how to price a product is especially challenging. Price a product too high and a business might have a steep drop-off in sales. A price too low may mean reduced profits. Understanding economics can give both buyers and sellers a lens to analyze prices, specifically **elasticity**, which shows how responsive consumers and producers are to changes in price.

We will also learn how markets affect the welfare of society and when a market fails to produce an optimal output, known as a **deadweight loss**. Lastly, we will look at what happens to markets when a government sets a price either above or below equilibrium (price ceilings and floors) and how tariffs affect consumers and producers.

Elasticity of Demand

Elasticity of demand measures how consumers respond to changes in price. When the price of a good increases, will consumers still buy it or leave the market? When demand is inelastic, consumers are insensitive to changes in price, meaning the change in quantity demanded is small relative to the change in price. With elastic demand, a price change leads to a large change in quantity demanded relative to the price change.

Calculating Price Elasticity of Demand

Use the formula below for calculating price elasticity of demand. Use absolute values for this formula, and ignore the negative sign.

$$\text{Price Elasticity of Demand } (Ed) = \frac{\% \text{ Change in Quantity Demanded } (Qd)}{\% \text{ Change in Price (P)}}$$

Also, you need to know how to calculate a percentage change in price and quantity to use the elasticity formula.

$$\% \text{ Change in Price or } Qd = \frac{\text{Change in P or } Qd}{\text{Initial P or } Qd}$$

Or, for another way to calculate a percentage change, you can just take the new number minus the old divided by the old number. The acronym for that is **N – OOO** (or **New Minus Old Over Old**).

Refer to Table 5.1 to make sure you get the elasticity of demand classifications correct.

TIP

Use this formula for calculating a percentage change. If you learned the midpoint method in class, it's no longer required on the AP exam.

Table 5.1 Elasticity Coefficient Value

Type of Elasticity	Elasticity Value
Perfectly Inelastic	$= 0$
Relatively Inelastic	< 1
Unit Elastic	$= 1$
Relatively Elastic	> 1
Perfectly Elastic	∞ (infinity)

TIP

Be sure to memorize the elasticity values on Table 5.1. They will show up on the test.

EXAMPLE

Suppose the price of designer blue jeans increases from $100 to $120 and the quantity demanded decreases from 10 to 9. First, calculate the percentage change for both price and quantity demanded: ($120 − $100)/$100 = 0.2 = 20% increase in price. (9 − 10)/10 = −0.1 = 10% decrease in the quantity demanded.

$$Ed = (-10\%)/(20\%) = 0.5$$

The price elasticity of demand is 0.5, or relatively inelastic. (Note that the negative sign is dropped!)

EXAMPLE

Suppose the price of apples decreases by 10% and the quantity demanded increases by 20%.

$$Ed = (20\%)/(-10\%) = 2$$

The price elasticity of demand is 2, or relatively elastic.

EXAMPLE

The price of eating at fast food restaurants has increased 5%, and the quantity demanded has decreased by 5%.

$$Ed = (-5\%)/(5\%) = 1$$

The price elasticity of demand is 1, or unit elastic.

EXAMPLE

If the price elasticity of demand for peanuts is 3 and the price of peanuts decreases by 5%, by what percent will the quantity demanded of peanuts increase? Note, here you are given different numbers but still use the same elasticity of demand formula.

$$3 = (x)/(5\%)$$

The percentage change in *Qd* is 15%

Another way to answer this: price elasticity of demand multiplied by the % change in price = % change in *Qd*. (3 × 5%) = 15%

Total Revenues Test to Determine Elasticity

Elasticity is important for firms as it affects their revenue and profits. Total revenue is the amount of money received from sales of a product. It is calculated by taking price × quantity.

The equation is TR = P × Q.

As shown in Table 5.2, if price increases and total revenue decreases, elasticity of demand is relatively elastic. If price increases and total revenue also increases, elasticity of demand is relatively inelastic. Lastly, if price changes and total revenue remains the same, elasticity of demand is unit elastic.

Table 5.2 Total Revenues Test (P × Q = Total Revenue) and Elasticity

Type of Elasticity	Relationship Between Price (P) and Total Revenues (TR)
> 1, Relatively Elastic	P and TR are inversely related
< 1, Relatively Inelastic	P and TR have a direct relationship
= 1, Unit Elastic	TR does not change when P changes

Perfect Elasticity

If demand is **perfectly elastic**, the price elasticity of demand is infinity. As price changes, the change in quantity demanded is infinite. For example, in Figure 5.1, at a price of P_1, buyers will buy any quantity. At any price above P_1, quantity demanded is zero, and at price P_1 and below, quantity demanded is infinite. (An easy way to remember the slope of a perfectly elastic demand curve is to call it "Mr. Flat.")

TIP

To remember the slope of perfectly inelastic or elastic curves, inelastic starts with an "i," which is a vertical letter, just like the perfectly inelastic curve. Perfectly elastic's curve is horizontal, just like the three dashes in the letter "E." Here's another: *inelastic* products are *insensitive* to changes in price.

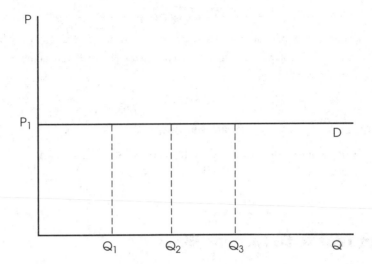

Figure 5.1 Perfectly Elastic Demand

If demand is **perfectly inelastic**, the price elasticity of demand is zero. As price changes, the change in quantity demanded is zero. For example, in Figure 5.2, at either P_1, P_2, or any price, the quantity demanded remains unchanged at Q_1. (An easy way to remember the slope of a perfectly inelastic demand curve is to call it "Mr. Stick.")

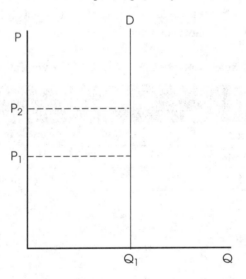

Figure 5.2 Perfectly Inelastic Demand

Elasticity Along a Demand Curve

On a downsloping, linear demand curve, the price elasticity of demand varies along the curve. Think of measuring elasticity as looking at a specific point on the demand curve. In general, the top left of the demand curve is the elastic range, the lower right section is the inelastic range, and the midpoint of the curve is unit elastic. As you can see in Figure 5.3, as the price decreases in the elastic range, total revenue increases. However, as price decreases in the inelastic range, total revenue falls. (You will see this concept again later. *A monopoly always produces in the elastic range of the demand curve.*)

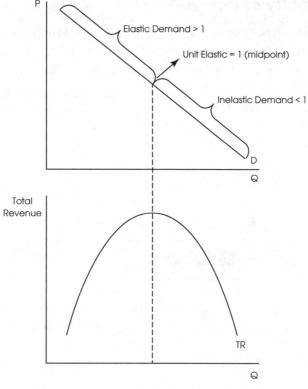

Figure 5.3

Three Questions to Determine Demand Elasticity

1. **ARE THERE ADEQUATE SUBSTITUTES AVAILABLE, OR IS THE GOOD A NECESSITY?** If a good is a necessity without any close substitutes, a consumer is likely to purchase the same quantity as the price changes. Diabetics who need a shot of insulin to survive do not have adequate substitutes; their demand for insulin is inelastic. If the price of Toyota cars increases, buyers likely can find a close substitute and buy a different brand. Hence, demand would be relatively elastic for new cars.

2. **CAN THE PURCHASE BE DELAYED?** If consumers have a longer time to make a buying decision, the demand for the product is generally more price elastic. If the purchase cannot be delayed, demand is more inelastic. For example, given a huge increase in the price of gasoline, demand for gas in the short term is unlikely to change much. In the longer term, consumers have time to shop for more fuel-efficient cars or arrange other forms of transportation, leading to more elastic demand with more time. Emergency medical care is another example of a purchase that cannot be delayed and has inelastic demand.

3. **DOES THE PURCHASE REQUIRE A LARGE PERCENTAGE OF INCOME?** If a good is a large part of one's budget, the good tends to be more price elastic. If a luxury boat increases in price by 10%, that amount can be several thousand dollars, a significant part of one's budget, leading to less quantity demanded. However, if the price of salt increases by 10%, that is likely a very small amount of one's monthly spending, making demand for salt relatively inelastic.

TIP

Here's an acronym to remember the elasticity of different sections of the demand curve. From top left to bottom right of the curve is EUI: Elastic, Unit Elastic, Inelastic. To remember EUI, just think Eat Up Idiots.

Cross-Price Elasticity of Demand

Cross-price elasticity of demand (CPED) measures how a price change in one product affects the quantity demanded of another product. Calculating this determines if products are complementary or substitute goods. If the CPED is a positive value, the two goods are substitutes, and if negative, they are complements.

$$\text{CPED} = \frac{\% \text{ D Quantity Demanded of Product X}}{\% \text{ D Price of Product Y}}$$
$$(\text{where D} = \text{change in})$$

Figure 5.4 Cross-Price Elasticity of Demand

> **TIP**
>
> Use absolute values (positive numbers) when calculating normal elasticity. However, pay attention to positives and negatives when using cross-price and income elasticity of demand.

EXAMPLE

Substitute Goods

Suppose the price of plastic wrap increases by 20% and the quantity demanded of waxed paper increases by 50%. (50%)/(20%) = 2.5. Since the answer is a positive number, these two goods are substitutes (see Figure 5.4).

EXAMPLE

Complementary Goods

Suppose the price of hot dogs increases by 20% and the quantity demanded of hot dog buns decreases by 10%. (−10%)/(20%) = −0.5. Since the answer is a negative number, these two goods are complements (see Figure 5.4).

Income Elasticity of Demand

In addition to consumers being constrained by prices in their purchasing decisions, they are also constrained by their budgets or incomes. Thus, we consider consumers' sensitivity in terms of their responses to changes in both prices and incomes. Income elasticity of demand shows how changes in income affect the quantity demanded of a good and can be determined using this formula:

$$\text{Income Elasticity of Demand} = \frac{\% \text{ D Quantity Demanded}}{\% \text{ D Consumer Income}}$$

This formula shows whether a good is an inferior or a normal good. Recall that with normal goods, there is a direct relationship between an individual's income and the quantity demanded. With a normal good, an increase in income leads to an increase in the quantity demanded. Conversely, with inferior goods, there is an inverse relationship between income and the quantity demanded. An increase in income results in a decrease in the quantity demanded for inferior goods. The ratio for normal goods will have a positive sign, and the ratio for inferior goods will have a negative sign. (See Figure 5.5.)

Figure 5.5 Income Elasticity of Demand

EXAMPLE

Suppose consumer incomes decrease by 5% and this leads to a 10% increase in the quantity demanded for spicy ramen noodles. (10%)/(−5%) = −2. Since the answer is negative, this means spicy ramen is an inferior good.

Price Elasticity of Supply

Elasticity also applies to the supply curve. Price elasticity of supply considers how a change in price affects the quantity supplied. The elasticity values for supply are exactly the same as demand. Timing is important when considering the elasticity of supply. The longer firms have to adjust, the more elastic their supply curves are, as it's difficult for many firms to significantly increase production in the short term. In the long run, a market or industry supply curve is usually perfectly elastic (remember this when studying perfect competition).

In Figure 5.6, the left part of the figure (the supply) is perfectly inelastic, where a change in price leaves the quantity supplied unchanged. The right part shows perfectly elastic supply, where at a price of P_1 or higher, producers will produce an infinite quantity, and there will be no production below P_1.

$$\text{Price Elasticity of Supply} = \frac{\% \text{ D Quantity Supplied}}{\% \text{ D Price}}$$

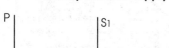

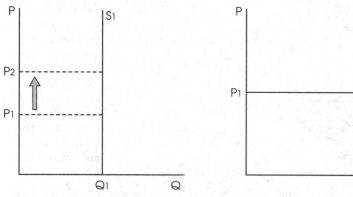

Figure 5.6 Price Elasticity of Supply

Consumer and Producer Surpluses

An important way economics measures the effectiveness of markets is to highlight and calculate consumer and producer surpluses. When both consumer and producer surpluses are maximized, economists consider this an efficient outcome. The **consumer surplus** is the difference between the highest price a consumer would pay for a product and the actual price paid.

TIP

If a demand curve is perfectly elastic, there is no consumer surplus. Likewise, if a supply curve is perfectly elastic, there is no producer surplus.

For example, if you bought a concert ticket for $20 but you would have a maximum of $50, the consumer surplus is $50 − $20 = **$30**. You would surely buy the ticket as the marginal benefit of buying the ticket is $50 and the marginal cost is $20. The demand curve displays the maximum price each consumer will pay, so this can be easily calculated and displayed graphically. For example, in Figure 5.7, the market for a bag of peanuts, the area of consumer surplus is the triangular area below the demand and above the equilibrium price of $5, or area ABC. To calculate the exact value of the consumer surplus, use the formula ½ (base × height) by taking the difference between $9 and $5 on the price axis times the quantity sold and multiplying by ½.

Or, ½ × ($9 − $5) × 30 = **$60**.

The **producer surplus** is the difference between the lowest price a producer would sell a product and the actual price received.

EXAMPLE

If you have an old cell phone that you sell on the Internet for $100 but you would have sold it for as low as $50, your producer surplus is $100 − $50 = **$50**. In Figure 5.7, the equilibrium price for a bag of peanuts is $5, but many sellers would have sold it for less than that and receive producer surpluses. The area of producer surplus is above the supply curve and below the equilibrium price of $5, or area **CDB**. To calculate the exact total value of the producer surplus, take the difference between $5 and $1 on the price axis times the quantity sold, and multiply by 1/2. Or, 1/2 × $4 × 30 = **$60**. Adding the consumer and producer surpluses together gives you the total surplus of $120.

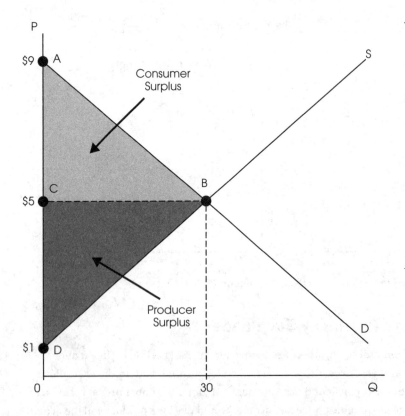

TIP

The area of consumer surplus can be located on a graph as the area below the demand curve, above price, and left of quantity. For producer surplus, find it above the supply curve, below price, and left of quantity.

Figure 5.7 Consumer and Producer Surpluses in the Peanut Market

Table 5.3 Consumer and Producer Surpluses (from Figure 5.7)

Equilibrium price and quantity	**$5, 30**
Consumer surplus	**Area: ABC**
	½ × ($9 − $5) × 30 = **$60**
Producer surplus	**Area: CBD**
	½ × ($5 − $1) × 30 = **$60**
Total surplus	**$60 + $60 = $120**

Government-Set Prices: Price Ceilings and Price Floors

Up until now we've assumed that prices in markets are free to rise and fall, regardless of how high or low they are. However, governments sometimes decide that prices in some markets are unfair and try to correct the market by fixing prices above or below the market price. Whatever good intentions policy makers have, these actions have predictable consequences that students of economics can foresee by learning the effects of price ceilings and floors.

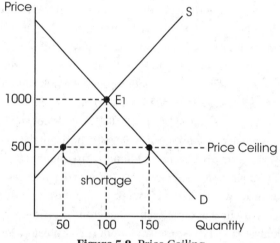

Figure 5.8 Price Ceiling

A **price ceiling** is a maximum legal price that can be charged for a product or service. One of the most common examples of price ceilings in the U.S. is limits on the price of rental housing units, also known as rent control. We can analyze the impact of these well-intended laws in the price ceiling graph shown in Figure 5.8. Suppose the competitive market equilibrium is at $1,000 for rent in a city and the government passes a law stating that the maximum price that can be charged is now $500. On the demand side, this lower price encourages more people to demand rental housing, and the quantity demanded increases from 100 to 150. For a price ceiling to impact the market, note that the price ceiling would have to be "binding" or set less than the equilibrium price of $1,000. Otherwise, the ceiling would be irrelevant, and the price would be $1,000. The major problem, however, occurs on the supply side for rental housing. The price ceiling makes it less attractive for landlords to offer housing for rent, decreasing their revenue and profits, and the quantity supplied falls from 100 to 50. Landlords might also respond by converting their rental units to owner-occupied condos or be less likely to maintain upkeep and repair their units. There is now disequilibrium and a shortage in the rental market, as buyers have a quantity demanded of 150, whereas only 50 units are available for rent, or a shortage of 100 units.

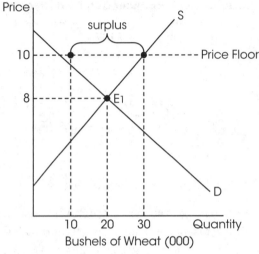

Figure 5.9 Price Floor

A **price floor is** a minimum legal price that can be charged for a product or service. A binding price floor is placed above the equilibrium price and occurs when society feels certain producers are not receiving enough income. Two common types of price floors are price supports for farmers and the minimum wage. Suppose an effective price floor is placed above the equilibrium price in the wheat market, as shown in Figure 5.9, and this results in an excess supply of a product being produced. A competitive market equilibrium would have a price of $8 and a quantity supplied and demanded of 20,000 bushels. At the price floor of $10 set by the government, producers are supplying 30,000 bushels but consumers will buy only 10,000 at that price, leading to a shortage of 20,000 (the horizontal difference between the demand and supply curves at $10). Some additional consequences of this price floor may be that the government purchases the excess supply (subsidizing farmers financed by taxpayers) and then storing the extra wheat. At the higher price, farmers may also devote more scarce land to the production of wheat as opposed to other crops consumers consume. Now we will look at how price controls affect consumer and producer surpluses with further graphical analysis.

> **TIP**
>
> A price ceiling is only binding (or effective) if it is placed below the equilibrium price, and a price floor only if above. If not, the equilibrium price where supply and demand meet will prevail in the market. Several previous AP exam questions have asked this!

Deadweight Loss with a Price Ceiling

When a market fails to maximize total surplus (the sum of consumer and producer surpluses), a deadweight loss is present. A **deadweight loss** is the loss of total surplus when a market fails to reach a competitive equilibrium. The loss of efficiency from price controls can be found by locating the area of the deadweight loss. In Figure 5.10, assuming a price ceiling is imposed on the peanut market, the new quantity bought and sold is 15, not 30. Note the loss of total surplus (deadweight loss) that arises, shown by the area **DBF**. Producer surplus is now area **EFC**, and consumer surplus is area **ADFE**.

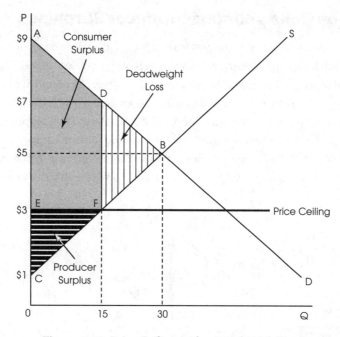

Figure 5.10 Price Ceiling with a Deadweight Loss

Deadweight Loss with a Price Floor

With a binding price floor, a maximum price is set above the competitive market price. If a price floor is imposed on the peanut market as in Figure 5.11, the new quantity in the market is 15, not 30. Note the loss of total surplus that arises, a deadweight loss, shown by the area **DBF**. Producer surplus is now area **EDFC**, and consumer surplus is area **ADE**.

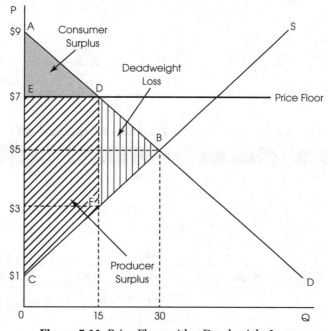

Figure 5.11 Price Floor with a Deadweight Loss

Impact of Taxes on Consumer and Producer Surpluses

While all governments need tax revenue to provide public services, taxation does result in a reduction of total surplus (a deadweight loss). Taxes can have varying impacts on consumers and producers depending on their respective price elasticities of demand or supply. In Figure 5.12, the equilibrium price of a pound of beef is $5. Suppose, however, that the government places an excise tax of $4 on the production of beef, measured graphically by the vertical distance between the supply curves (remember from Unit 4 that taxes are a supply curve shifter). An **excise tax** is a per-unit tax on the production or sale of a good. After the tax, the consumers pay a price of $7 for beef, but sellers only get $3 from the sale; the other $4 goes to the government as tax revenue. While many people think producers will pay all the $4 tax, in reality it is split between buyers and sellers. Buyers are paying the tax in the form of higher prices.

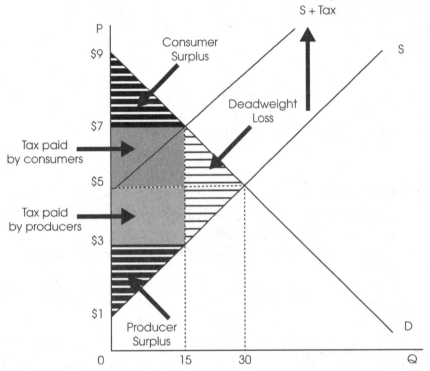

Figure 5.12 Incidence of the Tax on the Beef Market

> **TIP**
>
> The tax revenue portion of a tax graph (tax paid by consumers and producers) is not part of the deadweight loss. This money is revenue for the government.

Table 5.4 Before and After Tax Analysis of Figure 5.12

Before Tax		After Tax	
Price and quantity	**$5, 30**	Total size of tax	**$4**
Consumer surplus	½ × ($9 − $5) × 30 = **60**	Price for consumers	**$7**
Producer surplus	½ × ($5 − $1) × 30 = **60**	Price received by sellers	**$3**
Total surplus	$60 + $60 = **$120**	Consumer surplus	½ × ($9 − $7) × 15 = **15**
		Producer surplus	½ × ($3 − $1) × 15 = **15**
		Total tax revenue	($7 − $3) × 15 = **60**
		Tax paid by consumers	($7 − $5) × 15 = **30**
		Tax paid by producers	($5 − $3) × 15 = **30**
		Deadweight loss	½ × ($7 − $3) × **15 = $30**

Also note in Figure 5.12 the reduction in producer and consumer surpluses. As buyers pay a higher price, you can note how both consumer and producer surpluses have decreased. Part of this surplus goes to the government as tax revenue, but another part has disappeared, the deadweight loss. Consumers wanted to buy a quantity of 30 and producers wanted to sell 30, but only 15 units were bought and sold. The total deadweight loss in this case is $30 as seen in the calculations in Table 5.4.

Consumers and producers are usually both partially responsible for paying the tax (the tax incidence), but often one pays a greater percentage of the tax. The tax incidence is directly related to the price elasticity of supply and demand. If supply is more price elastic than demand (i.e., demand is more inelastic), consumers bear a greater burden of the tax than suppliers. Conversely, if demand is more price elastic than supply, sellers pay more of the tax. In fact, governments like placing taxes on items that have relatively inelastic demand, such as cigarettes or gasoline, as many people still buy them as price increases, placing a greater burden of the tax on consumers (and providing a consistent revenue stream for the government).

Table 5.5 summarizes who is responsible for paying a tax, or the tax incidence.

TIP

To master the tax graph, write down the price the buyer pays and the price received by the seller. The difference is the tax. In Figure 5.12, buyers pay $7 and sellers receive $3, so it is clear the tax is $4.

Table 5.5 Tax Incidence

Elasticities	Tax Incidence: Who pays the tax, consumers or producers?
Elasticity of demand > elasticity of supply	Producers pay more of the tax than consumers.
Elasticity of demand < elasticity of supply	Consumers pay more of the tax than producers.
Perfectly inelastic demand ($Ed = 0$)	Consumers pay all the tax.
Perfectly elastic demand ($Ed = \infty$)	Consumers pay none of the tax.
Perfectly inelastic supply ($Es = 0$)	Producers pay all of the tax.
Perfectly elastic supply ($Es = \infty$)	Producers pay none of the tax.

TIP

Regarding the tax incidence (who pays the tax), the curve that is more price inelastic pays more of the tax. Conversely, the more price elastic curve pays less.

A Tax Paid Mainly by Consumers

Now we will graphically show the tax incidence falling more on consumers in Figure 5.13. The equilibrium price and quantity is at Q_1 and P_1, but after the tax is imposed and the supply curve shifts up by the amount of the tax. P_T and Q_T are the after-tax price and quantity, with P_s the price received by sellers. Here you can see demand is more inelastic than supply, resulting in consumers paying a greater amount of tax.

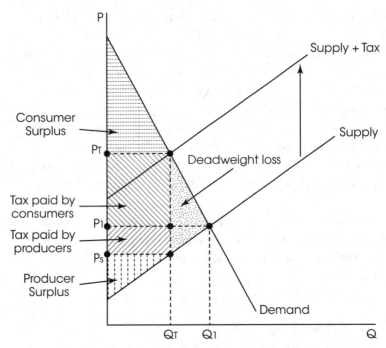

Figure 5.13 Consumers Paying a Larger Portion of a Tax

A Tax Paid Mainly by Producers

Now we will graphically show the tax incidence falling more on producers in Figure 5.14. The equilibrium price and quantity is at Q_1 and P_1, but after the tax is imposed and the supply curve shifts up by the amount of the tax. P_T and Q_T are the after-tax price and quantity, with P_S the price received by sellers. Here you can see supply is more inelastic (steeper) than demand, resulting in sellers paying a greater amount of tax.

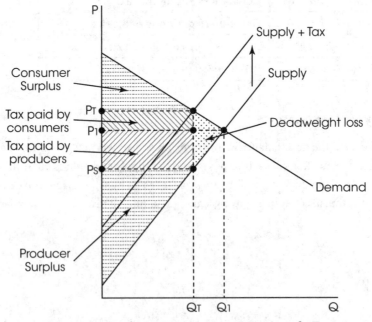

Figure 5.14 Producers Paying a Larger Portion of a Tax

Trade, Tariffs, and Quotas

If you have taken Macro in addition to Microeconomics, you likely have learned about international trade in detail. However, for the purposes of Micro, you should understand the effects of international trade on total surpluses, and how tariffs and quotas affect total welfare.

World Price with No Tariff or Quota

Let's look at the market for bananas in Figure 5.15. Here you can see the price and quantity before ($4, 40) and after ($2, 60) trade at the world price. Note at the world price consumer surplus is area ABDE because 60 were consumed, and producer surplus is C because only 20 were produced. Therefore, the total surplus (area ABCDE) is greater than before trade (area ABC). At the world price, consumers receive huge gains from the lower prices, but a peculiarity is that producer surplus shrinks from area BC to C. Despite the fact that the producer surplus decreases in size, there is still a large net positive gain in total surplus (areas D and E) from the large increase in consumer surplus. The amount of domestic consumption increases from 40 to 60 after trade, and the total amount of imports is the horizontal distance between the demand and supply curves at the world price, 60 − 20 = 40. See Table 5.6 for more details from the graph.

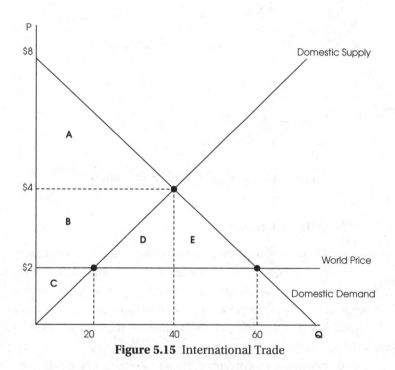

Figure 5.15 International Trade

Table 5.6 Before and After Trade Analysis of Figure 5.15

Before World Trade		After Trade at World Price	
Equilibrium price and quantity	$4, 40	Equilibrium price and quantity	$2, 60
Consumer surplus	A	Consumer surplus	ABDE
Producer surplus	BC	Producer surplus	C
Total surplus	ABC	Total surplus	ABCDE
Quantity of imports	—	Quantity of imports	60 − 20 = 40
Net gains from trade	—	Net gains from trade	DE

World Price with a Tariff

Recall that all taxes create a deadweight loss. A tariff is a tax on imports or exports, and a quota has a similar effect on trade that sets a limit on the quantity of goods imported or exported. To better understand the effect of tariffs on total surplus, look at Figure 5.16. At the world price, P_W, there is no deadweight loss and the amount of imports is from Q_1 to Q_4. After a tariff, the new price is P_T, and the quantity of imports has decreased. Areas that were consumer surplus before trade are now tax revenue from the tariff and deadweight loss.

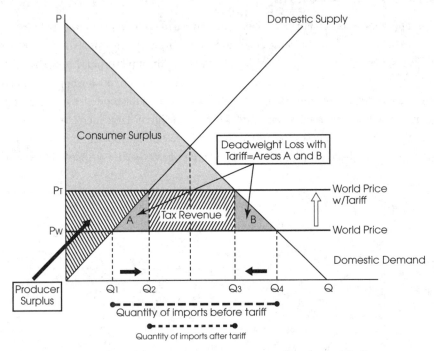

Figure 5.16 Trade at the World Price with Tariff

Trade at the World and Tariff Prices

Let's assume that domestic suppliers successfully lobby the government for a tariff on imported bananas because of a decline in profits for domestic producers. As shown in Figure 5.17, the imposition of a \$1 tariff on imported bananas increases the price of bananas to \$3 and reduces the quantity of domestic consumption from 60 to 50. Domestic producers are happy as their production increases from 20 to 30 and their producer surplus increases from area C to CH. However, the tariff has an undesirable effect on total surplus and results in a deadweight loss (areas D and G). A similar effect would take place if a quota was set as opposed to a tariff, except a quota will not provide tax revenue for the government like a tariff (areas F_1 and F_2 are the tax revenue). See Table 5.7 for further analysis of the impact of the tariff.

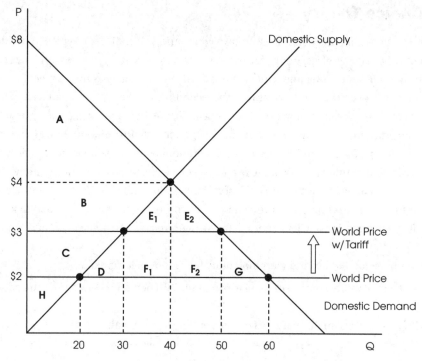

Figure 5.17 World Trade Before and After Tariff

Table 5.7 An Analysis of Trade Before and After a Tariff

World Price Before Tariff		World Price After Tariff	
Equilibrium price and quantity	$2, 60	Equilibrium price and quantity	$3, 50
Consumer surplus	$ABCDE_{1,2}F_{1,2}G$	Consumer surplus	$ABE_{1,2}$
Producer surplus	H	Producer surplus	CH
Total surplus	$ABCDE_{1,2}F_{1,2}GH$	Total surplus	$ABCE_{1,2}F_{1,2}H$
Net gains from trade	$DE_{1,2}F_{1,2}G$	Net gains from trade	$E_{1,2}F_{1,2}$
Quantity supplied (domestic)	20	Quantity supplied (domestic)	30
Quantity of imports	60 − 20 = 40	Quantity of imports	50 − 30 = 20
		Deadweight loss (net loss from tariff)	DG
		Tax revenue	$F_{1,2}$

Consumer Choice Theory

How does a consumer allocate a limited income among a wide variety of choices? A typical individual consumes a wide assortment of goods and services, from necessities such as clothes and groceries, and luxury items such as vacations and the latest iPhone. Consumers make these decisions rationally as they expect the benefits of the purchase outweigh the costs. This is known as utility in economics and is measured in what economists call utils. Think of utils as pleasure or satisfaction points. For example, one item that brings many people utils is the consumption of ice cream…up to a certain point. If one is experiencing **diminishing marginal utility**, it means that at some point as you consume a good or service, each additional unit consumed yields a decreasing additional amount of satisfaction or utility. Think of the first scoop of ice cream on a hot summer day. The first scoop of ice cream provides lots of utils. However, with each additional scoop, utility begins to eventually decrease and even will become negative at some point when you can't eat anymore. Assuming each scoop of ice cream costs the same, eventually the marginal cost will be more than the marginal benefit, and you would not pay for an additional scoop.

Table 5.8 shows both the total utility and marginal utility for scoops of ice cream.

- **Total utility** is the total utility amount of satisfaction or utility a person receives from the consumption of a good or service.
- **Marginal utility** is the extra amount of satisfaction or utility from consuming one more unit of a good or service.

Note that while total utility is increasing for scoops one through four, marginal utility is decreasing, yet positive. Total utility is at its highest point when marginal utility is zero.

Table 5.8 Scoops of Ice Cream

Quantity	Total Utility	Marginal Utility
0	0	—
1	20	20
2	35	15
3	45	10
4	50	5
5	50	0
6	45	−5

Figures 5.18 and 5.19 show the graphical relationship between total utility and marginal utility from consuming ice cream. Note that total utility increases at a decreasing rate and eventually declines. Marginal utility is the change in total utility and decreases with each additional ice cream scoop and turns negative when total utility is falling. Obviously, you can be sure that the sixth scoop of ice cream wouldn't be consumed, as the marginal utility is negative.

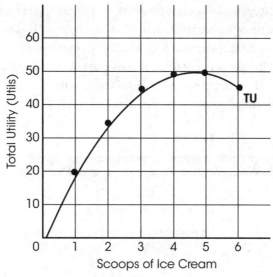

Figure 5.18

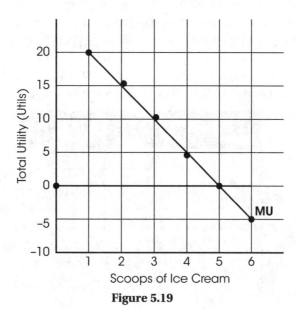

Figure 5.19

The Utility-Maximization Rule

As consumers face decisions about what items to consume, how can they choose which specific combinations of items will give the maximum amount of satisfaction (utility) given budget constraints? To maximize one's satisfaction, the **utility-maximization rule** should be used, which states that a consumer maximizes utility when the marginal utility per dollar spent for all items is equal given budget constraints. If the marginal utility per dollar is not equal, consumers will want to begin by buying the product with the highest marginal utility per dollar and spending less on the good with a lower marginal utility per dollar. When deciding what to purchase first, think of it as purchasing the good that gives you the most "bang for your buck." For example, if you are at a theme park and you need to decide how much money to spend on souvenirs vs. playing games, you can use the utility-maximization formula:

$$\frac{MU_X}{P_X} = \frac{MU_Y}{P_Y}$$

By applying this formula, you spend money until the marginal utility of good X (souvenirs) divided by the price of X equals the marginal utility of good Y (games) divided by the price of Y, given the budget constraint. As shown in Table 5.9, you consume more of the good with a higher marginal utility per dollar and less of the good with a lower marginal utility per dollar. Eventually, diminishing marginal utility will allow the sides to equal out, and the optimal combination of consumption will have been reached.

TIP

On FRQs regarding the utility-maximization question like in Table 5.10, the question will often change the prices and then ask how consumers will often change their consumption pattern. When this happens, just make another table listing the new marginal utility/new price and you will ace it.

Table 5.9

Using the Utility-Maximization Rule	
If MU/Px > MU/Py	Buy more of x and less of y
If MU/Px < MU/Py	Buy more of y and less of x
If MU/Px = MU/Py	Maintain current consumption level

Sample Question

Maria has $52 to spend at an amusement park and wants to spend her limited budget on souvenirs or playing games. Souvenirs cost $8 each, and games cost $4 each. Help her find the optimal combination of these items to maximize her utility using Table 5.10. Note the utility numbers are total, not marginal.

Table 5.10 Total Utility: Souvenirs vs. Games

Total Units	Total Utility (Souvenirs $8)	Total Utility (Games $4)
1	56	32
2	104	60
3	136	84
4	160	104
5	180	116
6	196	126
7	208	134

The utility-maximization formula $MU_x/P_x = MU_y/P_y$ uses marginal utility, but on an AP test question, you are often only initially given total utility. To solve this problem, look at the total utility data and make your own table of the marginal utility and the marginal utility/price for each product (done for you in Table 5.11). Start circling the item with the highest marginal utility per dollar and continue until you have spent all the income.

Table 5.11 Marginal Utility and Marginal Utility/Price

Total Units	Marginal Utility of Souvenirs	Marginal Utility S/Price S ($8)	Marginal Utility of Games	Marginal Utility G/Price G ($4)
1	56	⑦	32	⑧
2	48	⑥	28	⑦
3	32	④	24	⑥
4	24	③	20	⑤
5	20	2.5	12	③
6	16	2	10	2.5
7	12	1.5	8	2

This gives you the correct utility-maximization combination for Maria, which is **4 souvenirs and 5 games given the budget constraint of $52.**

EXAMPLE

Assume Carly spends all her weekly budget on gummy bears candy and yoga pants. Gummy bears cost $2, and yoga pants cost $40, and at her current consumption level, the marginal utility for gummy bears is 1 and for yoga pants it is 10. Applying the utility-maximization rule, should Carly maintain or change her consumption level, and why?

Answer: Change her consumption. The MU/P of gummy bears is 1/2 = .5, and MU/P for yoga pants is 10/40 = .25. Carly then should consume more gummy bears and less yoga pants as .5 > .25. Eventually the MU/P for gummy bears will equal the MU/P for yoga pants due to diminishing marginal returns.

SUMMARY

- Price elasticity of demand or the percentage of change in the quantity demanded of a particular good divided by the price of the same good demonstrates the sensitivity of consumers to price changes. $P \times Q = TR$ allows a revenue test, i.e., whether a price change will increase or decrease total revenue.
- Price elasticity of supply shows the sensitivity of producers or firms to price changes for their products.
- Price elasticity of demand or supply that has a numerical value > 1 is elastic, = 1 is unit elastic, or < 1 is inelastic.
- Cross-price elasticity of demand is the percentage change in the quantity demanded of one product in response to the percentage change in the price of a second product. If this ratio produces a positive sign, then the two products are good substitutes. If this ratio produces a negative sign, then the two products are complements.
- Income elasticity of demand measures the responsiveness of consumers to changes in their income. A positive income elasticity is a normal good, while a negative income elasticity is an inferior good.
- Consumer surplus is the difference between the highest price a consumer would pay and the actual price paid.
- Producer surplus is the difference between the lowest price a producer would sell for and the actual price of a sale.
- A price ceiling is a government-fixed maximum price that can be charged and results in a shortage and deadweight loss. To be effective or binding, it must be set below the equilibrium price, otherwise the equilibrium price prevails in the market.
- A price floor is a government-fixed minimum price that can be charged and results in a surplus and deadweight loss. To be effective or binding, it must be set above the equilibrium price, otherwise the equilibrium price prevails in the market.
- A tax on a good creates a deadweight loss, and the burden or incidence of the tax falls more on the person with the more inelastic demand or supply.
- A tariff does provide the government with tax revenue but also causes a deadweight loss.
- The theory of consumer choice includes understanding diminishing marginal utility, facing budget constraints, and z consumption choices with the utility-maximization rule.

Formulas

Calculating a Percentage Change:

$$\% \text{ Change in Price} = \frac{\text{Change in P}}{\text{Initial P}}$$

$$\% \text{ Change in } Qd = \frac{\text{Change in } Qd}{\text{Initial } Qd}$$

Price Elasticity of Demand:

$$E_d = \frac{\% \text{ D Quantity Demanded}}{\% \text{ D Price}}$$

Cross-Price Elasticity of Demand:

$$\text{CPED} = \frac{\% \text{ D Quantity Demanded of Product X}}{\% \text{ D Price of Product Y}}$$

Complements   Substitutes

←————————————●————————————→

–   +

Income Elasticity of Demand:

$$E_i = \frac{\% \text{ D Quantity Demanded}}{\% \text{ D Consumer Income}}$$

Inferior   Normal

←————————————●————————————→

–   +

Price Elasticity of Supply:

$$E_s = \frac{\% \text{ D Quantity Supplied}}{\% \text{ D Price}}$$

Utility-Maximization Rule:

$$\frac{\text{MU}_X}{\text{P}_X} = \frac{\text{MU}_Y}{\text{P}_Y}$$

Multiple-Choice Review Questions

1. When the price elasticity of demand coefficient ratio is 2, demand is

   (A) unit elastic.
   (B) relatively elastic.
   (C) perfectly elastic.
   (D) relatively inelastic.
   (E) perfectly inelastic.

2. Price times quantity measures

   (A) the international trade gap.
   (B) the budget deficit.
   (C) total revenue.
   (D) price elasticity of demand.
   (E) price elasticity of supply.

3. A positive sign on cross-price elasticity of demand indicates that the two products are

   (A) luxuries.
   (B) necessities.
   (C) substitutes.
   (D) complements.
   (E) independent.

4. If the quantity demanded of good X increases 25% while the price decreases 25%, this means the price elasticity of demand is

   (A) unit elastic.
   (B) relatively elastic.
   (C) perfectly elastic.
   (D) relatively inelastic.
   (E) perfectly inelastic.

5. If an excise tax is imposed on a supplier, the tax incidence will fall more heavily on consumers if

   (A) demand and supply are both unit elastic.
   (B) the price elasticity of demand is more inelastic than supply.
   (C) the price elasticity of supply is more inelastic than demand.
   (D) the price elasticity of demand is more elastic than supply.
   (E) the price elasticity of supply is perfectly inelastic.

6. Suppose a 10% decrease in the price of ice cream leads to a 15% increase in the quantity demanded of ice cream. What type of elasticity does this show?

   (A) Perfectly elastic
   (B) Relatively elastic
   (C) Unit elastic
   (D) Relatively inelastic
   (E) Perfectly inelastic

7. A 20% increase in the price of milk leads to a 10% decrease in the quantity of cereal purchased. The cross-price elasticity of demand between milk and cereal is

   (A) −0.5 and the two goods are substitutes.
   (B) −0.5 and the two goods are complements.
   (C) 0.5 and the two goods are complements.
   (D) −2 and the two goods are substitutes.
   (E) 2 and the two goods are complements.

8. If the cross-price elasticity of demand between goods X and Y is positive and the income elasticity of demand for good Y is negative, which of the following is correct?

   (A) Good Y is an inferior good, and good X is a normal good.
   (B) Good Y is an inferior good, and goods X and Y are complements.
   (C) Good Y is a normal good, and goods X and Y are substitutes.
   (D) Good Y is an inferior good, and goods X and Y are substitutes.
   (E) Good Y is an inferior good, and goods X and Y are complements.

9. The area above a supply curve, below the equilibrium price, and left of equilibrium quantity is the

   (A) deadweight loss.
   (B) consumer surplus.
   (C) producer surplus.
   (D) price ceiling.
   (E) price floor.

10. If the demand for gasoline is price inelastic in a competitive market, an increase in the price of gasoline will

    (A) result in a deadweight loss in the gasoline market.
    (B) cause an increase in the consumer surplus.
    (C) decrease the total revenue of gasoline producers.
    (D) increase the total revenue of gasoline producers.
    (E) decrease the total spending on gasoline by consumers.

11. A tariff that is imposed on a good that is imported to the United States will result in which of the following to consumer surplus, domestic producer surplus, and tax revenue?

	Consumer Surplus	Domestic Producer Surplus	Tax Revenue
(A)	Increase	Decrease	Decrease
(B)	Decrease	Increase	Decrease
(C)	Decrease	Increase	Increase
(D)	Increase	Increase	Increase
(E)	Decrease	No change	Decrease

12. Jane is shopping online and is spending $48 on T-shirts and music downloads. Given her budget constraint of $48 she is at her utility-maximization combination of spending. T-shirts cost $10. In addition, her marginal utility of T-shirts is 40 and for music downloads it's 8. What then is the price of music downloads?

    (A) 50¢
    (B) $1
    (C) $2
    (D) $3
    (E) $4

Use this chart for questions 13 and 14.

Quantity of Pizza	Marginal Utility from Pizza	Quantity of Music Downloads	Marginal Utility from Music Downloads
1	10	1	8
2	8	2	6
3	6	3	4
4	4	4	2
5	2	5	1

13. Samantha consumes both pizza and music downloads. The table above shows her marginal utility from these. What is her total utility from purchasing four music downloads?

    (A) 4
    (B) 14
    (C) 18
    (D) 20
    (E) 21

14. Now assume Samantha's weekly income is $12, the price of a pizza is $2, and the price of a music download is $1. What is the utility-maximization quantity of pizza and music downloads if she spends her entire $12 on these two goods?

	Pizza	Music Downloads
(A)	2	2
(B)	2	3
(C)	4	4
(D)	5	4
(E)	5	5

15. According to the principle of diminishing marginal utility, as more units of the same good are consumed

    (A) marginal utility stays the same.
    (B) total utility stays the same.
    (C) marginal utility decreases.
    (D) marginal utility increases.
    (E) marginal utility and total utility both increase.

16. An effective price ceiling is characterized by

    (A) a price set below the current (or equilibrium) market price of the good.
    (B) a price set above the current (or equilibrium) market price of the good.
    (C) a shift of the demand curve.
    (D) a shift of the supply curve.
    (E) a surplus of the good.

17. Which of the following would cause the price of a good to be fixed above the equilibrium price?

    (A) Consumers' incomes decreased
    (B) An effective price ceiling
    (C) Taxes for producers increased
    (D) The price of a substitute product decreased
    (E) An effective price floor

Free-Response Review Questions

1. Analyze the following graph of the sugar market and how a per-unit excise tax affects the following.

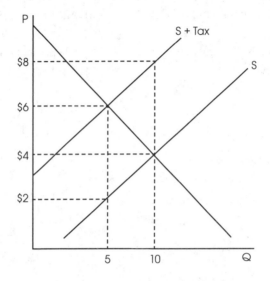

Sugar Market with Tax

(a) What is the size of the tax per unit on the sugar market?

(b) What is the total amount of tax revenue from the tax?
   (i) Is the tax incidence between consumers and producers equal, do consumers pay more of the tax than producers, or do producers pay more of the tax than consumers?

(c) What is the price that consumers pay for sugar after the tax?
   (i) What is the after-tax, per-unit price received by producers for each sale?

(d) What was the equilibrium price and quantity before the tax?

(e) Now assume the price elasticity of demand becomes more inelastic while supply remains constant. Who will now pay more of the burden of the tax? Consumers? Producers? Or will the burden of the tax be equal? Explain.

2. Assume Micah spends $14 on burgers and slices of pizza every week. A burger costs $4, and a slice of pizza is $2.
    Using the chart, answer the following questions.

Total Units	Marginal Utility of a Burger	Marginal Utility of a Slice of Pizza
1	20	12
2	16	10
3	12	8
4	8	6
5	4	4

(a) What is the total utility of consuming 4 burgers?

(b) What is the quantity of burgers and slices of pizza that will maximize Micah's utility given that he
     spends $14?

(c) Now suppose a 10% increase in the price of a burger leads to a 5% increase in the quantity of slices of
     pizza purchased. Calculate the cross-price elasticity between burgers and pizza, and note if burgers and
     pizza are complements, substitutes, or inferior goods. Show your work.

3. Analyze the following graph of the price of sugar in the United States before and after a tariff is imposed.

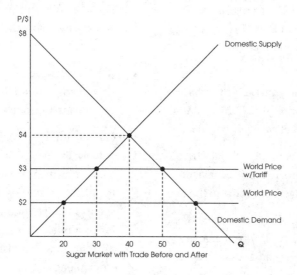

Sugar Market with Trade Before and After Tariff

(a) What is the price of sugar if there is no trade?

(b) Calculate the total consumer surplus both without trade *and* at the world price. Show your work.

(c) Calculate the total tariff revenue at the world price with a tariff. Show your work.

(d) What is the quantity of domestic supply at the world price both with and without
     a tariff?

4. Assume the market for chicken wings is in equilibrium.

    (a) Draw a correctly labeled graph of the chicken wing market, labeling the price P_E and the quantity Q_E at equilibrium.

    (b) Assume the government now decides the price of chicken wings is too high and decides to set an effective price ceiling in the market. Draw the price ceiling on the same graph drawn in (a), labeling the new price P_C, the new quantity supplied Q_S, and the new quantity demanded Q_D.

    (c) At the new price, is the chicken wing market in equilibrium, or does it have a shortage or a surplus? Explain.

Answer Explanations

1. **(B)** If the price elasticity is greater than 1, then a good is elastic. 1 is unit elastic, and between 0 and 1 is inelastic.

2. **(C)** Total revenue (TR) = P × Q. If an increase in P leads to TR increasing (a direct relationship) and vice versa, demand is inelastic. If a decrease in P leads to TR increasing (an inverse relationship) and vice versa, demand is elastic.

3. **(C)** This is an application of the cross-price elasticity equation: % change in QDx/% change in Py. If the number is positive, goods are substitutes; if negative, complements.

4. **(A)** The price elasticity of demand formula is % change in QD/% change in P: 0.25/0.25 = 1. A price elasticity of 1 is unit elasticity.

5. **(B)** With an excise tax, the more inelastic curve pays more of the tax. Demand is more inelastic than supply, and thus buyers pay more of the tax.

6. **(B)** This is an application of the cross-price elasticity equation: % change in QDx/% change in Py. 0.15/−0.10 = −1.5. Greater than 1 shows elastic demand, and as the number is negative, the two goods are complementary.

7. **(B)** This is an application of the cross-price elasticity equation: % change in QDx/% change in Py. −0.10/0.2 = −0.5. A negative number means the goods are complements.

8. **(D)** A positive cross-price elasticity of demand means the goods are substitutes, and a negative income elasticity means the good is inferior.

9. **(C)** Producer surplus is the difference between the minimum price a seller would have offered a good for sale and the actual price sold. This is shown graphically above the supply curve, below price, and left of quantity.

10. **(D)** When a good is price inelastic, an increase in P will lead to an increase in total revenue (TR). P × Q = TR.

11. **(C)** A tariff increases the price to consumers and reduces consumer surplus. Domestic producers will now be able to sell at a higher price, increasing the producer surplus, and the tariff is a tax that results in increased government revenue.

12. **(C)** The utility-maximization formula is MUx/Px = MUy/Py. Using the data, it is 40/$10 = 8/X. X = $2.

13. **(D)** To calculate Samantha's total utility from 4 downloads, add up the marginal utility of music downloads 1 through 4. 8 + 6 + 4 + 2 = 20.

14. **(C)** The utility-maximization formula is MUx/Px = MUy/Py. Divide the numbers in the MU column by the price of each good, and circle the highest numbers until the income of $12 is spent. The higher number gives you more "bang for your buck." Both sides equal out and utility is maximized with consumption of 4 pizzas and 4 downloads.

15. **(C)** Diminishing marginal utility means that satisfaction or utility decreases with consumption of each additional unit.

16. **(A)** An effective or binding price ceiling is always below the equilibrium price. If a price ceiling were set above the equilibrium price, it would be irrelevant and would not affect the price.

17. **(E)** An effective or binding price floor is always above the equilibrium price. If a price floor were set below the equilibrium price, it would be irrelevant and would not affect the price.

Free-Response Review Answers

1. (a) $4
   (b) $20. ($6 − $2) × 5 = $20
       (i) The tax burden is equally shared by producers and consumers. Both pay $10 in tax.
   (c) $6, where the demand curve and supply + tax curves meet
       (i) $2. The tax of $4 is subtracted from the sale price of $6, leaving producers with $2.
   (d) $4, quantity of 10
   (e) Consumers will now pay more of the tax or have a higher tax incidence. The more inelastic curve pays more of the tax. Here the demand curve is now more price inelastic than the supply curve.

2. (a) 56. 20 + 16 + 12 + 8 = 56
   (b) 2 burgers and 3 slices of pizza. As you can see with the new columns of both products' utility per dollar, circle the highest utility per dollar until both sides equal out and the budget constraint of $14 is met.

Total Units	Marginal Utility of a Burger	Marginal Utility B/Price B ($4)	Marginal Utility of Pizza	Marginal Utility P/Price P ($2)
1	20	(5)	12	(6)
2	16	(4)	10	(5)
3	12	3	8	(4)
4	8	2	6	3
5	4	1	4	2

   (c) Substitutes. The formula to calculate cross-price is the percentage change in the quantity demanded of good X/percent change in the price of good Y. 5%/10% = 0.5. Since that is positive, they are substitutes. If the number were negative, the two goods would be complements.

3. (a) $4
   (b) ½ × ($8 − $4) × 40 = $80 consumer surplus at the price before trade
       ½ × ($8 − $2) × 60 = $180 consumer surplus with trade at the world price
   (c) ($3 − $2) × (50 − 30) = $20
   (d) 20 at the world price without a tariff and 30 at the world price with the tariff

4. (a), (b) See the figure below for the correct graph.

   (c) An effective price ceiling is below the equilibrium price and leads to a shortage. At the price ceiling, the quantity demanded increases, as consumers want to buy more at a lower price. However, the quantity supplied decreases at the lower price as it is no longer profitable for some firms to produce at price P_C.

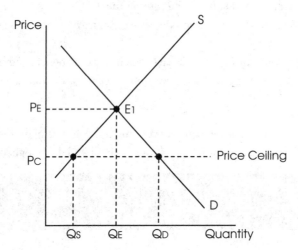

6

Costs of Production

Learning Objectives

In this chapter, you will learn:

→ Short run vs. long run
→ Law of diminishing marginal returns
→ Production function
→ Relationship of production curves to cost curves
→ Economies of scale
→ Implicit and explicit costs
→ Economic profit vs. accounting profit
→ Average costs and marginal costs, fixed costs and variable costs
→ Total costs and marginal costs

Introduction

In this chapter, we turn now to the behavior and costs of firms (businesses) when producing. The costs involved in production and how firms maximize profit are the key issues addressed. Sometimes students get overwhelmed with this information, with lots of curves and formulas to remember. However, with practice and review, you will be able to master the key concepts.

Short Run vs. Long Run

Concerning a firm's production, the distinction between the short and the long run is very significant. The difference between a short and long run in this context is not the difference between a 100-meter race and a marathon. The **long run** is when all resources used in production are variable and supply can adjust to changes in demand. The **short run**, however, is where at least one production input is fixed and supply cannot fully adjust to changes in demand. For example, when a farmer grows corn and the farmland he owns is fixed, he cannot change the amount of land in the short run. He can, however, hire more farmhands to work in the short run, as labor is a variable input.

The Production Function

In the short run, as variable inputs (such as labor) are added to fixed inputs (such as a factory), production first increases at an increasing rate (because labor specializes, making them more productive); then, production increases at a decreasing rate. Later, there is actually a decrease in total production as successively equal increments of variable inputs are added. This is an example of one of the most important concepts in Micro—the law of diminishing returns.

The **law of diminishing marginal returns** states that as a firm adds an increasing amount of variable resources (labor) to a fixed resource, the additional production each new worker adds (marginal product) will eventually decrease. For example, if grapes are to be pressed for juice with the use of workers' feet (a variable resource) and there is a fixed supply of grape vats to stomp in, increasing the number of workers will, initially, greatly increase the amount of pressed grapes. However, at some point, there will be a scramble among workers to find a suitable space for pressing grapes. As increasing numbers of workers are competing for space, this leads to smaller and smaller increases in output and diminishing marginal returns. If the firm continues to hire workers, at some point, production will even turn negative as overcrowded work spaces limit the space to smash grapes.

Graphing the Production Function

In Table 6.1 you can see the total product (TP), marginal product (MP), and average product (AP). Total product is the total production, while marginal product is the change in production with an additional worker, and average product is the total product divided by the number of labor inputs.

$$AP = \frac{\text{Total Output}}{\text{Variable Inputs}}$$

$$MP = \frac{\text{Change in Output}}{\text{Change in Input}}$$

Table 6.1 Production Function

Quantity of Input (workers hired)	Total Product (TP) (gallons of grape juice)	Marginal Product (MP)	Average Product (AP)
0	0	—	—
1	5	5	5
2	20	15	10
3	45	25	15
4	60	15	15
5	70	10	14
6	72	2	12
7	63	−9	9

Increasing returns { (rows 2, 3, 4)

Decreasing returns { (rows 5, 6)

Negative returns ← (row 7)

In Figure 6.1, graphing the info in the table, you can see, in stage one, **increasing marginal returns**, that total product is increasing at an increasing rate. Each worker in this stage adds more marginal product than the previous worker due to specialization of labor. In stage two, **diminishing marginal returns**, the law of diminishing marginal returns sets in, as each worker adds less and less to marginal product due to more variable resources being added to fixed resources (in this case, grape-stomping vats). Note that in stage two, total product is still increasing, however. In stage three, **negative marginal returns**, total product is falling, and marginal revenue turns negative as each additional worker hired leads to a negative amount of production. This occurs because the fixed workspace becomes overcrowded as workers get in each other's way. A business surely will not hire any workers in this last stage. (Note that MP always intersects AP at AP's highest point. If MP is higher than AP, AP is rising. If MP is below AP, AP is falling, as shown in Figure 6.2(a).)

TIP

Make sure you fully understand the law of diminishing marginal returns. You will see this concept several times on the exam.

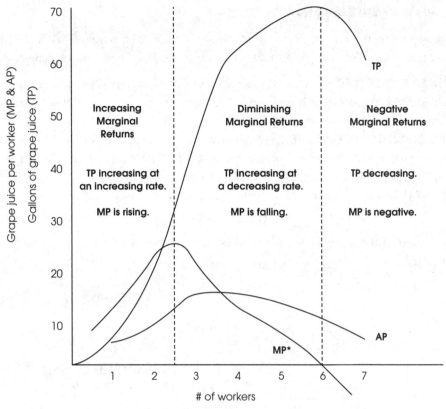

Figure 6.1 The Production Function

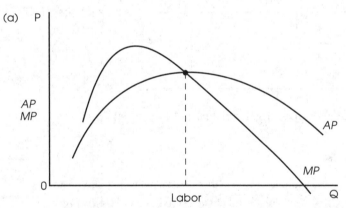

Figure 6.2(a) Average Product, Marginal Product

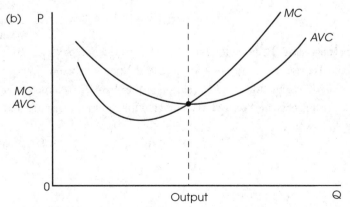

Figure 6.2(b) Average Variable Cost, Marginal Cost

TIP

The marginal product (MP) and marginal cost curves (MC) are mirror images of each other. The average product (AP) and average variable cost (AVC) curves are also mirror images. Also, total product (TP) is at its highest point where MP turns negative.

Production Costs in the Short Run

When a firm is producing in the short run, it incurs both fixed and variable costs. Recall that in the short run at least one resource is fixed. Total costs are comprised of two categories: **fixed costs** and **variable costs**.

1. **TOTAL FIXED COSTS (TFC)**: Total fixed costs are those that do not vary with changes in output. In the short run, these costs stay constant. Even when a firm's output is zero, these costs have to be paid. Examples are rent, insurance, and capital equipment.

2. **TOTAL VARIABLE COSTS (TVC)**: Total variable costs vary as output changes. Unlike fixed costs, when there is no production, variable costs equal zero. Examples of variable costs include changes in the number of employees, travel expenses, and energy costs related to production changes.

3. **TOTAL COST (TC)**: Total cost is the sum of both fixed and variable **costs.**

$$\text{Total Cost} = \text{TFC} + \text{TVC}$$

See Figure 6.3 for the relationship between these curves. Note that the difference between the TC and TVC curves is the total fixed cost.

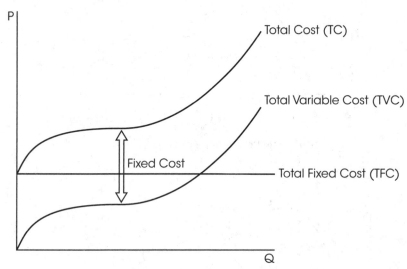

Figure 6.3 Total, Total Variable, and Total Fixed Costs

Average and Marginal Costs

Here are the formulas for calculating the averages of these three costs: **average fixed costs (AFC), average variable costs (AVC),** and **average total cost (ATC)**. *To calculate average costs, simply take the total and divide it by quantity as shown here:*

$$\text{AFC} = \frac{\text{TFC}}{\text{Q}} \qquad \text{AVC} = \frac{\text{TVC}}{\text{Q}} \qquad \text{ATC} = \frac{\text{TC}}{\text{Q}}$$

- **Marginal Cost (MC):** Marginal cost is the change in total cost from the production of one more unit of output. Marginal costs are the most important costs to firms. See below the formula to calculate MC. The MC calculation should be simple as the change in quantity is usually one. Note on the graph that the MC always intersects the AVC and ATC curves at their minimum points and drawing the MC graph is like drawing the Nike swoosh!

$$\text{MC} = \frac{\Delta \text{TC}}{\Delta \text{Q}}$$

> **TIP**
>
> If a firm has costs when total product is zero, they are fixed costs. Fixed costs are not counted when calculating AVC, TVC, or MC.

Curves: Relationships Between Cost and Product Curves

Figures 6.2(a) and (b) illustrate the inverse relationship between marginal cost and marginal product, and average product and average variable cost. The relationship of MP to AP is the exact opposite of the relationship of MC to AVC. In both cases, if the marginal curve is less than the average, the average must be declining. When the marginal curves are greater than the averages, the averages must be increasing. (*Think of it this way: The average curve is always chasing the marginal curve.*)

However, the MP curve intersects the AP curve at the *maximum* point on AP, but the MC curve intersects the AVC (and ATC) curve at the *minimum* point of the average curve. Why? When MP declines, each additional unit of labor adds less and less to total product due to diminishing marginal returns (remember that MP is the addition to total product). Thus, as each additional worker contributes less and less to total product, the marginal cost of production increases and heads the exact opposite way on the graph.

Now let's look at the AVC, ATC, and MC curves on the graph in Figure 6.4. As you see, the MC curve intersects both the AVC and ATC at its minimum points. Regarding the AFC curve, as you might expect, since total fixed costs don't change in the short run, AFC is going to decline as output increases, as shown here:

> In Figure 6.3 the distance between the AVC and ATC curves is the average fixed cost. As output increases, the AFC curve will decline. Hence, the difference between the ATC and AVC curves will gradually become smaller as output increases.

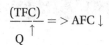

$$\frac{(TFC)}{Q\uparrow} => AFC \downarrow$$

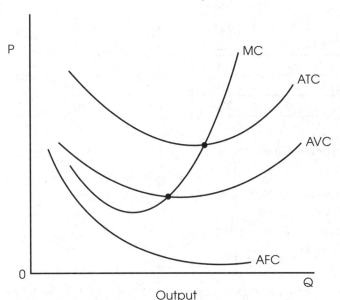

Figure 6.4 Average Variable Cost, Average Fixed Cost, Average Total Cost, and Marginal Cost

> **TIP**
>
> When drawing cost curves, be sure to draw the marginal cost curve intersecting ATC at its minimum point. Otherwise, you will lose a point on the AP test! It can be helpful to draw a dot at the minimum point on the ATC curve, then draw MC right through this point to show you know the correct intersection point.

Calculating Costs

It is important to know not only how to graph cost curves but also to understand the reason behind their slopes. First you will see in Table 6.2 some of the costs of production for the firm Eric's Easy Rider Bikes; try to fill out the rest on your own, then check the solution in Table 6.3. Eric's will experience the same issues of a typical firm in that they will eventually incur diminishing marginal returns. It's important to know how to calculate every one of these costs, and following the solution you will see multiple ways to calculate each of these costs. As there are multiple ways to calculate each, there's no reason any student couldn't learn how with some practice!

Table 6.2 Eric's Easy Rider Bicycles' Costs of Production

Q	Total Fixed Cost (TFC)	Marginal Cost (MC)	Total Variable Cost (TVC)	Total Cost (TC)	Average Variable Cost (AVC)	Average Total Cost (ATC)	Average Fixed Cost (AFC)
0	100	—	—		—	—	—
1	100	50		150		150	
2	100		75		37.5		50
3	100			225		75	
4	100	75			50		25
5	100		300			80	
6	100	125					

Table 6.3 Eric's Easy Rider Bicycles' Costs of Production (Solution)

Q	Total Fixed Cost (TFC)	Marginal Cost (MC)	Total Variable Cost (TVC)	Total Cost (TC)	Average Variable Cost (AVC)	Average Total Cost (ATC)	Average Fixed Cost (AFC)
0	100	—	—	100	—	—	—
1	100	50	50	150	50	150	100
2	100	25	75	175	37.5	87.5	50
3	100	50	125	225	41.67	75	33.33
4	100	75	200	300	50	75	25
5	100	100	300	400	60	80	20
6	100	125	425	525	70.83	87.5	16.67

Here are the many ways these costs can be calculated.

Calculating Total Fixed Cost (TFC):

- The cost at zero units of production is TFC, which is 100. Thus, TFC = 100.
- TFC = AFC × Q. At a quantity of two, $50 \times 2 = 100$.
- TFC = TC − TVC. At a quantity of two, $175 − 100 = 100$.
- TFC = AFC × Q. At a quantity of two, $50 \times 2 = 100$.

Calculating Marginal Cost (MC):

- As MC is a variable cost, take the marginal (additional) change in TVC. The TVC of producing 3 units is 125 and for 4 units is 200. $200 − 125 = 75$ (marginal cost of the 4th unit).
- Take the change in total cost. The TC of the 3rd unit is 225 and the 4th unit is 300.
  $300 − 225 = 75$ (marginal cost of the 4th unit).

Calculating Total Variable Cost (TVC):

- TVC = TC − TFC. At a quantity of two, $175 − 100 = 75$.
- TVC = AVC × Q. At a quantity of two, $37.5 \times 2 = 75$.
- Calculate the marginal costs up to the quantity desired. At a quantity of two, $50 + 25 = 75$.

Calculating Total Cost (TC):

- TC = TFC + TVC. At a quantity of two, 100 + 75 = 175.
- TC = ATC × Q. At a quantity of two, 87.5 × 2 = 175.
- Calculate the marginal costs up to the quantity desired and add that to TFC. At a quantity of two, marginal cost is 50 + 25, added to the FC of 100, and the TC is 175.

Calculating Average Variable Cost (AVC):

- AVC = TVC/Q. At a quantity of two, 75/2 = 37.5.
- AVC = ATC − AFC. At a quantity of two, 87.5 − 50 = 37.5.

Calculating Average Total Cost (ATC):

- ATC = TC/Q. At a quantity of two, 175/2 = 87.5.
- ATC = AVC + AFC. At a quantity of two, 50 + 37.5 = 87.5.

Calculating Average Fixed Cost (AFC):

- AFC = TFC/Q. At a quantity of two, 100/2 = 50.
- AFC = ATC − AVC. At a quantity of two, 87.5 − 37.5 = 50.

Taxes and Shifting Cost Curves

One of the most important shifters of cost curves is taxes. Per-unit and lump-sum taxes have differing effects on cost curves.

1. **PER-UNIT TAXES**: A per-unit tax is a tax on each additional unit of output produced. An excise tax, placed on sales of a specific product, is an example of a per-unit tax. With a per-unit tax, the amount of taxes paid increases as output increases; thus, it is a variable cost, not a fixed cost. If a per-unit tax is imposed on the production of a good for the firm shown in Figure 6.5, variable costs increase, shifting the MC, ATC, and AVC upward but not the AFC. The amount produced at the profit-maximizing quantity (MR = MC; more on that in later chapters) will then decrease from Q_1 to Q_2 due to the tax. (*Note:* Try not to be confused by all of the shifts shown in Figure 6.5. This merely shows the increases in AVC, ATC, and MC and their shifts upward.)

 TIP

A per-unit tax changes the MC and thus also the profit-maximizing MR = MC quantity.

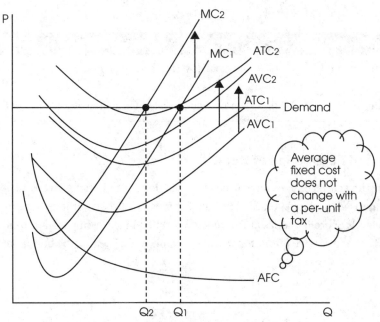

Figure 6.5 Shifting Cost Curves: A Per-Unit Tax

2. **LUMP-SUM TAXES**: A lump-sum tax is a fixed and unchanging tax regardless of the amount a firm produces. As such, this tax affects only fixed, not variable, costs: total and average costs change, but it has no impact on marginal and variable costs and their averages. In Figure 6.6, note how the lump sum will not affect the amount produced, Q_1, as marginal cost does not change, and thus the profit-maximizing output (MR = MC) is unchanged. The only curves that shift are the AFC and ATC, as the ATC is the total of the variable and fixed costs.

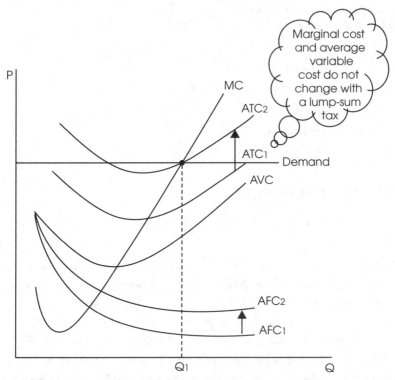

Figure 6.6 Shifting Cost Curves: A Lump-Sum Tax

See Table 6.4 for a summary of the effects of lump-sum taxes and per-unit taxes on the different cost curves.

Table 6.4

Type of Tax	Cost Curves Affected
Per-unit tax (excise tax)	Marginal cost (MC), average total cost (ATC), average variable cost (AVC)
Lump-sum tax	Average fixed cost (AFC), average total cost (ATC)

Long-Run Costs and Economies of Scale

Recall that in the short run at least one resource used in production is fixed. In the long run, however, all resources are variable as all inputs used in production can be changed. In Figure 6.7, hypothetical short-run plant size (capacity) at different levels of production is illustrated as five different short-run average total cost curves. If a long-run average total cost curve were present, it would be a long "U" skimming the bottom or minimum ATCs of the five curves.

The firm has an average total cost (ATC) curve I for production up to 1,000 units, ATC curve II for up to 1,500 units, and so on. The decision comes at production of 800 units whether to stay with plant size I and its related ATC curve or to expand capacity to plant size II. The advantage of expanding the plant size at this juncture would be to enjoy the economies of scale evident in II ATC. That is, at 800 units the firm could produce more efficiently on curve II ATC since it is downward sloping—lower per unit average costs—while curve I ATC is upward sloping at 800 units to its limit of 1,000 units. Thus, the firm could produce 800 to 1,000 units more cheaply with plant size II than with plant size I.

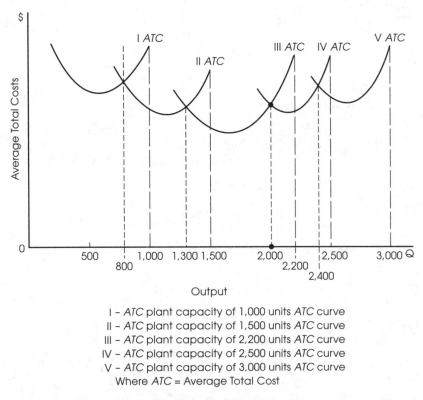

I – *ATC* plant capacity of 1,000 units *ATC* curve
II – *ATC* plant capacity of 1,500 units *ATC* curve
III – *ATC* plant capacity of 2,200 units *ATC* curve
IV – *ATC* plant capacity of 2,500 units *ATC* curve
V – *ATC* plant capacity of 3,000 units *ATC* curve
Where *ATC* = Average Total Cost

Figure 6.7 Adjustment in Plant Size (Capacity) from Short-Run to Long-Run Cost Curves

Stages of the Long-Run Average Total Cost Curve

1. **ECONOMIES OF SCALE** occur when the long-run average total cost curve (LRATC) decreases as output increases. This is equivalent to increasing returns to scale, where if inputs are increased by X percent, output increases more than X percent. Economies of scale occur as the firm increases its production with its first three factories, or ATC curves.
2. **CONSTANT RETURNS TO SCALE** occur when the long-run average total cost curve remains constant as production increases or decreases. This is shown in the middle portion of the graph in Figure 6.8(a).
3. **DISECONOMIES OF SCALE** occur when the long-run average total cost curve increases as a firm's output increases. This is also equivalent to decreasing returns to scale, where if inputs are increased by X percent, output increases less than X percent. This is shown in the upward-sloping portion of the graph in Figure 6.8(a).

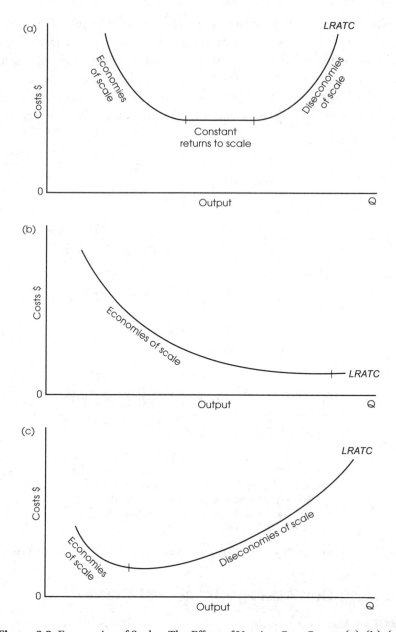

Figure 6.8 Economies of Scale—The Effect of Varying Cost Curves (a), (b), (c)

Returns to Scale

Many of the firms that experience economies of scale are capital-intensive industries that require large factories or extensive equipment to achieve profits, such as energy companies or auto manufacturers. As they increase the resources used in production, output can increase by an even greater amount, achieving increasing returns to scale. A simple way to measure returns to scale is to imagine a firm doubles all resources used in production and determine if output doubles, more than doubles, or less than doubles. See Table 6.5 for the possible outcomes.

Table 6.5 Returns to Scale

If a Firm Doubles All Inputs Used in Production . . .
and output more than doubles, the firm is experiencing **increasing returns to scale**.
and output less than doubles, it is **decreasing returns to scale**.
and output doubles, it is experiencing **constant returns to scale**.

Economic vs. Accounting Profit

There is a big difference between the way economists and accountants view profit. The major difference between these two is the way they measure costs. While every business has explicit costs like labor, rent, equipment, etc., economists also consider implicit costs, those not directly visible (opportunity costs) when calculating profit. Accountants are, not surprisingly, concerned only with **accounting profit**, which equals revenue-explicit costs. Economists, however (and you, since the title of the course you are taking right now is Economics), need to consider economic profit. **Economic profit** equals revenue minus explicit *and* implicit costs.

Normal Profit

Now that we know that economic profit is different from accounting profit, what happens if there is zero economic profit? While this situation might sound disastrous to an accountant, in economics it actually means a firm is doing well. Zero economic profit means resources employed in a firm could not be put to better use anywhere else.

This condition of zero economic profit is also known as a **normal profit**, which means resources cannot be made better off in any other activity. Still confused? Here is another example. Let's say famous basketball player LeBron James retires early from his basketball career to open a restaurant, Bron's Burrito Shop. In this restaurant, LeBron earns $3 million in revenue and has $2 million in explicit costs (e.g., direct costs such as rent, wages, food, and insurance) for an accounting profit of $1 million in his first year ($3 M in revenues − $2 M in expenses). However, as you likely know, LeBron is one of the most talented basketball players in the world and also could have earned $20 million a year if he were playing basketball. To an accountant, it looks like LeBron made a nice profit of $1 million. But to an economist, LeBron dropped the ball big time, to the tune of $19 million, as seen in Table 6.6.

Table 6.6 Bron's Burrito Shop: Accounting vs. Economic Profit

Sales from restaurant (revenue)	$3 million
Explicit costs	−$2 million
Accounting profit (revenues − explicit costs)	$1 million
Implicit costs (basketball salary)	−$20 million
Economic profit or loss (revenues − explicit and implicit costs)	$3 − (−$22) = −$19 million

Now let's assume a few years later LeBron earned $20 million in accounting profit at Bron's Burritos by expanding his firm in the long run. In this case, his economic profit would be zero. Why zero? While LeBron's accounting profit is positive ($20 million), his economic profit considers explicit costs and his implicit costs (the $20 million he could have earned playing ball if not running his restaurant). Considering this implicit cost ($20 M) gives LeBron zero economic profit and a normal profit.

Table 6.7 has a review of the two ways to measure profit, and since this is economics, the one on the left is most important. Just don't tell an accountant that!

Table 6.7 The Difference Between Economic and Accounting Profit

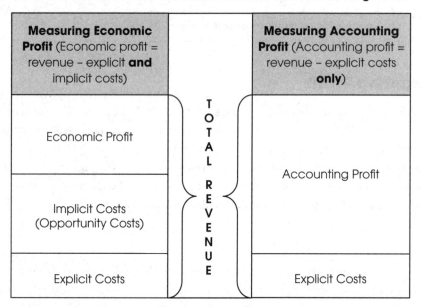

> **NOTE**
>
> **Accounting profit will always be larger than economic profit.**

SUMMARY

- The law of diminishing marginal returns is the range of output over which production increases at a decreasing rate; i.e., the additional units of production become smaller and smaller due to fixed resources.
- The MP curve *always* intersects the AP curve at the maximum point of the AP curve. The MC curve *always* intersects the AVC and ATC at their minimum points.
- Economic profits = revenue minus explicit *and* implicit costs.
- Accounting profits = revenue minus explicit costs.
- The marginal cost and marginal product curves are inverse, or mirror, images of each other.
- The three phases of the long-run average total cost curve are economies of scale, constant returns to scale, and diseconomies of scale.
- The vertical distance between ATC and AVC is the same as the vertical distance between AFC and the *x*-axis.
- A per-unit tax affects marginal cost and thus will change the profit-maximizing quantity (MR = MC). With a lump-sum tax, the tax paid stays the same regardless of output and will not change the MR = MC level of output.

Formulas

Total Cost (TC) = Total Variable Costs (TVC) + Total Fixed Costs (TFC)

Average Total Cost (ATC) = Average Variable Costs (AVC) + Average Fixed Costs (AFC) or

Total Costs/Q

Marginal Cost (MC) = $\Delta TC / \Delta Q$

Average Fixed Cost (AFC) = TFC/Q

Average Variable Cost (AVC) = TVC/Q

Multiple-Choice Review Questions

1. Which of the following is true?

   (A) TC = TVC + TFC
   (B) TFC = MC + ATC
   (C) AVC + AFC = TC
   (D) MC = TC − TFC
   (E) ATC = AVC + MC

2. If a business owner has a $100,000 accounting profit and could have made exactly $60,000 in his next best business opportunity, he has earned

   (A) $160,000 in economic profits.
   (B) $100,000 in economic profits.
   (C) $40,000 in economic profits.
   (D) neither an economic profit or loss.
   (E) none of the above.

3. With capital fixed at one unit with 1, 2, 3 units of labor added in equal successive units, production of the output increases from 300 (1 unit of labor) to 350 (2 units of labor) to 375 (3 units of labor). Which of the following is a correct interpretation?

   (A) This is long-run increasing returns to scale.
   (B) This is long-run decreasing returns to scale.
   (C) This is long-run constant returns to scale.
   (D) This is short-run diminishing marginal returns.
   (E) This is short-run increasing marginal returns.

4. There are economies of scale when

   (A) the tripling of all inputs doubles the output produced.
   (B) long-run average total cost decreases as output increases.
   (C) the short-run average total cost curve remains constant as output increases.
   (D) the long-run average total cost curve increases as output increases.
   (E) the short-run average total cost curve increases as output increases.

5. Marginal cost (MC) is equal to average variable cost (AVC) and average total cost (ATC) when

   (A) marginal cost (MC) intersects AVC and ATC at their maximum points.
   (B) AVC and ATC intersect MC at its maximum point.
   (C) MC intersects AVC and ATC at their minimum points.
   (D) AVC and ATC intersect MC at its minimum point.
   (E) the economy is in the recovery phase of the business cycle.

Refer to the graph below for question 6.

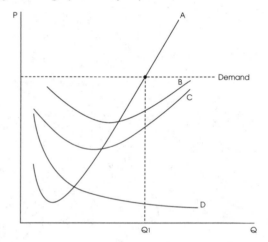

6. Which cost curves do A, B, C, and D represent, in order from A to D?

   (A) ATC, MC, AFC, AVC
   (B) MC, AFC, AVC, ATC
   (C) MC, ATC, AVC, AFC
   (D) AFC, MC, ATC, AVC
   (E) AFC, ATC, AVC, MC

7. Which of the following statements is true regarding the marginal cost (MC), average variable cost (AVC), and average total cost (ATC) curves?

   (A) If MC is greater than ATC and AVC, then ATC and AVC must be decreasing.
   (B) If MC is greater than ATC and AVC, then ATC and AVC must be increasing.
   (C) If MC is increasing, then ATC and AVC must be increasing.
   (D) If ATC and AVC are decreasing, MC must be decreasing as well.
   (E) If AVC is increasing, then both MC and ATC must be increasing.

8. If a firm's average total cost curve is increasing as output increases, the firm's marginal cost must be

   (A) less than average total cost.
   (B) greater than average total cost.
   (C) equal to average total cost.
   (D) less than average variable cost but greater than average total cost.
   (E) less than both variable and average total cost.

For questions 9 and 10 refer to the following table.

Number of workers	Number of hamburgers
1	20
2	40
3	65
4	80
5	90
6	95
7	90

9. The table refers to the quantity of hamburgers that can be produced in a day. What is the marginal product of the 4th worker?

   (A) 15
   (B) 20
   (C) 40
   (D) 80
   (E) 210

10. The table refers to the number quantity of hamburgers that can be produced in a day. With which worker will diminishing returns set in?

   (A) 2nd
   (B) 3rd
   (C) 4th
   (D) 5th
   (E) 6th

For questions 11, 12, and 13 refer to the following table.

Total output	Total cost
0	$20
1	$30
2	$38
3	$44
4	$50

11. In the table, what is the average variable cost of producing 3 units of output?

   (A) $8
   (B) $14.6
   (C) $16.6
   (D) $33
   (E) $44

12. In the table, what is the marginal cost of producing the 4th unit of output?

   (A) $2
   (B) $6
   (C) $12.5
   (D) $36.4
   (E) $50

13. In the table, what is the total variable cost of producing the 4th unit of output?

   (A) $12.5
   (B) $20
   (C) $30
   (D) $162
   (E) $182

14. If a per-unit tax is imposed on the production of wheat, which of the following shifts of cost curves is correct?

(A) There will be a downward shift of the ATC curve only, not the MC and AVC curves.

(B) There will be an upward shift of the ATC curve only, not MC and AVC.

(C) There will be an upward shift of the MC curve only, not ATC and AVC.

(D) There will be a upward shift of the MC, ATC, and AVC curves.

(E) There will be an increase in the AFC curve.

15. The vertical distance between the AVC and ATC measures

(A) marginal cost.

(B) total variable costs.

(C) revenue.

(D) total fixed cost.

(E) average fixed costs.

Free-Response Review Questions

1. (a) Draw a graph of the AFC, AVC, ATC, and MC curves for a typical firm.

   (b) Explain why the marginal cost curve intersects both the AVC and ATC at their minimum points.

2. (a) Complete the table below.

Output	TC	AFC	AVC	ATC	MC
1		$400	$100		$100
2		200	75		
3		133	70		
4		100	73		
5		80	80		
6		67	90		
7		57	103		
8		50	119		
9		44	138		
10		40	160		

   (b) Determine what total costs (TC) would be for zero output.

Answer Explanations

1. **(A)** There are two types of costs, variable and fixed. TC = TVC + TFC.

2. **(C)** Accounting profit = revenue minus explicit costs. Economic profit = revenue minus both explicit and implicit costs. Accounting profit is always greater than economic profit as there's always an opportunity cost. $100,000 accounting profit minus the implicit cost of $60,000 = $40,000 in economic profit.

3. **(D)** Diminishing marginal returns occur because as production increases, the additional output of each new worker decreases in the short run.

4. **(B)** Economies of scale occur when LRATC decreases as output increases. If LRATC increases as output increases, there are diseconomies of scale.

5. **(C)** Marginal cost intersects the ATC and AVC at their minimum points. If MC is below ATC and AVC, they are falling. If MC is above ATC and AVC, they must be rising.

6. **(C)** MC is shaped like the Nike swoosh. The vertical difference between AVC and ATC = AFC. ATC and AVC get closer to one another as output increases but never touch. AFC continues to fall as output increases.

7. **(B)** If MC is above ATC and AVC, they must be rising. If MC is below ATC and AVC, they are falling.

8. **(B)** MC always intersects ATC at its minimum point. ATC "chases" the MC curve, so if ATC is rising, its MC is greater. If ATC was falling, MC would be lower than ATC.

9. **(A)** Marginal product (MP) is the change in output from using an additional input. Total product (hamburgers) at the 3rd worker is 65 and at the 4th is 80. 80 − 65 = 15 MP for the 4th worker.

10. **(C)** Diminishing returns begin when marginal product starts to fall. MP is the change in total output (hamburgers). MP is increasing until the 4th worker, whose MP is 15 compared to an MP of 25 for the 3rd worker.

11. **(A)** Average variable cost is TVC/Q. If there's a cost at zero output, it's a fixed cost, which is 20 here. So, the TVC at 3 units is 44 − 20 = 24. 24/3 = 8.

12. **(B)** MC is the change in total cost from producing an additional unit. The change in total cost from producing units 3 to 4 = $6.

13. **(C)** If there's a cost at zero output, it's a fixed cost, which is 20. TVC = TC − TFC. $50 − $20 = $30.

14. **(D)** A per-unit tax is a variable cost placed on each additional unit of output. So, it increases MC, AVC, and ATC. Fixed costs are not affected by a per-unit tax, so AFC is unchanged.

15. **(E)** ATC = AVC + AFC, so the vertical difference between the AVC and ATC curves = AFC.

Free-Response Review Answers

1. (a)

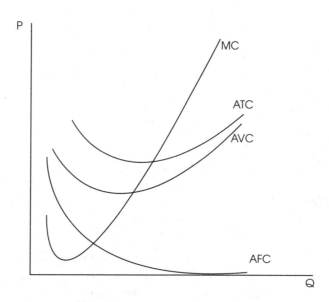

(b) When the MC curve is above ATC or AVC, that means the ATC and AVC must be increasing. If MC is below ATC and AVC, they both must be decreasing. The ATC and AVC curves are always "chasing" the MC curve.

2. (a)

Output	TC	AFC	AVC	ATC	MC
1	$500	$400	$100	$500	$100
2	550	200	75	275	50
3	610	133	70	203	60
4	690	100	73	173	80
5	800	80	80	160	110
6	940	67	90	157	140
7	1,120	57	103	160	180
8	1,350	50	119	169	230
9	1,640	44	138	182	290
10	2,000	40	160	200	360

AFC + AVC = ATC. TC = ATC × Quantity. MC = Change in Total Cost/Change in Q.

(b) Since TFC = AFC * Q, TFC = 400, at a quantity of 0, the only costs are fixed costs. Thus, TC = 400.

At zero output, TC = $400.

7

Perfect Competition

Learning Objectives

In this chapter, you will learn:

→ Market demand curve and firm's demand curve
→ Long-run equilibrium
→ Price takers
→ Strategies for profit maximization and loss minimization
→ Optimal output and efficiency
→ Evaluation of perfect competition in the long run
→ Adjustment from short-run to long-run equilibrium
→ Allocative and productive efficiency

Introduction to Market Structures

In this chapter, we will explore the first of four product markets in which firms operate. Studying product markets helps one understand why a farmer selling lettuce has much less pricing power than your local cable TV company. These different firms face vastly different levels of competition. The four market structures range from perfect competition to the imperfectly competitive models of monopolistic competition and oligopoly to monopoly. For each of these product markets, there is a set of characteristics that help us understand the different costs, efficiencies, and pricing strategies of the different markets. This chapter will address the most competitive product market—perfect competition (see Figure 7.1).

TIP

The largest number of questions on the AP Microeconomics exam come from the four market structures.

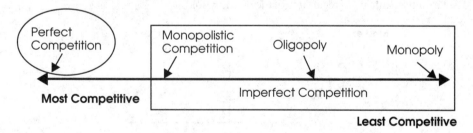

Figure 7.1

Profit-Maximizing Level of Output

Perfectly competitive firms and all other product markets maximize economic profit by producing where marginal revenue (MR) equals marginal cost (MC).

1. **ECONOMIC PROFIT** is total revenue minus economic costs (both explicit and implicit costs).
2. **MARGINAL REVENUE (MR)** is the change in total revenue from the sale of an additional product:

$$MR = \frac{\Delta TR}{\Delta Q}$$

3. **MR = MC** is the profit-maximizing level of output. Looking at Figure 7.2, you can see this firm will not produce a quantity less than 8, as MR is greater than MC; it can make additional profit by producing a greater quantity. If the firm produces a quantity of 10, MC > MR, the firm would lose money as it costs more to produce the 10th unit than the revenue received. Thus, the profit-maximizing level of output is 8 where MR = MC.

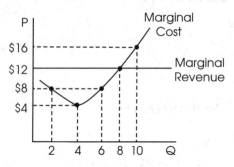

Figure 7.2

Perfect Competition

Perfectly competitive firms are characterized by large numbers of sellers that compete in national and global markets. Firms can easily **enter and exit a market**, and they are "**price takers**," where they have no influence on the price of the product they produce. Prices for each firm are determined in large markets where all firms (sellers) compete for the buyers of the same identical products. That is, the price is set in these markets and each firm must charge the "market price." To charge more would result in the loss of sales to other firms

> **Important**
>
> All profit-maximizing firms in every market structure produce where **Marginal Revenue (MR) = Marginal Cost (MC)**.

that produce the same product. Thus, each firm sells at the equilibrium price set in the market, as displayed in the market graph of a perfectly competitive firm in Figure 7.3. Note that on the firm graph (on the right), the perfectly elastic demand curve shows that demand is also equal to marginal revenue, average revenue, and price. The MR = D = AR = P is perfectly elastic regardless of how many units the firm sells. The price stays constant and each additional unit sells for the same price regardless of the quantity sold.

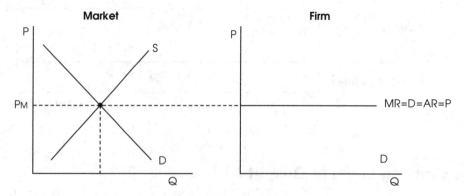

Figure. 7.3 Perfect Competition

When adding the cost curves to a firm graph you can see the profit-maximizing quantity for the firm in Figure 7.4 at Q_1, where MR = MC. Note again that the market on the left comprises thousands of firms and determines the market price. The firm is a "price taker," and that is why the MR = D = AR = P curve for the firm is perfectly elastic.

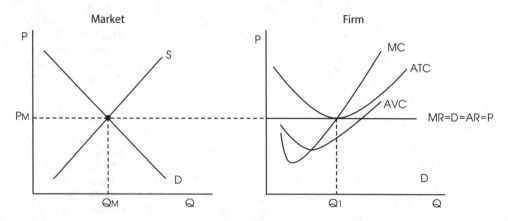

Figure 7.4 Perfect Competition (Efficiency)

TIP

To remember the labels on a perfectly competitive firm, MR = D = AR = P, you can just remember Mr. Darp and label it MR = D = AR = P. This will get you credit for a correct label on the AP exam.

Efficiency and Perfect Competition

A perfectly competitive firm in long-run equilibrium, such as in the Firm graph in Figure 7.4, results in a situation that is unique to perfect competition and not found in other markets—efficiency. There are two types of efficiency that are met by these firms in long-run equilibrium.

1. **ALLOCATIVE EFFICIENCY** is when a firm produces the socially optimal output level where **P = MC**. This output level means the exact amount that society desires is being produced. Producing more or less than this amount would be inefficient.

2. **PRODUCTIVE EFFICIENCY** is when a good is being produced where **P = minimum ATC**, which is the lowest possible cost.

As a perfectly competitive firm produces where P = MC, it is **allocatively efficient. This means that the exact amount of a product that society desires is being made**. A perfectly competitive firm in long-run equilibrium also produces where P = minimum ATC. This is known as **productive efficiency, which means goods are being produced at the lowest possible cost using the fewest possible resources**.

TIP

Be sure to practice drawing the perfect competition graphs side-by-side.

Perfect Competition's Profit-Maximizing Quantity

As mentioned previously, firms in all market structures maximize profits by producing where MR = MC. If we refer to the short run, price as reflected by the demand curve remains horizontal but can increase or decrease in the short run; therefore, there can be profits or losses in the short run. Firms maximize profits or minimize losses by producing the optimal output, that is, the level of output at which MR = MC. Thus, if you are given a graph, a table, or a set of output and price levels, you need to find the MR = MC quantity in the short run. For example, if price is $14, find the optimal output in Figure 7.5:

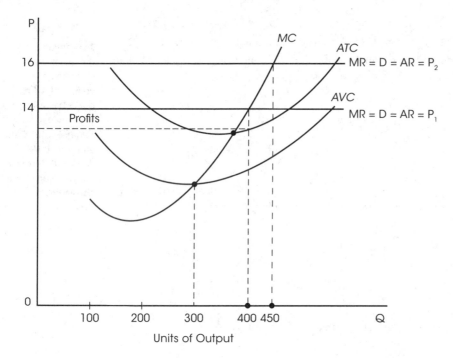

Figure 7.5 Determination of Profits

TIP

To calculate profits, go to the profit-maximizing quantity, MR = MC, and draw a straight dotted line to the optimal quantity. From that quantity, draw up to the firm's demand curve, which gives you the profit-maximizing price. Compare that price to the ATC curve at the same quantity. The formula for profit is (Price − Average Total Cost) × Quantity, for either an economic profit or loss. And if price is below AVC, the firm should shut down.

Where MR = MC, drop a line perpendicular to the horizontal axis and the output of 400 would be the optimal output, the level at which profits would be maximized. As a follow-up question, what would the firm do if the price increased to $16? Would the firm produce at 300, 350, 400, or 450 units of output? To determine the answer, follow the general criterion of best output at MC = MR. Thus, with a price (MR) of $16, MR = MC at an output level of 450. Hence, the best (optimal) output level will be 450.

CHARACTERISTICS OF PERFECT COMPETITION

- The demand curve is horizontal, or perfectly elastic, and also is MR = D = AR = P

- Easy entry and exit

- Firms are "price takers"

- Products are identical

- Zero economic profits in the long run

- Allocatively efficient (P = MC) in long-run equilibrium

- Productively efficient (P = minimum ATC) in long-run equilibrium

The Shut-Down Rule

The shut-down rule states that firms should not produce when price falls below AVC. Yes, a firm might still produce even if it is making economic losses. Why? If it is operating above AVC but below ATC, then it is at least covering all of its variable costs and at least some of its fixed costs (remember that the area between the ATC and AVC is average fixed costs). A firm at this point would lose more money by shutting down than staying open. If a firm's MR = MC level of output is where P < AVC, as shown in Figure 7.6, it is more economical to shut down production and simply incur fixed costs.

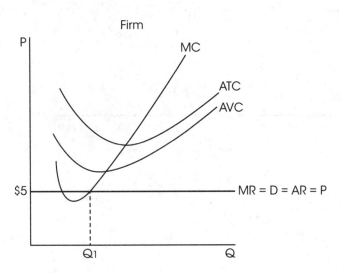

Figure 7.6 Shut-Down Case

TIP

There is always a question or two on the AP exam on the shut-down rule. Remember that a firm will shut down when P < AVC, and a firm will produce when P > AVC despite economic losses.

Determining Profit

1. *To determine total profits or total losses at the profit-maximizing level of output (MR = MC), use the following: Quantity × Price − Average Total Cost, Q(P − ATC). If P > ATC, then the firm would be realizing* profits. For example, if a firm has an optimal output level of 10 units at a price of $20 and an average total cost of $10, total profits would be $100. Total profits = Q(P − ATC), or 10(20 − 10) = $100 profit. Conversely, if at the MR = MC quantity of 10 units price was $20 and ATC was $22, there would be losses (ATC > Q). Total losses would be Q(ATC − P) or 10(22 − 20) = losses of $20.

2. *Compare the profit-maximizing price with Average Variable Cost (AVC). If P = AVC or P > AVC, the firm* continues to operate. If AVC < P, then the firm would shut down and incur losses (total fixed costs, which must be paid in the short run). The MR = MC rule would not apply here; the best output level is zero units of output.

3. *If the firm continues to produce (P > AVC), then the best* output is where MR = MC.

4. *To determine total profits or losses*, first determine whether at best output P > ATC or ATC > P. In the former case, profits are realized. In the latter case, losses are incurred. If Q is the optimal output, then for total profits, Q(P − ATC); for total losses, Q(ATC − P).

Useful Hint

The marginal cost curve is the supply curve for a firm. However, this is only where P > AVC; when P < AVC the firm will shut down and there will be no supply.

DECISION MAKING FOR THREE SITUATIONS

1. Shut-down case (see Figure 7.6). (P < AVC, therefore, shut down; total losses = TFC). At the market price of $5, the average variable cost is higher than price at every level of output. Therefore, the firm should shut down (at least temporarily) since its cost of continuing production is greater than its revenue. It has no revenue to apply to fixed costs and cannot recover its variable costs at the price of $5 per unit. Its optimal or best output is zero, and its minimal total costs are equal to its total fixed costs.

2. Profit-maximization case (see Figure 7.7). P > AVC, which suggests that the firm should continue to produce as long as MR > MC up to the level of output at which MR = MC; this level of output will maximize profits.

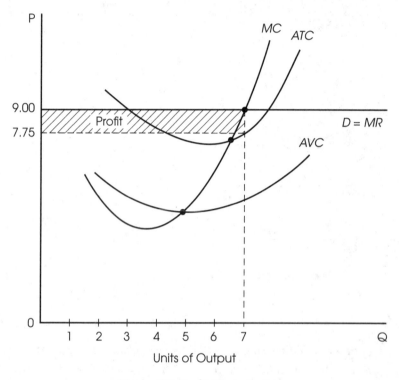

Figure 7.7 Profit Maximization

At the market price of $9, the firm covers its ATC (P > AVC) and, thus, continues to produce as long as MR > MC up to the level of output at which MR = MC, or if there is no level of output at which MR = MC, the highest level of output MR > MC would be the optimal output. In this case MR = MC at the $7 units of output. The optimal (best) output is 7, at which profits are maximized. Total profits at 7 units of output would be Q(P − ATC) = total profits. Profits are maximized when the Q is the optimal level of output (MR = MC). So, Q(P − ATC) becomes 7(9 − 7.75) = 8.75.

3. Loss minimization (see Figure 7.8). P > AVC, which suggests that the firm, in the short run, will continue to produce as long as MR > MC up to the level of output at which MR = MC even if there are losses. We want the level of output at which we minimize the total losses (MR = MC).

At a market price of $6 per unit this level would be at 5 units of output (MR = MC). Total losses would be Q(ATC − P) where Q is the optimal or best output; that is, total losses are minimized. Thus, Q(ATC − P) becomes 5(7.60 − 6) = 8.00. This is the rectangular area in the graph below, noted as "losses" (loss permit at best output × number of units). If they shut down, it loses total fixed costs. TFC = AFC * Q = (ATC − AVC) * 5 = 18.

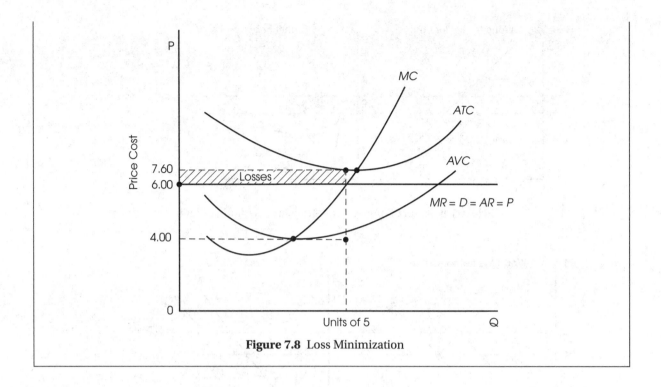

Figure 7.8 Loss Minimization

Perfect Competition in the Long Run

While perfectly competitive firms do not earn economic profits in the long run, they often do in the short run. Due to the market having easy entry and exit, profits will attract new competition and firms, while losses create incentives to leave the market. Questions regarding the short- and long-term adjustment in perfect competition are frequent on both the free-response and multiple-choice questions. Here are some scenarios with graphs for you to better understand this concept.

Scenario 1

This market is made up of the world's corn farmers, and as corn is a global commodity, the price of corn is traded on the world market. The firm graph comes from Farmer Bob's corn farm in the Midwest. Demand has currently increased for corn in the world market, causing the price of corn to rise (a move from E_1 to E_2 in the corn market in Figure 7.9). As Farmer Bob is a price taker, he has no influence over the price of corn in the world market. However, as he realizes the price of corn has increased, he increases production to the profit-maximizing quantity (MR = MC) and is earning economic profits for the first time in many years (see Figure 7.9).

Farmer Bob and other corn farmers are elated that they are earning economic profits. In an efficient market like corn, however, with easy entry and exit, and economic profits being made, competition is never far away. Entrepreneurs see profits to be made, and after an adjustment period, also known as the long run, many new firms enter the corn market. As shown in Figure 7.10, these new firms increase the supply in the world market, increasing from S_1 to S_2 and moving to a new equilibrium, E_2 to E_3, reducing the price in the market from PM_2 to PM_3. Farmer Bob now sees his economic profits disappear. He has no choice but to take the new price in the market, which makes his new perfectly elastic demand curve fall from MR = D = AR = P_2 to MR = D = AR = P_3. Farmer Bob and other firms will always produce at the profit-maximizing quantity of MR = MC, which is now qf_3, where he originally began producing. Even though economic profits for Farmer Bob have gone away, he still is breaking even and earning a normal profit, so not all is lost.

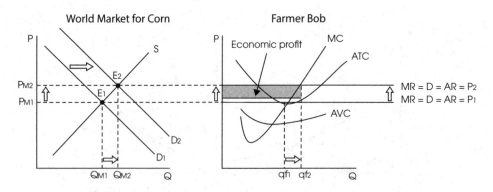

Figure 7.9 Perfect Competition (Short-Run Economic Profits)

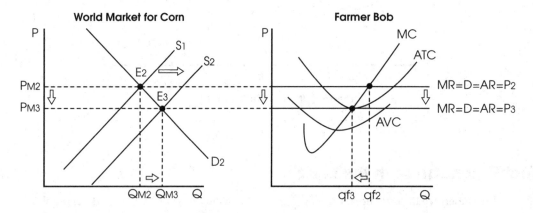

Figure 7.10 Perfect Competition (Long-Run Adjustment)

Scenario 2

Perfectly competitive firms find themselves incurring an economic loss. Should the firm with an economic loss shut down? To review, if a firm is producing where price is above AVC, it should continue to produce in the short run. The firm incurs a smaller loss than if it were to shut down, as it can cover the variable costs and some of the fixed costs.

In the scenario in Figure 7.11, P < ATC, so the shaded rectangle shows the economic loss. Farmer Bob, however, realizes he is still above AVC and continues to produce corn despite economic losses, as he can still cover his variable costs and some of his fixed costs. Many other corn farmers see losses and decide to leave the industry. The industry again goes through a long-run adjustment; this time, as farmers leave the world market, the supply decreases and the world price increases, as shown in Figure 7.12.

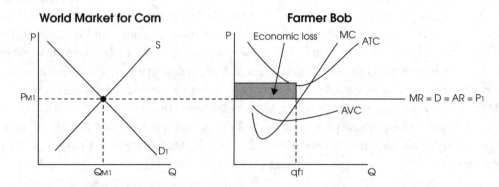

Figure 7.11 Perfect Competition (Short-Run Economic Profits)

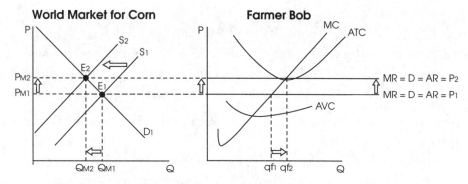

Figure 7.12 Perfect Competition (Firms Leave in Long Run)

As supply shifts in the world market to the left and price increases from P_{M_1} to P_{M_2}, the price taken by Farmer Bob increases so that he is now breaking even, earning neither an economic profit or loss, but a normal profit. This is a perfect example of a perfectly competitive firm in long-run equilibrium. Then the firm is productively (P = minimum ATC) and allocatively (P = MC) efficient, earning a normal profit.

Perfect Competition Graphing Identification

Check out Figure 7.13, and see if you can locate and understand the coordinates and the dollar value at the profit-maximizing quantity for the following: average revenue, marginal revenue, price, total revenue, total cost, average fixed cost, average total cost, and total profit or loss. Find the solutions in Table 7.1.

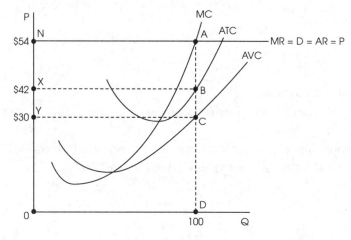

Figure 7.13

Table 7.1

Concept	Coordinates	Dollar Value
Average revenue (AR), marginal revenue (MR), price (P)	DA	$54
Total revenue (TR)	0DAN	$5,400
Total cost (TC)	0DBX	$4,200
Average fixed cost (AFC)	CB	$12
Average total cost (ATC)	DB	$42
Total profit	XBAN	$1,200

SUMMARY

The perfectly competitive market is characterized by a large number of sellers, availability of perfect substitutes, perfectly elastic demand function, price takers, no barriers to entry or exit, productive and allocative efficiency, zero economic profits, and pricing at marginal cost and at minimum average cost in the long run.

- A perfectly competitive firm's demand curve is perfectly elastic and equals marginal revenue, average revenue, and price.
- The major criterion for determining the optimal (best) output for the firm operating under perfect competition, in the short run, is to produce that level of output at which MR = MC. The specific criteria and steps to determine the best output are:
  1. The firm will produce, in the short run, as long as price is greater than or equal to average variable cost (AVC). If price is less than AVC, the firm should shut down and take as losses its total fixed costs.
  2. The firm (if number 1 is satisfied) will produce up to the level of output at which MR = MC. This will either maximize profits or minimize losses.
- The evaluation of perfect competition in the long run would reveal that firms are operating efficiently by utilizing the available technology with zero economic profits, price equal to minimum average cost, and price equal to marginal cost (socially efficient pricing). Firms are directed by the market in their pricing (price takers).
- The adjustment of firms from the short run to the long run is accommodated by the absence of barriers to entry or exit. The entry of new firms attracted by short-run profits and the exit of firms discouraged by losses ultimately results in the restoration of market equilibrium as described in the previous paragraph.

Formulas

$P < AVC$ firms shut down in the short run

$MR = D = AR = P$ perfectly competitive firm's demand function

$MR = MC$ profit-maximizing criterion

$P = MC$ socially optimal price (under perfect competition in the long run); efficiency

$P = \textbf{minimum average cost}$ in the long run for a perfectly competitive firm

$Q(P - ATC) = $ profit or loss

$MR = \dfrac{\Delta TR}{\Delta Q}$ marginal revenue

Multiple-Choice Review Questions

1. The individual firm, operating under perfect competition, is characterized as:

    (A) a price maker.
    (B) one of a few sellers.
    (C) a price strategist.
    (D) a price taker.
    (E) interdependent.

2. Firms maximize their profits by producing a level of output at which

    (A) $MC = AFC$.
    (B) $MC = MR$.
    (C) $P = ATC$.
    (D) $MR = AVC$.
    (E) $P = AVC$.

3. In the short run, a firm should shut down if

    (A) price $>$ ATC.
    (B) price $<$ AVC.
    (C) price $<$ ATC.
    (D) price $=$ ATC.
    (E) $MR = MC$.

4. The demand curve for the firm operating under perfect competition is

    (A) upward sloping to the right.
    (B) downward sloping to the right.
    (C) a perfectly vertical line.
    (D) a perfectly horizontal line.
    (E) concave to origin.

5. Which of the following is not correct for a perfectly competitive firm, in long-run equilibrium?

    (A) Price $=$ minimum average total cost.
    (B) Price $=$ marginal revenue.
    (C) Price $=$ minimum average variable cost.
    (D) Price $=$ marginal cost.
    (E) Normal profits.

6. All of the following are true about a perfectly competitive firm in long-run equilibrium except

    (A) economic profit $=$ zero.
    (B) $P > ATC$.
    (C) $P =$ minimum ATC.
    (D) $P > AVC$.
    (E) $P = MC$.

7. Which of the following is true about this profit-maximizing, perfectly competitive firm?

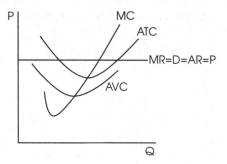

    (A) The firm should shut down as $P < AVC$.
    (B) The firm is covering AVC but not ATC.
    (C) The firm is incurring economic losses, and firms will enter the industry in the long run.
    (D) The firm is incurring economic losses, and firms will leave the industry in the long run.
    (E) The firm is earning economic profits, and firms will enter the industry in the long run.

8. A profit-maximizing, perfectly competitive firm is producing where marginal revenue is greater than the marginal cost. What actions should this firm take?

    (A) Increase the quantity they are producing
    (B) Decrease the quantity they are producing
    (C) Increase their marginal cost
    (D) Leave the industry
    (E) Increase production so that $MC > MR$

9. Assume the market for grapes is perfectly competitive. Now assume there is an increase in demand for grapes in the global market. How will this affect a firm currently producing grapes in the short run?

(A) Economic profits will decrease due to increased production costs.

(B) Average total costs will decrease.

(C) The firm's demand curves will shift up, leading to economic profits.

(D) The firm's demand curves will shift down, leading to economic losses.

(E) The firm's demand curve will shift up, but the firm will not make economic profits.

Free-Response Review Question

1. Assume the market for soybeans is perfectly competitive and in long-run equilibrium, and Sam's Soybeans is a small farm in the market.

   (a) Draw correctly labeled side-by-side graphs of both the market for soybeans and the firm, labeling the market equilibrium P_M and Q_M and labeling Sam's Soybeans equilibrium P_F and q_F.

   (b) Is Sam's Soybeans earning economic profits, economic losses, or a normal profit?

   (c) Now assume that in the soybean market there is a huge drought that ruins the soybean harvest of thousands of farmers (but not Sam's). Show on the same graph as above what would happen to the new equilibrium price and quantity in both the market and firm, labeling the firm P_{M2} and Q_{M2} and Sam's Soybeans P_{F2} and q_{F2}.

   (d) Shade in the area of economic profit or loss for Sam's Soybeans at the new equilibrium.

Answer Explanations

1. **(D)** A perfectly competitive firm "takes" the price from the competitive market of thousands of buyers and sellers. The firm has no impact over the price its product earns in the market.

2. **(B)** All profit-maximizing firms in all market structures produce where marginal revenue = marginal cost. This is one of the most important concepts to understand for the AP exam.

3. **(B)** P < AVC is the shut-down point. Firms should still produce in the short run when incurring economic losses if P > AVC but less than ATC; this way firms can at least cover all their variable costs and some of their fixed costs, which would be incurred either way in the short run.

4. **(D)** The perfectly competitive firm takes the price set in the market and is a perfectly elastic, horizontal demand curve that also equals marginal revenue, average revenue, and price (otherwise known as "MR. DARP").

5. **(C)** Price = minimum average total cost, which indicates productive efficiency, not variable cost.

6. **(B)** Price = ATC at long-run equilibrium. Perfectly competitive firms break even in long-run equilibrium, earning a normal profit but zero economic profit.

7. **(E)** At the MR = MC profit-maximizing quantity, the firm is earning economic profits as P > ATC. As perfectly competitive firms can easily enter and exit the industry, the economic profits will attract new firms.

8. **(A)** If MR > MC, a firm can increase profit by producing until MR = MC.

9. **(C)** The price earned by the firm will increase, shifting its demand curves upward, leading to greater output and short-run economic profits.

Free-Response Review Answer

1. (a) See the graph and check for correct labels, prices, and quantities.

    (b) Sam is earning a normal profit. A normal profit is the break-even point, where
         P = ATC and resources could not be put to better use anywhere else.

    (c) Supply now shifts to the left in the market, causing the price to go up in the market, and as Sam's
         Soybeans is a price taker, the price for the firm increases as well.

    (d) See the graph for the economic profit.

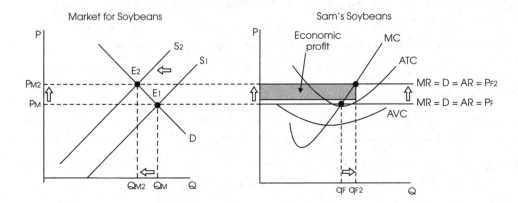

8

Monopoly

Introduction

A monopoly is a market structure where one single firm constitutes an entire industry and no close substitutes exist for consumers. It is important to note that a monopoly is on the opposite end of the market structure continuum than perfect competition, as shown in Figure 7.1 at the beginning of Chapter 7. Unlike perfect competition, there are high barriers to entry for a monopoly as other firms are prevented from entering and competing. Monopolies are "price makers" as opposed to "price takers" as they are *both* the industry and the firm at the same time—so goodbye to side-by-side graphs!

Demand and Marginal Revenue in a Monopoly

Monopolies (and all imperfectly competitive firms) have downsloping demand curves, with marginal revenue less than demand. When a monopoly wants to sell more units, it must lower its price for all buyers; when price decreases from, say, $200 to $150, the additional (marginal) revenue received decreases faster than price, from which the demand curve is derived. See the separate demand and marginal revenue curves in Figure 8.1. So say goodbye to Mr. Darp where MR = D from perfect competition because he's gone as MR < D with a monopoly.

Table 8.1 exemplifies the reasoning behind the differing marginal revenue and demand curves, that marginal revenue is less than price (the demand curve) and does not equal price like in perfect competition. This is because if a monopoly wants to sell more product, it must lower the price for all units sold, resulting in marginal revenue falling faster than price. Note that marginal revenue eventually becomes negative. This is why the MR curve falls below the quantity axis in Figure 8.1 and is the inelastic range of the demand curve. A monopolist will not produce in this range, as the additional revenue from a sale is negative.

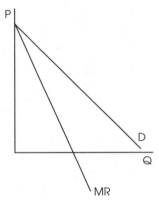

Figure 8.1 Monopoly

Table 8.1 Price and Marginal Revenue

Price	Qd	TR	MR
$6	0	0	—
$5	1	5	5
$4	2	8	3
$3	3	9	1
$2	4	8	−1
$1	5	5	−3

The Nature of a Monopoly

A **monopoly** by definition is a firm that is a single seller of a product for which there are no close substitutes. It is at the opposite end from perfect competition on the spectrum of market competitiveness.

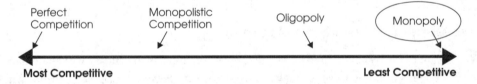

The key to the market power of a monopoly is the difficulty competitors have entering the industry. Here are a few reasons for these high barriers to entry:

- **GOVERNMENT POWER.** The government may give sole production rights to a single firm.
- **RESOURCE CONTROL.** A firm may control the resources required for production of a product, such as a diamond company controlling all the diamond mines.
- **ECONOMIES OF SCALE.** A firm that becomes very large may gain significant production advantages over its rivals by being able to produce with lower costs. (Reminder: Economies of scale means that long-run average total costs decrease as a firm grows in size.) Thus, competitors cannot compete as they may have higher production costs.
- **COPYRIGHTS OR PATENTS.** Here the government grants sole production rights of a product to a single firm, such as new medical drugs.

A Monopolist's Demand Curve

A profit-maximizing monopoly will always produce in the elastic range of the demand curve (the upper half of the demand curve). In this range, marginal revenue is positive; as a monopolist lowers prices to increase profits, total revenue increases. A monopolist will not produce in the inelastic range, as the marginal revenue is negative; a decrease in price here decreases total revenue. Note the position in Figure 8.2 where the marginal revenue curve travels below the quantity axis, at all prices below P_1, the inelastic range. Also, total revenue is at its highest point when marginal revenue is 0, shown at P_1 in Figure 8.2.

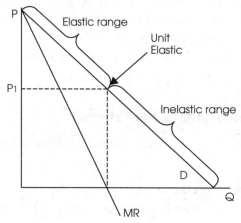

Figure 8.2 Elastic and Inelastic Range

Graphing a Monopoly

A monopoly is unique in that it is both the firm **and** the industry, and "price maker." In a monopoly, there is only one graph because the firm is the industry, which is sharply different from perfect competition's side-by-side graphs and perfectly elastic demand curve. Like all profit-maximizing firms, a monopolist determines price and output at where MR = MC. A monopoly graph is shown in Figure 8.3.

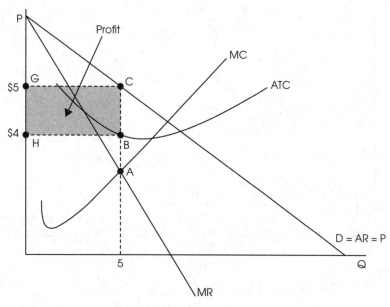

Figure 8.3 Monopoly Profits

To calculate economic profit in Figure 8.3, draw a vertical dashed line at the profit-maximizing quantity, MR = MC (point A), extended down to the quantity of 5 and back up to the demand curve (point C) and then horizontally to the price axis (point G), where the price is $5. The profit is shown on the graph to be the rectangular area, HGCB. The numerical profit value is calculated by taking (P − ATC) × Q, or ($5 − $4) × 5 = 5. Another way to get this same exact answer is to subtract total cost from total revenue. **Total revenue** is calculated by taking the price mulitplied by quantity at the profit-maximizing point ($5 × 5 = $25). The **total cost** is calculated by heading to the ATC curve from the profit-maximizing quantity (point B) and then taking the price at the ATC, $4 (point H) times the quantity of 5. Total cost then is $4 × 5 = $20. TR − TC = profit ($25 − $20 = $5 profit). Last, you may be asked to calculate **per-unit profit**, which is P − ATC ($5 − $4 = $1) or total profit divided by quantity ($5/5 = $1). Be sure not to confuse per-unit with total profit! In this case, take total profit divided by the quantity ($5/5 equals a per-unit profit of $1).

TIP

When answering monopoly graph questions, the first step is to locate the profit-maximizing quantity at MR = MC and find the price from the demand curve at that quantity. This is key to interpreting a monopoly graph.

Monopolies and Efficiency (The Deadweight Loss Returns)

Aside from perfect competition, none of the other market structures is productively or allocatively efficient, leading to a misallocation of resources.

1. **ALLOCATIVE EFFICIENCY** is producing the exact amount of output that society wants, where P = MC. Monopolies, however, produce where P > MC based on society's needs.

2. **PRODUCTIVE EFFICIENCY** is when products are being produced at the lowest minimum cost, where P = minimum ATC. Monopolies, however, produce where P > ATC.

While it is good to be the monopolist, both in the board game and in real life, it is generally bad for consumers and society overall. The situation that is present in all imperfectly competitive markets (but not perfect competition!) is known as the deadweight loss. To review, it is the loss of welfare to society resulting from market inefficiency causing a reduction of consumer and producer surpluses.

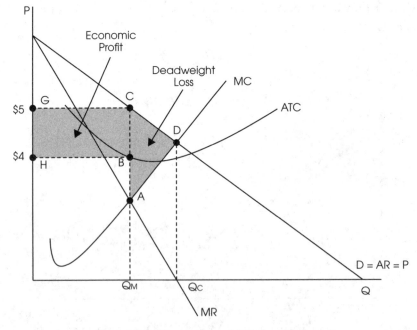

Figure 8.4 Monopoly and Deadweight Loss

In Figure 8.4:

1. The deadweight loss is measured by the area of ACD. If this were a competitive market producing at Q_C, there would be no deadweight loss, and the area would be part of either consumer or producer surplus. The monopoly is not allocatively efficient as $P \neq MC$.

2. The monopoly also does not produce at minimum ATC. This means it is not productively efficient as $P \neq$ minimum ATC.

3. For help identifying and labeling deadweight loss, imagine drawing an arrow pointing at the output as if it were a competitive market. When labeling deadweight loss with a monopoly or monopolistically competitive firm, it will always be below the demand curve, above marginal cost, and to the left of the profit-maximizing quantity. Students have found this technique helpful in identifying the deadweight loss, as it is frequently asked on the AP Microeconomics exam.

Interpreting a Monopoly Graph

It is an important skill to be able to interpret several different versions of a monopoly graph. The graph shown in Figure 8.5 looks slightly different than the previous graphs in this chapter. Do you notice the difference? Well, if you haven't found it already, the marginal cost, average cost, and long-run average total cost curves have all the same perfectly elastic slope for simplicity's sake, as opposed to their normal slope seen in the previous graphs and probably in your class. Don't let these different-shaped curves distract you from the basics: firms still produce at MR = MC and profit is still calculated the same way.

Please see Table 8.2 for questions and answers to several commonly asked questions using Figure 8.5.

Price Discrimination

If a monopoly or any imperfectly competitive firm had its way, it would charge each customer exactly the maximum price that each customer would be willing to pay. As a practical matter, this would be very difficult or impossible to do since the firm would not know the maximum price for each customer (the costs of identifying these differences would be high relative to any information revealed), and the policy would likely fall victim to some customers discovering they had paid more than others for the same product. Perhaps you should not ask other passengers on an airline what they paid for their tickets unless you got a very good price.

Although the above suggests perfect price discrimination with perfect information about each consumer, we can still find many examples of price discrimination. For example, movie theaters may charge less for an afternoon (matinee) movie than for a movie in a more popular time such as evening or night. Senior citizens may be charged lower prices for lodging, museum attendance, and transportation. Some discounts simply promote better allocation of scarce commodities such as space on highways at commuter rush times or one's time. Price discrimination works best if the following conditions are operative:

1. Separate markets for consumers based on different price elasticities' relatively elastic demand. This really means that customers with elastic demand have more choices of substitute products. Customers with relatively inelastic demand have less sensitivity to the price of a particular product since they have fewer substitute choices.

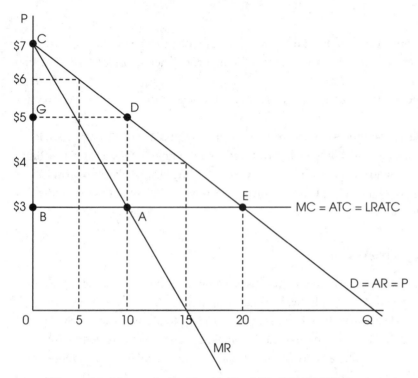

TIP

A monopoly graph with flat cost curves similar to Figure 8.5 has occasionally appeared on AP exams. Be sure to practice it.

TIP

On the AP test, students are frequently asked to draw a monopoly graph. Make sure to practice it and be able to locate the profit or loss and the deadweight loss.

Figure 8.5 Monopoly Graph with Flat MC, ATC, LRATC Curves

Table 8.2 Monopoly Graph Questions and Answers from Figure 8.5

Question	Answer
1. What is the **profit-maximizing quantity**?	10, where MR = MC
2. What is the **price** at the profit-maximizing quantity?	$5
3. Locate the area and calculate the **economic profit** at the profit-maximizing quantity.	Area: GDAB 10 × ($5 − $3) = $20
4. Locate the area and calculate the **deadweight loss** at the profit-maximizing quantity.	Area: DAE ½ × (20 − 10) × ($5 − $3) = $10
5. Locate the area and calculate the **consumer surplus** at the profit-maximizing quantity.	Area: CDG ½ × ($7 − $5) × 10 = $10
6. Below what price is **marginal revenue** negative and in the **inelastic range of demand**?	$4 as below this MR is negative. A monopolist will always produce on the elastic portion of the demand curve, or ≥ $4 in this example.
7. At what quantity is there **unit elasticity**?	15; marginal revenue equals zero at Q15.
8. At the profit-maximizing quantity, are there **economies of scale, diseconomies of scale,** or **constant returns to scale**?	Constant returns to scale, as LRATC is flat. When LRATC is declining, it's economies of scale; increasing, it's diseconomies of scale.
9. What is the **allocatively efficient quantity**?	20, where P = MC
10. At the **allocatively efficient quantity,** what is **consumer surplus**?	Area: EBC ½ × ($7 − $3) × 20 = $40

2. There must not be opportunities for the resale of the product.
3. The price differences are not based on cost differences.
4. The firm is a price maker—it has a pricing strategy that looks to charge a higher price and realize more profits.

Price Discrimination Shown Graphically

For a monopolist who practices perfect price discrimination, the monopoly graph has a few distinctive features that are commonly asked on the AP exam:

1. **DEMAND = MARGINAL REVENUE.** An important distinction to make is that with perfect price discrimination, demand and marginal revenue are no longer separate curves. See Figure 8.6.
2. **NO CONSUMER SURPLUS.** Every consumer is paying the highest price he or she is willing to pay.
3. **PROFITS INCREASE.**

All of these are shown in Figure 8.6.

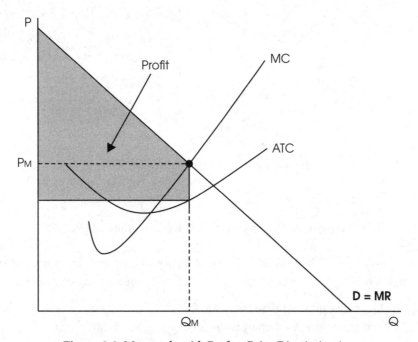

Figure 8.6 Monopoly with Perfect Price Discrimination

Note that profit (shaded area) increases significantly at the profit-maximizing point (MR = MC) while the consumer surplus has disappeared and turned into profit for the monopoly.

Natural Monopolies and Regulation of Monopolies

Occasionally there is significant cost advantage when only one firm produces in a market. A firm in this situation is a **natural monopoly** and realizes economies of scale, where LRATC continues to decrease as output increases. Due to this and very high fixed costs that serve as barriers to entry, one firm can serve a market at lower costs than several firms. Electricity or water companies are examples of natural monopolies.

Due to the significant cost savings of having one producer in these industries, governments allow some monopolies such as utility companies to operate. However, that's not the end of the story. Due to the fear of high prices and poor quality and service (typical of markets with no competition), governments regulate natural monopolies with the goal of increasing efficiency and reducing deadweight loss.

Here are the two scenarios available for regulating a monopoly, with unregulated monopolies included for comparison.

1. **SOCIALLY OPTIMAL PRICING.** Here government regulators will force the monopoly to have allocatively efficient pricing at P = MC. However, socially optimal is likely below the average total cost of production, which may force a firm to go out of business or require a large subsidy from taxpayers.
2. **FAIR-RETURN PRICING.** Regulators set the price = ATC wishing to let the monopoly break even and earn a normal profit, covering its implicit and explicit costs. However, this price is higher than is socially optimal but is less than the unregulated monopoly price.
3. **UNREGULATED MONOPOLY.** The bulk of this chapter has discussed unregulated monopolies, who produce at the profit-maximizing quantity of MR = MC, and underproduce and overcharge.

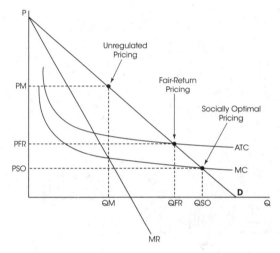

Figure 8.7 Monopoly with Price Discrimination

Yes, you guessed it, this graph will look slightly different than previous monopoly graphs, as ATC is continually falling within the range of production. Figure 8.7 shows some of these three pricing strategies.

- P_{SO} and Q_{SO} refer to socially optimal pricing at P = ATC.
- P_{M} and Q_{M} refer to an unregulated monopoly with output where MR = MC.

CHARACTERISTICS OF A MONOPOLY

- One firm selling a unique product
- The demand curve is downsloping, with MR < D
- High barriers to entry
- Firm is a "price maker"
- Economic profits in the long run
- Not allocatively efficient (P > MC)
- Not productively efficient (P > minimum ATC)

Formulas

MR = MC profit-maximizing level of output

Regulated Monopolies (pricing at)

a. Fair-Return Price:

Price = average total cost (at intersection of demand curve and average total cost curve)

b. Socially Optimal Price:

Price = marginal cost (at the intersection of demand curve and marginal cost curve)

Multiple-Choice Review Questions

Use the figure below to answer questions 1 and 2.

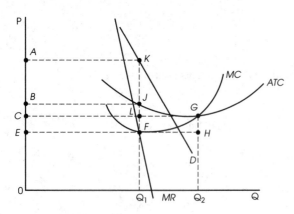

One firm constitutes the market

Use the figure below to answer questions 3, 4, and 5.

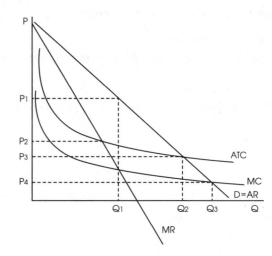

1. The total profits for this monopolist are identified by

   (A) CEFL.
   (B) ABJK.
   (C) BCLF.
   (D) CEHG.
   (E) BEFJ.

2. The total costs for the monopolist are identified by

   (A) CEFL.
   (B) CEHG.
   (C) ABJK.
   (D) $E0Q_1F$.
   (E) $B0Q_1J$.

3. The socially optimal price would be

   (A) P_1.
   (B) P_2.
   (C) P_3.
   (D) P_4.
   (E) none of the above.

4. The unregulated monopolist's price would be

   (A) P_1.
   (B) P_2.
   (C) P_3.
   (D) P_4.
   (E) none of the above.

5. The "fair-return" price of the regulated monopolist would be

   (A) P_1.
   (B) P_2.
   (C) P_3.
   (D) P_4.
   (E) none of the above.

Use the figure below to answer questions 6 and 7.

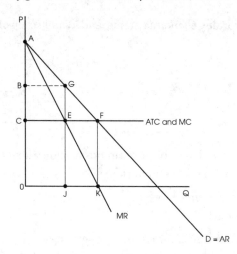

6. If this is a perfectly competitive market, the consumer surplus would be area

   (A) ABG.
   (B) ACF.
   (C) BCEF.
   (D) COKF.
   (E) GEF.

7. After the unregulated, profit-maximizing monopolist takes over, the consumer surplus is

   (A) ABG.
   (B) ACF.
   (C) BCEG.
   (D) COKF.
   (E) GEF.

8. If a monopoly increases production in the elastic region of the demand curve, which of the following is true?

   (A) Marginal revenue and total revenue are negative.
   (B) Marginal revenue is negative, and total revenue is increasing.
   (C) Marginal revenue is negative, and total revenue is decreasing.
   (D) Marginal revenue is positive, and total revenue is decreasing.
   (E) Marginal revenue is positive, and total revenue is increasing.

9. Which of the following are true about profit-maximizing monopolies?

   I. They produce on the inelastic portion of their demand curves.
   II. Marginal revenue is less than demand.
   III. They are "price takers."
   IV. Price is greater than minimum ATC.

   (A) I and II only
   (B) I, II, and III only
   (C) II and IV only
   (D) I and III only
   (E) I, III, and IV only

10. Which of the following is true of a natural monopoly?

   (A) As output increases, the long-run average total cost curve decreases.
   (B) As output increases, the long-run average total cost curve increases.
   (C) As output increases, the long-run average total cost curve remains constant.
   (D) The fair-return price is where an unregulated natural monopoly will produce.
   (E) The socially optimal price is greater than the marginal cost.

Free-Response Review Questions

1. Draw a correctly labeled graph of an unregulated monopoly earning economic profits, and identify each of the following on your graph.

   (a) The profit-maximizing quantity and price, labeled Q_M and P_M
   (b) The area of economic profit, shaded in
   (c) The deadweight loss, also shaded in
   (d) The allocatively efficient quantity, labeled Q_C

2. Grant's Gas Guzzlers is a used car lot operating as a geographic monopoly due to its remote location without any competition. Grant's Gas Guzzlers continues to produce despite having economic losses.

   (a) Why might Grant's Gas Guzzlers remain open despite the economic loss?
   (b) Now assume Grant's Gas Guzzlers is earning economic profits.

      (i) At the profit-maximizing price, at what segment of the demand curve is the firm operating at: the inelastic, unit elastic, or elastic range?
      (ii) If Grant's Gas Guzzlers increases its prices, what will happen to total revenue?

   (c) Now assume Grant's Gas Guzzlers' fixed costs increase. What will happen to its profit-maximizing quantity? Explain.

Answer Explanations

1. **(B)** From the MR = MC quantity of Q_1, head up to the demand curve (K), down to the ATC (J), then over to the price axis (B), and up to the price (A). If you were asked to calculate the dollar value of the profit, take $Q \times (P - ATC)$.

2. **(E)** From the MR = MC quantity of Q_1, head up to the ATC curve (J), then to the monopolist's price (B), and down to the x-axis (0). If you were asked to calculate the dollar value of total costs, take $ATC \times Q$.

3. **(D)** The socially optimal price is where P = MC, or P_4, at the quantity of Q_3.

4. **(A)** An unregulated profit-maximizing monopoly will produce where MR = MC. Q_1 is the quantity; head up to the demand curve and over to the price axis where price is P_1.

5. **(C)** The fair-return price is where P = ATC, or P_3.

6. **(B)** In a perfectly competitive market, quantity comes from where P = MC, or K, and the price is C. The consumer surplus is found below the demand curve, above the price, and left of quantity (K), and is ACF.

7. **(A)** The monopolist MR = MC quantity is J, and from heading straight up to the demand curve and over to the price axis, the price is B. The consumer surplus is found below the demand curve, above the price (B), and left of quantity (J), and is ABG.

8. **(E)** If production increases in the elastic range, marginal revenue is always positive and thus total revenue will increase. Therefore, a monopoly will always produce in the elastic range of their demand curve.

9. **(C)** In a monopoly, MR < D and P > minimum ATC. Monopolies produce in the elastic of their demand curve and are "price makers," not takers.

10. **(A)** The economic case for a natural monopoly (like a utility or an energy company) is that its LRATC decreases as output increases.

Free-Response Review Answers

1.

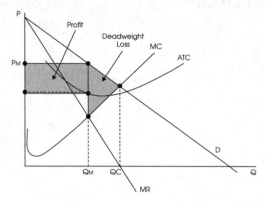

2. (a) At this profit-maximizing level of output, price must be above average variable cost. At this price, the firm can at least pay all the variable costs and some of the fixed costs by staying in business.

   (b) (i) The elastic range
      (ii) Decrease—monopolies always produce on the elastic portion of their demand curve. As price increases, total revenue decreases in the elastic range.

   (c) It will remain the same. Fixed costs don't affect marginal revenue or marginal cost, the profit-maximizing quantity. Fixed costs only change the total costs and fixed costs.

9

Imperfect Competition: Monopolistic Competition and Oligopoly

Learning Objectives

In this chapter, you will learn:

→ Monopolistic competition and nonprice competition
→ Differentiated products
→ Price > marginal cost
→ Barriers to entry and exit
→ Oligopolies and interdependence
→ Game theory and strategies on prices/output
→ Nash equilibrium

Introduction

In the two previous chapters, we reviewed the "bookends" of market structures: perfect competition and monopoly. Now we will look at the two other imperfect competitors: monopolistic competition and oligopoly. Monopolistic competition has many more firms than oligopolies, but oligopolies represent dominant industries in terms of market share, assets, and control over prices. Look at Figure 9.1 to see where they lie on the continuum of market structure competition.

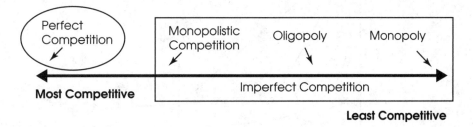

Figure 9.1

Monopolistic Competition

Firms that are monopolistically competitive have characteristics of both a monopoly and perfect competition. They are monopolies in the sense that they sell their own product that is slightly differentiated from competitors. Consider your favorite fast food joint: its burgers and other items are marginally different from its competitors, so in this sense it has some monopoly power. For example, McDonald's burgers are slightly different from Wendy's. However, there are also many competitors due to easy entry and exit, and in this sense, it's a very competitive market—hence the name "monopolistic competition."

Characteristics of Monopolistic Competition

1. **EASY ENTRY AND EXIT:** As it is easy to enter this market, when new firms arrive, it decreases the demand for existing firms in the market. When firms leave the market, it increases demand for the firms still producing. The intense competition also results in a very elastic demand curve for firms.
2. **ZERO ECONOMIC PROFIT IN THE LONG RUN:** Due to easy entry and exit, any shortrun profits will attract new firms until economic profits have disappeared.
3. **DIFFERENTIATED PRODUCTS AND NONPRICE COMPETITION:** These firms use nonprice competition such as advertising to differentiate their products from their competition with the goal of increasing demand for their own products.
4. **INEFFICIENCY:** Monopolistically competitive firms are not allocatively efficient, as price does not equal MC. Price is actually greater than MC for these firms. They also are not productively efficient, as price does not equal minimum ATC.
5. **MR < D:** Just like a monopoly, the marginal revenue is less than demand, and they are both downsloping.

Graphing Monopolistic Competition: From the Short to the Long Run

In the short run, there are dynamic shifts in demand in an intense competitive environment. Thus, we can expect that some firms will realize profits as demand for their products increases, sometimes at the expense of rival firms, some of which will incur losses even to the extent of leaving the industry. Thus, in the short run, we can illustrate both situations with the following graphs.

In Figure 9.2, the firm is earning economic profits in the short run. As a result of these economic profits, new firms see opportunities for profit and enter the industry. But in the long run, these new entrants to the industry will reduce the market share of existing firms. This decreases the demand and marginal revenue for the existing firms, resulting in a new long-run output level seen in Figure 9.4 at the break-even point.

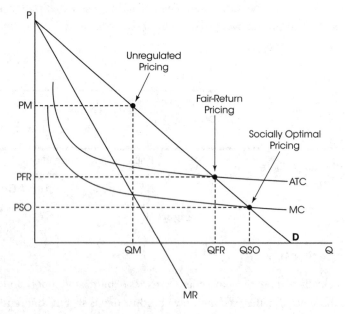

Figure 9.2 Monopolistically Competitive Firm—Short-Run Profits

In Figure 9.3, the firm is incurring losses in the short run. As firms are losing money, some start to leave the industry, as there is easy entry and exit. As firms leave the industry, market share increases for the remaining firms. Demand and MR then shift to the right for the existing firms, ending up in the long-run equilibrium shown in Figure 9.4.

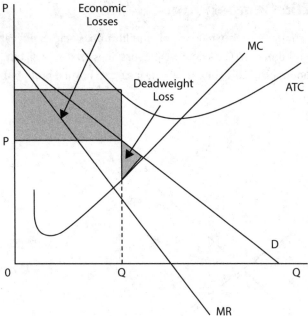

Figure 9.3 Monopolistically Competitive Firm—Short-Run Losses

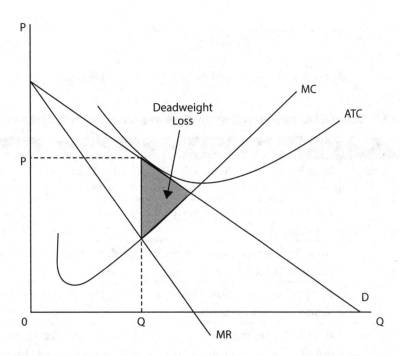

Figure 9.4 Monopolistically Competitive Firm in Long-Run Equilibrium

Efficiency and Monopolistic Competition

As seen in Figure 9.5, a monopolistically competitive firm in long-run equilibrium is neither allocatively efficient (P $\neq$ MC) nor productively efficient (P $\neq$ minimum ATC). A deadweight loss does exist as well, but it is generally not as large as a monopoly. Also, a monopolistically competitive firm earns a normal profit but no economic profits in long-run equilibrium.

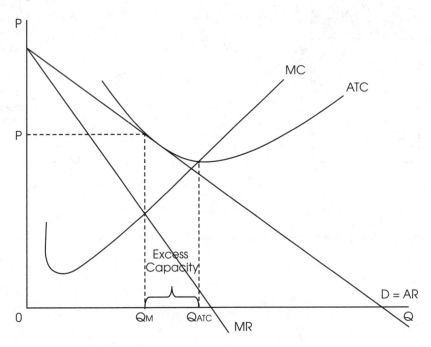

Figure 9.5 Monopolistic Competition: Excess Capacity

Table 9.1 Comparison: Perfect Competition and Monopolistic Competition

	Perfect Competition	**Monopolistic Competition**
Long-run profits (Economic)	Zero; Price = Minimum ATC	Zero; Price = ATC (*not* at minimum ATC)
Efficiency/ inefficiency	Efficient = Market prices weed out the inefficient firms	Inefficient (excess capacity, underutilization of capacity)
Product differentiation	None. Products are homogeneous (identical in each product market).	Differentiation is necessary for survival.
P and MC	P = MC (socially optimal) efficient allocation of resources.	P > MC. Allocatively inefficient.
P and MR	P = MR. No pricing strategy. All firms take prices from the market.	P > MR. Pricing strategy. Some extent of price making.

Excess Capacity

Another key feature of monopolistically competitive firms is the presence of excess capacity, shown graphically in Figure 9.5. A monopolistically competitive firm produces at Q_M, while a productively efficient firm (P = minimum ATC) would produce at Q_{ATC}. As an example of excess capacity, one might visualize four gas stations on the four corners of a busy intersection. The total demand, on average, for gasoline is considerably less than the available supply; therefore, each station is not able to utilize all of its pump capacity. Each station does not sell enough gas to spread its high fixed costs over the amount of gas sold, so the stations quickly exhaust any economies of scale and do not reach minimum ATC. This is a classic case of underutilization or excess capacity. Suppose that two gas stations would have the right capacity to handle the demand. They could then spend the fixed costs over a greater number of gallons of gas and achieve some efficiency. With easy entry and exit, there tend to be too many competitors given a certain demand.

Interpreting a Monopolistic Competition Graph

Look at the graph in Figure 9.6 and find the coordinates and dollar value for the following at the profit-maximizing quantity: price, average revenue, total revenue, total cost, average total cost, consumer surplus, and profit or loss. (See solutions in Table 9.2.)

TIP

When drawing a monopolistic competition graph in long-run equilibrium, make sure the demand curve is tangent with the *ATC* before its minimum point. (See Figure 9.4 or Figure 9.5.)

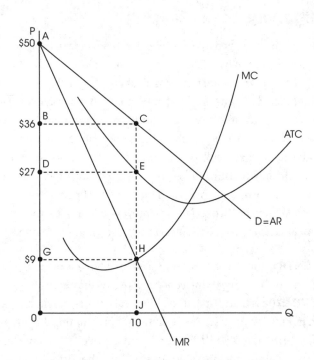

Figure 9.6 Monopolistic Competition Graph

Table 9.2 Solutions to Figure 9.6

Concept	Coordinates	Dollar Value
Price (P), Average revenue (AR)	JC	$36
Total revenue (TR)	BCJ0	$360
Average total cost (ATC)	JE	$27
Total cost (TC)	DEJ0	$270
Consumer surplus (CS)	ACB	$70
Profit or loss	BCED	$90 profit

SUMMARY: MONOPOLISTIC COMPETITION

1. Relatively easy entry
2. Differentiated products
3. Advertising, nonprice competition
4. Inefficient, excess capacity
5. Large number of buyers and sellers
6. Long-run *equilibrium*: zero economic profits
7. Allocatively inefficient: P > MC
8. P > MR
9. Deadweight loss

Introduction to Oligopoly

An **oligopoly** is a market structure characterized by a very small number of firms that have market dominance. Some examples of oligopolies in the real world can be found in the soft drink, airline, and cell-phone industries. The key to understanding an oligopoly is the "interdependence" of rival oligopolists. Oligopolists must closely consider the actions of other firms, as the output and price decisions of one firm can have a significant impact on an entire market. For example, Company X may want to raise its prices in an attempt to increase profits. However, if its oligopoly rival Company Y is expected to lower its prices to undercut the sales of Company X, then X may not raise its prices in the first place. This interdependence may actually lead to lower prices or, at least, no increase in prices.

The firms in this example and in oligopolistic markets have a strong incentive to collude. **Collusion** is an agreement (usually illegal) drawn up to agree on what price and quantity will be produced in a market. To solve this problem, in the United States there is an **antitrust policy** to prevent oligopolies from becoming monopolies with no competition for the benefit of consumers and society. Here are some other characteristics of oligopolies:

1. **HIGH BARRIERS TO ENTRY.** The industry is comprised of only a few firms. If it were easy to enter the industry, you would see many more firms due to the economic profits they earn.
2. **A FEW POWERFUL FIRMS** (less than 10) that sell identical or differentiated products.
3. **PRICE LEADERSHIP.** If there is a price leader or dominant firm among the other oligopolists, the leader can "set" the price to maximize profits and other firms simply price at the same level since they are unable to gain market share by maintaining their previous prices. The other firms in the market face smaller profits given their lower volume of production.
4. **COLLUSION.** Oligopolies sometimes decide to form a **cartel**, which is a group of firms that act together and have a formal agreement not to compete. These oligopolists may decide that "if you can't beat 'em, you might as well join 'em." That is, rivals may divide markets among themselves according to regional areas or product specializations. Cartels, such as OPEC (Organization of Petroleum Exporting Countries), may have production limits or price agreements among its members in an effort to set or control prices (and act like a monopoly). However, oligopolistic firms that have colluded have a strong incentive to cheat, which is modeled in the next section in the game theory payoff matrix.

It's Game Time: Modeling Oligopoly with Game Theory

Game theory is the study of how people and firms act strategically in the context of a game. As rival oligopolistic firms attempt to maximize profits, the success of a strategy is dependent on the actions taken by the other firms. A firm may have a **dominant strategy**, which is the best choice for a player regardless of what the other player chooses. See Figure 9.7 for an example of a payoff matrix between two firms in the same market.

Firm A's numbers are underlined, and Firm B's are circled. The first number will always be for the player on the left and the last number for the player on the top of the payoff matrix.

Figure 9.7 shows the potential profits for two competing firms when they price both high and low (assume each firm wants to maximize profit). Can you locate each firm's dominant strategy, if there is one? For Firm A, pricing low is the dominant strategy because if Firm B chooses a high price, Firm A will receive a profit of $40 if they price low and a profit of $25 if they go high. If Firm B chooses a low price, Firm A will get $10 if it goes low but $0 if Firm A chooses a high price. As $40 > $25 and $10 > $0, Firm A is better off choosing a low price regardless of what Firm B does. Firm B's dominant strategy is also to go low, as this strategy is best regardless of what Firm A does ($35 > $25 if Firm A goes high and $10 > $5 if Firm A goes low).

Now assume that both A and B decide to collude and both price high and earn $25. Each side now has an incentive to cheat on their agreement. For example, if A prices high and B reneges on the agreement and switches to a low price, B's profits will increase to $35 from $25, while A will lose out, earning $0. This is why many collusive agreements in the real world are hard to maintain since the incentive to cheat is strong in oligopolistic markets.

Nash Equilibrium and the Prisoner's Dilemma

- In Figure 9.7, it turns out that both Firm A and Firm B have a dominant strategy of pricing low. As both firms have a dominant strategy of pricing low, they end up in the bottom right corner, with a profit of $10 each. The game has reached equilibrium with both players choosing their respective dominant strategies. When players choose the action that is best for them given the actions of the other players, it is said to reach a **Nash equilibrium**. Another way to think of Nash equilibrium is that it occurs when the game ends with both sides voluntarily choosing the same cell.

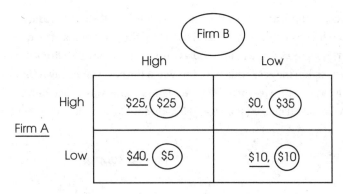

Figure 9.7 Game Theory Payoff Matrix

- The respective dominant strategies led both firms to set prices low and earn a profit of $10; however, if both sides had chosen high, they would each have had a greater profit of $25 each. As each firm acts in its own interest by choosing its best strategy considering the other player's actions, a less than ideal outcome results. This is known as the **prisoner's dilemma**. In a traditional prisoner's dilemma game, police arrest two suspects that they interrogate in separate rooms. A confession is the dominant strategy for both, yet when they both confess they receive longer prison sentences than if they had remained silent and not confessed.

> **TIP**
>
> Students find it helpful to circle or underline each player's respective numbers on the payoff matrix as to not mix up each firm's numbers, as shown for you in Figure 9.7.

A frequently asked question on the AP exam is to determine the dominant strategy, if any, for a player. A dominant strategy is not always present. A situation like this is depicted in Figure 9.8.

Can you locate the firm (A or B) in Figure 9.8 below that does not have a dominant strategy? (Once again, the numbers are underlined or circled for the respective players.)

If Grant's Garage prices high, Red's Bug Zappas is better off pricing high, as $45 is better than $35. However, if Grant's Garage prices low, Red's Bug Zappas is better off pricing low, as $20 is greater than $10. It is clear Red's Bug Zappas does not have a dominant strategy. Grant's Garage does have a dominant strategy, as pricing high ($50 > $40 and $40 > $25) will leave them better off regardless of what Red's Bug Zappas does.

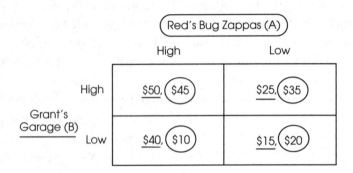

Figure 9.8 Game Theory Payoff Matrix

If both players know the information in the matrix, a Nash equilibrium can still be reached despite Red's Bug Zappas not having a dominant strategy. Red's Bug Zappas knows Grant's Garage will choose its dominant strategy of pricing high. Aware of this, Red's Bug Zappas will choose to go high, and the respective profits for Grant's Garage and Red's Bug Zappas will be $50 and $45. So even if one side does not have a dominant strategy, a student can still discern the outcome in the game, given that both sides know the information in the payoff matrix.

One more question that may appear on the AP exam is to show the effect of a subsidy (a government payment to producers) on the payoff matrix. If asked this, don't make this question harder than it really is. In Figure 9.9, the matrix shows the profits of the same firms if they locate east or west. A question may ask what happens when the government awards a $5 subsidy to each firm who locates to the west of the city. Note the subsidy was added only to each firm's west profits on the payoff matrix (shown as +5); you should add them together on the AP exam.

TIP

You will be sure to see game theory payoff matrix questions on the AP exam, certainly on the multiple-choice and maybe in the free-response section. The good news is that you will not be required to graph an oligopoly, unlike the other market structures, but be sure you have the payoff matrix down pat.

Red's Bug Zappas

		East	West
Grant's Garage	East	$50, $45	$25, $35 + $5
	West	$40 + $5, $10	$15 + $10, $20 + $5

Figure 9.9 Game Theory Payoff Matrix with Added Subsidy (West)

Now that we have covered all four market structures, you can use this Venn diagram to compare and contrast the major characteristics of each in Figure 9.10.

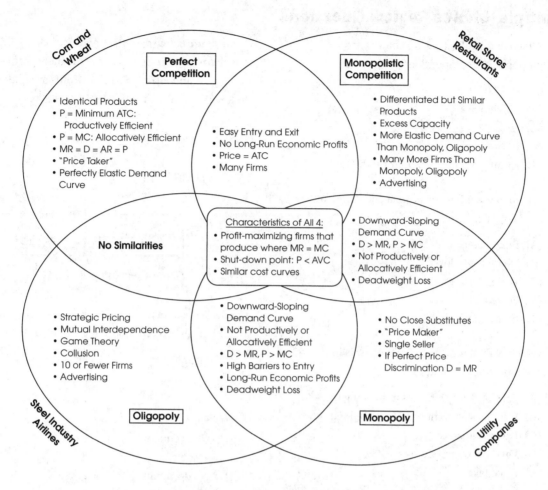

Figure 9.10 Four Market Structures

SUMMARY: OLIGOPOLY

1. Formidable barriers to entry
2. Differentiated or similar products
3. Interdependence
4. Few firms, controlling major shares of market
5. Allocatively inefficient: price > marginal cost, excess profits
6. Price > marginal revenue
7. Productively inefficient: P ≠ minimum ATC
8. Collusive activities and cooperative arrangements
9. Deadweight loss

Formulas

MR = MC profit-maximizing criterion for monopolistic competition and oligopoly

P > MC relationship between price (P) and marginal cost (MC) for both monopolistic competition and oligopoly

P > ATC relationship between P and ATC for both monopolistic competition and oligopoly

Multiple-Choice Review Questions

1. Which of the following is a characteristic of monopolistic competition?

    (A) $P > MC$
    (B) Efficiency
    (C) $D = MR$
    (D) $P = MR$
    (E) Homogeneous or similar products

2. Which of the following is *not* a characteristic of oligopolies?

    (A) Price takers
    (B) Deadweight loss
    (C) Strong barriers to entry
    (D) Few firms
    (E) Interdependence

3. Which of the following is a characteristic of monopolistic competition?

    (A) Economically efficient in the long run
    (B) Pricing at minimum ATC in the long run
    (C) Excess capacity
    (D) Very few competitors
    (E) Price taker

Use the figure below to answer questions 4 and 5. The game theory matrix below shows the daily profits for both Firm A and Firm B. Firm A's profits are underlined, and Firm B's are circled.

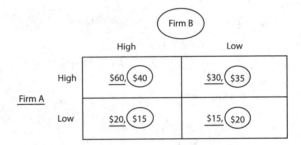

Game Theory Payoff Matrix

4. Given the data in the game theory matrix, what are both firms' dominant pricing strategies?

	Firm A	Firm B
(A)	Low	No dominant strategy
(B)	High	Low
(C)	No dominant strategy	High
(D)	No dominant strategy	Low
(E)	High	No dominant strategy

5. Given the data in the game theory matrix, if both firms know all of the information in the matrix and cooperate in their pricing, what will each firm choose?

	Firm A	Firm B
(A)	High	High
(B)	High	Low
(C)	Low	High
(D)	Low	Low
(E)	No dominant strategy	

6. Which of the following is true of oligopolies?

    I. They make strategic decisions considering competitors' actions.

    II. There are low barriers to entry.

    III. They are neither allocatively nor productively efficient.

    IV. They are "price takers" in the market.

    (A) I only

    (B) I and II only

    (C) I, II, and IV only

    (D) I and III only

    (E) I, III, and IV only

7. In this market structure, short-run profits attract new competition, causing the demand curve to shift to the left and decrease for existing firms in the market, resulting in zero economic profit in long-run equilibrium.

    (A) Perfect competition

    (B) Monopoly

    (C) Monopolistic competition

    (D) Oligopoly

    (E) All of these

8. In game theory, this is the *best* choice for one player regardless of what the other player chooses.

    (A) Nash equilibrium

    (B) Dominant strategy

    (C) Prisoner's dilemma

    (D) Interdependence

    (E) Collusion

9. If a lump-sum tax is imposed on a monopolistically competitive firm, which of the following will happen to the price and quantity sold in the market?

    (A) Price will increase and quantity will increase.

    (B) Price will decrease and quantity will increase.

    (C) Price will increase and quantity will decrease.

    (D) Price will decrease and quantity will decrease.

    (E) Price and quantity will remain unchanged.

Free-Response Review Questions

1. Assume Carly's Cafe is a coffee shop that is operating in a monopolistically competitive industry. Carly's Cafe is earning economic profits.

    (a) Draw a correctly labeled graph of Carly's Cafe, and include the following on the graph:

    (i) The profit-maximizing price and quantity, labeled P_M and Q_M

    (ii) The area of economic profits, shaded in

    (iii) The productively efficient output level, Q_P

    (iv) The quantity of excess capacity

    (b) What will happen to the number of firms in this monopolistically competitive industry in the long run? Explain.

2. In a remote town, there are only two indoor entertainment complexes, Fields' Fun House and Amazing Jake's. The figure below shows the profits for each firm if they price tickets high or low. Analyze the matrix, and answer the following questions. Fields' Fun House is the first number in each cell, and Amazing Jake's is the second number.

Amazing Jake's

		High	Low
		High	Low
Fields' Fun House	High	$30, $35	$20, $30
	Low	$15, $15	$5, $20

Game Theory Payoff Matrix

    (a) What type of market structure do these two firms operate in?
    (b) Is there a dominant strategy for Amazing Jake's? Explain.
    (c) If Field's goes low, where will Jake's go?
    (d) What is the game's Nash equilibrium?

Answer Explanations

1. **(A)** A monopolistically competitive firm is not allocatively efficient as P > MC. Only in perfect competition does P = MC in long-run equilibrium.

2. **(A)** Price takers is a characteristic only of perfect competition.

3. **(C)** A key characteristic of monopolistically competitive firms is that there is excess capacity. Firms aren't productively efficient as they don't produce at the minimum ATC.

4. **(E)** A dominant strategy is when a firm has a best choice regardless of what action the other player chooses. Firm A's dominant strategy is to go high, as $60 > $20 if A goes high and $30 > $15 if A goes low. Firm B does not have a dominant strategy. If B chooses high and A goes high, $40 > $35, but if A goes low, $15 < $20, so B would be better off choosing low if A goes low.

5. **(A)** Firm A will use its dominant strategy and go high. B knows A will go high and then will also go high as $40 > $35 that B would get if they went low. This is also the game's Nash equilibrium, which is the outcome when each player chooses what is best for them given the actions of the other players.

6. **(D)** Oligopolies make strategic decisions using game theory and are inefficient like every market structure except perfect competition.

7. **(C)** With monopolistic competition, firms can easily enter and exit the market, so profits attract competition, resulting in zero economic profit in long-run equilibrium.

8. **(B)** See the explanation for question 5 for a further explanation of a Nash equilibrium.

9. **(E)** A lump-sum tax does not affect either MR or MC, so the profit-maximizing quantity of MR = MC is unaffected, and P and Q will be unchanged. Only a per-unit tax or subsidy affects Q and P.

Free-Response Review Answers

1. (a) See figure below. Note that productive efficiency is where MC and ATC meet. The area of overcapacity is between current output Q_M and Q_P.

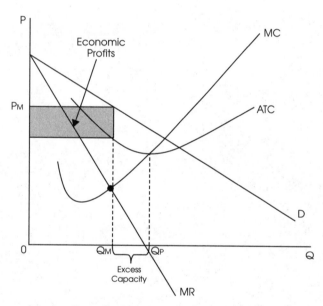

Monopolistically Competitive Firm—Short-Run Profits

(b) As Carly's Cafe is earning economic profits, new firms will enter the industry, decreasing demand for the existing firm's products. The demand will decrease and shift left for Carly's Cafe and similar existing firms, returning to the long-run equilibrium with no economic profits or losses.

2. (a) Oligopoly

    (b) No. Jake's best move depends on Fields' move. If Jake's goes high, it would earn $35 if Fields' goes high, which is greater than $15 if Fields' goes low. However, if Jake's goes low, it would earn $30 if Fields' goes high but $20 if Fields' goes low. So if Jake's goes low, $20 > $15 but $30 < $35. If it chooses high, $35 > $30 but $15 < $20. Thus, it has no dominant strategy.

    (c) Low, as $20 > $15

    (d) Both would go high. Fields' would use its dominant strategy, going high. Jake's doesn't have a dominant strategy, but as Jake's knows Fields' will go high, its best option then is to go high as well.

10

Resource Markets with Applications to Labor

Learning Objectives

In this chapter, you will learn:

→ Product markets and resource markets: the connections
→ Marginal revenue product
→ Derived demand
→ Monopsony vs. competitive labor markets

Introduction to Factor Markets

As you are reading this far in the book, you probably have a good understanding of supply and demand and product markets. The good news is that this unit applies the fundamentals of supply and demand that you have already learned. However, this section is concerned not with the product markets but with the markets for land, labor, capital, and entrepreneurship (the factor or resource markets). The key difference to note here is that this is the exact opposite of the product markets: *Now firms are the demanders in the factor markets, not consumers, and suppliers are not firms but individuals with their labor.* The demand curve is now made of firms searching for inputs, not consumers in the market for goods and services. This chapter will help explain issues such as why a career as a doctor is likely much more lucrative financially than one as a college professor. It is not the result of some type of conspiracy against professors but the workings of supply and demand that determine wages in the labor market.

Key Concepts of Factor Markets

1. **DERIVED DEMAND** relates the product and factor markets together. There is demand for the factors of production (land, labor, capital, entrepreneurs) because this demand is derived from the goods that are produced by these inputs. For example, there is demand for shoemakers because there is demand for shoes; the demand for shoemakers is derived from the demand for shoes from consumers in the product market.

2. **THE MARGINAL REVENUE PRODUCT (MRP)** is the addition to a firm's revenue when an additional input is employed. The MRP is represented graphically by a downsloping demand curve that tells a firm what hiring an additional unit of labor will contribute to its revenue.

3. **THE MARGINAL FACTOR COST (MFC)** (also sometimes called marginal resource cost or MRC) is the additional cost of employing an additional input like a machine or worker. A firm maximizes its profits by continuing to hire inputs as long as MRP > MFC up until the point where MRP = MFC.

4. **THE LEAST-COST RULE** of multiple inputs states that to minimize costs (as any profit-maximizing firm will do) a firm will adjust the ratio of inputs until (L is labor and K is capital):

$$\frac{MP_L}{P_L} = \frac{MP_K}{P_K}$$

5. **A MONOPSONY** occurs when there is a single buyer of labor. This is the "monopoly of the factor markets." Similar to how a monopoly overcharges and underproduces, a monopsony underhires and pays workers less than would occur in a competitive market.

6. **FACTORS** that can shift the demand and supply for certain resources, for example, a decrease in the cost of robots to produce cars will decrease the demand for assembly line car workers.

Marginal Revenue Product (MRP) and Marginal Factor Cost (MFC)

TIP

Many employees feel they are extremely valuable and irreplaceable by their employer. Although this may be true, the more likely scenario is that a business owner is probably more concerned with whether the additional revenue generated from an employee is greater than the cost of hiring the worker.

> **Most AP exam questions assume a perfectly competitive output market, where MR = P. So the MRP formula you can use is MP × P, which is also MP × MR (in perfect competition).**

The first step to determine the value of labor is to measure its marginal revenue product. The **marginal revenue product (MRP)** is the addition to a firm's revenue when an additional input is employed. This can also be calculated as follows:

$$MRP = \frac{\Delta \text{ in Total Revenue}}{\Delta \text{ in Resource Quantity}} \text{ or } MP \times P \text{ (in perfect competition) or } MP \times MR$$

The next essential step to determine the value of labor in the factor market is to calculate the marginal factor (resource) cost (MFC). The **marginal factor cost (MFC)** is the additional cost to the firm from hiring an additional input like a machine or worker. If there is a competitive labor market, the MFC also equals the wage.

$$MFC = \frac{\Delta \text{ in Total Resource Cost}}{\Delta \text{ in Resource Quantity}} = \text{Wage}$$

For a more detailed analysis of the profit-maximizing resource employment in a perfectly competitive labor market, look at Table 10.1. At 4 workers, the MRP of $30 is greater than the cost of the labor, $20. At this point, the firm would continue to hire workers until MRP = MFC at 5 units of labor. This is just an application of basic economic concepts, thinking at the margin, and weighing the marginal costs versus the benefits. If the costs are greater than the benefits, a worker would not be hired, as is shown with the 6th unit of labor. The MFC ($20) is greater than the MRP ($10), so the optimal number of workers hired is 5 (MRP = MFC).

> **Profit-Maximizing Rule For Employing Resources: MRP = MFC**
>
> A firm maximizes its profits by continuing to hire inputs used in production if the MRP > MFC up until the profit-maximizing point where **MRP = MFC**. If MRP < MFC, the firm will no longer use that input as it costs the firm more than it brings in revenue.

Table 10.1 How Many Workers Should Be Hired?
product price = $10, wage = $20

Units of Labor	Total Product	Marginal Product (ΔQ/ΔL)	Marginal Revenue (P = MR)	Marginal Revenue Product (MP * MR)	Marginal Factor Cost (MFC = Wage)
0	0				
1	5	5	10	50	$20
2	16	11	10	110	$20
3	22	6	10	60	$20
4	25	3	10	30	$20
5	27	2	10	20	$20
6	28	1	10	10	$20
7	26	−2	10	−20	$20

The Three Shifters of Resource Demand

In addition to **derived demand**, the demand in the product market that in turn creates a demand for the inputs used in production, there are other factors that influence the demand for labor. Here are the three shifters of resource demand.

1. **CHANGES IN THE PRODUCT DEMAND.** An increase in the price of a product then increases MRP and the resources used in production. An increase in the price of airplanes would also increase the MRP of airplane builders and would shift the demand curve (MRP) to the right, as shown in Figure 10.1. This would result in more labor being hired, as the optimal quantity increases from Q_1 to Q_2.

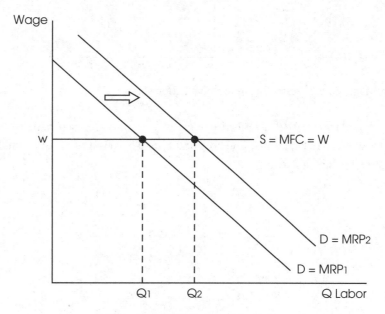

Figure 10.1 The Demand for Labor

2. **CHANGES IN PRODUCTIVITY.** An increase in technological progress increases marginal product and thus MRP as well (as MRP = MR * MP), shifting the MRP curve to the right from MRP_1 to MRP_2 (see Figure 10.1). Increases in productivity can make a firm more profitable and give it a greater incentive to employ more resources and utilize the increased productivity of resources.

3. **CHANGES IN THE PRICES OF OTHER RESOURCES.**
   - *Substitute resources.* If the price of farm machinery decreases relative to farm laborers, more machinery would be utilized, and this would decrease the MRP of farm labor, shifting the MRP from MRP_2 to MRP_1 in Figure 10.1.
   - *Complementary resources.* If the price of lumber used to build new houses decreases, more homes will be built, increasing demand and thus MRP for construction workers, shifting the MRP curve to the right from MRP_1 to MRP_2.

Perfectly Competitive Labor Market

A **perfectly competitive labor market** is comprised of many firms hiring many workers with similar skills and abilities. Just as perfectly competitive firms are price takers in product markets, here the firms are **wage takers**; each individual firm is only hiring a small percentage of the industry total, has no influence on the market wage, and must pay its hired workers the market-determined wage rate. This wage is shown as w in the labor market and as S = MFC = W for the firm in Figure 10.2.

NOTE

The graph for a perfectly competitive market for labor is very similar to the perfectly competitive one in the product market, except the horizontal firm graph is not demand but supply, labeled MFC. This graph often appears on the FRQ section of the AP exam.

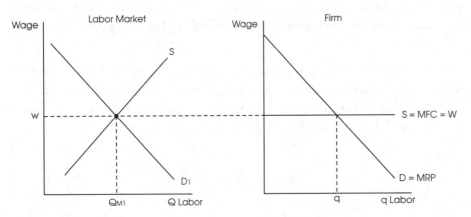

Figure 10.2 Perfectly Competitive Labor Market

Be sure to note the differences between a perfectly competitive *product market* (Chapter 7) and a perfectly competitive *labor market* shown in Figure 10.2. The horizontal curve is the supply of labor, not a demand curve as in a perfectly competitive product market.

Minimum Wage

An effective minimum wage can have a significant effect on a labor market and individual firms. If the government sets an effective minimum wage (which is a type of price floor, previously discussed), the wage will increase, but the quantity hired in this labor market and the firm will decrease, as shown in Figure 10.3.

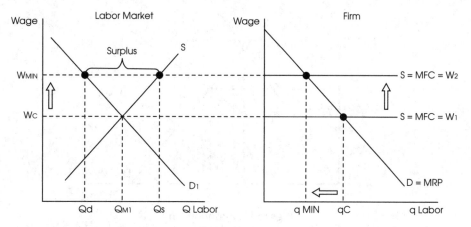

Figure 10.3 Perfectly Competitive Labor Market with Minimum Wage

After the effective minimum wage is instituted in the labor market on the left, the quantity of labor supplied increases (Q_s), but the quantity demanded decreases to Q_d, which will be the new amount of labor hired in the market. As the individual firm on the right is a wage taker, the wage increases shifting from W_1 to W_2, meaning that less labor is demanded as the quantity decreases from q_C to q_{MIN}.

Monopsony

Similar to the way a monopoly uses its market power to adversely affect product markets, a monopsony has a similar effect on factor markets.

- A **monopsony** is a single buyer of labor, for example, a small-town coal mine. Recall how a monopoly has two downsloping curves, with marginal revenue less than demand, as it must lower prices for all to increase sales, which decreases marginal revenue. A monopsony has not two downward- but two upward-sloping curves, S and MFC (Figure 10.4). The MFC curve increases at a faster rate than the supply curve as a monopsony cannot wage discriminate. As it hires additional workers, it must pay higher wages to them as well as to every other worker previously hired. This results in the MFC curve being higher than supply.

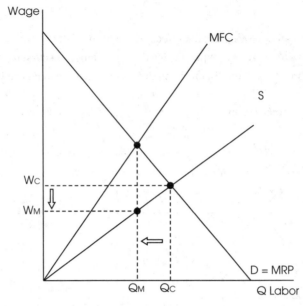

Figure 10.4 Monopsony

In Figure 10.4, the quantity of labor hired in a monopsonistic labor market would be at Q_M, where MFC = MRP, but note the wage paid, W_M. They pay a wage based on the supply curve at Q_M, so a monopsony hires fewer workers and pays less than would occur in a competitive market (Q_C and W_C).

Least-Cost Rule

You well know by now that firms maximize profits by either increasing revenue or decreasing costs (or both). Similar to when we learned about utility maximization by consumers in Chapter 5, producers attempt to find the cost-minimizing combination from two different inputs (labor and capital) used in production with the least-cost rule. (If you remember how to solve utility-maximization problems from Chapter 5, it will come in handy.)

> **The least-cost rule** of multiple inputs states that to minimize costs, a firm will adjust the ratio of inputs until the marginal product of labor divided by the price is equal to the marginal product of capital divided by the price (L is labor and K is capital):
>
> $$\text{Least-Cost Rule} = \frac{MP_L}{P_L} = \frac{MP_K}{P_K}$$

As firms use more and more of one resource, for example, labor, the productivity of the input (labor) eventually declines due to diminishing marginal returns. If $MP_L/P_L > MP_K/P_K$, the firm will hire more labor and decrease its use of capital. Eventually the MP of labor will decline, the MP of capital will increase, and the ratios of marginal product per dollar will be equal. The same holds true with the diminishing returns of capital usage. To solve a least-cost rule problem, look at Table 10.2. If the firm has only $35, and a robot costs $10 and a factory worker costs $5, what is the optimal use of resources? Just like with consumers' utility maximization, make a chart of the MP/P for each, start by choosing the highest number, and continue until all money has been spent (in this case $35). The highest MP/P number is like getting the most "bang for your buck."

Table 10.2 Least-Cost Rule

Number of Robots/ Factory Workers	MP_K (Robots)	MP_K/P_K (Price K = $10)	MP_L (Factory Workers)	MP_L/P_L (Price L = $5)
1	30	③	20	④
2	20	②	15	③
3	10	1	10	②
4	5	0.50	5	1

In Table 10.2, hiring 2 robots and 3 factory workers is the optimal cost-minimizing point given the production constraint of $35. This is the point where $\frac{MP_L}{P_L} = \frac{MP_K}{P_K}$ or 2 = 2 in this example.

SUMMARY

- The marginal revenue product (MRP) of a resource represents the demand for labor, and marginal factor cost (MFC) of a resource represents the cost of labor.
- A firm maximizes its profits by hiring the number of units of employees at which MRP = MFC.
- The three shifters of the labor demand curve are changes in the demand for the product, changes in productivity, and changes in the prices of other resources.
- The least-cost rule is $\frac{MP_L}{P_L} = \frac{MP_K}{P_K}$.
- A monopsony is when there is a single buyer of labor, and graphically the MFC curve is higher than the supply curve. A monopsony hires labor at the quantity where MFC = MRP but pays a wage rate from the lower supply curve at the quantity hired.
- The demand for a resource is derived from the demand for a product to which the resource has contributed.
- A firm in the perfectly competitive labor (resource) market is a price taker in terms of the wage rate paid by the firm for its workers. The supply (of workers) curve is perfectly horizontal at the competitive market wage rate.

Formulas

Least-Cost Rule = $\frac{MP_L}{P_L} = \frac{MP_K}{P_K}$

Marginal Revenue Product = $\frac{\Delta \text{ in Total Revenue}}{\Delta \text{ in Resource Quantity}}$ or MP × P (in perfect competition) or MP × MR

Marginal Factor Cost = $\frac{\Delta \text{ in Total Resource Cost}}{\Delta \text{ in Resource Quantity}}$ = Wage

Optimal hiring point: MRP = MFC

Multiple-Choice Review Questions

Labor Units	Total Output	MP	Output Price*	TR	MFC**	MRP
1	5	5	10	50	60	
2	20	15	10	200	60	
3	30	10	10	300	60	
4	35	5	10	350	60	
5	35	0	10	350	60	

*Output price constant at $10 indicates a perfectly competitive product market.
**Labor price constant at $60 indicates a perfectly competitive labor market.

1. With the data in the table above, how many units of labor would the employer hire?

   (A) 1
   (B) 2
   (C) 3
   (D) 4
   (E) 5

2. If for two resources, labor (L) and capital (K), the ratios of their marginal physical products are

$$\frac{MP_L}{P_L} > \frac{MP_K}{P_K}$$

   the firm should:

   (A) increase capital (K) use and hire less labor until the ratios are equal.
   (B) hire more labor (L) and use less capital until the ratios are equal.
   (C) lower the price of capital (P_K).
   (D) lower the price of labor (P_L).
   (E) seek union membership for labor (L).

3. Which of the following will NOT cause a decrease in labor demand?

   (A) A decrease in the price of the product being produced
   (B) A decrease in the price of machinery of the good being produced
   (C) A decrease in the technical progress used in producing the good
   (D) A decrease in supply of the good
   (E) A decrease in the demand of the good

Use this chart for question 4.

Number of Workers	Bushels of Grapes
1	30
2	50
3	65
4	75
5	80
6	84

4. In perfectly competitive product and labor markets, if a bushel of grapes sells for $5 and each worker hired costs $25, how many workers should be hired?

   (A) 1
   (B) 2
   (C) 3
   (D) 4
   (E) 5

5. An increase in the demand for fidget spinners will likely cause which of the following?

   (A) A decrease in the wages of fidget spinner producers
   (B) An increase in the demand for the workers who produce fidget spinners
   (C) A decrease in the price of the capital used to produce fidget spinners
   (D) A decrease in the price of substitute goods for fidget spinners
   (E) All of the above

6. When compared to a perfectly competitive labor
    market, a monopsony will

    (A) pay more but hire fewer workers than a
         perfectly competitive market.
    (B) pay less but hire more workers than a
         perfectly competitive market.
    (C) pay more and hire more workers than a
         perfectly competitive market.
    (D) pay less and hire fewer workers than a
         perfectly competitive market.
    (E) pay the same and hire the same amount of
         workers as a perfectly competitive market.

7. Assume the marginal product of robots is 10,000
    and the price of a robot is $1,000, while the
    marginal product of labor is 81 and the price of
    labor is $9. What should the firm do?

    (A) Make no changes to the amount of capital
         and labor used
    (B) Decrease the amount of capital and decrease
         labor
    (C) Decrease the amount of capital and increase
         labor
    (D) Increase the amount of capital and increase
         labor
    (E) Increase the amount of capital and decrease
         labor

Use the figure below to answer question 8.

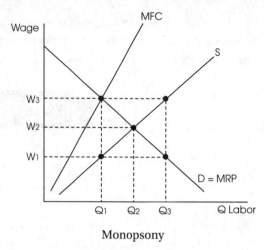

Monopsony

8. Based on the figure, what is the wage and quantity
    of labor hired for the monopsony?

	Wage	Quantity of Labor
(A)	W_1	Q_1
(B)	W_1	Q_3
(C)	W_2	Q_2
(D)	W_3	Q_1
(E)	W_3	Q_3

Free-Response Review Questions

1. The I. M. Green Company is a profit-maximizing firm that produces and sells avocados in perfectly competitive product and labor markets. Each avocado sells for $2, and the wage rate is $20 per day. See the short-run production table for avocados below.

Quantity of Labor	Number of Avocados per Day
1	20
2	50
3	75
4	90
5	100
6	105
7	108

   (a) What is the marginal revenue product of the 2nd worker?

   (b) After which worker hired do diminishing marginal returns begin?

   (c) What is the marginal product of the 4th worker?

   (d) How many workers will be hired at a wage of $20 a day?

   (e) If fixed costs are $30 and 5 labor units are hired, what is the economic profit or loss?

   (f) Now assume the wage rate increases to $30. How many workers will now be hired?

2. Abby's Apple Farm is a firm that operates in both perfectly competitive product and labor markets.

   (a) Using side-by-side graphs for the labor market and Abby's Apples, label the Farm Labor Market's equilibrium wage and quantity W_M and Q_M, and Abby's Apples equilibrium wage and quantity of labor hired W_F and Q_F.

   (b) Now assume that there is a significant increase in the number of farm laborers in the market willing to work. What will happen to the following?

      (i) Will the wage for workers in the Farm Labor Market increase, decrease, or remain the same?

      (ii) Will the quantity of labor hired at Abby's Apples increase, decrease, or remain the same? Explain.

   (c) Abby's Apples is minimizing its costs with the cost-minimizing input combination. Assume each apple-picking robot harvests 1,000 apples per hour and rents for $50 an hour, and each farm laborer costs $10 an hour. How many apples does each apple farm laborer harvest per hour? Show your work.

Answer Explanations

1. **(C)** The profit-maximizing amount of resources is where MRP = MFC. MRP = MP × P. A firm will hire workers if MRP > MFC. The MRP in the chart from 1 labor unit going down is 50, 150, 100, 50, 0. As the MFC is constant at 60, you would not hire the 4th labor unit as the cost is $60 while it brings in only $50 in revenue. 3 workers are the optimal amount as it is the last worker where MRP > MFC. Beyond 3, MRP < MFC.

2. **(B)** As the MP/P of labor is higher than the MP/P of capital, a firm should hire more labor and use less capital to minimize costs, until both sides equal out. (When the MP/P of one side is greater than the other, a firm gets more production there for the price paid and should employ more of it.)

3. **(D)** Labor demand is the MRP. All answers would decrease MRP except a decrease in supply of the good, which would increase the price. MRP = MP × P, and if P increases, MRP increases.

4. **(E)** The profit-maximizing amount of resources is where MRP = MFC. MFC is constant at $25, and MRP = MP × P. MRP > MFC until the 5th worker, where MRP = MRC. The 6th worker's MRP is $20 and costs $25 (MFC), so the 6th worker will not be hired.

5. **(B)** This is an example of derived demand. The demand for workers to produce fidget spinners is "derived" from the product market, where consumers purchase them.

6. **(D)** Similar to how a monopoly in the product market produces less and charges more than a competitive market, a monopsonist in the labor market pays workers less and hires less labor compared to firms in a competitive market.

7. **(E)** The optimal combination of resources is where MP/P of labor = MP/P of capital. For labor it is currently 81/$9 and 10,000/$1,000 for capital, or 9 labor < 10 capital. The firm therefore is getting more "bang for their buck" by using capital as 10 > 9. The firm should use more capital and employ less labor to minimize their costs; eventually, diminishing returns will set in and both sides will equal out.

8. **(A)** The profit-maximizing amount of labor hired is where MRP = MFC, so the quantity is Q_1. However, the wage paid comes from the supply curve, which is W_1. Note that if this were a competitive labor market, the quantity hired would be Q_2 and the wage would be W_2.

Free-Response Review Answers

1. (a) $60. 30 × $2 = $60.

   (b) 2nd worker

   (c) 15. 90 − 75 = 15.

   (d) 5 workers. MRP ($20) = MFC ($20).

   (e) $70. Total revenue is 100 × $2 = $200. Total cost is $130. $200 − $130 = $70.

   (f) 4 workers. MRP ($30) = MFC ($30).

2. (a)

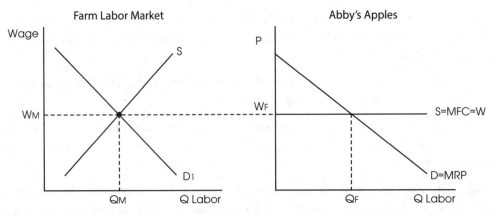

Perfectly Competitive and Abby's Apples Farm Labor Markets

   (b) (i) Decrease

      (ii) Increase. As Abby's Apples is a "wage taker," its workers take the wage set in the Farm Labor Market. This wage decreased, and since the MRP curve for labor is downsloping and the horizontal MFC curve shifts downward, the quantity of labor demanded increases.

   (c) 200. Using the cost-minimizing input combination formula:

$$\text{Least-cost rule} = \frac{MP_L}{P_L} = \frac{MP_K}{P_K}$$

$$x/\$10 = 1,000/\$50, \text{ thus } 200/\$10 = 1,000/\$50$$

11

Government and Public Sector: Market Failure, Externalities, Public Goods, Efficiency

Learning Objectives

In this chapter, you will learn:

- → Positive and negative externalities
- → Public goods and private goods
- → Market failure
- → Income distribution
- → Types of taxes

Introduction

In previous chapters, we have discussed the benefits of markets in that they can lead to the efficient allocation of resources. However, there are situations where free markets fail to satisfy society's wants by producing too much or too little of something. These situations are known as **market failures**. A market failure is when a market fails to provide an efficient allocation of resources, and there can be a role for government to intervene and attempt to promote a more desirable social outcome.

Market Failure and Externalities

One argument for government involvement in a market is to increase efficiency by correcting market failures, leading to production at the socially efficient quantity where **marginal social benefit (MSB)** = **marginal social cost (MSC)**. With a market failure, private markets fail to produce at the efficient outcome where at MSB = MSC; this distortion results in **externalities**, the costs or benefits that affect a third party or people not involved in the production or consumption of a good.

Marginal Social Benefit (MSB) = Marginal Social Cost (MSC)

What is the optimal amount of production when all the costs and benefits are taken into consideration? It's MSB = MSC. In my classroom, I ask students what they are willing to sacrifice to help the environment. I start by asking who recycles. Almost everyone raises their hand (at this point the marginal social benefit of recycling is much greater than the marginal social cost). I then ask: Who is willing to forgo a shower 3 times a week to save water? Who will give up their car? As the questions progress in the amount of personal sacrifice required to help the environment, the number of hands up gradually falls. By the end, rightly or wrongly, most students feel that the social cost of these huge sacrifices begins to outweigh their perceived benefits. At some point, students feel the cost (MSC) of living with some pollution outweighs the benefit (MSB) of sacrificing many modern conveniences.

For another example, consider the benefits to a midsize city building new playgrounds, illustrated in Figure 11.1. We all know that good parks make for good city living, but how many new playgrounds should be built? If the city builds the amount of playgrounds at Q_1, heading straight up the graph from that point you can see MSB > MSC, indicating society wants more built. No one wants a playground on every corner (well, almost no one), so if the quantity at Q_3 is produced, MSC > MSB and society wants fewer built. The optimal amount of playgrounds is at Q_2, P_2, the sweet spot where MSB = MSC.

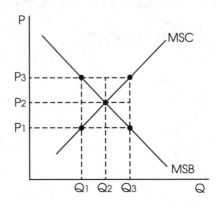

Figure 11.1

Externalities

Externalities can arise due to both producer and consumer activity. When consumer actions result in external or spillover costs being imposed on third parties, it is a consumption externality. Cigarette consumption causing secondhand smoke (a negative externality) or immunity from the consumption of a vaccine (a positive externality) are examples of consumption externalities. When producer actions result in external or spillover costs being imposed on third parties, it is a production externality. A firm dumping hazardous chemicals into a local river (a negative externality) or the government subsidizing higher-education institutions (a positive externality) are examples of production externalities.

Positive Externalities

Even though a college student surely benefits from the knowledge they acquired, the market for higher education does not realize all the benefits for society. A better-educated population also results in lower crime rates, a more productive economy, and increased tax revenues; these spillover benefits to third parties not directly involved in the transaction make education a positive externality. If a market with **positive externalities** like education is left alone, it will have a marginal social benefit (MSB) greater than the marginal social cost (MSC) at the market quantity. To remedy the issue, the government can provide a **per-unit subsidy** to either consumers or producers equal to the **marginal external benefit (MEB)**. A per-unit subsidy is a government payment for production or consumption of each unit. It induces greater output of the desired good and is more effective in reaching social efficiency than a **lump-sum subsidy** not based on production quantity. For example, the government subsidizes items that provide positive externalities such as solar panels, electric cars, the arts, and education.

TIP

Students on past AP exams have had trouble locating the deadweight loss at the market equilibrium on externality graphs. A helpful tip is to imagine an arrow pointing the optimal output where "the socials meet," MSB = MSC, originating between the two curves.

Positive Externality in Production

In Figure 11.2, there is a deadweight loss at the market quantity where supply and demand meet (Q_{MKT}). The good is underproduced as marginal social benefit (MSB) > marginal social cost (MSC). A per-unit subsidy for producers the size of the marginal external benefit (MEB) can remedy this, increasing production to the socially optimal quantity (Q_s) where marginal social benefit (MSB) = marginal social cost (MSC).

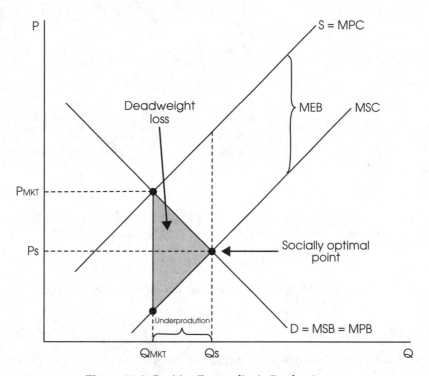

Figure 11.2 Positive Externality in Production

Positive Externality in Consumption

In Figure 11.3, there is a deadweight loss at the market quantity where supply and demand meet (Q_{MKT}). The good is underproduced as marginal social benefit (MSB) > marginal social cost (MSC). A per-unit subsidy for consumers the size of the marginal external benefit (MEB) can remedy this, increasing demand and thus output to the socially optimal quantity (Q_s) where marginal social benefit (MSB) = marginal social cost (MSC) at Q_s and P_s.

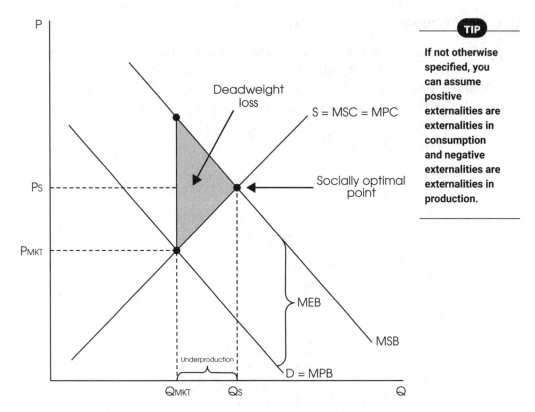

Figure 11.3 Positive Externality in Consumption

Negative Externalities

Similar to how government can promote positive externalities, the government can attempt to prevent **negative externalities** and remedy the related market failure by taxing goods that impose spillover costs on third parties. Some examples of negative externalities include secondhand smoke, airplane noise, and pollution. With a negative externality, the market is producing more of a good than is socially desirable. These externalities spill over to individuals who are neither consumers nor producers of a product. For example, consider a firm that is polluting the environment. Without government intervention, the market is producing at a cost that is greater to society than the polluting firm. If left alone, it will have a marginal social cost (MSC) greater than the marginal social benefit (MSB) at the market quantity. To remedy the issue, the government can impose a **per-unit tax** to either consumers or producers equal to the **marginal external cost (MEC)**. A per-unit tax increases the cost of production or consumption of each unit and induces a reduced output. It also gives a greater incentive for social efficiency than a **lump-sum tax** not based on production quantity. For example, the government taxes items that result in negative externalities such as gasoline and cigarettes.

Negative Externality in Production

In Figure 11.4 at the market quantity (Q_{MKT}), there is a deadweight loss as the good is overproduced. A per-unit tax on producers by the size of the marginal external cost (MEC) can remedy this, decreasing production (supply) to the socially optimal amount (Q_s) where marginal social benefit (MSB) = marginal social cost (MSC).

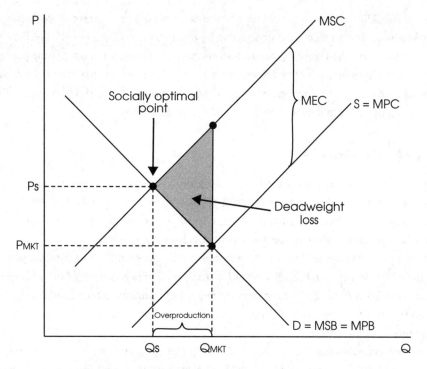

Figure 11.4 Negative Externality in Production

Negative Externality in Consumption

In Figure 11.5 at the market quantity where supply and demand meet (Q_{MKT}) there is a dead-weight loss as the good is overproduced. A per-unit tax on consumers the size of the marginal external cost (MEC) can remedy this, reducing demand and thus output to the socially opti-mal amount (Q_s) where marginal social benefit (MSB) = marginal social cost (MSC).

TIP

For help labeling the deadweight loss at the market equilibrium, imagine an arrow pointing to the optimal output where MSB = MSC, originating between the two supply curves.

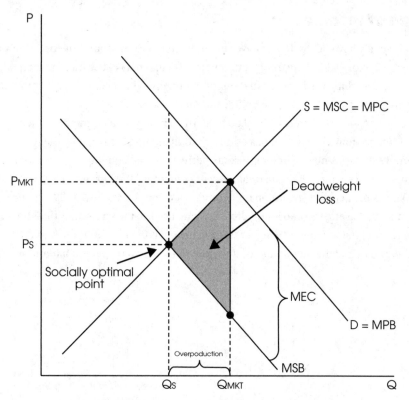

Figure 11.5 Negative Externality in Consumption

Per-unit taxes or subsidies are not the only idea economists have to solve externalities, however. Economist Ronald Coase proclaimed that an efficient outcome can be reached without the aid of government. And you guessed it—his idea is named the **Coase theorem**. According to the Coase theorem, private parties can solve the issues created by externalities on their own. For example, a polluting firm may pay the affected parties to compensate for the harm of pollution. Or homes next to a new airport may receive soundproof windows from an airline company, all resolving the externalities without government intervention.

Public vs. Private Goods

A **private good** both has exclusion and is a rival in consumption. For example, a person may be excluded from the benefits of private goods by not being willing or able to pay the price; if I bought the last seat to a sold-out major league baseball playoff game, someone else is denied the fun of watching the game in person. Also, if there are 40,000 seats available, one more ticket for me means one less for someone else.

Public goods are nonexclusive and nonrival, as one person's consumption of a public good does not exclude others from benefiting from it, unlike a sold-out baseball game. Examples of public goods are national defense, clean air, or a lighthouse. If a person pays no federal income tax, which funds the military, that person would not be denied any of the benefits of national defense. Everyone benefits from the public good of national defense whether they have paid or not.

As public goods are nonexclusive, they do pose a dilemma known as the **free-rider problem**. This means that people know they can benefit from public goods without paying for them. If all consumers are free riders, demand drops to zero for the product. For example, if a private company in your city wishes to put on a big fireworks show, they would have a hard time finding people willing to pay to watch. People who live nearby know they can see and benefit from the fireworks without paying and be "free riders." Due to the free-rider problem, private firms will not supply public goods (or fireworks shows), and if society wants a public good to be produced, it will have to direct government to do it. When this occurs, governments collect taxes for public goods and provide things, such as national defense and even your city's taxpayer-funded fireworks show.

The Distribution of Income

If you follow the news, you likely have heard debates over income inequality, or about the top 1% of income earners versus the bottom 99%. Economists debate many different factors that may cause income inequality; several frequently mentioned reasons include the increase in demand for highly skilled labor, global competition, past discrimination, education levels, and differences in ability and motivation.

At this stage of the book, you are probably not shocked to learn economics has a graph for income inequality, called the **Lorenz curve**, which shows how much of a country's total income is earned by the number of households. As shown in Figure 11.6, the 45-degree line represents perfect income equality, also shown at point B. At point B, 50% of families are receiving 50% of the total percent of income. The Lorenz curve part of the graph (shaped like a banana) shows the actual distribution of income. For example, at point A, 50% of the population has only 25% of the income, displaying income inequality. You can also infer from point A that the remaining 50% of the population earns 75% of total income. The bigger the gap between the Lorenz curve and the perfect equality line, the bigger the amount of income inequality (or the more the Lorenz curve has a banana shape, the more inequality).

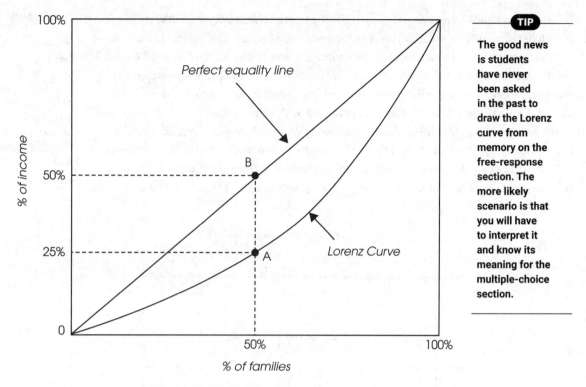

Figure 11.6 The Lorenz Curve

In comparing Figure 11.6 to Figure 11.7, you can see the greater amount of separation between the Lorenz curve and the perfect equality line (or a bigger banana curve). If fact, at point A in Figure 11.7, 50% of the population earns only 10% of the income, and the remaining 50% earns 90% of total income.

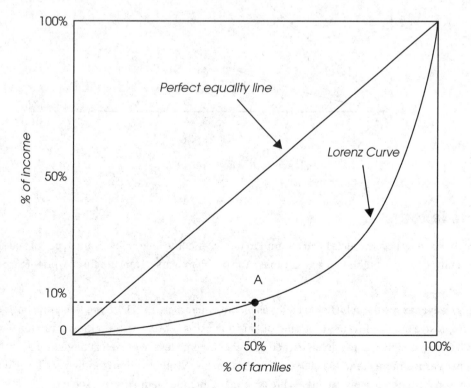

Figure 11.7 The Lorenz Curve

Another related calculation of inequality is the **Gini coefficient**. The coefficient ranges from 0 to 1; a value of 1 would represent all income going to one family, whereas a value of 0 would represent all families receiving the same amount of income. In Figure 11.8, a Gini coefficient of 0 would indicate the perfect equality line. The Gini coefficient is useful as it makes it simple to compare inequality rates among countries or geographical areas. For example, with the latest data available at publication, the United States has a higher Gini coefficient (or more income inequality) than many western European countries such as France but a lower Gini coefficient than some South American countries such as Brazil.

You can also use the Lorenz curve to calculate the Gini coefficient. To do so, take the area between the Lorenz curve and the line of perfect equality, area A in Figure 11.8, and divide it by the total area of A and B.

> **TIP**
>
> A Gini coefficient closer to 0 would mean there is less income inequality, whereas a number closer to 1 would mean more inequality.

$$\text{Gini Coefficient} = \frac{A}{A + B}$$

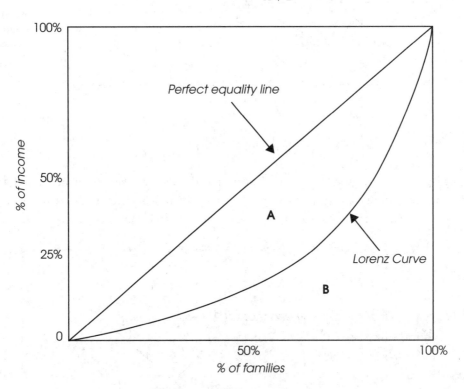

Figure 11.8 The Lorenz Curve

Types of Taxes

Taxation can be used by governments in an attempt to reduce income inequality. Some types of taxes may help reduce inequality; however, others can actually make the problem worse. Here are three types of taxes with examples:

- A **progressive tax** results in higher tax rates as income increases. The U.S. federal income tax is an example of a progressive tax. The first few thousand dollars one earns is taxed at lower rates (even for very rich people like Bill Gates) and then every dollar earned at higher income levels is taxed at higher rates. By the time Bill Gates has earned more than $400,000 or so (at the time of this publication) for the year, he is in the highest tax bracket. A progressive tax can lessen the amount of income inequality in a society.

- A **proportional tax** imposes the same tax rates on everyone regardless of income. Whether a person makes $100 or $100,000 a year, each person pays the same percentage of total income in taxes.
- A **regressive tax** is where the average tax burden decreases as percent of income rises. The sales tax on consumption is a good example of a regressive tax. High-income earners are more likely to save some of their income, whereas low-income earners likely spend all or a greater percentage of their income earned. So as a percent of total income, a sales tax tends to be a greater burden on low-income earners, making it a regressive tax.

SUMMARY

- Externalities become the basis for government taxes or subsidies. Any government action stems from the costs or benefits occurring to others than the market buyers and sellers.
- Appropriate government action would be to place a per-unit tax on a polluter for the value of the *negative externality*. The outcome would be an efficient level of output at which marginal social benefits (MSB) = marginal social costs (MSC).
- The government should place a per-unit subsidy on production of a product that creates a positive externality, until the optimal output level where MSB = MSC.
- The government should place a per-unit tax on production of a product that creates a negative externality, until the optimal output level where MSB = MSC.
- The Lorenz curve shows how much of a country's total income is earned by the number of households.
- The Gini coefficient or ratio measures income inequality. A ratio closer to 1 shows more income inequality, whereas a number closer to 0 shows more income equality.
- Due to the free-rider problem, public goods are provided by governments.

Formulas

$MSB = MSC$ the allocatively efficient quantity, considering externalities:

If $MSB > MSC$, it's a positive externality.

If $MSC > MSB$, it's a negative externality.

$MPB + MEB = MSB$

$MPC + MEC = MSC$

Multiple-Choice Review Questions

1. Which of the following is true about a public good?

   (A) One person's consumption means others get less.
   (B) Consumers can be excluded from its benefits by not paying for it.
   (C) One more unit of a public good for some consumers means one less unit for other consumers.
   (D) One person's consumption does not exclude others from consuming it.
   (E) Everyone pays the same amount for the good.

2. If there is a negative externality associated with a firm's production of a private good, which of the following is an action by government that would most likely move the market to an efficient outcome?

   (A) Shut down the firm
   (B) Give the firm a per-unit subsidy
   (C) Place a per-unit tax on the firm
   (D) Relocate the firm
   (E) None of the above

3. If there is a positive externality associated with the production of a private good, which of the following is an action of government that would most likely move the market to an efficient outcome?

   (A) Shut down the firm
   (B) Give the firm a per-unit subsidy
   (C) Place a per-unit tax on the firm
   (D) Relocate the firm
   (E) None of the above

4. For a polluting steel company, a government action to achieve an efficient outcome would produce what effect on the market equilibrium price and output?

   (A) Output would increase; price would not change.
   (B) Output would increase; price would decrease.
   (C) Output would increase; price would increase.
   (D) Output would decrease; price would decrease.
   (E) Output would decrease; price would increase.

5. All of the following are true regarding externalities except:

   (A) marginal social cost = marginal private cost + marginal external cost.
   (B) marginal social benefit = marginal private benefit + marginal external benefit.
   (C) a per-unit subsidy is a solution to a positive externality.
   (D) if MSB > MSC, it is referring to a positive externality.
   (E) the socially efficient production quantity is where MPB = MPC.

6. If there are positive externalities present when a good is produced, which of the following is true?

   (A) The marginal social benefit is greater than the marginal social cost, and the problem can be corrected with a per-unit subsidy.
   (B) The marginal social benefit is greater than the marginal social cost, and the problem can be corrected with a lump-sum subsidy.
   (C) Consumers should be taxed so they will buy less of the good.
   (D) The marginal private benefit is greater than the marginal social benefit, and the problem can be corrected with a per-unit tax.
   (E) The marginal social benefit is less than the marginal social cost, and the problem can be corrected with a lump-sum tax.

7. One reason public goods are underproduced is because they cause free riders. What problem do free riders cause?

   (A) Binding price ceilings
   (B) Income inequality
   (C) Positive externalities
   (D) Smaller market demand
   (E) Increased market demand

8. Which of the following is an example of a positive externality?

   (A) Paying to watch a basketball game
   (B) Paying to download a new game
   (C) Enjoying you neighbor's flower garden
   (D) Enjoying loud music while disturbing your neighbors
   (E) Hearing loud construction noise next door

9. Which of the following government policies will likely shift the Lorenz curve outward?

   (A) Decreasing the sales tax
   (B) Making the tax system regressive
   (C) Making the tax system progressive
   (D) Making the tax system proportional
   (E) Imposing a per-unit tax on gasoline

Free-Response Review Question

1. Assume Firm A has been polluting rivers and lakes near its factory while producing steel, causing a negative externality in production. Draw a correctly labeled market for Firm A showing each of the following:

   (a) The private market equilibrium price and quantity, labeled P_M and Q_M

   (b) The socially optimal quantity and price of production, labeled P_S and Q_S

   (c) The deadweight loss at the market equilibrium

   (d) Explain what government action could result in a socially optimal outcome.

Answer Explanations

1. **(D)** A public good is nonexcludable and nonrival. If a public good is provided to some, it is provided to all. An example is national defense.

2. **(C)** The solution to a negative externality is a per-unit tax equal to the size of the marginal external cost to society. This increases the marginal cost of producing additional units of a good, reducing quantity.

3. **(B)** The solution to a positive externality is a per-unit subsidy equal to the size of the marginal external benefit to society. This lowers the marginal cost of producing additional units of a good, increasing the quantity produced.

4. **(E)** This company is producing a good with a negative externality, and the efficient outcome for society is to decrease the quantity produced and increase the price.

5. **(E)** The socially efficient production quantity is where marginal social benefit (MSB) = marginal social cost (MSC).

6. **(A)** With a positive externality, society desires more of a good than is produced by the free market, which is why MSB > MSC. A per-unit subsidy can solve the externality.

7. **(D)** Free riders or the free-rider problem arises when people realize they can consume a public good without paying. This problem and the nonexcludability of public goods necessitates that the government provide them.

8. **(C)** When one person's use of a good affords benefits to a third party not directly involved in the transaction, this is a positive externality—for example, enjoying the fresh smell of your neighbor's flowers.

9. **(B)** A regressive tax means people with lower incomes pay a greater percent of their income in taxes than those with higher incomes. This would shift the Lorenz curve outward, as this displays greater income inequality.

Free-Response Review Answer

1. (a), (b), (c)

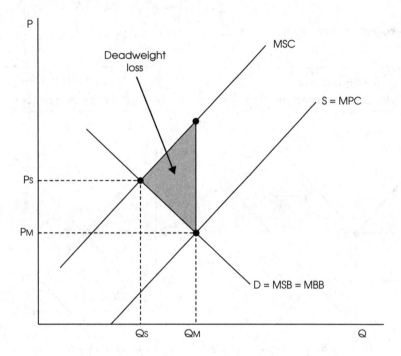

(d) The government could place a per-unit tax on the production of steel, equal to the marginal external cost (the difference between the MPC and MSC curves).

Key Microeconomics Graphs

The following are graphs that students may be asked to graph based on past exams.

Supply and Demand

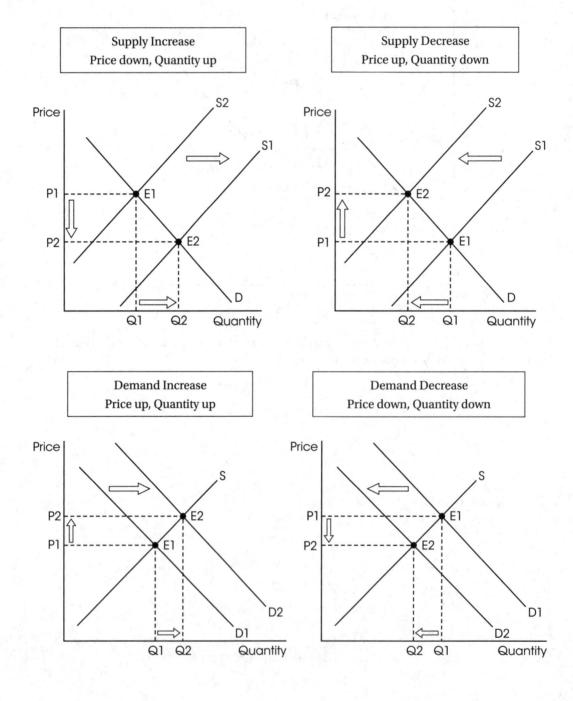

Consumer and Producer Surpluses

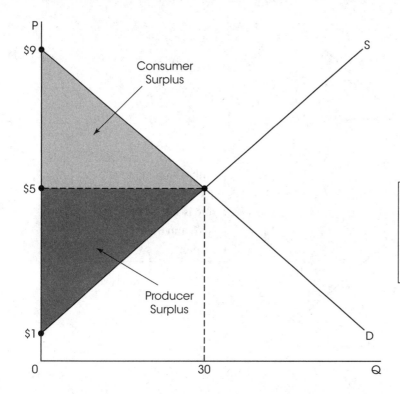

Calculate the area of consumer or producer surplus triangle by using this formula: ½ (Base × Height).

Price Ceiling

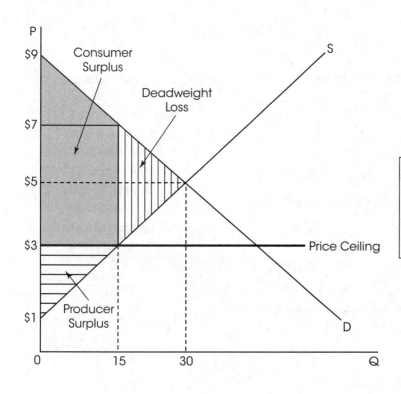

With a binding price ceiling, the quantity sold is 15 and the price is $3, and there is a shortage.

Price Floor

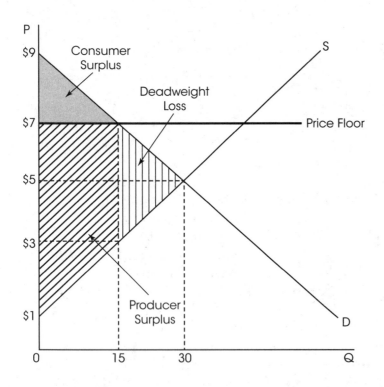

With a binding price floor, here the quantity sold is 15 and the price is $7, and there is a surplus.

Supply and Demand with Tax

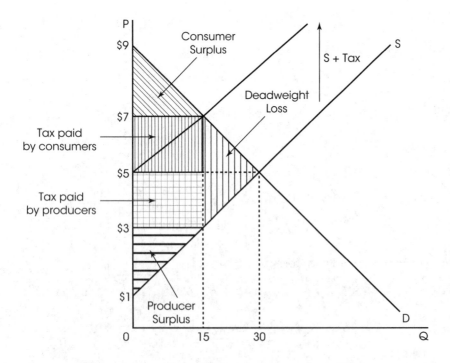

The vertical distance between the curves S and S + Tax is the size of the tax. After the tax the new price is $7 and the quantity is 15. While consumers pay $7, producers receive $3 after the tax is paid.

Tax with Burden Falling More on Consumers

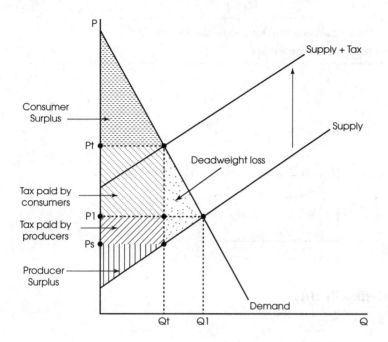

As the demand curve is more inelastic than the supply curve, consumers pay more of the tax.

Tax with Burden Falling More on Producers

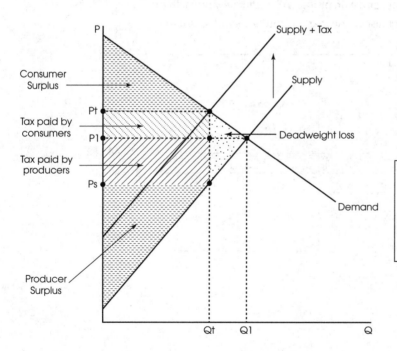

As the supply curve is more inelastic than the demand curve, producers pay more of the tax.

Perfect Competition in Long-Run Equilibrium

The firm is earning zero economic profit and is in long-run equilibrium. The firm takes the price in the market and is a price taker.

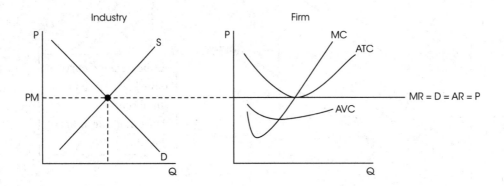

Perfect Competition Earning Short-Run Profits

The firm is earning economic profits in short-run equilibrium as a result of an increase in demand in the industry. As perfectly competitive markets have low barriers to entry and exit, profits will attract new firms, in the long run supply will increase in the market, and firms will return to zero economic profit.

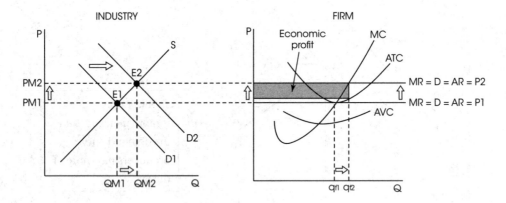

Perfect Competition Incurring Short-Run Losses

The firm is incurring economic losses in the short run as a result of a supply increase in the industry decreases the price received by firms. As perfectly competitive markets have low barriers to entry and exit, in the long run losses will force some firms to leave the industry and the remaining firms will return to zero economic profit.

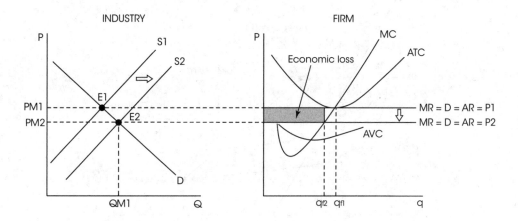

Monopoly in Long-Run Equilibrium

Monopolies earn economic profits in long-run equilibrium. At the profit-maximizing $MR = MC$ quantity (Q_M), price (P_M) comes from the demand curve.

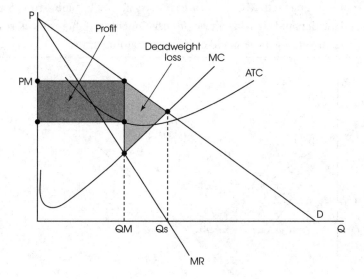

Natural Monopoly

> A natural monopoly's regulated pricing could be at the fair-return price
> (P = ATC) or the socially optimal price (P = MC). An unregulated monopoly
> produces where MR = MC, and price comes from the demand curve. The
> average total cost of a natural monopoly decreases as output increases.

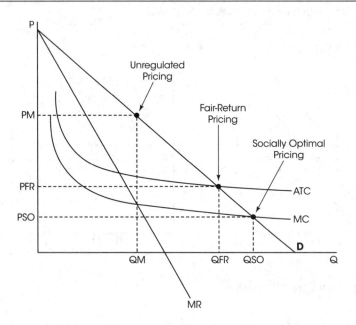

Monopolistic Competition in Long-Run Equilibrium

> Monopolistically competitive firms earn zero economic profit in long-run equilibrium, and
> the demand curve is tangent to ATC. There is easy entry and exit; if short-run profits exist,
> firms enter, and the demand curve decreases for existing firms. If there are short-run losses,
> some firms leave, increasing the demand curve for remaining firms.

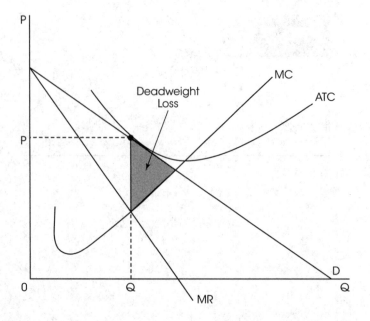

Perfectly Competitive Labor Market

A firm that hires workers in a perfectly competitive labor market has to hire at the wage set in the labor market and are wage takers. The profit-maximizing quantity of an input hired is where marginal revenue product (MPR) = marginal factor (resource) product (MFC).

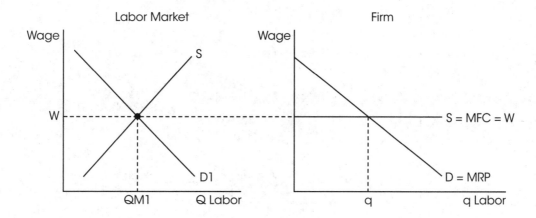

Positive Externality in Production

At the market quantity where supply and demand meet (Q_{MKT}), there is a deadweight loss as the good is underproduced. A per-unit subsidy the size of the marginal external benefit (MEB) can remedy this, increasing production to the socially optimal amount (Q_S) where marginal social benefit (MSB) = marginal social cost (MSC).

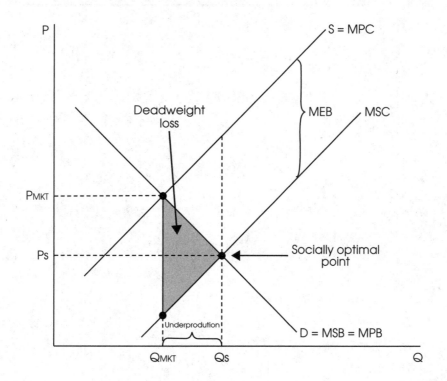

Positive Externality in Consumption

At the market quantity where supply and demand meet (Q_{MKT}) there is a deadweight loss as the good is underproduced. A per-unit subsidy to consumers the size of the marginal external benefit (MEB) can remedy this, increasing demand and thus output to the socially optimal amount (Q_S) where marginal social benefit (MSB) = marginal social cost (MSC).

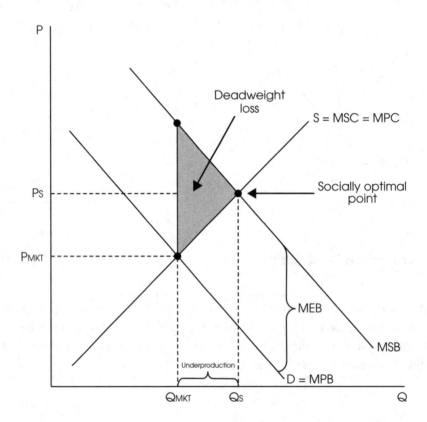

Negative Externality in Production

At the market quantity (Q_{MKT}), there is a deadweight loss as the good is overproduced. A per-unit tax on producers by the size of the marginal external cost (MEC) can remedy this, decreasing production to the socially optimal amount (Q_S) where marginal social benefit (MSB) = marginal social cost (MSC).

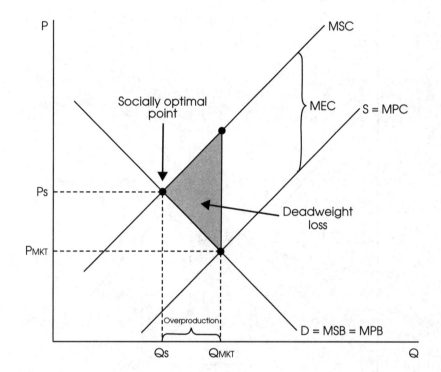

Negative Externality in Consumption

> At the market quantity where supply and demand meet (Q_{MKT}), there is a deadweight loss as the good is overproduced. A per-unit tax the size of the marginal external cost (MEC) on consumers can remedy this, reducing demand and thus output to the socially optimal amount (Q_S) where marginal social benefit (MSB) = marginal social cost (MSC).

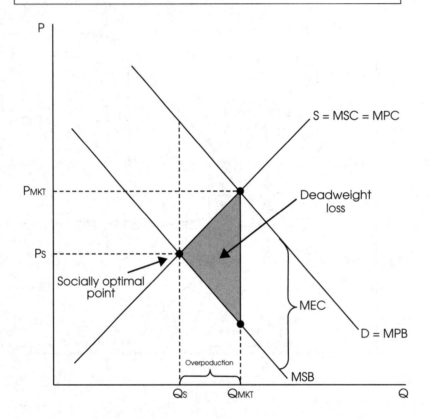

ANSWER SHEET
Microeconomics

Multiple-Choice Questions

1. Ⓐ Ⓑ Ⓒ Ⓓ
2. Ⓐ Ⓑ Ⓒ Ⓓ
3. Ⓐ Ⓑ Ⓒ Ⓓ
4. Ⓐ Ⓑ Ⓒ Ⓓ
5. Ⓐ Ⓑ Ⓒ Ⓓ
6. Ⓐ Ⓑ Ⓒ Ⓓ
7. Ⓐ Ⓑ Ⓒ Ⓓ
8. Ⓐ Ⓑ Ⓒ Ⓓ
9. Ⓐ Ⓑ Ⓒ Ⓓ
10. Ⓐ Ⓑ Ⓒ Ⓓ
11. Ⓐ Ⓑ Ⓒ Ⓓ
12. Ⓐ Ⓑ Ⓒ Ⓓ
13. Ⓐ Ⓑ Ⓒ Ⓓ
14. Ⓐ Ⓑ Ⓒ Ⓓ
15. Ⓐ Ⓑ Ⓒ Ⓓ

16. Ⓐ Ⓑ Ⓒ Ⓓ
17. Ⓐ Ⓑ Ⓒ Ⓓ
18. Ⓐ Ⓑ Ⓒ Ⓓ
19. Ⓐ Ⓑ Ⓒ Ⓓ
20. Ⓐ Ⓑ Ⓒ Ⓓ
21. Ⓐ Ⓑ Ⓒ Ⓓ
22. Ⓐ Ⓑ Ⓒ Ⓓ
23. Ⓐ Ⓑ Ⓒ Ⓓ
24. Ⓐ Ⓑ Ⓒ Ⓓ
25. Ⓐ Ⓑ Ⓒ Ⓓ
26. Ⓐ Ⓑ Ⓒ Ⓓ
27. Ⓐ Ⓑ Ⓒ Ⓓ
28. Ⓐ Ⓑ Ⓒ Ⓓ
29. Ⓐ Ⓑ Ⓒ Ⓓ
30. Ⓐ Ⓑ Ⓒ Ⓓ

31. Ⓐ Ⓑ Ⓒ Ⓓ
32. Ⓐ Ⓑ Ⓒ Ⓓ
33. Ⓐ Ⓑ Ⓒ Ⓓ
34. Ⓐ Ⓑ Ⓒ Ⓓ
35. Ⓐ Ⓑ Ⓒ Ⓓ
36. Ⓐ Ⓑ Ⓒ Ⓓ
37. Ⓐ Ⓑ Ⓒ Ⓓ
38. Ⓐ Ⓑ Ⓒ Ⓓ
39. Ⓐ Ⓑ Ⓒ Ⓓ
40. Ⓐ Ⓑ Ⓒ Ⓓ
41. Ⓐ Ⓑ Ⓒ Ⓓ
42. Ⓐ Ⓑ Ⓒ Ⓓ
43. Ⓐ Ⓑ Ⓒ Ⓓ
44. Ⓐ Ⓑ Ⓒ Ⓓ
45. Ⓐ Ⓑ Ⓒ Ⓓ

46. Ⓐ Ⓑ Ⓒ Ⓓ
47. Ⓐ Ⓑ Ⓒ Ⓓ
48. Ⓐ Ⓑ Ⓒ Ⓓ
49. Ⓐ Ⓑ Ⓒ Ⓓ
50. Ⓐ Ⓑ Ⓒ Ⓓ
51. Ⓐ Ⓑ Ⓒ Ⓓ
52. Ⓐ Ⓑ Ⓒ Ⓓ
53. Ⓐ Ⓑ Ⓒ Ⓓ
54. Ⓐ Ⓑ Ⓒ Ⓓ
55. Ⓐ Ⓑ Ⓒ Ⓓ
56. Ⓐ Ⓑ Ⓒ Ⓓ
57. Ⓐ Ⓑ Ⓒ Ⓓ
58. Ⓐ Ⓑ Ⓒ Ⓓ
59. Ⓐ Ⓑ Ⓒ Ⓓ
60. Ⓐ Ⓑ Ⓒ Ⓓ

Microeconomics Practice Test

Two hours are allotted for this exam: 1 hour and 10 minutes for Section I, which consists of multiple-choice questions; and 50 minutes for Section II, which consists of three mandatory essay questions.

Section I—Multiple-Choice Questions

TIME—1 HOUR AND 10 MINUTES
NUMBER OF QUESTIONS—60
PERCENT OF TOTAL GRADE—66$^{2}/_{3}$

DIRECTIONS: Each of the questions below are followed by five suggested answers or completions. Select the one that is best in each case and then fill in the corresponding circle on the answer sheet.

1. Which of the following is NOT a characteristic of perfectly competitive industry?

    (A) Free entry into the industry
    (B) Product differentiation
    (C) Perfectly elastic demand curve for firms
    (D) Homogeneous products
    (E) Many sellers and many buyers

2. Which of the following is a characteristic of monopolistic competition in the long run?

    (A) Strong barriers to entry
    (B) Homogeneous products
    (C) Zero economic profits
    (D) Minimum average total cost equals price
    (E) Allocative efficiency

3. Which of the following is (are) characteristic of an oligopoly?

    I. Formidable barriers to entry
    II. Mutual interdependence
    III. Relatively few sellers

    (A) I only
    (B) II only
    (C) III only
    (D) I and III only
    (E) I, II, and III

4. Which of the following is a characteristic of a monopoly?

    (A) A price that is always in the elastic range of the demand curve
    (B) Price equal to marginal revenue
    (C) Perfectly elastic demand curve
    (D) Low barriers to entry
    (E) Zero economic profits

5. Compared to perfect competition in long-run equilibrium, a monopoly has

    (A) more choices of products for consumers.
    (B) allocative efficiency.
    (C) lower prices.
    (D) a price less than marginal cost.
    (E) a price greater than marginal cost.

6. With the presence of a negative externality, which of the following would correct the externality?

    (A) A per-unit subsidy
    (B) A per-unit tax
    (C) A lower price
    (D) A higher level of output
    (E) A government-created task force

7. With the presence of a positive externality, which of the following would correct the externality?

(A) A per-unit subsidy
(B) A per-unit tax
(C) A higher price
(D) A lower level of output
(E) A government-created task force

8. Which of the following is true regarding externalities?

(A) Marginal social cost = marginal private cost + marginal social benefit.
(B) Marginal social benefit = marginal private benefit – marginal social cost.
(C) Marginal social cost = marginal private cost + marginal external benefit.
(D) Marginal social cost = marginal private cost + marginal external cost.
(E) Quantity of externality = marginal private costs.

9. Which of the following is true?

(A) Average total cost = total fixed costs divided by the number of units produced.
(B) Average total cost = average variable costs divided by the total number of units produced.
(C) Average total cost = average variable cost plus marginal cost.
(D) Average total cost = average variable cost plus average fixed cost.
(E) All of the above.

10. Which of the following is true about the relationship of the average total cost (ATC) curve and the marginal cost (MC) curve?

(A) ATC and MC are always equal.
(B) ATC and MC are never equal.
(C) The ATC curve intersects the MC curve at the minimum point of the MC curve.
(D) The MC curve intersects the ATC curve at the minimum point of the ATC curve.
(E) The MC curve intersects the ATC curve at the maximum point of the ATC curve.

Question 11 is based on the figure below.

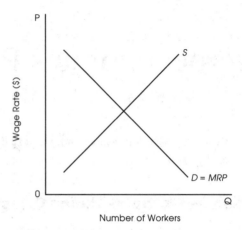

11. Which of the following will happen when a new computerized system for a firm increases the marginal productivity of its workers?

(A) The marginal revenue product curve will shift to the left, which will cause the wage rate to decrease.
(B) The supply curve will shift to the right, causing the wage rate to decrease.
(C) The marginal revenue product curve will shift to the right, causing the wage rate to increase.
(D) The supply curve will shift to the left, causing the wage rate to increase.
(E) The marginal revenue product curve will shift to the right and the supply curve will shift to the left, leaving the wage rate unchanged.

12. Which of the following is true about an effective price floor?

(A) It is used to correct government policy.
(B) It is used when the equilibrium price is too high.
(C) It will be located above the equilibrium price.
(D) It will be located below the equilibrium price.
(E) It is when the stock market has closed at a new low.

13. Which of the following is true about an effective price ceiling?

   (A) It is used to correct government policy.
   (B) It is used when equilibrium prices are too low.
   (C) It will be located above the equilibrium price.
   (D) It will be located below the equilibrium price.
   (E) It is when the stock market has closed at a new high.

14. Which of the following situations best exemplifies the concept of consumer surplus?

   (A) It refers to a consumer who no longer has any outstanding debts.
   (B) The federal government has taken in more revenue than it has paid out in expenditures.
   (C) A consumer does not buy a pizza as it costs more than the highest price she is willing to pay.
   (D) A consumer pays less for a pizza than the highest price she is willing to pay.
   (E) A consumer buys a pizza for the exact highest price she is willing to pay.

Number of Workers	Widgets Produced per Two Weeks
1	40
2	70
3	95
4	115
5	130
6	130

15. Given the data in the table above and knowing that workers are paid $1,250 every two weeks and that widgets are sold to retailers at $50, how many workers would be hired?

   (A) Two
   (B) Three
   (C) Four
   (D) Five
   (E) Six

Questions 16–19 are based on the monopoly graph below.

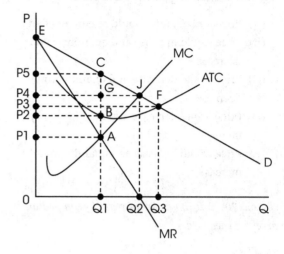

16. An unregulated, profit-maximizing monopoly will produce at which quantity and price?

   (A) Q_1, P_5
   (B) Q_1, P_2
   (C) Q_1, P_1
   (D) Q_2, P_4
   (E) Q_3, P_3

17. If this monopoly were regulated as a natural monopoly and ordered to produce at the socially optimal quantity, what would be the quantity and price?

   (A) Q_1, P_5
   (B) Q_1, P_2
   (C) Q_1, P_1
   (D) Q_2, P_4
   (E) Q_3, P_3

18. What is the area of economic profit if this was an unregulated, profit-maximizing monopoly?

   (A) 0, P_2, B, Q_1
   (B) 0, P_5, C, Q_1
   (C) P_2, P_5, C, B
   (D) P_1, P_5, C, A
   (E) 0, P_1, A, Q_1

19. If a lump-sum tax were now placed on this unregulated monopoly, what would happen to the new
profit-maximizing quantity and price?

(A) Price and quantity would remain unchanged
(B) Price would increase and quantity would
decrease
(C) Price would decrease and quantity would
decrease
(D) Price would decrease and quantity would
increase
(E) Price would increase and quantity would
increase

*Questions 20–22 are based on the perfectly competitive
market depicted below.*

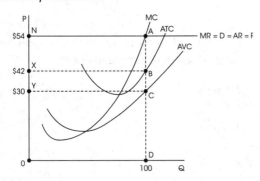

20. At a market price of $54, the area of profits or
losses is

(A) 0, Y, C, D
(B) 0, X, B, C
(C) X, N, A, B
(D) Y, X, B, C
(E) 0, N, A, D

21. Based on the graph, what is the total fixed cost at
the profit-maximizing quantity?

(A) $54
(B) $1,200
(C) $2,400
(D) $3,000
(E) $5,400

22. What will happen to the number of firms in the
long run in this industry based on the profit conditions in this perfectly competitive firm?

(A) The number of firms will increase as the existence of economic profits attracts more firms.
(B) The number of firms will decrease as the existence of economic profits attracts fewer firms.
(C) The number of firms will decrease as the
existence of economic losses causes firms to
leave
(D) The number of firms will increase as the existence of economic losses attracts more firms.
(E) The number of firms will remain unchanged
as all the profits in the industry are gone.

23. If a 10% increase in the price of good A leads
to a 20% decrease in the quantity demanded of
good B, then

(A) the cross-price elasticity is 0.5 and the goods
are complements.
(B) the cross-price elasticity is –2 and the goods
are complements.
(C) the cross-price elasticity is 2 and the goods
are complements.
(D) the income elasticity is 2 and the goods are
inferior.
(E) the income elasticity is 0.5 and the goods are
normal.

24. If the government announces that the drinking of
red grape juice reduces the risk of heart attacks,
which of the following will be correct in terms of
changes in supply, demand, and the price of red
grape juice?

	Supply	Demand	Price of Grape Juice
(A)	Increases	Decreases	Increases
(B)	No change	No change	Decreases
(C)	No change	Increases	Increases
(D)	Decreases	Increases	Decreases
(E)	Decreases	Decreases	Decreases

Questions 25–28 are based on the figure below.

Market for Coffee

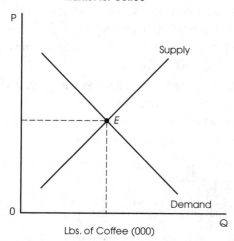

Lbs. of Coffee (000)

25. If the demand for coffee increases and at the same time increases in productivity lower production costs, what would happen to the new price and quantity?

Price	Quantity
(A) Increase	Increase
(B) Indeterminate	Increase
(C) Increase	Decrease
(D) Decrease	Indeterminate
(E) Decrease	Decrease

26. If the government provides a subsidy to the producers of coffee, which of the following will occur?

(A) A shift to the left of the supply curve
(B) A shift to the left of the demand curve
(C) A move along the supply curve to the right
(D) A shift to the right of the demand curve
(E) A shift to the right of the supply curve

27. If the producers of coffee have to pay an increase in wages and fringe benefits to their workers, which of the following is correct?

(A) A shift to the left of the supply curve
(B) A shift to the left of the demand curve
(C) A move along the supply curve to the right
(D) A shift to the right of the demand curve
(E) A shift to the right of the supply curve

28. If the price of coffee increases (a normal good), which of the following is most likely to happen?

(A) An increase in the quantity of coffee consumers want to purchase
(B) No change in the quantity of coffee consumers want to purchase
(C) A decrease in the quantity of coffee consumers want to purchase
(D) An increase (shift) in the demand for coffee
(E) A decrease (shift) in the demand for coffee

Use the following graph for Question 29.

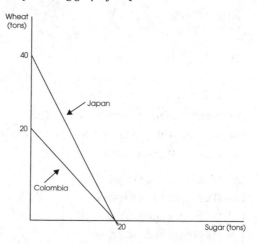

29. The production possibilities graph shows how much each country can produce in a year. According to the graph, which of the following is true?

(A) Colombia has an absolute advantage in the production of wheat.
(B) Japan has a comparative advantage in the production of sugar.
(C) Colombia has a comparative advantage in the production of wheat.
(D) Japan cannot benefit from trade with Colombia.
(E) Japan has a comparative advantage in the production of wheat.

Questions 30–31 are based on the figure below.

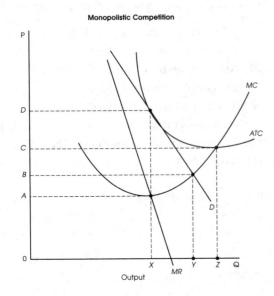

Monopolistic Competition

30. For this firm operating under monopolistic competition, which of the following is the profit-maximizing output and price?

    (A) OX output and OA price
    (B) OX output and OD price
    (C) OX output and OB price
    (D) OZ output and OC price
    (E) OZ output and OA price

31. At the profit-maximizing output, which of the following is correct?

    (A) Economic profits are zero, and the firm is operating efficiently.
    (B) Economic profits are above normal, and output is greater than under perfect competition.
    (C) Economic losses are present.
    (D) Price is less than marginal cost.
    (E) Economic profits are zero, and the firm is operating inefficiently.

32. Which of the following best exemplifies economies of scale?

    (A) As a firm's output decreases, long-run average total cost decreases.
    (B) As a firm's output increases, long-run average total cost increases.
    (C) As a firm's output increases, long-run average total cost decreases.
    (D) As a firm's output increases, long-run average total cost remains constant.
    (E) As a firm becomes larger, it becomes less productive.

33. Which of the following is correct?

    (A) In the long run, all inputs are variable.
    (B) In the short run, all inputs are variable.
    (C) In the long run, supply is not able to adjust fully to changes in demand.
    (D) In the short run, supply is able to adjust fully to changes in demand.
    (E) A short run is any distance less than one mile.

34. If a firm decreases its prices by 15 percent and the quantity demanded increases by 30 percent, which of the following is correct?

    (A) The price elasticity of demand is unit elastic.
    (B) The price elasticity of demand is perfectly elastic.
    (C) The price elasticity of demand is relatively elastic.
    (D) The numerical coefficient of elasticity is equal to one.
    (E) The numerical coefficient of elasticity is less than one.

35. At its current level of output, a firm uses two inputs in the production process, labor and robots. Robots produce an output of 1,000 units a day and cost $500, and labor produces 200 units a day and costs $100. In order to lower total production costs, how should the firm change its use of labor and robots?

(A) Increase both amounts of labor and robots.
(B) Use more robots and less labor.
(C) Use more labor and fewer robots.
(D) Use less labor and fewer robots.
(E) Maintain the current level of robots and labor.

36. When marginal cost equals price in a perfectly competitive product market in long-run equilibrium, which of the following is NOT true?

(A) There is allocative efficiency as price = marginal cost.
(B) There is productive efficiency as price = minimum average total cost.
(C) The perfectly competitive firm is earning economic profits.
(D) The market is producing the amount of goods desired by society.
(E) The firm is earning a normal profit.

37. Which of the following is a correct statement?

(A) Average total cost equals marginal cost plus average fixed costs.
(B) Average total cost equals marginal costs plus average variable costs.
(C) Average total cost equals average fixed costs plus average variable costs.
(D) Total fixed costs vary with output.
(E) Total fixed costs equal total variable costs at zero output.

38. Which of the following describes a monopolistically competitive market?

(A) A small number of firms with high barriers to entry and exit
(B) A large number of firms with high barriers to entry and exit
(C) A small number of firms and allocative efficiency
(D) It produces products with no close substitutes
(E) Low barriers to entry and exit and excess capacity

Questions 39–41 are based on this monopoly graph.

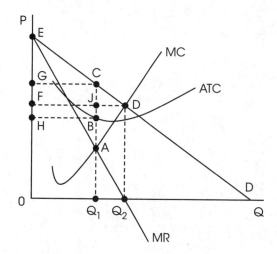

39. If this firm was producing at the socially optimal quantity, what area would be the consumer surplus?

(A) ECG
(B) CDA
(C) EDF
(D) GCBH
(E) GCJF

40. The deadweight loss as the result of the monopoly producing at the profit-maximizing quantity is the area of

(A) ECG
(B) CDA
(C) EDF
(D) GCBH
(E) GCJF

41. The consumer surplus of the monopoly producing at the profit-maximizing quantity is

(A) ECG
(B) CDA
(C) EDF
(D) GCBH
(E) GCJF

Use the following graph for Questions 42, 43, and 44.

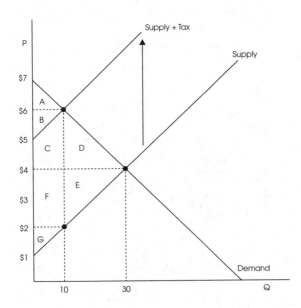

42. The market shown in the graph has had a per-unit tax placed on its production. What are the after-tax consumer and producer surpluses?

	Consumer Surplus	Producer Surplus
(A)	ABCD	FEG
(B)	AB	FG
(C)	A	G
(D)	BCD	FE
(E)	ABCFG	DE

43. The market shown in the graph has had a per-unit tax placed on its production. What is the tax incidence, or burden of the tax paid by consumers and producers?

	Consumer Tax Incidence	Producer Tax Incidence
(A)	BC	F
(B)	ABCD	FEG
(C)	A	G
(D)	BCD	FE
(E)	ABCFG	DE

44. The market shown on the graph has had a per-unit tax placed on its production. What is the after-tax price paid by consumers and the after-tax price received by producers?

	Price for Consumers	Price Received by Sellers
(A)	$4	$4
(B)	$6	$2
(C)	$7	$1
(D)	$4	$2
(E)	$5	$1

45. If, for each additional unit of a variable input added, the increases in output become smaller, which of the following correctly identifies the concept?

(A) Diminishing marginal returns
(B) Diminishing marginal utility
(C) Increasing marginal utility
(D) Increasing marginal productivity
(E) Constant costs

46. Which of the following is correct about the demand for labor?

(A) The demand for labor is independent of the demand for other inputs or resources.
(B) The demand for labor is independent of the demand for the products produced by labor.
(C) The demand for labor is independent of the availability of other inputs or resources.
(D) The demand for labor is derived from the demand for the products produced by labor.
(E) The demand for labor is derived from the demand for labor unions.

47. If an increase in the price of good Y causes the quantity demanded of good X to increase, this means the two goods are

   (A) complementary goods.
   (B) substitute goods.
   (C) inferior goods.
   (D) normal goods.
   (E) independent goods.

Use the following graph for Question 48.

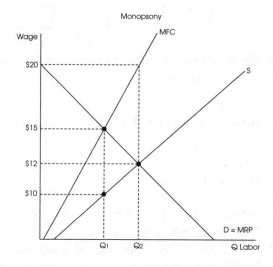

48. The graph shows a monopsony labor market. What is the profit-maximizing wage and quantity of workers hired by the monopsonist?

Wage	Quantity
(A) $12	Q_2
(B) $20	Q_2
(C) $15	Q_1
(D) $12	Q_1
(E) $10	Q_1

49. Under what conditions would a firm continue to hire labor in a perfectly competitive labor market?

   (A) When the marginal revenue product is greater than the marginal factor cost
   (B) When labor costs less than capital
   (C) When the marginal revenue product is positive
   (D) When the marginal factor cost is greater than the marginal revenue product
   (E) When the average product is increasing

50. What law best describes a production possibilites curve that has a bowed out or concave shape from the origin?

   (A) The law of productive efficiency
   (B) The law of diminishing marginal utility
   (C) The law of increasing opportunity cost
   (D) The law of supply
   (E) The law of demand

51. According to the table, what is the fixed cost, marginal cost, and average total cost of producing the 4th unit?

Output	Total Cost
0	$20
1	$30
2	$35
3	$50
4	$80
5	$115

	Fixed Cost	Marginal Cost	Average Total Cost
(A)	$20	$30	$20
(B)	$20	$50	$20
(C)	$20	$80	$60
(D)	$30	$30	$115
(E)	$110	$80	$47.5

Use the following game theory matrix for Questions 52 and 53.

Firm Y

		High	Low
	High	$60, $45	$50, $35
Firm X			
	Low	$40, $10	$15, $20

52. This game theory payoff matrix shows the possible profit for two firms deciding to price high or price low. Firm X will earn the profit to the left in each cell, and Firm Y's profit is to the right in each cell. Which of the following statements is correct?

(A) Firm X's dominant strategy is to price low.
(B) Firm X's dominant strategy is to price high.
(C) Firm Y's dominant strategy is to price low.
(D) Firm Y's dominant strategy is to price high.
(E) Neither firm has a dominant strategy.

53. This game theory payoff matrix shows the possible profit for two firms deciding to price high or price low. Firm X will earn the profit to the left in each cell, and Firm Y's profit is to the right in each cell. Assume each firm knows all the information in the payoff matrix. All of the following statements are correct EXCEPT

(A) if the two firms collude, Firm X will price high and Firm Y will price high.
(B) if Firm X prices low, then Firm Y will price low.
(C) Firm Y does not have a dominant strategy.
(D) the game will reach a Nash equilibrium with both pricing high.
(E) if Firm Y prices high, Firm X will price low.

54. Assume Celine's Crab Shack earned an accounting profit of $20,000 this year. However, the owner and head chef, Celine, is also a talented artist who could have earned $30,000 painting and $2,000 in interest from the money she invested in her restaurant. Based on this information, which of the following statements is correct about Celine?

(A) She has incurred an economic loss as a chef.
(B) She has gained economic profits as a chef.
(C) She has a negative accounting profit as a chef.
(D) She is earning a normal profit as a chef.
(E) Her explicit costs are $12,000 as a chef.

55. For a profit-maximizing, nonprice-discriminating monopolist, marginal revenue is

(A) equal to price.
(B) negative when the firm is maximizing profit.
(C) more than the price.
(D) a perfect elastic curve.
(E) less than the price.

56. Assume that people like mustard on their hot dogs. Due to increases in the cost of production, the supply of hot dogs decreases. How will this affect the market for mustard?

(A) The demand for mustard will increase as hot dogs and mustard are complements.
(B) The quantity demanded of mustard will increase as hot dogs and mustard are complements.
(C) The demand for mustard will go down as hot dogs and mustard are complements.
(D) The supply of mustard will increase to offset the hot dog market.
(E) The demand and supply of mustard will remain unchanged.

Use this graph for Question 57.

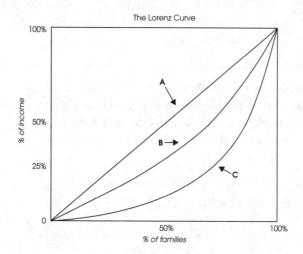

57. On the Lorenz curve, all of the following are true except

   (A) line A shows more income inequality than line B.
   (B) line A shows perfect income equality.
   (C) line B shows less income inequality than line C.
   (D) line C shows greater income inequality than line A.
   (E) on line A, 50% of families earn 50% of the total income.

58. If a government passes an effective minimum wage law, in which of the following situations will the change in employment be the smallest?

   (A) If labor demand is relatively elastic
   (B) If labor demand is unit elastic
   (C) If labor demand is relatively inelastic
   (D) If labor demand is perfectly elastic
   (E) If labor supply is relatively elastic

59. Assume the government imposes a 20% excise tax on all food sold in a country. Which of the following is true?

   (A) This is a proportional tax.
   (B) This is a regressive tax.
   (C) This is a progressive tax.
   (D) The quantity demanded for food will not change, as it is perfectly inelastic.
   (E) There will be no additional tax revenue from this tax.

Use the following table to answer Question 60.

Number of Times	Marginal Utility from Movies	Marginal Utility from Trampoline Park
1	30	15
2	20	10
3	10	5
4	5	2
5	0	1

60. Assume Joe has only $45 to spend on entertainment. What combination of movies, which cost $10 per movie, and visits to the trampoline park, which cost $5 per visit, would maximize his utility?

   (A) Going to the movies and trampoline park 2 times each
   (B) Going to the movies and trampoline park 3 times each
   (C) Going to the movies 2 times and the trampoline park 3 times
   (D) Going to the movies 3 times and the trampoline park 5 times
   (E) Going to the movies 4 times and the trampoline park 5 times

Section II—Free-Response Questions

TIME—60 MINUTES

PERCENT OF TOTAL GRADE—33$^1/_3$

DIRECTIONS: You have 60 minutes to answer all three of the following questions. It is suggested that you spend approximately half your time on the first question and divide the remaining time equally between the next two questions. Include correctly labeled diagrams, if useful or required, in explaining your answers. A correctly labeled diagram must have all axes and curves clearly labeled and must show directional changes.

Students should consider doing a "sketch" (main points, quick graph, etc.) of the answer before actually answering the free-response questions. Be sure to label the axes, curves, and show directional shifts on all graphs. Good luck!

1. Farmer Fred produces corn in a perfectly competitive market. Farmer Fred is earning economic profits.

   (a) Draw correctly labeled, side-by-side graphs of both the market for corn and for Farmer Fred, showing each of the following:

      (i) The equilibrium price and quantity in the corn market labeled P_{M1} and Q_{M1}.

      (ii) The equilibrium price and quantity for Farmer Fred labeled P_{F1} and Q_{F1}.

      (iii) Farmer Fred's economic profit shaded in.

   (b) As Farmer Fred is earning economic profits, what will happen in the market for corn as the economy adjusts to long-run equilibrium? In two newly drawn, side-by-side graphs of the corn market and Farmer Fred, show the following with correct labels:

      (i) The initial equilibrium price and quantity in the corn market, P_{M1} and Q_{M1}.

      (ii) The initial equilibrium price and quantity showing short-run economic profits for Farmer Fred, P_{F1} and Q_{F1}.

      (iii) The new long-run equilibrium price and quantity in the corn market labeled P_{M2} and Q_{M2}.

      (iv) The new long-run equilibrium price and quantity in the corn market for Farmer Fred labeled P_{F2} and Q_{F2}.

   (c) At the new long-run equilibrium, is Farmer Fred earning an economic profit, an economic loss, or a normal profit?

   (d) Now assume that in the corn market, the price of corn has decreased 20% while the quantity demanded at that price has increased 40%. Is the price elasticity of demand unit elastic, relatively elastic, perfectly elastic, relatively inelastic, or perfectly inelastic? Explain.

2. A firm has a patent that makes it the only producer in the market. The firm is currently earning economic profits in long-run equilibrium.

    (a) Draw a correctly labeled graph with each of the following:

        (i) The profit-maximizing quantity and price produced by the firm, labeled Q_m and P_m.

        (ii) The area of economic profit clearly shaded and labeled.

        (iii) The area of deadweight loss clearly shaded and labeled.

    (b) Now assume that the firm is producing at the socially optimal quantity. Label this quantity Q_s on the same graph from 2a.

    (c) As a profit-maximizing monopolist, what area of the demand curve will the monopolist operate: where demand is elastic, inelastic, or unit elastic?

    (d) Now assume the monopoly is producing at the quantity where total revenue is maximized and then the firm produces increases production beyond that amount. Will marginal revenue be negative, positive, or zero? Explain.

3. After an outbreak of the flu, a public relations campaign by the government is encouraging more people to get flu shots, arguing that it produces a positive consumption externality.

    (a) Draw a correctly labeled graph of this positive consumption externality, showing each of the following:

        (i) The equilibrium market price and quantity, labeled P_M and Q_M.

        (ii) The socially optimal equilibrium price and quantity, labeled P_S and Q_S.

        (iii) The area of deadweight loss, shaded in.

    (b) At the market quantity, is the marginal social benefit greater than, less than, or equal to the marginal private benefit?

    (c) What type of action would you recommend to bring production to the socially optimal quantity? Explain.

Answer Explanations

Multiple-Choice Questions

1. **(B)** (Chapter 7) The other answers are all characteristics of a perfectly competitive industry. Products are homogeneous (the same, identical) under perfect competition.

2. **(C)** (Chapter 9) All of the other characteristics listed as choices are *not* appropriate for monopolistic competition. Choices B, D, and E are characteristics of perfect competition in the long run; choice A is characteristic of oligopoly and monopoly.

3. **(E)** (Chapter 9) All of these are characteristics of an oligopoly. Review the Venn diagram in Chapter 9 for more characteristics of an oligopoly.

4. **(A)** (Chapter 8) A profit-maximizing monopolist will always price in the elastic range of the demand curve. In the inelastic range of the demand curve, additional output will lower the price *and* decrease total revenue (unlike the elastic range or the demand curve, where total revenue increases as output increases). Review the Venn diagram in Chapter 9 for more characteristics of a monopoly. To change the other choices to fit a monopoly, you would have to rewrite choices B, C, D, and E as follows:

   B: $P > MR$
   C: downward-sloping demand curve
   D: complete barriers to entry
   E: presence of economic profits

5. **(E)** (Chapter 8) With a monopoly, the price paid by consumers is greater than the cost of production, or $P > MC$. Thus, a monopolist is not allocatively efficient, which leads to monopolies having a deadweight loss. The optimal output from society's viewpoint is where $P = MC$, where perfectly competitive firms produce at long-run equilibrium. See the Venn diagram in Chapter 9 for more characteristics of a monopoly compared to perfect competition.

6. **(B)** (Chapter 11) The rule to follow is a per-unit tax for a negative externality and a per-unit subsidy for a positive externality. Both would internalize or correct the externality.

7. **(A)** (Chapter 11) See number 6.

8. **(D)** (Chapter 11) The marginal social cost is made up of the marginal private cost, but it also includes the costs imposed on other parties not involved in a transaction, known as marginal external costs. So the marginal private cost is added to the marginal external cost to equal the marginal social cost.

9. **(D)** (Chapter 6) $ATC = AVC + AFC$

10. **(D)** (Chapter 6) If marginal cost (MC) is less than average total cost (ATC), ATC will be decreasing. If MC is greater than ATC, ATC will be increasing. Therefore, MC intersects ATC at its minimum point. This also holds true for MC and average variable cost.

11. **(C)** (Chapter 10) On the graph you will see the demand for workers curve (D) is equal to the marginal revenue product (MRP) of the workers. Thus, if the price for the product (P_X) stays constant and if the computerized system increases MP_L (marginal productivity), the MRP_L will increase as a shift of $D(MRP_L)$ to the right.

12. **(C)** (Chapter 5) A binding or effective price floor is placed above the equilibrium price, leading to a surplus. If a price floor is placed below the equilibrium price, it is ineffective and the price will be at the equilibrium quantity.

13. **(D)** (Chapter 5) A binding or effective price ceiling is placed below the equilibrium price, leading to a shortage. If a price ceiling is placed above the equilibrium price, it is ineffective and the price will be at the equilibrium quantity.

14. **(D)** (Chapter 5) The consumer surplus is the difference between the highest price that a buyer would pay and the actual price paid. If you would have paid $10 to see a movie but actually paid $5, the consumer surplus would be $5.

15. **(B)** (Chapter 10) First, construct a third column headed marginal product (MP), which would be the difference in widgets for each additional worker hired (e.g., 30 MP as the difference between 40 widgets for one worker, and 70 widgets for two workers). Second, construct a fourth column headed MRP_L (marginal revenue product), which is the function of $MP_L \times P_L$. Then you will find the *number* of workers (first column) hired that will maximize the profits of the firm doing the hiring. This number will be the level of hiring at which $MP_L \times P_L$ (or wage rate, which = $1,250). Thus,

(1) Number of Workers	(2) Widgets Produced for Two Weeks	(3) MP_L	(4) MRP_L $MP_L \times P_L$
1	40	40	$1,600
2	70	30	$1,500
3	95	25	$1,250
4	115	20	$1,000
5	130	15	$750
6	130	0	—

Since the widgets are sold at $50, column 4 is $MP_L \times P_L$ ($50). The profit-maximizing level is three workers whose MRP_L is $1,250, which is equal to the wage paid every two weeks of $1,250 per worker.

16. **(A)** (Chapter 8) The reference is to the graph supplied for Questions 16–19. The profit-maximizing output and the selling price are determined by the intersection of marginal cost and marginal revenue (MR = MC). The price, P_5, is read from the demand curve or by extending a vertical line from the intersection of MR and MC to the demand curve (point C); the related point on the price axis is P_5. Similarly, the best output is Q_1, which is found by dropping a vertical line from the intersection of MC and MR to the quantity (horizontal) axis.

17. **(D)** (Chapter 8) The socially optimal price is where P = MC, and since price is shown by the demand curve, the answer is Q_2, P_4.

18. **(C)** (Chapter 8) From the profit-maximizing quantity of Q_1 (located from the MR = MC output level), head up to the demand curve at point C and then over to the price axis to find the price, Q_5. From point C, head down to the ATC curve at point B, then left to P_2. Then you have the profit rectangle of P_2, P_5, C, B. It is also helpful to know that profits or losses are (P – ATC) $\times$ Q.

19. **(A)** (Chapter 8) A lump-sum tax does not change either MC or MR (from the profit-maximizing quantity of MR = MC), so quantity and price will remain unchanged. A per-unit tax does change MR and MC but not a lump-sum tax.

20. **(C)** (Chapter 7) Profits for a perfectly competitive firm are found where MR = MC, point A on the graph. From A head down to the ATC curve at point B, then left for the ATC of $42 (X) and up to the price of $54 (N). Thus, the profit rectangle is XNAB. The profit-maximizing quantity is 100 (D).

21. **(B)** (Chapter 6) Total fixed cost (TFC) is the difference between the average total cost (ATC) and average variable cost (AVC) curves multiplied by the profit-maximizing quantity at MR = MC. It can be calculated here by taking the area BC ($12) × quantity (100). $12 × $100 = $1,200.

22. **(A)** (Chapter 7) As the firm is earning short-run profits, this will attract new firms to the industry, as firms face easy entry and exit under perfect competition.

23. **(B)** (Chapter 5) Cross-price elasticity of demand (CPED) is calculated by taking the % change in QDx/% change in Py. –20%/10% = –2. As the CPED is negative, it means the two goods are complements. If the CPED was positive, the goods would be substitutes.

24. **(C)** (Chapter 4) The government announcement would result in an increase in demand for red grape juice. With supply constant, the price for red grape juice would increase as the demand curve shifts to the right.

25. **(B)** (Chapter 4) We know for sure that the demand and supply curves will increase and shift to the right. This will definitely increase the new quantity, but price is indeterminate. It is not clear how far each curve will shift to the right, which determines the new price. So price is indeterminate.

26. **(E)** (Chapter 4) In the chapter on supply and demand, there is a list of factors that will cause shifts in the supply and demand curves. When the government provides a subsidy to the producer, there is a decrease in the cost of production that encourages more production (shift to the right of the supply curve).

27. **(A)** (Chapter 4) An increase in costs of production such as wage increases will lead to a decrease in supply.

28. **(C)** (Chapter 4) An increase in the price of coffee, a normal good, will cause the quantity demanded to decrease, moving along a fixed demand curve. Note that this is not a change in demand, as there is no shift in the curve, just a change in the quantity demanded.

29. **(E)** (Chapter 2) Absolute advantage is easy to find and is just the maximum amount that can be produced of a good. So it is a tie for sugar, but Japan has the absolute advantage in producing wheat. Even if one country has an absolute advantage in producing both products, a country can still benefit from trade. A country should specialize in the product in which it has a lower opportunity cost, which is a comparative advantage. To calculate comparative advantage, it is helpful to put the numbers in a chart (see the following example) to calculate the opportunity cost. To calculate the opportunity cost, take the opposite number and put it over the side for which you are calculating the opportunity cost. For example, Japan's opportunity cost of producing wheat is 20/40, or ½. For Colombia, it's 20/20, or 1. So Japan has the comparative advantage in wheat, as its relative opportunity cost (½) is lower than Colombia's (1). Likewise, Colombia has the comparative advantage in sugar; its opportunity cost (1) is lower than Japan's (2), and it will specialize in sugar.

	Wheat	Sugar
Japan	40	20
Colombia	20	20

	Wheat	Sugar
Japan	20/40	40/20
Colombia	20/20	20/20

30. **(B)** (Chapter 9) This is the typical tendency for monopolistic competitors—price equals average total cost (not at minimum ATC), allowing firms normal profits (zero economic profits). At MC = MR, price is at OD and output is at OX.

31. **(E)** (Chapter 9) See the answer for 30 above for zero economic profits. The firm operates inefficiently since P > minimum ATC, and P > MC.

32. **(C)** (Chapter 6) With economies of scale, as production increases there are savings in average costs of production. When output increases more than proportionately to increases in input, the firm is getting more output per added input or, in effect, there is a decrease in cost of production.

33. **(A)** (Chapter 6) In other words (in contrast to the other choices), supply is able to adjust fully to changes in demand in the long run. In the short run, some inputs are fixed in quantity, and supply is unable to adjust fully to the changes in demand.

34. **(C)** (Chapter 5) Using the price elasticity of demand formula, 30/15 = an elasticity coefficient of 2, which makes demand relatively elastic.

$$\frac{\% \,\Delta \text{ Quantity}}{\% \,\Delta \text{ Price}}$$

Elasticity Coefficient Value

Type of Elasticity	Elasticity Value
Perfectly inelastic	= 0
Relatively inelastic	< 1
Unit elastic	= 1
Relatively elastic	> 1
Perfectly elastic	∞ (infinity)

35. **(E)** (Chapter 10) The least-cost rule for using inputs is $MP_x/P_x = MP_k = P_k$. 1,000/$500 robots = 200/$100 labor. 2 robots = 2 labor. In this case, the firm already has the least-cost labor combination as both sides equal out. They should make no change to their current combination.

36. **(C)** (Chapter 7) Earning economic profits in the long run is the only choice that is not a characteristic of perfectly competitive markets; instead, it is a characteristic of oligopolies or monopolies.

37. **(C)** (Chapter 6) The two types of costs, fixed and variable, are added together to get total cost. Variable costs can change in the short run, while fixed costs stay constant in the short run.

38. **(E)** (Chapter 9) A major characteristic of monopolistically competitive firms is that they produce where P = ATC, but only when ATC is falling, which results in excess capacity. Also, there is strong competition, as firms can easily enter and exit.

39. **(C)** (Chapter 8) The socially optimal quantity is where the monopoly reaches allocative efficiency (P = MC). The consumer surplus is the area above the price, below the demand curve, and left of quantity at Q_2.

40. **(B)** (Chapter 8) To find the deadweight loss, locate the difference between the allocatively efficient output (Q_2, where P = MC) and the monopolist's profit-maximizing output (Q_1, where MR = MC). Between Q_1 and Q_2, the area above MC and below D is the deadweight loss, area CDA.

41. **(A)** (Chapter 8) At the profit-maximizing output, MR = MC, a monopoly charges a higher price than at the socially optimal price shown in question 39. Hence, the consumer surplus is now the smaller area ECG.

42. **(C)** (Chapter 5) The after-tax price is $6, so the consumer surplus is the area under the demand curve and above the price of $6, or area A. While consumers pay $6, the tax is $4, so the sellers only receive $2 after the tax. The producer surplus is the area above the supply curve and below the price received by sellers, area G.

43. **(A)** (Chapter 5) The tax incidence is the amount of the tax burden sellers and buyers pay. The tax burden for consumers is the difference between the before- and after-tax prices × quantity, or ($6 – $4) × Q, and that is the area BC. For producers, it is the difference between the price received before and after the tax × quantity, or ($4 – $2) × Q, and that is the area F.

44. **(B)** (Chapter 5) From where the supply curve + tax meets the demand curve, head to the axes to see the price ($6) and quantity (10) for buyers. From the after-tax equilibrium quantity of 10, go to the original supply curve before tax and over to the price axis for the price received by sellers ($2). Or take the after-tax price minus the size of the tax to get the after-tax price received by sellers ($6 – $4 = $2).

45. **(A)** (Chapter 6) This is an essential concept to understand—diminishing marginal returns or productivity, the eventual decline in productivity as more and more of a variable input is added in short-run production.

46. **(D)** (Chapter 10) This is a very important concept—derived demand.

47. **(B)** (Chapter 4) If the increase in price of one good causes demand to go up for another product, then they are substitute goods, like coffee and tea. If a price increase of one good causes demand to go down for another product, then they are complementary goods, like hot dogs and hot dog buns.

48. **(E)** (Chapter 10) A monopsony, where one firm controls the market for labor, hires less labor and at lower wages than would a competitive labor market. The quantity hired is where marginal factor cost (MFC) = marginal revenue product (MRP), but note the wage paid is at the supply curve at the quantity where MFC and MRP meet, not the wage where MFC = MRP. A monopsony-controlled labor market would have a wage of $10 at Q_1, and a competitive labor market would have a wage of $12 at Q_2.

49. **(A)** (Chapter 10) All firms will continue to hire up until the point where marginal revenue product (MRP) = marginal factor cost (MFC). If the MRP > MFC, a firm will continue to hire until MRP = MFC.

50. **(C)** (Chapter 2) When a production possibilities curve has this shape, it is indicative of increasing opportunity costs. This means resources are not completely adaptable to other uses, so as more of one product is produced, gradually more and more of the other product is sacrificed.

51. **(A)** (Chapter 6) When output is 0, total cost is $20, meaning that it is a fixed cost. As output moves from 3 to 4, total cost moves from $50 to $80. The difference between these is the marginal cost, or $30. The average total cost is calculated by taking the total cost at an output of 4, $80, divided by 4, which is $20.

52. **(B)** (Chapter 9) A dominant strategy is a player's best choice regardless of the opponent's actions. Firm X's dominant strategy is to go high and earn $60 if Firm Y goes high and $50 if Y goes low. If X went low, it would earn only $40 and $15 depending on Y's move, much less than X's high numbers of $60 and $50. Firm Y does not have a dominant strategy as if X goes high, Y would be better off going high, but if X went low, Y would be better off going low.

53. **(E)** (Chapter 9) Since $60 > $40, Firm X would prefer to charge a high price and get $60 profit. So E is not true.

54. **(A)** (Chapter 6) Economic profit is different from accounting profit in that it considers both implicit and explicit costs. She has $20,000 in accounting profit, but she could have earned $30,000 as an artist and earned $2,000 in interest if she invested her restaurant money. So she could have earned a total of $32,000 as an artist compared to $20,000 as a restaurateur. So her economic loss is $12,000.

55. **(E)** (Chapter 8) For a nonprice-discriminating monopolist, marginal revenue is less than price. For a monopolist to increase sales, he must lower prices for all buyers. So when price falls for all buyers, marginal revenue falls at a greater rate than price. For any firm that has a downward-sloping demand curve and charges all customers the same prices, marginal revenue will be less than price.

56. **(C)** (Chapter 4) The decreasing supply in the hot dog market will increase the price of hot dogs. As mustard and hot dogs are complementary goods, the increase in price of hot dogs will decrease the demand for mustard, shifting the mustard demand curve to the left. If the price of one good increasing causes demand to decrease for another good, they are complementary goods. If the price of one good increasing causes another good's demand to increase, they are substitute goods.

57. **(A)** (Chapter 11) The bigger the curve or "banana" shape of the Lorenz curve, the greater the income inequality. This graph shows the degree of income inequality in a country. So line C displays greater income inequality, and line A shows perfect income equality.

58. **(C)** (Chapter 5) If labor demand is relatively inelastic, firms will continue to hire workers despite wage increases. So as wages increase, firms with relatively inelastic labor demand curves will continue to hire more labor than if labor demand was more elastic, where labor demand would be more sensitive to wage increases.

59. **(B)** (Chapter 11) A regressive tax takes a greater percentage of total income from lower income groups. So even though this seems like a proportional tax, lower income groups may spend all of their income, whereas higher income groups are more likely to have saved some income. Lower income groups are thus likely to pay a greater percentage of their income on the food tax.

60. **(B)** (Chapter 5) The formula for utility maximization is $MU_x/P_x = MU_y/P_y$. When solving these problems, it is helpful to also make a chart of the MU/P for each good. Start by choosing and circling the goods that give the highest utility per dollar on your chart, and continue until you run out of money. As you can see in the table below, the utility-maximizing combination of going to the movies and trampoline park 3 times each, given the $45 to spend, is correct.

Number of Times	Marginal Utility from Movies	Marginal Utility/ Price, MU/P	Marginal Utility from Trampoline Park	Marginal Utility/ Price, MU/P
1	30	③	15	③
2	20	②	10	②
3	10	①	5	①
4	5	0.5	2	0.4
5	0	0	1	0.2

Free-Response Questions

Here are the correct answers for the free-response section. Please be advised that you can earn partial credit if at least some of your answer is correct. You can also receive points for labeling your graphs correctly, even if you make the wrong shift.

1.

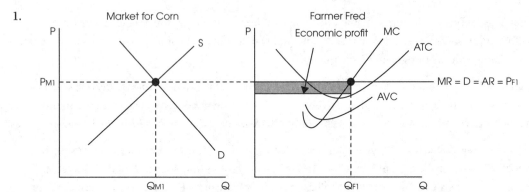

(a) Note that Farmer Fred is a price taker and takes the price in the corn market. The profit-maximizing quantity is at MR = MC; from there head to the demand curve and quantity axis for P_{F1} and Q_{F1}. Note that a perfectly competitive firm has a perfectly elastic demand curve, labeled MRDARP (marginal revenue, demand, average revenue, and price). P at the end is labeled P_{F1}, giving the correct point for the correct label. Remember, for labeling profit, go to the profit-maximizing quantity, and start drawing the profit box between the demand curve and the ATC, and head over to the price axis to complete the profit rectangle.

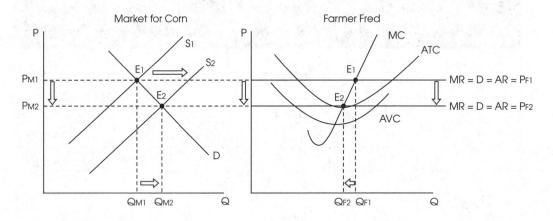

(b) Economic profits being made in a perfectly competitive market attract competition, as there is easy entry and exit for firms. The economic profit causes the supply curve in the market on the left to increase, causing the market price of corn to fall to P_{M2}. Farmer Fred has no control over the price at which he sells, so he "takes" that price, and his economic profit is gone. His price then falls to MR = D = AR = P_{F2}, and the quantity falls to Q_{F2} at his new equilibrium, E_2, at the minimum of the ATC.

(c) Fred is earning a normal profit because price = ATC. A normal profit = zero economic profit. (Remember the difference between accounting and economic profit? Zero economic profit does not mean there is no accounting profit. In fact, with a normal profit, he could not be doing better anywhere else. So zero economic profit is actually not bad!)

(d) Relatively elastic demand. You need to calculate the price elasticity of demand using the formula (% Δ in QD/% Δ in P), so that 40%/20% gives an elasticity coefficient of 2, which signifies relatively elastic demand. For review, here is the chart for elasticity coefficients that are important to know.

Elasticity Coefficient Values	
Type of Elasticity	Elasticity Value
Relatively elastic	> 1
Perfectly elastic	∞ (infinity)
Relatively inelastic	< 1
Perfectly inelastic	$= 0$
Unit elastic	$= 1$

2.

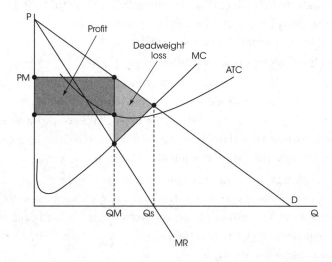

(a) See graph. The profit-maximizing quantity comes from the profit-maximizing quantity of MR = MC and the price from the demand curve. Deadweight loss is located as an "arrow" pointing to the socially optimal quantity where P = MC and above the MC curve and below D between Q_m and Q_s. Profit is P − ATC × Q.

(b) See graph. The socially optimal or allocatively efficient quantity is where P = MC. Price comes from the demand curve.

(c) Elastic. A profit-maximizing monopolist will always produce on the elastic range to maximize profits.

(d) Negative. Total revenue is maximized where MR = 0. An additional unit will put the marginal revenue curve below the axis, so it would be negative and in the inelastic range of the demand curve.

3.

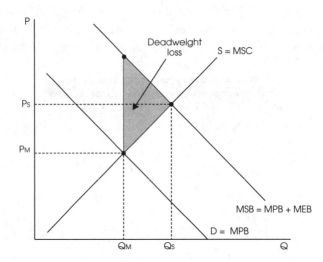

(a) (i) The private market underproduces the socially optimal amount of a good or service when a positive externality is present. The private market quantity is where marginal private benefit (MPB) is equal to the marginal social cost (MSC).

  (ii) The socially optimal output of a good is where MSB = MSC.

  (iii) To correctly find the area of the deadweight loss, imagine it is an arrow pointing to the socially optimal quantity, originating from the side with two curves, with the length of the arrow tip the difference between Q_M and Q_S. It would be pointing the other way with a negative externality.

(b) The MSB is greater than the MPB at the market quantity. The difference between these two points is the marginal external benefit (MEB) that the market does not produce.

(c) An effective policy solution would be a per-unit subsidy equal to the marginal external benefit. A per-unit subsidy lowers the marginal cost of production by giving money to a firm for each additional unit produced. As a review, a lump-sum subsidy gives a fixed payment to a firm regardless of production quantity. A per-unit tax (for negative externalities) is more effective for solving externalities than a lump-sum subsidy or tax.

Macroeconomics

BARRON'S ESSENTIAL 5

As you work toward achieving that 5 on your AP Macroeconomics exam, here are five essentials that you **MUST** know above everything else:

Understand the aggregate supply/aggregate demand model. This concept is critical for doing well on the exam. It is likely to appear on a free-response question and will be used to answer multiple-choice questions.

- As with any diagram, be able to label all axes and curves.

- You should know what can shift the aggregate supply and aggregate demand curves.

- You should be able to use the model to conclude what will happen in the long run and in the short run when one or both of the curves shifts.

Vocabulary is important. Very few, if any, of the questions on the AP exam will ask you to define a specific term, but you need to know the definition of technical ones.

- For instance, a multiple-choice question may ask about closing an inflationary gap. You will be at a total loss if the term "inflationary gap" is not in your vocabulary.

- Be sure you know the terms listed at the end of each chapter.

Monetary and fiscal policy are critical concepts. One of the most important things a student learns in introductory macroeconomics is that monetary and fiscal policy can be used to help fight unemployment and inflation.

- Be able to demonstrate how monetary and fiscal policy work on an aggregate supply/aggregate demand diagram.

- There are several reasons why monetary and fiscal policy may not work. You should be able to list and explain these reasons.

- Monetary and fiscal policy are not as effective in economies that rely heavily on international trade. You should be able to explain why.

Diagrams are more important than formulas. Important formulas are listed at the end of each chapter.

- Easy formulas, such as Fisher's Hypothesis or the formula for the unemployment rate, are more likely to come into play on the exam.

- Specific diagrams, such as the supply and demand for loanable funds, are often required. Be sure to label all axes and curves. If you forget a label, use something general like "Q" for quantity or "D" for demand.

Be definite in your conclusions to free-response questions. Some questions are complex and have different conclusions in different circumstances. Nevertheless, be definite in your response.

- If you use the wrong approach on a free-response question but your conclusion is correct, you will still earn points. State your conclusion clearly.

- You can earn points on a free-response question just for having the appropriate graph correctly labeled. To obtain full credit, explain what is happening on the graph and reach the correct conclusion.

12

The National Economic Accounts

Learning Objectives

In this chapter, you will learn:

- → The accounts
- → Gross domestic product
- → The expenditure approach
- → The income approach
- → The value-added approach
- → Real GDP
- → The underground economy
- → Per capita GDP
- → Limitations of GDP

The Accounts

The National Economic Accounts (NEA) make up a comprehensive group of statistics that measure various aspects of the economy's performance. For instance, if everyone's income in the United States was summed together, how much would that be? The figure for personal income in 2021 was $21,077.2 billion. What were corporate profits in 2021? $2,805.8 billion. Personal income and corporate profits are two examples of the hundreds of statistics included in the NEA.

The NEA include a variety of measures of income and production. The most recent updates on these figures are published by the Department of Commerce in a periodical titled the "Survey of Current Business." On the Internet, updates are available at *www.bea.gov*, the home page of the Bureau of Economic Analysis (BEA), an agency within the Department of Commerce.

Gross Domestic Product

The premier statistic for measuring the overall performance of the economy is gross domestic product (GDP). GDP measures the dollar value of production within the nation's borders. Generally speaking, the more that is produced, the healthier the economy.

The BEA provides "flash" estimates of GDP for each quarter about 30 days after the quarter ends, but these rough estimates are subject to large revisions. The annual estimates of GDP are more reliable, but they, too, are subject to revision.

An amazing feature of these estimates is that they are available on such a timely basis. Consider all of the goods and services produced in the United States in a year, from toothpicks and airplanes to haircuts and surgery. How does the BEA keep track of all this production? For 2021, GDP was estimated to be $23.0 trillion.

How did the BEA arrive at this figure? A small army of statisticians and analysts keeps track of production and sales of a wide variety of goods and services. For instance, one person is responsible for Popsicle sticks, toothpicks, and tongue depressors. This person gets in touch with the major suppliers and retailers of these products. From this survey an estimate of the number of toothpicks sold is obtained. There is a difference between the number of toothpicks sold and the number produced, but this difference will be accounted for later.

The survey of manufacturers and retailers also yields an average price of toothpicks. Then the number of toothpicks sold is multiplied by their price to get the dollar value of toothpick sales.

The dollar values of all other products sold are added to the figure for toothpicks to obtain an estimate of total sales of goods and services. The resulting figure is known as "final sales" and is part of the NEA. But it is not GDP. GDP measures *production*, not sales. There may be goods that are produced but not sold. They will show up in inventories at the manufacturers or at the retailers. Therefore, the change in business inventories is added to final sales to arrive at GDP.

Table 12.1 shows the calculation of GDP for a hypothetical economy that produces only two products—pizza and soda. In the year 2019, four pizzas are produced at an average retail price of $10; 12 sodas are produced at a price of $2. GDP is $64. In the year 2020, pizza production is up to five pizzas and the price has increased to $11. Soda production is up to 15 units, but the price has fallen to $1. GDP is $70.

Table 12.1 Calculating GDP

Year 2019		
Production	**Price**	**Value**
4 Pizzas	$10	$40
12 Sodas	$2	$24
		GDP = $64
Year 2020		
Production	**Price**	**Value**
5 Pizzas	$11	$55
15 Sodas	$1	$15
		GDP = $70

This is a general overview of how GDP is estimated. In practice, many more complications arise. Some of these complications will come to light as we examine the expenditure and the income approaches to calculating GDP.

The Expenditure Approach

Consumption Expenditures

If you look up the estimates of GDP online, don't expect to see the dollar value of toothpicks sold or produced. That level of detail would require a publication much thicker than the *Oxford English Dictionary*. Instead, the BEA lumps together all the goods and services sold to households and calls this consumption expenditures.

Government Expenditures

However, state, local, and federal governments also make expenditures. The things that are produced and sold to governments are summed together and referred to as government expenditures. Some of the products that governments buy are unique to this category. For instance, fighter jets are sold to our federal government but not to individual households. On the other hand, our government purchases many of the same items bought by households, such as personal computers; but the price and quantity of personal computers purchased by the government will be different than that of households.

Investment Expenditures

Expenditures by businesses on plant and equipment are called investment expenditures; thus, the term "investment" means something very different in its economic sense. It does not refer to households buying stocks or bonds. The complete definition of investment is business expenditures on plant and equipment plus residential construction plus the change in business inventories. The change in business inventories was mentioned in the previous section. It changes the figure for final sales into GDP. The BEA lumps the change in inventories in with business spending on plant and equipment and residential construction to get what it calls investment.

Exports and Imports

Many goods and services are produced here and sold abroad. These are called exports. Some of the expenditures made by households, government, and businesses will be on goods and services from abroad. These imports should not be included in our GDP since they represent production outside our nation's borders. That is why imports are subtracted from exports to get "net exports."

GDP represents production. Some of the goods and services produced go to households, some go to government, some go to businesses, and some are sold abroad. Imports are subtracted out because these products were not made domestically, yet they are counted in consumption expenditures by households, purchases by government, and investment by firms.

The expenditure approach to calculating GDP is often summarized with the formula:

$$GDP = C + I + G + X$$

where C is consumption expenditures by households

I is investment by firms

G is government purchases

X is net exports = exports − imports

The formula appears deceptively simple. Remember that to obtain the figure for C, consumption expenditures, quite a bit of effort is required. The average price and quantity sold of millions of products must be gathered. The same must be done for I, G, and X.

Table 12.2 shows the components of the expenditure approach to calculating GDP with their values for 2021. Notice that about 70 percent of all the goods and services produced go to households.

Table 12.2 The Expenditure Approach to GDP—2021

	(Billions of Dollars)
Consumption expenditures	15,741.6
Government expenditures	4,052.7
Investment	4,120.0
Net exports	− 918.2
GDP	22,996.1

Source: U.S. Department of Commerce, Bureau of Economic Analysis

The Income Approach

The BEA takes the trouble to calculate GDP in a manner completely different from the expenditure approach outlined above. This second way of calculating GDP is known as the income approach. The income approach yields several statistics that are incorporated into the NEA and provides a check on the expenditure approach.

Theoretically, both techniques for calculating GDP will result in exactly the same figure because when anything is produced, whether it is a stick of gum or a skyscraper, just enough income is generated in the production process to equal the value of what is produced.

Consider a toaster that retails for $15. Suppose it costs $10 to manufacture:

Labor	$6
Materials	$3
Overhead	$1

Since the toaster retails for $15, then $5 in profits were made when it was sold. So, if everyone who had anything to do with the manufacture of the toaster chipped in the income they made, it would equal $15 exactly. Workers made $6; raw material owners made $3; the utility company (overhead) made $1; and the owner of the toaster company made $5. Altogether, this comes to $15.

Notice that if the toaster sold for $15.01, then $5.01 in profits would have been earned and the principle would still hold true: whenever anything is produced, just enough is earned to buy it back. Therefore, an alternate way to measure GDP, which measures production, would be to add up all the income that was earned in the economy. That is the income approach to calculating GDP.

Table 12.3 outlines the income approach for calculating GDP. Wages and salaries are the predominant type of income. But there is also proprietors' income, rental income, and interest income. Corporate profits must also be included because this represents corporate income and corporations are owned by their shareholders. There are some adjustments that must be made once all the types of income are summed together. Specifically, indirect business taxes (such as business licenses) and depreciation must be added in.

Table 12.3 The Income Approach to GDP—2021

	(Billions of Dollars)
Compensation of employees	12,598.7
Proprietors' income	1,821.9
Rental income	726.5
Interest income	1,640.7
Corporate profits	2,805.8
Depreciation	3,847.9
Miscellaneous items	3,402.5
GDP	22,996.1

Source: U.S. Department of Commerce, Bureau of Economic Analysis

The Value-Added Approach

There is a third approach to calculating GDP, the value-added method, that is similar to the income approach. Instead of considering who earned income during the production process, the value-added approach considers how much of the final retail price of the product was added by each producer or industry.

Returning to the toaster example, suppose one factory obtained the raw materials and refined them by getting them ready for assembly. That factory then ships the refined parts to another firm. The second factory assembles the toaster and markets it.

The first factory started with nothing, brought together the raw materials, and refined them. It sold the refined toaster parts to the second factory for $7. So the first factory created $7 worth of value.

The second factory finished the production process and then marketed and sold the toaster for $15. The second factory added $8 of value. GDP is calculated by adding up the value of the toaster at each stage of the production process: $0 + $7 + $8 = $15.

As with the expenditures and income approaches, there are many complications to calculating GDP via the value-added method. The U.S. Bureau of Economic Analysis does not use the value-added approach, only the expenditure and income approaches. However, many nations use the value-added method not only to estimate GDP but also to tax producers at each stage of the production process.

Real GDP

GDP measures production, but one cannot conclude that more was produced simply because this year's GDP was greater than last year's because prices may have risen. The rise in prices could offset a decline in production volume, resulting in a higher figure for GDP. Clearly, if the prices of the goods and services produced changes, so will GDP, regardless of production.

There is, however, a simple way to correct for price changes: When calculating GDP for different years, use prices from just one of those years. This way the prices are constant from one year to the next and any change in GDP must be due to a change in production.

The BEA routinely makes this correction, and the resulting figure is known as "real GDP" or "constant-dollar GDP." In order to make the distinction, regular GDP is sometimes referred to as "nominal" or "current-dollar GDP." The year from which prices are taken to calculate real GDP is called the base year. It does not matter which year is chosen as the base year. The important feature is that prices are held constant so that any changes in real GDP are the result of changes in the amount of production.

Table 12.4 shows how to calculate real GDP using the information from Table 12.1. The base year is 2019.

> **TIP**
>
> Any economic statistic with the term "real" inserted in front of it means that the statistic has been adjusted for inflation, i.e., real interest rate, real consumer spending.

Table 12.4 Calculating Real GDP

Year 2019		
Production	**Price**	**Value**
4 Pizzas	$10	$40
12 Sodas	$2	$24
		Nominal GDP = $64

Production	**Base Year Price**	**Value**
4 Pizzas	$10	$40
12 Sodas	$2	$24
		Real GDP = $64

Year 2020		
Production	**Price**	**Value**
5 Pizzas	$11	$55
15 Sodas	$1	$15
		Nominal GDP = $70

Production	**Base Year Price**	**Value**
5 Pizzas	$10	$50
15 Sodas	$2	$30
		Real GDP = $80

In 2019, real and nominal GDP are equal since the base year is 2019. In 2020, real GDP is calculated using 2020 production levels and 2019 prices. Since real GDP increased from 2019 to 2020, production must have increased since prices were held constant at their base year values.

Table 12.5 shows nominal and real GDP over the years. An astute reader could deduce that 2012 is the base year since real and nominal GDP are equivalent in that year. Once nominal and real GDP have been calculated, it is a simple matter to obtain a measure of price changes. But this statistic will be discussed in the next chapter when inflation and price indexes are taken up.

Table 12.5 Nominal and Real GDP

Year	Nominal GDP (billions of $)	Real GDP (billions of chained 2012 $)
2012	16,254.0	16,254.0
2013	16,843.2	16,553.3
2014	17,550.7	16,932.1
2015	18,206.2	17,390.3
2016	18,659.1	17,680.3
2017	19,479.6	18,079.1
2018	20,527.2	18,606.8
2019	21,372.6	19,032.7
2020	20,893.7	18,384.7
2021	22,996.1	19,427.3

Source: U.S. Department of Commerce, Bureau of Economic Analysis

The Underground Economy

Each year there are trillions of dollars of goods and services that are produced and never counted in GDP. All of this production falls into what is called the underground economy. The first thing that comes to mind with regard to the underground economy is illegal items and activities, but illegal production and ill-gotten income are the smaller part of the underground economy.

Marry your auto mechanic, the saying goes, and you will lower GDP. This is true because when you took your car to the shop to be repaired, the BEA was able to estimate the transaction and include it in GDP under household consumption. Now that the mechanic is your spouse, the auto repairs are done out back under the shade tree. The BEA does not attempt to measure this sort of production.

Anything households do for themselves and that does not pass through a market goes unmeasured. This amounts to quite a bit of production—the backyard gardens, the lawn maintenance, the cleaning, the babysitting, etc. One estimate of underground household production puts it at 30 percent of official GDP.

Illegal gambling services, prostitution, and drugs are not counted in official GDP estimates. The house painter who insists on being paid in cash to avoid taxes is part of the underground economy.

By adding together the legal and illegal sides of the underground economy, some analysts get a figure that is 150 percent of the official figure. That implies that production in the United States in 2019 was closer to $32.0 trillion than the official figure of $21.4 trillion.

Other Things Not Counted in GDP

The underground economy is a subset of total production that is not counted in GDP but, technically speaking, should be. The illegal nature of the goods and services involved often prohibits estimation. However, there is a list of things that are not counted in GDP and rightly so.

1. For instance, it would be incorrect to count **secondhand sales** in GDP. When you sell your 1997 Ford truck, this does not represent production in the current year. The truck was counted in the GDP of 1997, and there is no reason to count it, or any portion of it, again simply because it is being resold.
2. **Transactions that are purely financial** are not, and should not be, counted in GDP. If you buy 100 shares of IBM stock, this does not directly represent any new production. Someone got your money, and you got their shares of IBM. This swap does not affect GDP except for any brokerage services provided.

3. **Intermediate sales** are not included in GDP. These are sales to firms that will incorporate the item into their final product. An example will help here. When a corporation that makes Popsicles buys Popsicle sticks, this is an intermediate sale. When a person buys a Popsicle, he cannot avoid buying the stick as well. This latter transaction is counted in GDP and valued at the price of the Popsicle and the stick. So the stick would be counted twice if the purchase of sticks by the manufacturer was included in GDP and the final sale to the consumer was also counted.

As another example of an intermediate transaction, the purchase of flour by a baker is not counted in GDP because the flour will get counted when the bread is purchased by a household. However, when a baker buys a delivery truck, this is not an intermediate transaction, and the purchase gets counted in GDP under investment expenditures.

Per Capita GDP

Japan is an amazing country in many ways. Japan produces about 145 times as much as Montana each year, yet both are about the same size. Of course, the population of Japan is about 128 times that of Montana. In order to compare which has a higher standard of material well-being, divide the production of each by its population:

Japan: per capita GDP = GDP/Population = $5.4 trillion/126.5 million = $42,700
Montana: per capita GDP = GDP/Population = $46.2 billion/1.1 million = $42,000

Japan and Montana have about the same standard of living since their per capita GDPs are about equal. Table 12.6 shows that living standards are disparate across the globe.

Table 12.6 GDP and GDP per Capita for Selected Countries 2019

Country	GDP	Per Capita
China	$22.5 trillion	$22.5 trillion/1.4 billion = $16,000
Japan	$5.2 trillion	$5.2 trillion/125.4 million = $41,600
Sierra Leone	$13.4 billion	$13.4 billion/8.3 million = $1,600
Sweden	$548 billion	$548 billion/10.4 million = $52,700
USA	$20.5 trillion	$20.5 trillion/332.0 million = $61,700

Source: United Nations

Limitations of GDP

Two countries could have the same per capita GDP, but one of the nations could be more congested with people and traffic, more crime ridden, less safe from foreign invasion, more stressed socially, and more unequal in terms of rich and poor. GDP does not account for any of these factors.

The limitations of GDP as a measure of the quality of life are well documented. If one nation's GDP is greater than another's, it simply means more is being produced. The things being produced may all be going to a few select families. Or the high-production nation could be working longer hours on average with little or no vacation time. In short, greater production does not necessarily imply better living conditions.

New statistics that account for at least some of these factors have been developed. There is the Genuine Progress Indicator that combines 26 statistical indicators including GDP. And there are "happiness" indexes that survey a nation's population to determine average satisfaction with life. But none of these more complete statistics has come close to surpassing GDP as the premier way to measure living standards.

SUMMARY

- The NEA are a bank of internally consistent statistics that measure various aspects of the economy's performance. Basically, the NEA measure production and income in their various forms. An implicit assumption behind the statistics is that more production and more income means a better economy.

- Some economists have questioned this assumption. Are we really better off when we produce more gadgets and gizmos, and pollute the environment in the process? Is it possible for more to be produced and more income to be earned while the quality of life deteriorates? Another criticism of the NEA concerns leisure time. Don't rising production levels sometimes result in less leisure time? If so, this is not reflected in the statistics where the negative side effects of increased production levels are not taken into account.

- Despite these criticisms, the NEA are the best measures available for gauging the economy's health. GDP measures production. However, whenever anything is produced, an equivalent amount of income is generated, to the penny. Thus, GDP also measures earned income.

There are three approaches to estimating GDP: 1) the expenditure approach, 2) the income approach, and 3) the value-added approach. The U.S. Bureau of Economic Analysis calculates GDP with the expenditure approach and the income approach.

Real GDP is GDP adjusted for price changes. If real GDP increases from one period to the next, then production must have increased since prices were kept constant at their base period level.

Formulas

$$GDP = C + I + G + X$$

$$GDP \text{ per Capita} = \frac{GDP}{Population}$$

Multiple-Choice Review Questions

1. Which of the following is counted in U.S. GDP?

   (A) Final goods and services purchased by the government
   (B) Both the peaches used by a bakery to make peach pies and the peach pies
   (C) Museum purchases of ancient art
   (D) Imported goods and services
   (E) Sales of antiques

2. Which of the following is counted in GDP?

   (A) The estimated value of housework
   (B) The value of illegally produced goods and services
   (C) The value of stocks, bonds, and other financial assets
   (D) The change in business inventories
   (E) Secondhand sales

3. According to the way in which economists use the word, the bulk of "investment" is done by

   (A) households.
   (B) businesses.
   (C) government.
   (D) foreigners.
   (E) all of the above.

4. In the equation GDP = C + I + G + X, X stands for

   (A) exports.
   (B) expenditures.
   (C) exports minus imports.
   (D) imports minus exports.
   (E) export taxes.

5. GDP measures

   (A) production within a nation's borders.
   (B) production by a nation's citizens wherever they may be.
   (C) total income earned producing goods and services.
   (D) (B) and (C)
   (E) (A) and (C)

6. Suppose a nation produces only two goods: pizza and soda. In 2018, 20 pizzas are sold at $10 each and 10 sodas are sold at $1 each. In 2016, the base year, 10 pizzas were sold at $8 each and 10 sodas were sold at $1 each. Therefore, nominal GDP in 2018 is _____ and real GDP in 2018 is _____.

   (A) $30; $20
   (B) $170; $90
   (C) $210; $100
   (D) $110; $90
   (E) $210; $170

7. Imagine an economy that produces only two goods: cheese and crackers. Calculate GDP for this economy if cheese retails for $3 a pound and 10 pounds are produced while crackers sell for $2 a pound and 20 pounds are produced.

   (A) $35
   (B) $70
   (C) $150
   (D) $1,200
   (E) Not enough information is given to calculate GDP.

8. Suppose a nation produces only two goods: pizza and soda. In 2018, 20 pizzas are sold at $10 each and 10 sodas are sold at $1 each. In 2016, the base year, 10 pizzas were sold at $8 each and 10 sodas were sold at $1 each. Therefore, real GDP in 2016 is _____.

   (A) $90
   (B) $110
   (C) $170
   (D) $210
   (E) $330

9. Your grandparents buy the vacation house they used to rent every year.

   (A) GDP decreases by the amount of the purchase because C decreases.
   (B) GDP increases by the amount of the purchase because I increases.
   (C) GDP is unaffected because it is a secondhand sale.
   (D) GDP decreases because I decreases.
   (E) I increases, but C decreases.

10. The cabbages you grow in your summer garden are

    (A) counted in GDP under C.
    (B) counted in GDP under I.
    (C) counted in GDP but not NDP.
    (D) not counted in GDP.
    (E) counted in final sales but not GDP.

11. If your grandparents have a new home built for their retirement, this would primarily affect

    (A) consumption.
    (B) government purchases.
    (C) investment.
    (D) exports.
    (E) imports.

12. If a U.S. citizen buys a television made in Korea by a Korean firm, then this action by itself ____ U.S. net exports and ____ Korean net exports.

    (A) increases; does not affect
    (B) increases; decreases
    (C) increases; increases
    (D) decreases; decreases
    (E) decreases; increases

13. Given:

Government expenditures	$300
Depreciation	$200
Investment	$400
Consumption expenditures	$900
Taxes	$100
Corporate profits	$500
Exports	$200
Imports	$300

    GDP equals _____.

    (A) $1,500
    (B) $1,700
    (C) $1,800
    (D) $2,100
    (E) $2,900

14. Which of the following events has no effect on GDP?

    (A) You buy a 1957 Chevy from a friend.
    (B) The Department of Transportation repaves a road.
    (C) Your friends make a music CD that doesn't sell any copies.
    (D) A college buys computers.
    (E) You buy a bottle of French wine.

15. Which of the following will have an effect on GDP?

    (A) You lose $50 betting with a friend.
    (B) You fix your brother's car without buying any new parts.
    (C) Your father's firm makes computers and exports them to China.
    (D) You buy 1,000 shares of stock in a corporation.
    (E) Your wealthy uncle buys a painting by Picasso.

Free-Response Review Questions

1. Explain the difference between nominal GDP, real GDP, and GDP per capita.

2. Suppose that production and prices rise from one year to the next but population stays constant. Will each of the three statistics above rise, fall, or remain unchanged? Explain your reasoning.

3. In what type of situation is GDP per capita more appropriate than nominal or real GDP?

4. Is GDP an overestimate or an underestimate of all that is produced in a nation? Explain.

Answer Explanations

1. **(A)** Final purchases by federal, state, and local governments are the "G" in GDP $= C + I + G + X$.

2. **(D)** The change in business inventories is included in investment, the "I" in GDP $= C + I + G + X$.

3. **(B)** Investment includes spending on residential structures and the change in business inventories. However, the biggest part of investment is business purchases of plant and equipment.

4. **(C)** X stands for net exports, which are exports minus imports.

5. **(E)** GDP measures total production within the nation's borders. However, whenever anything is produced, an equivalent amount of income is earned by the people involved in the production process. Therefore, GDP also measures total income earned.

6. **(E)** The information in the question is captured in the following table:

Year	Price of Pizza	Quantity of Pizza	Price of Soda	Quantity of Soda
2016	$8	10	$1	10
2018	$10	20	$1	10

Nominal GDP in 2018 $= \$10 \times 20 + \$1 \times 10 = \$210$

Real GDP in 2018 $= \$8 \times 20 + \$1 \times 10 = \$170$

Nominal GDP in 2018 is price times quantity for each good in 2018 added together. Real GDP is calculated in the same manner except the prices are from the base year.

7. **(B)** The information in the question is captured in the following table:

Price of Cheese	Quantity of Cheese	Price of Crackers	Quantity of Crackers
$3	10	$2	20

Nominal GDP $= \$3 \times 10 + \$2 \times 20 = \$70$

8. **(A)** The information in the question is captured in the following table:

Year	Price of Pizza	Quantity of Pizza	Price of Soda	Quantity of Soda
2016	$8	10	$1	10
2018	$10	20	$1	10

Real GDP in 2016 = $8 × 10 + $1 × 10 = $90

The base year is 2016, so real and nominal GDP are equal.

9. **(C)** This is a secondhand sale, and those are not counted in GDP.

10. **(D)** The cabbages are not counted in GDP because they were not sold in a market.

11. **(C)** New residential construction is included in investment even if the home is built by a household.

12. **(E)** The television is an import for the U.S. and decreases U.S. net exports = exports − imports. The television is an export to Korea, and Korean exports increase.

13. **(A)** GDP = C + I + G + X. From the table, C = $900; I = $400; G = $300; X = $200 − $300. Putting all this together: GDP = $900 + $400 + $300 + $200 − $300 = $1,500.

14. **(A)** Your purchase of the Chevy is a secondhand sale. All the other responses fit into a component of GDP.

15. **(C)** Exports are included in GDP. None of the other responses reflect activities included in GDP.

Free-Response Review Answers

1. Nominal GDP measures the production of goods and services within a nation's borders. Nominal GDP could increase because of an increase in output or an increase in the prices of the goods and services produced. Real GDP measures production but adjusts for any price changes. Real GDP does not change if prices change because it values current output in terms of prices of the given base period. Only one thing can cause real GDP to change, and that is a change in output. GDP per capita is production per person.

2. If production and prices rise while population stays constant, then all three statistics—GDP, real GDP, and GDP per capita—will rise. GDP rises if production or prices rise. Real GDP rises if production rises. Per capita GDP rises if GDP rises and population does not.

3. GDP per capita is most appropriate for making international comparisons of GDP. The GDP of the United States is much greater than that of Switzerland, but production per person, and therefore living standards, are not all that different between the two nations.

4. GDP is a vast underestimate of output because of all the production that is not counted. Items that do not go through standard markets are not counted. This includes illegal drugs and gambling but also home car repair and household vegetable gardens. All of this uncounted production is known as the underground economy. Estimates are that the underground economy could be half the size of the official economy.

13

Inflation and Unemployment

Learning Objectives

In this chapter, you will learn:

→ The twin evils
→ Inflation
→ Unemployment

The Twin Evils

Both *inflation* and *unemployment* exert an enormous toll on the economy and, therefore, on the standard of living. The cost of unemployment is obvious: an important resource, labor, is being underutilized. This implies that we are not producing as much as if we were using our resources fully. In economic terms, we are producing inside the production possibilities frontier. Moreover, the households that are experiencing unemployment face real hardships.

The costs associated with inflation are less obvious. Many people understand that rising prices can hurt families on fixed incomes, but this is only a minor issue because most incomes keep pace with rising prices. When prices rise, someone benefits—the owners of the firms that produce the goods and services whose prices are rising. In general, rising prices imply rising incomes, so falling real incomes are not a major cost of inflation.

We will see that a more significant cost associated with inflation is the inefficiencies that ensue when people respond to rising prices. Again, a nation will be producing at a point inside the production possibilities frontier if it does not use its resources efficiently.

In addition, inflation arbitrarily takes purchasing power from some households and puts it in the hands of others. A massive redistribution of wealth is yet another cost of inflation.

The costs to society of rising prices are much more subtle than the blunt and obvious damages caused by unemployment. Nevertheless, it is unclear which economic evil is more pernicious. Only normative conclusions are possible on this question.

Inflation

The Consumer Price Index

Inflation is a sustained increase in most prices in the economy. The inflation rate is the rate at which prices are rising. Disinflation is when the inflation rate is decreasing. So prices are still rising, only not as briskly. Deflation is when prices are falling.

Each month the Bureau of Labor Statistics (BLS) checks prices on 90,000 items at more than 23,000 retail and service outlets. The BLS checks prices only in urban areas. Because prices are liable to be different in different regions, the BLS checks prices on the same items in twenty metropolitan areas.

The result of all this effort is the predominant measure of the cost of living in the United States—the consumer price index (CPI). The CPI measures the average change over time in the prices paid by urban consumers for a market basket of consumer goods and services. The BLS computes the CPI for each month.

Consider a simple example where the typical household in the economy consumes 5 packages of cheese and 8 boxes of crackers in a month. If the price of cheese rises to $2.25 from $2.00 and the price of crackers climbs to $1.50 from $1.25, then the CPI rises to 116.25 from 100. The calculations are shown in Table 13.1. The assumption is that period 1 is the base period, the period to which all other periods are compared.

Table 13.1 Calculating the Consumer Price Index

Period 1			
Item	Price	Amount	Cost
Cheese	$2.00	5	$10.00
Crackers	$1.25	8	$10.00

Total cost = $20.00

$$\text{CPI} = \frac{\text{Total Cost This Period}}{\text{Total Cost Base Period}} \times 100 = \frac{20.00}{20.00} \times 100 = 100$$

Period 2			
Item	Price	Amount	Cost
Cheese	$2.25	5	$11.25
Crackers	$1.50	8	$12.00

Total cost = $23.25

$$\text{CPI} = \frac{\text{Total Cost This Period}}{\text{Total Cost Base Period}} \times 100 = \frac{23.25}{20.00} \times 100 = 116.25$$

Period 3			
Item	Price	Amount	Cost
Cheese	$2.35	5	$11.75
Crackers	$1.60	8	$12.80

Total cost = $24.55

$$\text{CPI} = \frac{\text{Total Cost This Period}}{\text{Total Cost Base Period}} \times 100 = \frac{24.55}{20.00} \times 100 = 122.75$$

In period 3, the CPI rises to 122.75. To calculate the inflation rate between any two periods, take the percentage change in the CPI. For example, the inflation rate between periods 2 and 3 is:

$$\text{Inflation Rate} = (122.75 - 116.25)/116.25 = 0.0559 = 5.59\%$$

The inflation rate between periods 1 and 3 is:

$$\text{Inflation Rate} = (122.75 - 100.00)/100.00 = 0.2275 = 22.75\%$$

These calculations indicate that the cost of living for a typical family in this economy increased 5.59 percent between periods 1 and 2 and 22.75 percent between periods 1 and 3.

In the real world, many complications arise when calculating the CPI that are not apparent in this simple example. For instance, what should be done when the quality of a product changes? The price of automobiles has risen dramatically since the 1950s but so has the quality of the product. A new car these days comes with seat belts and air bags—safety devices that were not available in earlier versions of the product. Quality improvements such as this account for some portion of the price increase. The CPI overstates the amount of inflation since it does not account for all quality improvements.

This is just one example of how the CPI can overstate cost of living increases. A 1996 study from a bipartisan commission concluded that the CPI overstates inflation by more than one percentage point a year. The discrepancy is important because most income maintenance programs, such as Social Security, adjust their benefit payments with the CPI.

The GDP Deflator

Inflation can be measured with another statistic—the GDP deflator. In the previous chapter we discussed how GDP and real GDP are calculated. Both of these statistics can be used to obtain the GDP deflator through a simple formula:

$$\text{GDP Deflator} = (\text{GDP}/\text{Real GDP}) \times 100$$

In 2021 GDP was $22,996.1 billion, while real GDP equaled $19,427.3 billion. Therefore, the GDP deflator for 2021 was 118.4 (= (22,996.1/19,427.3) × 100). Table 13.2 shows GDP, real GDP, and the GDP deflator over the years.

To calculate the inflation rate between any two years, simply take the percentage change in the GDP deflator. By what percent did prices rise from 2012 to 2021? 12.4 percent (= (112.4 − 100.0)/100.0). In other words, there was 12.4 percent inflation between 2012 and 2021.

Table 13.2 GDP, Real GDP, and the GDP Deflator

$\text{GDP Deflator} = \dfrac{\text{Nominal GDP}}{\text{Real GDP}} \times 100$		$\text{Real GDP} = \dfrac{\text{Nominal GDP}}{\text{GDP Deflator}} \times 100$

Year	Nominal GDP (billions of $)	Real GDP (billions of chained 2012 $)	GDP Deflator
2012	16,254.0	16,254.0	100.0
2013	16,843.2	16,553.3	101.8
2014	17,550.7	16,932.1	103.7
2015	18,206.2	17,390.3	104.7
2016	18,659.1	17,680.3	105.5
2017	19,479.6	18,079.1	107.7
2018	20,527.2	18,606.8	110.3
2019	21,372.6	19,032.7	112.3
2020	20,893.7	18,384.7	113.6
2021	22,996.1	19,427.3	118.4

Source: U.S. Department of Commerce, Bureau of Economic Analysis

The GDP deflator, like the CPI, measures the level of prices in the economy. The inflation rates derived from the GDP deflator, however, do not match the inflation rates obtained from the CPI. Both inflation gauges suggest the same general pattern of inflation over the years.

The GDP deflator ignores import prices. If the price of imported cars increases, the CPI would rise in response but not the GDP deflator. However, the CPI ignores price changes for nonconsumer items. If the price of army helmets increases, the GDP deflator will increase but not the CPI. Still, for most years the CPI and the GDP deflator do not differ markedly.

In some instances we may have data on the GDP deflator and GDP; then we can calculate real GDP with the following formula:

$$\text{Real GDP} = (\text{GDP/GDP Deflator}) \times 100$$

In 2021 GDP was $22,996.1 billion and the GDP deflator equaled 118.4. Therefore, real GDP was $19,427.3 billion ($= (22,996.1/118.4) \times 100$).

The Costs of Inflation

Many people think that the most damaging aspect of inflation is that it erodes purchasing power. It is true that any household whose income does not keep pace with inflation will be hurt. But for the vast majority of households, incomes keep pace with, if not exceed, price increases.

To understand why, consider the circular flow diagram presented earlier in the text. If the prices paid for goods and services produced by firms increases, firms take in more revenue. If this revenue is not passed back to households in the form of higher wages, the firms make more profits. But someone owns the firms and the profits become their income. More specifically, the profits are returned to households in the form of dividends. So higher prices always translate into higher levels of income.

1. Inflation can be detrimental even if a household's income rises as fast as prices. This is because the value of savings accounts, trust funds, and other forms of financial wealth will be worth less than before the inflation. In other words, inflation erodes the purchasing power of savings. Savings play an important role in the economy. Households, businesses, and governments often need to borrow funds. Inflation discourages savings.

2. Another problem with inflation is the resources that are wasted dealing with higher prices. Firms have to print new brochures, restaurants need to produce new menus, and price lists in all the media will have to be revised. This takes time and effort. Resources that could have been used more productively are deployed to cope with rising prices. The misallocation of resources because of inflation is sometimes called "menu costs."

3. A final issue associated with inflation has to do with borrowing and lending in inflationary conditions. Lenders can be hurt by inflation because the dollars they loaned out are repaid at a later date with dollars that are not worth as much because of inflation. Imagine lending a friend $100 for a year at 10 percent interest. A year later the friend repays you $110. But suppose prices had risen 12 percent over the course of the loan. Your $110 could not even buy what your $100 could a year ago.

By the same token, borrowers could benefit from inflation because they get to repay their borrowings with inflated dollars. Why don't banks get hurt by inflation? Aren't they big lenders? They are, but they are also smart enough to add an inflation surcharge onto the interest rate that they charge. When a bank lends $100 to your friend it might charge 12 percent—10 percent for the real return and 2 percent to cover the cost of inflation that the bank expects over the course of the loan.

The idea that some lenders would protect themselves from inflation by charging higher interest on loans was codified into a formula by Irving Fisher in the early 1900s; the formula is known as "Fisher's Hypothesis":

$$\text{Nominal Interest Rate} = \text{Real Interest Rate} + \text{Expected Inflation}$$

The nominal interest rate is the rate actually paid. The real interest rate is the actual return the lender receives net of inflation.

The end result is that lenders who do not anticipate inflation will be hurt, but the borrower would benefit in this case. The biggest lender in the economy is households if you consider putting money in a bank account a loan to the bank. Notice that the nominal interest rate paid by banks on savings accounts is not adjusted upward for expected inflation. Households are big lenders who do not anticipate inflation; therefore, they will be hurt by rising prices.

TIP

Inflation can be measured with a variety of statistics. The most common measures of inflation are the percentage change in the consumer price index and the percentage change in the GDP deflator.

The federal government is the biggest borrower in the United States' economy. It stands to benefit from inflation because it can repay its borrowings with inflated dollars.

If you think about it, inflation works just like a tax, because households are major lenders and the government is a major borrower. It is as if Uncle Sam reaches into your wallet every night while you sleep and slips out just a little cash so that you don't even notice. The inflation tax is the result of the federal government benefiting from inflation while households are harmed. This redistribution of wealth from lenders to borrowers is yet another cost of inflation.

The costs of inflation are summarized in Table 13.3.

Table 13.3 The Costs of Inflation

- Financial wealth is eroded
- Savings are discouraged
- Menu costs—resources are misallocated with rising prices
- Inflation tax—wealth is redistributed from lenders to borrowers

Unemployment

The Types of Unemployment

The costs associated with unemployment are obvious. Households will encounter hardships, maybe even hunger. Unemployment means that a resource, labor, is not being used to its fullest potential. We are producing inside the production possibilities frontier. We could be producing more and enjoying more goods and services.

Unemployment is a problem during recessions—periods when real GDP is declining. During a recession, fewer goods and services are being produced. The amount of labor and other resources required for production is reduced, and people find themselves out of work.

The unemployment rate is defined as the number of unemployed persons divided by the labor force. The labor force does not include retired persons, those too young to work, and anyone who has not been actively seeking employment. In order to be counted as unemployed, you have to be out of work and looking for a job.

The Bureau of Labor Statistics (BLS) reports the unemployment statistics based on two broad surveys taken each month. One survey contacts employers and asks about employment levels at various business establishments, while the other survey interviews households.

Economists classify the unemployed into five general categories:

1. Those who are able to work, but not actively seeking employment because they are discouraged about their prospects for finding employment, are referred to as *discouraged workers* or the *hidden unemployed*. This situation is unfortunate because these people lack basic skills or suffer from other problems and have a difficult time finding work. Discouraged by their prospects, they no longer bother to pursue employment. These people do not show up in the unemployment statistics because they are not considered to be part of the labor force, thus the name "hidden" unemployment.

2. A form of unemployment that does show up in the official statistics is *structural unemployment*. The structurally unemployed are out of work because the economy is structured, or set up, to their disadvantage. For instance, there may be welders looking for work in Cleveland, but the welding jobs are in Dallas. Or welders may be out of work in Boston, but there are plenty of secretarial jobs open in that same area. Since it is often difficult for a person to relocate or retrain, structural unemployment is not easily remedied.

3. Some persons are able to find work for only a portion of the year due to the seasonal nature of their jobs. These individuals are considered to be *seasonally unemployed* as long as they actively look for work in the off-season. Farmers and construction workers may fall into this category.

4. As mentioned previously, unemployment rises during the contractionary phase of the business cycle. Individuals who lose their jobs during a recession and the corresponding slowdown in production are said to be *cyclically unemployed*. They are out of work specifically because of the business cycle. Hopefully, these people will be back to work when production picks up during the next expansion.

5. Finally, a number of persons are not working because they are between jobs. Someone who is scheduled to begin a new job next month and does not presently hold a job is considered to be *frictionally unemployed*. It is unlikely that people will be able to switch jobs without some time off. Indeed, some people take advantage of this time to relax or move their households and get their affairs in order. Also, someone who quits one job to look for another is considered to be frictionally unemployed. Finally, new entrants into the labor market, such as graduates looking for work or a stay-at-home parent reentering the work force, are considered frictionally unemployed.

TIP

People who are not actively looking for work are not in the labor force and therefore are not counted as unemployed.

In 2021 the labor force was estimated to be 161.2 million persons, while the unemployed numbered 8.6 million. This implies an unemployment rate of 5.3 percent ($= 8.6/161.2$). Some analysts contend that the unemployment picture is actually much worse than this figure indicates. For one, the 5.3 percent does not count hidden unemployment. Remember, those too discouraged to look for work are not counted as being unemployed or even in the labor force. They are simply not counted.

Another factor to consider is that persons who are working part-time are counted as if they are fully employed, even if they would like to have a full-time job. Again, the reported statistic of 5.3 percent understates the unemployment problem.

A related point to keep in mind is that 5.3 percent is the average unemployment rate across the nation. There are sections of the country where the rate is much higher and sections where it is lower. Moreover, it is well-known that the unemployment rate is worse for certain groups within the population, such as teenagers.

Economists consider the economy to be at full employment when the unemployment rate falls into the 4 to 5 percent range since frictional and structural unemployment account for about that much of the unemployment rate. When the unemployment rate falls into the 4 to 5 percent range, there is little or no cyclical unemployment.

A related concept is the natural rate of unemployment. This is the amount of unemployment that exists when the economy is producing on its production possibilities frontier. If there is no cyclical unemployment, then the economy is operating on its production possibilities frontier and at its natural rate of unemployment.

Despite the criticisms of the unemployment statistic, the fact remains that it is tabulated in the same manner each time, so that a drop in the rate means a larger portion of the labor force is working. The unemployment rate is a useful statistic, but care should be taken with its interpretation.

SUMMARY

- Inflation and unemployment are serious economic problems. Inflation causes the misallocation of resources and an arbitrary redistribution of income. Inflation is typically a problem when the economy is overheated—growing faster than normal. But inflation can also occur during recessions. Later we shall see why.

- Unemployment occurs when the economy is operating below its potential. Our most important resource is labor, and unemployment exists when this resource is not being fully utilized. We could have produced more and enjoyed more goods and services if not for the unemployment.

- We have reviewed the major statistics that measure unemployment and inflation and found that they are not perfectly accurate. It is important to understand how the numbers are generated so that their potential deficiencies can be anticipated. For instance, if the price of imported oil is rising rapidly, it is critical to know that the GDP deflator will not reflect this increase. The GDP deflator does not include the prices of imported products. The CPI does.

The most important question concerning inflation and unemployment has been ignored in this chapter: What causes inflation and unemployment? A complete answer is provided in the chapters ahead.

Formulas

$$\text{CPI} = \frac{\text{Total Cost This Period}}{\text{Total Cost Base Period}} \times 100$$

$$\text{Inflation Rate} = \frac{\text{CPI (This Period)} - \text{CPI (Previous Period)}}{\text{CPI (Previous Period)}} \times 100$$

$$\text{GDP Deflator} = (\text{Nominal GDP/Real GDP}) \times 100$$

$$\text{Real GDP} = (\text{Nominal GDP/GDP Deflator}) \times 100$$

$$\text{Nominal Interest Rate} = \text{Real Interest Rate} + \text{Expected Inflation}$$

$$\text{Unemployment Rate} = \text{Number of Unemployed/Civilian Labor Force}$$

Multiple-Choice Review Questions

1. If the price of olives imported into the United States decreases, then the GDP deflator will ____ and the CPI will _____.

   (A) decrease; decrease
   (B) decrease; remain unchanged
   (C) remain unchanged; decrease
   (D) remain unchanged; remain unchanged
   (E) decrease; increase

2. If the CPI goes to 150 from 120, then prices

   (A) increased 20 percent.
   (B) increased 25 percent.
   (C) decreased 30 percent.
   (D) increased 30 percent.
   (E) increased 150 percent.

3. According to experts, the CPI

   (A) overstates increases in the cost of living.
   (B) understates increases in the cost of living.
   (C) accurately estimates changes in the cost of living.
   (D) could over- or underestimate changes depending on the season.
   (E) should be abandoned in favor of the GDP deflator.

4. When products improve in quality the CPI will

   (A) automatically increase.
   (B) automatically decrease.
   (C) become negative.
   (D) overestimate the inflation rate.
   (E) underestimate the inflation rate.

5. If the price of imported industrial robots increases, then the CPI will ___ and the GDP deflator will ___ .

   (A) increase; increase
   (B) not be affected; not be affected
   (C) increase; not be affected
   (D) not be affected; increase
   (E) increase; decrease

6. If nominal GDP equals $5,000 and real GDP equals $4,000, then the GDP deflator equals

   (A) 0.8.
   (B) 1.25.
   (C) 125.
   (D) 300.
   (E) 800.

7. If nominal GDP equals $6,000 and the GDP deflator equals 200, what does real GDP equal?

   (A) $30
   (B) $1,200
   (C) $3,000
   (D) $12,000
   (E) $1,200,000

8. Which of the following is NOT a major cost of inflation?

   (A) Resources will be misallocated.
   (B) Wealth will be redistributed.
   (C) Savings will be discouraged.
   (D) Real incomes will fall.
   (E) Financial wealth will be eroded.

9. The term "menu costs" refers to

   (A) fewer choices due to inflation.
   (B) financial assets being worth less due to inflation.
   (C) "à la carte" savings falling.
   (D) food prices rising due to inflation.
   (E) resource misallocation due to inflation.

10. Given the information in the table, what is the unemployment rate in Ecoville?

Data for Ecoville

total population	6,000
adult population	4,000
unemployed population	200
labor force	2,000

    (A) 5 percent

    (B) 10 percent

    (C) 20 percent

    (D) 30 percent

    (E) 50 percent

11. Rising prices are a problem because

    (A) money in household savings accounts can now buy fewer goods and services.

    (B) household incomes generally do not rise with prices.

    (C) the economy could run out of money.

    (D) borrowers have to repay loans with more dollars.

    (E) households are encouraged to save more.

12. Fisher's Hypothesis states that

    (A) the real interest rate equals the nominal interest rate plus the inflation rate.

    (B) the nominal interest rate equals the real interest rate minus the inflation rate.

    (C) the nominal interest rate equals the unemployment rate plus the real interest rate.

    (D) the nominal interest rate equals the unemployment rate minus the real interest rate.

    (E) the nominal interest rate equals the real interest rate plus the inflation rate.

13. Sue loses her job at a shoe factory when the economy falls into a recession. Sue is

    (A) frictionally unemployed.

    (B) cyclically unemployed.

    (C) seasonally unemployed.

    (D) structurally unemployed.

    (E) a discouraged worker.

14. There is a strong demand for welders in California but Bill, an unemployed welder, lives in New York. Bill is

    (A) frictionally unemployed.

    (B) cyclically unemployed.

    (C) structurally unemployed.

    (D) considered to be a hidden worker.

    (E) not counted in the ranks of the unemployed.

15. It is unlikely that the unemployment rate will ever fall to zero because of

    (A) frictional unemployment.

    (B) cyclical unemployment.

    (C) government policies.

    (D) corporate policies.

    (E) the aged and infirm in our population.

Free-Response Review Questions

Inflation exerts significant costs on the economy. Specifically, explain how inflation

1. causes a misallocation of resources.

2. discourages savings.

3. redistributes wealth from lenders to borrowers.

Answer Explanations

1. **(C)** The GDP deflator will not pick up a change in the price of an imported good. However, the CPI will since imported olives are a consumer staple.

2. **(B)** The percentage change in the CPI gives the inflation rate. In this case, the percentage change in the CPI is calculated:

   Inflation rate = percentage change in the CPI = $\frac{150-120}{120} = \frac{30}{120} = \frac{1}{4} = 0.25 = 25$ percent

3. **(A)** The CPI overstates increases in the cost of living for the average family for several reasons. For instance, the quality of products generally increases, so some of any price increase is justified and is not inflation.

4. **(D)** The CPI does not account for quality improvements in products except in a few instances.

5. **(B)** The CPI will not be affected because industrial robots are not a typical consumer item. Only typical consumer prices are considered. The GDP deflator is not affected because the robots are imported. The GDP deflator considers only domestic products.

6. **(C)** The GDP deflator = $\frac{\text{nominal GDP}}{\text{real GDP}} \times 100 = \frac{\$5,000}{\$4,000} \times 100 = 1.25 \times 100 = 125$

7. **(C)** Real GDP = $\frac{\text{nominal GDP}}{\text{GDP deflator}} \times 100 = \frac{\$6,000}{200} \times 100 = \$30 \times 100 = \$3,000$

8. **(D)** When prices rise, incomes in the aggregate rise proportionally. This is because most people earn more when the products they are producing sell for more.

9. **(E)** When prices change, catalogs, menus, computer programs, and more need to be changed. This takes time, effort, and resources that could have been used doing something more productive.

10. **(B)** The unemployment rate = $\frac{\text{number of unemployed}}{\text{labor force}} = \frac{200}{2,000} = \frac{1}{10} = 0.10 = 10$ percent

11. **(A)** As prices rise, money in savings accounts can buy fewer goods and services.

12. **(E)** The equation for Fisher's Hypothesis appears with other formulas at the end of this chapter.

13. **(B)** Unemployment due to a lack of demand in the economy is called cyclical unemployment.

14. **(C)** Unemployment due to a mismatch in the location of employers and unemployed people with the skills to fill positions is known as structural unemployment.

15. **(A)** At any given time, there are people who are between jobs. This is called frictional unemployment.

Free-Response Review Answers

1. Inflation causes a misallocation of resources. Resources are spent dealing with rising prices and the repercussions of rising prices. Instead, these resources could have been spent producing more goods and services for the constituents of the economy to enjoy. For example, some firms will have to print new catalogs and revise their websites when the prices of their products change. This time and effort would not have been expended if prices had not risen. Some households will take the trouble to stock up on goods whose prices are expected to rise. The effort and storage costs are another misallocation of resources.

2. Inflation erodes the value of financial assets. Savings accounts, trust funds, and other accounts cannot buy as many products when the prices of those products rise. Why save if inflation will simply eat away at the value of savings?

3. Inflation allows borrowers to repay their loans with dollars that are not worth as much as the ones they borrowed. Lenders, on the other hand, are being repaid with dollars that have lost some of their value. Shrewd lenders understand this and charge higher rates of interest to cover the inflation that may occur over the course of a loan. However, lenders who do not anticipate inflation will be hurt while those who borrow from them will benefit.

14

Money and Banking

Learning Objectives

In this chapter, you will learn:

→ M1, M2, and the monetary base
→ Fiat money
→ The functions of money
→ The Federal Reserve System
→ The money expansion process
→ Policy tools of the Federal Reserve

M1, M2, and the Monetary Base

Money is anything that society generally accepts in payment for a good or service. This is a very broad definition and allows for many things to be counted as money. There have been societies that accepted beads and clamshells in exchange for goods and services.

Currency—coins issued by the Treasury and paper money issued by the Federal Reserve—is a widely accepted form of payment in the U.S. However, checkable deposits are widely accepted as well. Households and firms regularly use their checking accounts to pay bills and make purchases. Economists call checking accounts at banks *demand deposits*. Checking accounts at savings and loans, credit unions, and the like are referred to as *other checkable deposits*.

Additionally, deposits in savings accounts are counted as money. Unlike demand deposits and other checkable deposits, savings deposits cannot be drawn on with checks, debit cards, or auto payments. However, it is easy to move funds from savings into checking or cash. Savings deposits are highly *liquid*—they can be turned into cash rapidly and without loss.

The M1 definition of money is currency, demand deposits, and *other liquid deposits*. Other liquid deposits are other checkable deposits plus deposits in savings accounts. Another definition of money, M2, includes everything in M1 plus small time deposits and retail money market funds. It is OK to be unfamiliar with small time deposits and retail money market funds. They are defined with other new terms at the end of the chapter. What is important for the AP exam is to understand that these financial assets are not as liquid as savings accounts. For that reason, small time deposits and retail money market funds are relegated to M2. Figure 14.1 shows the differences between M1 and M2.

> **TIP**
>
> Most people think of money as currency, but currency is the smallest component of the money supply in the United States.

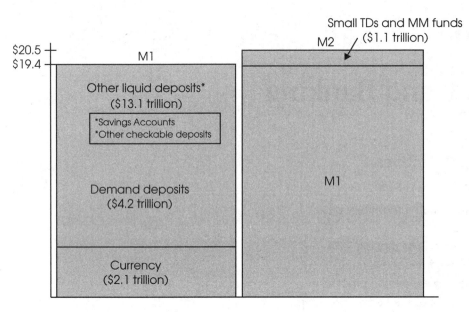

Figure 14.1 M1 and M2 in 2021

The amount of money in the U.S. economy in 2021 was $19.4 trillion or $20.5 trillion depending on which definition is used. Currency—coins and Federal Reserve Notes—was the smallest portion of the money stock. The bulk of the money supply is in the form of demand deposits and other liquid deposits.

An important detail to keep in mind is that currency inside a bank is not considered part of currency in circulation. Once coins and paper money find their way into depository institutions, they are no longer in circulation. It would result in double counting. The cash got into the bank's vault when someone made a deposit into checking or savings. The amount deposited into checking and savings accounts is counted in M1 and M2. It would be incorrect to count the deposited cash now as well.

We have already seen that the difference between banks and savings and loans, credit unions, and mutual savings associations can be important. Checking accounts at commercial banks are "demand deposits." Checking accounts at the other depository institutions are called "other checkable deposits." Aside from this and some legal technicalities, the distinction is not critical for economic analysis. This text follows the tradition in the field of money and banking of referring to all depository institutions as "banks" except when necessary.

Table 14.1 The Money Supply in the United States, 2021 (Trillions of Dollars)

M1		M2	
Currency	2.1	M1	19.4
Demand deposits	4.2	Small TDs and retail MM funds	1.1
Other liquid deposits	13.1	Total	20.5
Total	19.4		

Source: Federal Reserve Bank of the United States

Fiat Money

The United States has a lot of gold in Fort Knox and a smaller stash in the vault of the Federal Reserve Bank of New York, but none of this gold is used to back the money supply. The United States, and every other nation, uses *fiat money*. This means that the coins and paper money have nothing standing behind them except the fact that they are *legal tender*.

Legal tender means that the coin or paper money must be accepted in exchange for goods or services by the decree of the government. Still, Confederate currency was legal tender during the Civil War and even die-hard Southerners wouldn't accept it. That is because far too much of it was supplied by the Confederate authorities. This reveals the key to understanding how fiat currency works—its supply must be kept relatively limited.

From 1873 until 1933, the United States was on some form of the gold standard. The money supply was backed by gold or a combination of gold and silver. The primary advantage of the gold standard is that the supply of money must be kept limited since the supply of gold is limited. However, this system can be too confining when an increase in the supply of money is warranted and there is not an increase in the amount of gold held by the government.

A fiat monetary system is more flexible in that the gold holdings of the government need not increase in order to expand the nation's supply of money. By the same token, nations that do not keep the supply of their fiat currency limited will see it diminish in value, sometimes to the point of becoming worthless.

The Functions of Money

Most people think that money is good for only one thing—spending. True, textbooks refer to money as a "medium of exchange." Money is a much more efficient way to exchange goods and services than barter. Barter requires a double coincidence of wants; you have to find someone who has what you want and wants what you have in exchange. Money obviates the need for this and allows us to spend our time more productively.

However, people use money in another way all the time: to make comparisons. Which corporation is bigger, Procter and Gamble or Pfizer? The assets of Pfizer are worth about $267 billion, while the assets of Procter and Gamble are worth $320 billion; Pfizer is smaller than Procter and Gamble by this measure. Notice that dollar figures were used to make this comparison. This is using money as a unit of account. Consider another example. Suppose you win a drawing and you can have the grand prize, a Ford Mustang, or $10,000. Most people would take the car based on the comparison that a new Ford Mustang is worth well over $10,000. Again, money is being used to compare things.

Finally, money also serves as a store of value. You can work hard for 40 years and stuff 20 percent of each paycheck under your mattress. After you retire, you can live like a king. This is using money to store the value of your hard labor during your working years. Of course, money is a poor store of value during inflationary times. The $600,000 under the mattress can buy less and less as prices rise. On the other hand, money is an excellent store of value during deflations. The $600,000 can buy more and more goods and services as prices fall.

Table 14.2 The Functions of Money

- Medium of exchange—money is used to buy goods and services
- Unit of account—money is used to measure and compare
- Store of value—money is used to accumulate wealth

The Federal Reserve System

To understand how the money supply can be changed, it is necessary to understand the Federal Reserve System, or Fed, for short. The Fed is the central bank of the United States. This means that it controls the money supply and supervises all the depository institutions within the country. All of the banks, savings and loans, credit unions, and mutual savings banks report to the Fed each week. The Fed can audit any of these institutions at any time and would have to approve any mergers and acquisitions.

The Fed operates as the bank of banks. If you need a loan, you might go to a bank. If a bank needs a loan, it may borrow from the Fed. If you feel uncomfortable carrying around a lot of cash, you might deposit some of that cash in your account at a bank. If a bank feels uncomfortable having a lot of cash in its vault, it may deposit some of that vault cash in its account at the Fed.

FACTS ABOUT THE FED

1. There are 12 branches of the Fed located in major cities throughout the nation. This makes it convenient for banks and other depository institutions to do their banking.
2. The main headquarters of the Fed is in Washington, D.C.
3. The President of the United States appoints the seven members of the Board of Governors of the Federal Reserve System.
4. The President also appoints one of the members to be the chairman of the Board of Governors and another member to be the vice chairman.
5. All the members of the Board of Governors serve 14-year terms.
6. The Board of Governors makes the important decisions concerning the money supply. Should M1 and M2 be increased? Decreased? Held steady?

The Fed is a quasi-governmental institution. The people working at the Fed are paid by the federal government, but the Fed is not part of the executive, legislative, or judicial branches of government. The Board of Governors makes decisions concerning the money supply in complete autonomy. The Fed is not responsible to the President or Congress, although it regularly reports to both on its operations and intentions for the money supply.

Fractional Reserve Banking

Banks and other depository institutions keep only a fraction of the money deposited with them on hand. Most of any given deposit is used to make loans or other investments. Nevertheless, banks have plenty of cash on hand to meet their withdrawal needs. A bank manager's worst nightmare is to run short of cash.

Imagine a customer's deposit of $100 as a demand deposit. The bank may keep $10 on hand for withdrawal needs. With the other $90, the bank can make loans or buy investments. This, after all, is how the bank makes a profit. The $10 held aside by the bank are called *required reserves*. The $90 left over are called *excess reserves*.

T-accounts

In order to understand fractional reserve banking, it can be instructive to look at the balance sheet, or T-account, of a hypothetical commercial bank. Recent exams in AP Macroeconomics have featured multiple-choice and free-response questions that require knowledge of T-accounts.

T-accounts are an accounting tool that may be used for recording transactions. On the left side of a T-account, we record transactions involving the bank's assets. Changes in the bank's liabilities are recorded on the right-hand side of the ledger. Consider the balance sheet of Bank A when a customer deposits $100 into a checking account:

Commercial Bank A

Assets	Liabilities
+$100 currency	+$100 demand deposits

The bank has $100 more currency in its vault. That is an asset. But the bank also has a new liability: $100 in a customer's checking account that it must be prepared to reimburse at any moment. Notice that this transaction, by itself, has no effect on the money supply. The currency inside a bank's vault is not part of M1 or M2, but demand deposits are included in both. The customer's deposit lowers currency holdings of the public by $100. However, checking accounts are increased by $100.

Say the bank holds $10 of this deposit as required reserves and the remaining $90 are excess reserves. The transaction above could just as well be recorded as:

Commercial Bank A

Assets	Liabilities
+$10 required reserves	+$100 demand deposits
+$90 excess reserves	

TIP

A balance sheet must always stay balanced. If an amount is deducted from one side, then an equal amount must be added to the same side, or deducted from the other side.

Now consider what happens when the bank makes a loan with its excess reserves.

Commercial Bank A

Assets	Liabilities
+$10 required reserves	+$100 demand deposits
+$90 excess reserves	
−$90 excess reserves	
+$90 loan	

The bank no longer has $90 in excess reserves, but it has another asset—$90 in loans that hopefully will be repaid some day in the future with interest.

Suppose the person receiving the loan used it to buy flowers and at the end of the day the florist deposits the $90 in his checking account at Bank B:

Commercial Bank B

Assets	Liabilities
+$9 required reserves	+$90 demand deposits
+$81 excess reserves	

The bank holds 10 percent of the deposit aside as required reserves. The remaining $81 is excess reserves. However, it is critical to notice that this deposit increased the money supply, be it M1 or M2, by $90. How so? Demand deposits are part of the money supply, and they went up by $90. Did the currency holdings of the public decrease by $90? Did demand deposits at any other bank fall because of this transaction? No. When a bank makes a loan, it creates money because it leads to increases in demand deposits and other liquid deposits.

A similar scenario occurs if Bank A uses its $90 in excess reserves to buy an investment rather than make a loan. Suppose Bank A buys a collectible doll as a financial investment. Whoever sold Bank A the doll deposits the $90 in their bank, say Bank B:

Commercial Bank A		Commercial Bank B	
Assets	Liabilities	Assets	Liabilities
−$90 excess reserves		+$9 required reserves	+$90 demand deposits
+$90 collectible doll		+$81 excess reserves	

Bank B shows an increase in demand deposits of $90, which are part of M1 or M2, and no bank has lost demand deposits because of the transaction. The point of this analysis is to show that banks create money when they make loans or buy financial assets.

The process works in reverse as well. Banks destroy money when loans are repaid or they sell financial investments. To show money destruction, let's say Bank A sells its collectible doll some years later for $90. (Alas, the doll did not provide any financial reward.) The doll's new owner pays with a check from Bank B:

Commercial Bank A		Commercial Bank B	
Assets	Liabilities	Assets	Liabilities
−$90 collectible doll		−$9 required reserves	−$90 demand deposits
+$90 excess reserves		−$81 excess reserves	

Demand deposits in the banking system decrease by $90 without a compensating increase, thus decreasing M1 or M2. You may be thinking that the money supply is uncontrolled since it depends on banks' preferences for making loans or buying financial investments. But that is incorrect. Under normal circumstances, banks can be counted on to use just about all their excess reserves for loans or investments because that is how profits are maximized. In the next section, we shall see that the Fed controls the money supply by controlling the amount of reserves banks have for loans and investments.

The Money Expansion Process

Imagine that a counterfeiter prints up $1,000 in phony bills and spends the fake money at a jewelry store. At the end of the day, the jeweler deposits the counterfeit money into his bank. The bank, not detecting the phony bills, credits the jeweler's transaction account by $1,000. The bank holds $100 of the $1,000 aside as required reserves. The remaining $900 can be used as the bank sees fit. Typically, excess reserves such as these $900 are used to make loans or buy investments since that is how the bank makes profits.

Now suppose the bank loans the $900 to someone applying for a home improvement loan. The $900 ends up being spent on paint. The owner of the paint store deposits the $900 into demand deposits. Notice that this deposit is boosting demand deposits by $900 and demand deposits are part of the money supply as measured by M1 or M2. In other words, the money supply is increased when banks make loans with their excess reserves.

And this is not the end of the story. The bank that received the $900 deposit from the paint store will hold 10 percent of the deposit, or $90, as required reserves. The rest of the deposit is excess reserves, and the bank can use these in any way it wishes. Suppose the bank buys some real estate as an investment with the $810 in excess reserves. Whoever sold the real estate to the bank now has a check for $810. If this check is deposited into a demand deposit, the money supply will be going up again, this time $810.

Again, this is not the end of the story. The bank that receives the deposit of $810 will hold 10 percent, or $81, aside as required reserves. The remaining $729 is excess reserves that the bank may use to make a loan or buy an investment.

When all is said and done, the original $1,000 in counterfeit money will have led to a $10,000 increase in the money supply. This is because of the money expansion process where banks create transaction account money by using their reserves to make loans or buy investments. Table 14.3 outlines the money expansion process for this example.

Remember that money deposited into demand deposits or other liquid assets is part of the money supply. When counterfeiters deposit $1,000 into their demand deposit account, the money supply ends up increasing by $10,000. This is because of all the subsidiary deposits that occur because of the original $1,000 deposit. The column labeled "demand deposits and other liquid deposits" sums to $10,000.

Two formulas help us determine how much the money supply will increase because of a deposit from outside the system. The first formula is for the money multiplier:

$$\text{Money Multiplier} = 1/\text{Reserve Requirement}$$

In our case, the reserve requirement is 10 percent:

Money Multiplier $= 1/0.10 = 10$

Table 14.3 The Money Expansion Process

	Demand Deposits and Other Liquid Deposits	Required Reserves	Excess Reserves
Bank 1 (Counterfeiter's bank)	$1,000	$100	$900 (used to make a loan)
Bank 2 (Paint store's bank)	900	90	810 (used to buy real estate)
Bank 3 (Real estate seller's bank)	810	81	729
Bank 4	729	72.90	656.10
.	.	.	.
.	.	.	.
.	.	.	.
	$10,000		

This demonstrates that any deposit from outside the banking system, such as counterfeit money, will change the money supply by 10 times the amount of the deposit.

The second formula gives the change in the money supply because of the initial change in bank reserves:

Change in the Money Supply $=$ Money Multiplier $\times$ Change in Bank Reserves

In our example, the money multiplier is 10 and the initial change in bank reserves is the $1,000 in counterfeit money:

Change in the Money Supply $= 10 \times \$1,000 = \$10,000$

If the reserve requirement was 5 percent and the counterfeiters deposited $4,000 in fake money, the change in the money supply would be:

Money Multiplier $= 1/0.05 = 20$

Change in the Money Supply $= 20 \times \$4,000 = \$80,000$

Notice that the money expansion process is thwarted if banks decide to hold *precautionary reserves*—reserves over and above those strictly required. The process assumes banks make loans with their excess reserves. To the extent that banks choose to hold precautionary reserves, the money multiplier is diminished.

Another factor that affects the size of the money multiplier is the extent to which households and firms hold cash. A preference for holding cash means fewer deposits. Fewer deposits mean banks have less to make loans and buy investments. This is *cash drain*. On the other hand, the more comfortable society is with keeping money in accounts rather than cash, the more reserves banks have to work with. This expands the monetary base and the money supply.

Policy Tools of the Federal Reserve

The previous examples illustrate why counterfeiting is considered to be such a serious crime. A small amount of counterfeit money can lead to a significant change in the money supply because of the monetary expansion process, but the examples also suggest how the Fed could change the money supply.

The Fed could print money and deposit it into a bank and the monetary expansion process would take over. The money supply would increase by a multiple of the Fed's deposit. And what's more, the initial deposit isn't counterfeit. But this would be unfair to banks that did not receive Fed deposits.

In order to decrease the money supply, the Fed could simply ask some banks to hand over some of their reserves. This is obviously unfair, but those banks could now make fewer loans and investments. The money supply would shrink by a multiple of the amount the Fed extracted.

There are several fair and appropriate ways the Fed could alter the ability of banks to make loans and buy investments. Each of these methods involves the Fed increasing or decreasing bank reserves. With more reserves in the banking system, loans and investments increase and the money supply expands. With fewer reserves, loans and investments contract and the money supply decreases by a multiple of the initial change in reserves.

The monetary base is defined as bank reserves plus currency in circulation. To change the money supply, the Fed changes the monetary base by altering bank reserves and then the money supply changes by a multiple of the change in the monetary base Figure 14.2 shows this.

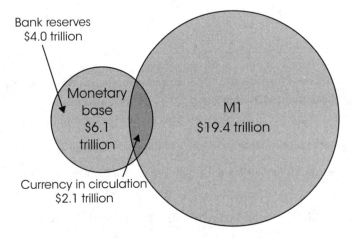

Figure 14.2 The Money Supply is a Multiple of the Monetary Base

As it turns out, there are several ways the Fed could change the monetary base and, therefore, the money supply. These methods are the policy tools of the Fed.

1. The Fed could stipulate that banks hold more required reserves. If the reserve requirement was increased, banks would have fewer excess reserves and could make fewer loans and investments. This would decrease the money supply. To increase the money supply, the Fed would lower reserve requirements.

2. Another policy tool involves the *discount rate*. The discount rate is the rate of interest the Fed charges when it makes loans to depository institutions. Remember that if you want a loan you might go to a bank, whereas a bank that needs a loan may go to the Fed.

   If the Fed lowers the discount rate, more banks are encouraged to borrow. These borrowings by banks from the Fed increase bank reserves. The money supply will increase by a multiple of the borrowings from the Fed.

As an illustration, suppose the Fed lowers the discount rate by half of a percentage point. Say that the lower discount rate encourages banks to borrow $12 million more than usual from the Fed. Assuming a 10 percent reserve requirement, the money supply would then increase by $120 million:

$$\text{Money Multiplier} = 1/\text{Reserve Requirement}$$

$$\text{Money Multiplier} = 1/0.10 = 10$$

$$\text{Change in the Money Supply} = \text{Money Multiplier} \times \text{Change in Bank Reserves}$$

$$\text{Change in the Money Supply} = 10 \times \$12 \text{ million} = \$120 \text{ million}$$

If the Fed wanted to decrease the money supply, then the discount rate should be raised. Raising the discount rate discourages banks from borrowing from the Fed, and banks, therefore, have fewer reserves. A decrease in reserves translates into a multiple decrease in the money supply.

3. The third policy tool available to the Fed to make changes in the monetary base and therefore in the money supply is *open market operations*. Open market operations are when the Fed buys and sells government securities in the secondary market. Government securities are IOUs that the government issues when it borrows money. They sometimes go by the names Treasury bills, bonds, or notes. The federal government of the United States has borrowed trillions of dollars from individuals and corporations, both foreign and domestic.

    When the government borrows money, it issues a Treasury security to the lender that states the amount of the loan, the rate of interest, and the length of the loan. However, the lender need not hold the government security until it matures. At any time, the lender may sell the government security to another investor. This is done in the *secondary market*.

    Lenders wishing to sell government securities that have a relatively high rate of interest attached to them will experience a profit in the secondary market, while those with relatively low rates will experience a loss. But the Fed does not buy and sell government securities in the secondary market with an eye toward making financial gains. The Fed participates in the secondary market for government securities in order to change the money supply.

    Imagine what happens when the Fed buys government securities in the secondary market. The Fed pays for the securities with a check that the seller deposits in a bank account. This deposit is an increase in bank reserves from outside the system. The money supply will increase by a multiple of this increase in bank reserves.

    To take a specific example, if the reserve requirement is 10 percent and the Fed wants to increase the money supply by $50 million, then the Fed would buy $5 million worth of government securities in the secondary market.

$$\text{Money Multiplier} = 1/\text{Reserve Requirement}$$

$$\text{Money Multiplier} = 1/0.10 = 10$$

$$\text{Change in the Money Supply} = \text{Money Multiplier} \times \text{Change in Bank Reserves}$$

$$\text{Change in the Money Supply} = 10 \times \$5 \text{ million} = \$50 \text{ million}$$

If the Fed wanted to decrease the money supply, it would sell government securities in the secondary market. Persons or corporations that buy the securities will pay with a check. The Fed cashes the check to draw the reserves out of the banking system and does not deposit proceeds of the sale back into the banking system. In this way, bank reserves are depleted. The money supply falls by a multiple of the decline in bank reserves. Specifically, if the Fed sells $6 million worth of government securities in the secondary market and the reserve requirement is 5 percent, then the money supply will fall by $120 million.

$$\text{Money Multiplier} = 1/\text{Reserve Requirement}$$

$$\text{Money Multiplier} = 1/0.05 = 20$$

$$\text{Change in the Money Supply} = \text{Money Multiplier} \times \text{Change in Bank Reserves}$$

$$\text{Change in the Money Supply} = 20 \times -\$6 \text{ million} = -\$120 \text{ million}$$

4. In 2008, the Fed started paying depository institutions interest on reserves. If the Fed changes this interest rate, it affects how many reserves are held.

To induce banks to hold more reserves, the central bank increases the interest rate it pays on reserves. Since banks earn more on idle reserves, they make fewer loans and investments, leading to a decrease in the money supply.

To increase the money supply, the Fed decreases the interest rate on bank reserves. Since banks earn less on their idle reserves, they reduce them by making more loans and investments. Remember, the money supply expands when banks use their reserves to make loans and buy investments.

Table 14.4 summarizes the policy tools of the Fed.

Table 14.4 Policy Tools of the Federal Reserve

Tool	Description	To Increase Money Supply	To Decrease Money Supply
Change reserve requirements	Change the percentage of each deposit that banks hold aside	Lower the reserve requirement	Raise the reserve requirement
Change the discount rate	Change the rate of interest the Fed charges on bank borrowings	Lower the discount rate	Raise the discount rate
Open market operations	Buy or sell government securities in the secondary market	Buy government securities	Sell government securities
Change the interest rate paid on reserves	The Fed can increase or decrease the rate of interest on reserves that banks hold	Lower the interest rate paid on reserves	Raise the interest rate paid on reserves

SUMMARY

- Money is anything generally accepted to pay for goods and services. Certainly, currency, demand deposits, and other liquid deposits are generally accepted. This definition of money is known as M1. Many experts think that other highly liquid assets should be considered money. These include small time deposits and retail money market funds. Adding these things to M1 gives M2, another prevalent definition of money.

- The money supply in the United States, like other nations, is not backed by gold or silver or any precious commodity. Fiat money is money because the government says it is money. Experience has shown that it is extremely important to keep the supply of fiat money relatively limited if it is to function correctly.

- Money is good for spending (a medium of exchange), for comparing things (a unit of account), and as an investment vehicle (a store of value). The United States is on a fractional reserve system where depository institutions keep only a fraction of each deposit on hand. Most of the money deposited in a bank is used to make loans and buy investments.

- Precautionary reserves and cash drain affect the size of the money multiplier. When depository institutions decide to hold extra or precautionary reserves, fewer loans and investments are made. This diminishes the money supply. Cash drain is the decision by households and firms to hold more of their money as currency rather than deposits. Bank reserves are diminished, and the monetary base shrinks.

- The Federal Reserve is the central bank of the United States and controls the money supply. It does this with open market operations or altering the discount rate, reserve requirements, or the interest rate paid on bank reserves. Any of these three techniques changes the monetary base. The money supply changes by a multiple of the change in the monetary base.

Formulas

Money Multiplier = 1/Reserve Requirement

Change in the Money Supply = Money Multiplier × Change in Bank Reserves

Multiple-Choice Review Questions

1. Which of the following is not included in M1?

   (A) Coins
   (B) Federal Reserve Notes
   (C) Demand deposits
   (D) Small time deposits
   (E) Other checkable deposits

2. Which of the following is not included in M2?

   (A) Currency
   (B) Demand deposits
   (C) Other checkable deposits
   (D) Savings accounts
   (E) Credit cards

3. Which of the following statements is true?

   (A) Some of the things included in M2 are not as liquid as the things in M1.
   (B) M2 is smaller than M1.
   (C) M1 is backed by gold, and M2 is backed by silver.
   (D) The biggest component of M1 is currency.
   (E) The biggest component of M2 is currency.

4. Fiat money

   (A) is not backed by any precious commodity.
   (B) can be exchanged for gold.
   (C) is backed by gold but cannot be exchanged for it.
   (D) is not legal tender.
   (E) can be backed by gold or silver.

5. Given the table, M1 = ___.

1. Federal Reserve Notes	2. $2
3. Savings Deposits	4. $9
5. Other Liquid Deposits	6. $17
7. Other Checkable Deposits	8. $8
9. Coins	10.$3
11.Currency	12.$5
13.Credit Card Debt	14.$22
15.Demand Deposits	16.$9

   (A) $21
   (B) $22
   (C) $31
   (D) $36
   (E) $53

6. Required reserves

   (A) can be used by banks to make loans or buy investments.
   (B) can be held in a bank's vault or its account at the Fed.
   (C) must be kept in a bank's vault.
   (D) must be used to make loans.
   (E) ensure that banks will have enough cash on hand to meet their withdrawals.

7. The secondary market for government securities is

   (A) where used items are traded.
   (B) located in smaller cities.
   (C) where the government borrows money.
   (D) where government securities that have already been issued may be bought or sold.
   (E) where government securities are issued.

8. If the reserve requirement is 2 percent, then the money multiplier is

   (A) 5.
   (B) 5 percent.
   (C) 50.
   (D) 50 percent.
   (E) one-half.

9. If the Fed buys bonds in the secondary market

    (A) the monetary base will increase.
    (B) the monetary base will decrease.
    (C) the monetary base will not be affected.
    (D) the discount rate would be affected.
    (E) reserve requirements would have to be increased in tandem.

10. Which of the following could potentially lead to an expansion of the money supply?

    (A) The central bank increases the discount rate.
    (B) The central bank decreases the interest rate on bank reserves.
    (C) The federal government increases its spending.
    (D) The central bank increases reserve requirements.
    (E) Taxes are reduced.

11. Assume the reserve requirement is 10 percent. If the central bank sells $29 million worth of government securities in an open market operation, then the money supply can

    (A) increase by $2.9 million.
    (B) decrease by $2.9 million.
    (C) increase by $290 million.
    (D) decrease by $290 million.
    (E) increase by $26.1 million.

12. Assume the reserve requirement is 5 percent. If the central bank buys $4 million worth of government securities in an open market operation, then the money supply can

    (A) increase by $1.25 million.
    (B) decrease by $1.25 million.
    (C) increase by $20 million.
    (D) decrease by $20 million.
    (E) increase by $80 million.

13. An increase in the discount rate _____ the monetary base and therefore M1 _____ .

    (A) increases; is unaffected
    (B) increases; increases
    (C) increases; decreases
    (D) decreases; increases
    (E) decreases; decreases

14. Increasing the interest rate paid on reserves incentivizes depository institutions to hold _____ reserves and make _____ loans and investments.

    (A) more; riskier
    (B) more; more
    (C) more; fewer
    (D) fewer; more
    (E) fewer; fewer

15. If depositors across the economy decide to hold less currency and more demand deposits, then bank reserves _____ and M1 _____ .

    (A) increase; decreases
    (B) increase; increases
    (C) decrease; decreases
    (D) decrease; increases
    (E) decrease; is unaffected

Free-Response Review Questions

1. Assume the reserve requirement is 10 percent. If the central bank buys $10,000 worth of government securities in the secondary market, will the money supply expand or shrink? By exactly how much after all is said and done?

2. Explain why the money supply changes when the central bank buys $10,000 worth of government securities in the secondary market. Why is the change in the money supply more than $10,000?

3. Suppose that depository institutions did not use all of their excess reserves to make loans and buy investments. For example, if the reserve requirement was 10 percent, depository institutions would hold 20 percent of their deposits idle. How would this affect your answer to question 1 above?

Answer Explanations

1. **(D)** Small time deposits are not a component of M1. See Table 14.1

2. **(E)** Credit cards are not a component of M2. See Table 14.1.

3. **(A)** The small time deposits and retail money market funds in M2 are less liquid than any component of M1.

4. **(A)** Fiat money is not backed by gold, silver, or any commodity.

5. **(C)** $31 = Other Liquid Deposits + Currency + Demand Deposits. Or alternatively, $31 = Savings Deposits + Other Checkable Deposits + Federal Reserve Notes + Coins + Demand Deposits

6. **(B)** Required reserves can be held in either of two locations: the depository institution's vault or its account at the regional Federal Reserve Bank.

7. **(D)** Open market operations occur in the secondary market for U.S. Treasury securities. In this market, the securities the U.S. Treasury has already used to borrow money are traded.

8. **(C)** Money Multiplier $= \dfrac{1}{\text{reserve requirement}} = \dfrac{1}{0.02} = 50$

9. **(A)** The money supply increases because the Fed pays for the bonds. The seller hands the bond to the Fed and receives money.

10. **(B)** When the central bank decreases the interest rate paid on bank reserves, it incentivizes banks to hold fewer of them and to make more loans and buy more investments instead. This increases the money supply. None of the other responses increase the money supply.

11. **(D)** The money expansion process is determined by calculating the money multiplier and then magnifying any change in bank reserves by that multiplier. In this case, the money multiplier equals 10:

Money Multiplier $= \dfrac{1}{\text{reserve requirement}} = \dfrac{1}{0.10} = 10$

The change in bank reserves is negative $29 million. This is because when the Fed sells government securities, the buyer pays with money out of their bank account. The Fed takes the money and puts it out of circulation. This lowers bank reserves.

Potential change in the money supply $= 10 \times -\$29$ million $= -\$290$ million

12. **(E)** The money expansion process is determined by calculating the money multiplier and then magnifying any change in bank reserves by that multiplier. In this case, the money multiplier equals 20:

$$\text{Money Multiplier} = \frac{1}{\text{reserve requirement}} = \frac{1}{0.05} = 20$$

The change in bank reserves is $4 million. This is because when the Fed buys government securities, it pays with money that finds its way into checking accounts. This increases bank reserves.

Potential change in the money supply $= 20 \times \$4\text{ million} = \$80\text{ million}$

13. **(E)** Increasing the discount rate discourages banks from borrowing from the Fed. Bank reserves decrease since banks are borrowing fewer reserves. The monetary base decreases because bank reserves are the major component of the monetary base. M1 decreases because the money supply is a multiple of the monetary base.

14. **(C)** Banks hold more reserves if they get paid more interest on them. That implies banks will make fewer loans and investments.

15. **(B)** Bank reserves increase since people want to hold less currency and more in deposits. This means banks can make more loans and buy more investments, increasing the money supply.

Free-Response Review Answers

1. If the central bank buys $10,000 worth of government securities in the secondary market, the money supply expands. When the central bank pays for the securities, the sellers will deposit their checks into the banking system. The reserves of the banking system will increase by $10,000. The money supply will increase by 10 times that amount, or $100,000, because the money multiplier is 10 in this case. (Money multiplier $= 1/0.10 = 10$.)

2. The money supply increases because when the central bank buys securities in the secondary market, this increases the reserves of banks where the checks are deposited. The reserves of these banks go up by $10,000. Now these banks are holding more reserves than they are required to by the Fed's reserve requirements. The banks make loans and buy investments with these excess reserves, and this serves to increase demand deposits and other liquid deposits. Demand deposits and other liquid deposits are part of the money supply.

3. If banks do not use all of their excess reserves to make loans and buy investments, then the money expansion process is not as effective. When a bank makes a loan, this money ends up as a deposit elsewhere, usually at another bank. If banks prefer to hold extra reserves, then the loans will not be as large and the increase in the money supply also will not be as large. If banks have a 10 percent reserve requirement and hold 10 percent more in extra reserves, this means that the money multiplier is 5 ($= 1/(0.1 + 0.1) = 1/0.2$) and the money supply will expand to only $50,000, not $100,000.

15

Monetary Theory

| **Learning Objectives**

In this chapter, you will learn:

→ The equation of exchange
→ The loanable funds market
→ The money market

The Equation of Exchange

The equation of exchange models how a change in the money supply affects the macroeconomy. The logic behind the equation goes back to John Stuart Mill (1806–1873). Irving Fisher (1867–1947), an economics professor at Yale, is credited with writing down the formula for the first time.

$$M \times V = P \times Y$$

where M is the money supply

V is the velocity of money

P is the price level

Y is the quantity of output or real GDP

The money supply can be defined as M1 or M2. The velocity of money is the number of times the typical dollar of M1 or M2 is used to make purchases during a year. The price level, P, can be measured with the GDP deflator.

Since $P \times Y$ = nominal GDP, the equation of exchange is sometimes written as:

$$M \times V = \text{Nominal GDP}$$

The equation of exchange is a tautology. That is, it is true by definition. It does not matter if we consider a tiny economy with three people that uses seashells for money or a modern industrial economy like the United States; the money supply times the velocity of money must equal the average price of all that is produced times the amount of output.

People are surprised to learn that the velocity of M1 these days is less than 3. It seems as if the average dollar is used more than 3 times a year. But remember, M1 is currency and also demand deposits and other liquid deposits. If someone maintains a minimum balance of $1,000 in a checking account, then those 1,000 dollars have a velocity of zero.

It is well-known that checking account dollars turn over, on average, much less than paper dollars. And savings deposits can sit for years without being used. The average velocity of all of these things combined is less than 3.

The equation of exchange can be manipulated algebraically. Suppose we know the money supply (M1) and $P \times Y$ (nominal GDP). Then we can solve for V:

$$M \times V = P \times Y$$

$$\$19 \text{ trillion} \times V = \$23.0 \text{ trillion}$$

$$V = 1.2$$

Indeed, this is how we know the velocity of M1 is 1.2.

The equation of exchange can be used to make some interesting deductions. Suppose that the velocity of money and real GDP are constant. Then if the money supply increases 10 percent, prices would have to increase 10 percent as well:

$$\uparrow M \times \overline{V} = \uparrow P \times \overline{Y} \quad \text{(The bars over the V and Y indicate they are constant.)}$$

But Y is real GDP, and we know real GDP is not constant. V is the velocity of money, and that is not constant either.

However, suppose the changes in Y and V are relatively small. Then we could conclude that a 10 percent increase in the money supply would increase prices about, but not exactly, 10 percent. In the past, Y and V have changed slowly for extended periods of time. However, there have been times when Y or V or both have shifted suddenly and significantly.

The idea that inflation is almost proportional to the growth rate of the money supply is known as the quantity theory of money. Many, if not most, professional economists believe this theory is true, especially in the long run.

Real life has provided many tests of the quantity theory. The most interesting evidence comes from hyperinflations. According to this theory, if a nation is experiencing 7,000 percent inflation, then the money supply must have increased 7,000 percent. Indeed, this was exactly the case in Brazil in the early 1990s. The Brazilian government ordered the central bank to deposit more and more money into its coffers in order to pay back loans. Once the money was put in circulation, prices started to rise.

There are many examples of hyperinflations throughout history, and every single one of them was caused by hefty increases in the money supply.

The Theory of Monetary Neutrality (aka The Classical Dichotomy)

The theory of monetary neutrality states that a change in the money supply will affect nominal variables in the economy but not real variables. This idea is based on the equation of exchange and the assumptions that V and Y are relatively stable.

In this case, an increase in the money supply increases prices almost proportionally. This includes the price of labor and other inputs into the production process. After the price level increases, a business can sell its production for 10 percent more, but the price of production materials also increases 10 percent. Why would the business produce more or less?

The total revenue of the business has gone up 10 percent, and so have total costs. These are nominal values. But the amount of production, say 400 gizmos per week, has not changed. Nor has the number of employees at the firm. These figures, 400 gizmos and 200 employees, are real variables.

More formally, nominal variables are expressed in dollar amounts while real variables are expressed in physical amounts (or are nominal variables adjusted for price changes). The amount of M1 in the economy is a nominal figure while the number of unemployed persons is a real variable. Nominal GDP, of course, is a nominal variable while real GDP is, well … real.

Getting back to the theory of monetary neutrality, if the money supply rises 20 percent and so do all prices including wages and salaries, then why would a family spend more or less on groceries? The family's income (a nominal variable) has risen 20 percent, but the number of sacks of groceries that income buys per week (a real variable) has not changed.

Therefore, the theory of monetary neutrality can be stated as "a change in the money supply affects only nominal variables; nothing real in the economy is affected." That can be shortened and made more dramatic: Money doesn't matter.

Most economists buy this dramatic idea if wages and salaries are given time to adjust to the higher prices. If you think about it, it makes sense. Why would the amount of currency in circulation or on deposit in accounts affect living standards? The maximum a nation can produce and therefore consume depends on resources and technology. If the money supply is increased, do we somehow get more resources or technological progress?

At the same time, most economists think an increase in the money supply will indeed increase production and therefore employment (both real variables) in the short run. We will postpone the explanation of this difference between the short run and the long run for later.

The Loanable Funds Market

Savings are critical for the macroeconomy to function properly. Businesses often need loans to expand or tide them over during a period of low cash flow. Similarly, households require loans to buy big-ticket items like vehicles and houses. But even everyday items such as chewing gum are often bought with a loan from a credit card issuer. The United States federal government is a big borrower. Borrowing would not be possible if there were no savings in the economy. Any lenders, foreign or domestic, are rewarded with interest payments.

Financial intermediation is the task of getting funds from savers (lenders) to spenders (borrowers). See Figure 15.1. Banks, savings and loans, credit unions, investment banks, mutual funds, hedge funds, and other institutions act as financial intermediaries. These institutions absorb savings and move the funds to borrowers willing to pay interest in order to obtain the loan of funds.

Financial intermediation is a vital and massive undertaking in a modern economy. Markets can help move the funds from savers to borrowers willing to pay the most interest. Imagine someone who wants a loan to buy a car. A bank is often the financial intermediary in this case. Funds from depositors are loaned out to the car buyer. The rate of interest on the loan is determined by supply and demand. The greater the supply of funds available for car loans, the lower the interest rate. If, on the other hand, the demand for car loans grows, then the interest rate will increase.

Think about who demands loanable funds in the U.S. economy: 1) individuals and households such as our car buyer above; 2) businesses; and 3) local, state, and federal governments. In addition, foreign businesses and governments can be demanders of U.S. loanable funds.

Who supplies loanable funds in the U.S. economy? The exact same list as the demanders. Individuals and households are one of the largest suppliers of loanable funds in the U.S. economy since deposits into savings accounts comprise a big chunk of loanable funds. Businesses supply loanable funds. Some firms use their profits to buy financial instruments such as Treasury securities. That amounts to supplying loanable funds to the federal government, the demander in this case. However, some state and local governments actually run surpluses. That is, they take in more in taxes than they spend. The surpluses are typically put to work earning interest. So, these governments are suppliers of loanable funds. Finally, foreign banks and businesses are suppliers of loanable funds, often to the U.S. federal government.

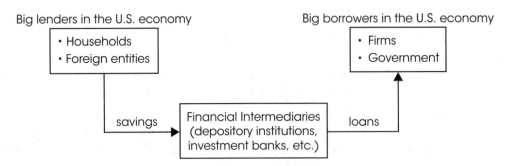

Figure 15.1 Financial Intermediation in the United States

The market for loanable funds considers the supply and demand for all types of loans, not just car loans. There are loans to help a business get started; loans to help buy a house; loans for college tuition; and many more. So there are many interest rates, but we might consider the average rate on all the various sorts of loans. This rate represents the cost, or price, of obtaining a typical loan.

With this average interest rate on the vertical axis, we can draw the supply and demand for loanable funds. The analysis is carried out with the real, or adjusted for inflation, rate of interest. This is because the real rate of interest reflects the true cost of borrowing money and the true reward for lending money.

The real interest rate is the nominal interest rate minus the inflation rate. Suppose the bank charges 7 percent for a car loan. That is the nominal interest rate. If the inflation rate is 2 percent over the course of the loan, then the bank earned 5 percent in real interest.

$$\text{Nominal interest rate} = \text{real interest rate} + \text{inflation}$$
$$7 \quad = \quad 5 \quad + \quad 2$$

Notice that when the real rate of interest is high, the quantity of funds demanded will be relatively low. The high cost prohibits some borrowers and discourages others. When the real rate of interest is low, the quantity of funds demanded is higher. Thus, the demand curve slopes downward.

The supply of funds curve slopes upward. If the real interest rate is high, suppliers of funds are encouraged to bring more to market. It is just the opposite if the going rate is relatively low. Thus, the supply of funds curve is upward sloping.

Where the two curves cross is the equilibrium point that determines the rate that will prevail in the market (r_e) and the quantity of funds that will be loaned out (Q_e). See Figure 15.2.

There is a reason to expect the equilibrium rate and quantity to prevail. Suppose the rate was higher. Here, the quantity supplied is greater than the quantity of funds demanded. This surplus of funds, like a surplus in any market, drives the price, in this case the interest rate, down. If the real interest rate was lower than the equilibrium rate, then an excess demand for funds would exist. Suppliers of funds, realizing they could loan out all they have, raise their asking rate for the loans.

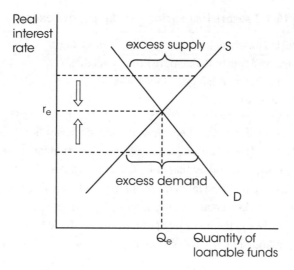

Figure 15.2 The Market for Loanable Funds

Once the equilibrium is established, there is no tendency for things to change, unless one or both of the curves shift. Of course, these curves are shifting almost all the time and the market is always adjusting to its new equilibrium point.

Consider what can cause the curves to shift. Let's take the supply curve first (see Figure 15.3). Suppose consumers change in their preferences and decide it is better to put more funds away for future use, as opposed to spending now. This will increase the supply of loanable funds shifting the supply curve to the right. The new equilibrium point occurs at r_e' and Q_e', where the interest rate is lower and the quantity of funds borrowed and loaned out is greater. This makes sense: if more funds are available, you should be able to obtain some at a lower rate and more funds will be loaned out.

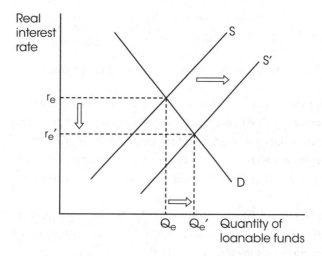

Figure 15.3 An Increase in the Supply of Loanable Funds

What else could cause more funds to come into the market? Foreign savers may increase their desire to lend in the domestic market. This is known as capital inflow. A separate factor increasing the supply of funds is an increase in saving due to a change in incentives. For instance, taxes on the interest earned from saving could be lowered. As a final example, consider what would happen if income in the economy increased. People would spend more, but they would save more as well and this is an increase in the supply of loanable funds.

Table 15.1 Factors Increasing the Supply of Loanable Funds

- A change in consumer preferences in favor of saving
- Foreigners deciding to make more funds available
- More saving due to a change in incentives
- Income increases

Of course, these factors also work in reverse: the supply of funds curve shifts left if consumers decrease their savings, or foreigners decide to send fewer funds over, or taxes on interest income are increased, or income falls.

Now let's consider what shifts the demand for loanable funds (see Figure 15.4). Suppose business opportunities blossom in the economy. There could be a lot of innovation, or good ideas for investing. This will increase the demand for loanable funds and shift the demand curve to the right. The new equilibrium point occurs at r_e' and Q_e', where the interest rate is higher and the quantity of funds borrowed and loaned out is greater. This makes sense: if funds are in greater demand, then it will cost you more to get some and more funds will be loaned out.

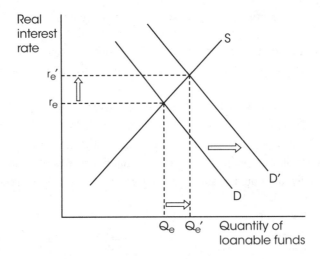

Figure 15.4 An Increase in the Demand for Loanable Funds

Another factor shifting the demand for funds to the right is an increase in expected future sales. Firms will want to increase production immediately, and many firms need to borrow the funds to ramp up production.

If new production techniques are developed, then firms will want to adopt them if they are cost-effective. It can be expensive to implement new technologies in the production process. Often new equipment and supplies are required and financed by borrowing. Thus, the adoption of new technologies can increase the demand for loanable funds.

Finally, consider what happens in the loanable funds market when the government decides to increase deficit spending. These funds must be borrowed, and that increases the demand for loanable funds. The subsequent rise in interest rates is often referred to as "crowding out."

Table 15.2 Factors Increasing the Demand for Loanable Funds

- More business opportunities present themselves
- Expected future sales increase
- New technologies are adopted
- Government borrowing increases

Again, all these demand shifters work conversely. The demand for loanable funds decreases, and the demand curve shifts left if business opportunities dry up, expected future sales decrease, new technologies require less plant and equipment, or the government reduces deficit spending.

The supply and demand for loanable funds determines the interest rate, and the level of the interest rate is critical. When interest rates rise, fewer investment projects are profitable. So fewer projects are undertaken, and that means less plant and equipment in the economy.

The supply of loanable funds is not the same as the money supply. The supply of loanable funds is determined by savers. The supply of money is determined by the Federal Reserve. However, the market for loanable funds is an important component in any theory about how a change in the money supply affects the economy. If the Fed changes the money supply, then borrowing and saving in the loanable funds market will be affected. That, in turn, will affect the real interest rate. However, the nominal interest rate is determined in the money market.

The Money Market

The supply and demand for money make up the money market. The Fed determines the supply of money in the economy. The demand for money is determined by how much households, firms, governments, and foreigners want to hold.

Figure 15.5 models the money market. The vertical axis measures the nominal interest rate. Nominal means "not adjusted for inflation." There are many interest rates in the economy: the rates on a car loan, a home loan, a student loan, and many more. You can think of "the" nominal interest rate as an average of all these various rates. Or you can pick one rate in particular. Interest rates are not all the same, but they tend to move in the same direction.

The horizontal axis of the diagram measures the quantity of money supplied and demanded. Where the two curves cross is the equilibrium point. R_e is the equilibrium interest rate, and Q_e is the amount of money supplied and demanded. M_s is the supply of money, and M_d is the demand for money.

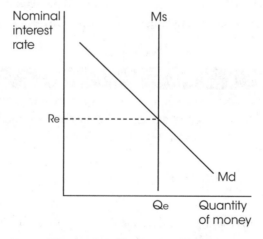

Figure 15.5 The Money Market

The supply of money curve is vertical because it is not affected if the nominal interest rate moves higher or lower. The supply of money is determined by the Fed. If the Fed decides to increase the money supply, then M_s shifts rightward. A decrease in the money supply shifts M_s to the left.

Table 15.3

The Supply of Money	
Why is it vertical?	The amount of money supplied to the economy is determined by the Fed and is not affected by a change in the nominal interest rate.
What can shift it?	The Fed changes the amount of money in the economy

The demand for money is the amount of money households, firms, government, and foreign entities want to hold as currency and in their demand deposits and other liquid deposits.

The quantity of money demanded is affected by several factors including the nominal interest rate. When interest rates are high, households and firms pare down the amount of money they hold in their wallets and transaction accounts where it earns little or no interest. They would rather place that money where it can earn these high rates of interest. It makes no sense to hold a lot of money in one's wallet or checking account if it can be loaned, for example, to the U.S. government at an attractive rate.

At low interest rates, households and firms do not mind demanding a lot of money. The funds would not earn much if they were loaned out and the funds will be on hand should interest rates rise. If the nominal interest rate changes, then there will be movement along the M_d curve. Remember our tip: when the factor causing the change is on the vertical axis, there is movement along the curve, not a shift.

Another factor affecting the demand for money is income. When income rises, households and firms want to have more money on hand because they are conducting more transactions or more expensive transactions. Imagine when you graduate from college and land a great job. Your income will increase dramatically, and you will most definitely have more money in your wallet or in your bank accounts. You will need it to live your splendid new life. An increase in income for the entire economy shifts M_d rightward. This time the factor causing the change, a change in income, is not on the vertical axis, so the entire curve shifts.

The demand for money is also affected by the price level. If prices in the economy increase, people and firms will keep more money on hand in order to conduct their daily transactions and M_d shifts rightward.

Table 15.4

The Demand for Money	
Why is it downward sloping?	A rise in the nominal interest rate induces people and firms to place their funds where it can earn the higher return. This means they have less on hand.
What can shift it?	▪ A change in income ▪ A change in the price level

Let's put the money market model through its paces. Suppose the price level in the economy rises. What will happen to interest rates and the amount of money supplied and demanded? An increase in the price level increases the demand for money since people and businesses need more on hand to make their usual purchases. An increase in money demand is modeled with a rightward shift in M_d.

CHAPTER 15: MONETARY THEORY   293

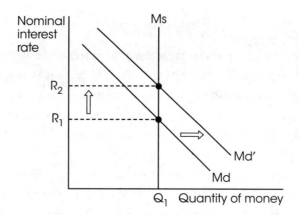

Figure 15.6 An increase in the Demand for Money

The equilibrium interest rate rises from R_1 to R_2, but the equilibrium quantity of money in the economy stays unchanged at Q_1. The Fed did not change the money supply, so when households and firms demand more money due to higher prices, interest rates rise (see Figure 15.6).

In another example, suppose the Fed increases the money supply.

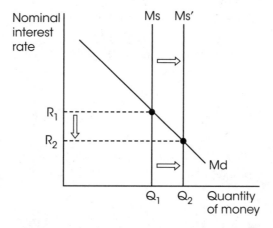

Figure 15.7 An Increase in the Supply of Money

The equilibrium nominal interest rate falls from R_1 to R_2. The supply of money increases from Q_1 to Q_2, the amount determined by the Fed. The model of the money market is indicating that an increase in the money supply lowers the nominal interest rate (see Figure 15.7).

SUMMARY

- The equation of exchange is the basis for the quantity theory of money and the theory of monetary neutrality. The equation itself cannot be disputed. $M \times V = P \times Y$ for any and every economy.

- The quantity theory of money and the theory of monetary neutrality depend on several assumptions about the equation of exchange. Those assumptions, and therefore the theories themselves, can be argued. However, most economists think these theories hold valuable insights into the workings of the macroeconomy.

- In addition, this chapter reviewed the market for loanable funds and the money market. Mastering the graphs portraying these markets is essential for doing well on the AP exam in Macroeconomics. You should be able to draw the graphs and correctly label the axes and lines within. Moreover, you should know what can shift the supply and demand curves for both of these models. These are not simple concepts to master, but working on the review questions below is a step in the right direction.

Formulas

Equation of Exchange: $M \times V = P \times Y$ or $M \times V = $ Nominal GDP

Nominal Interest Rate: Nominal Interest Rate = Real Interest Rate + Inflation

Multiple-Choice Review Questions

1. Based on the equation of exchange, if
   $M = 100$, $V = 3$, and $Y = 150$, then $P =$

   (A) 1/2.
   (B) 1.
   (C) 1.5.
   (D) 2.
   (E) 600.

2. According to the quantity theory of money, a
   decrease in the money supply would

   (A) raise the price level and output in the
       economy.
   (B) lower the price level and output in the
       economy.
   (C) raise the price level in the economy.
   (D) lower the price level in the economy.
   (E) raise the price level and lower output in the
       economy.

3. According to the assumptions of the quantity
   theory of money, if the money supply increases by
   5 percent, then

   (A) nominal and real GDP would rise by
       5 percent.
   (B) nominal GDP would rise by 5 percent; real
       GDP would be unchanged.
   (C) nominal GDP would be unchanged; real GDP
       would rise by 5 percent.
   (D) neither nominal GDP nor real GDP would
       change.
   (E) nominal GDP would be unchanged; the price
       level would rise by 5 percent.

4. According to the classical dichotomy, if the money
   supply rises 5 percent, then

   (A) the velocity of money will fall 5 percent.
   (B) the price level will rise almost proportionally.
   (C) the GDP deflator will fall 5 percent.
   (D) the price level will fall about 5 percent.
   (E) real GDP rises 5 percent.

5. According to the classical dichotomy, which of the
   following is influenced by monetary factors?

   (A) Nominal wages
   (B) Unemployment
   (C) Real GDP
   (D) Tonnage of steel produced in the U.S.
   (E) The standard of living

6. The principle of monetary neutrality implies that
   an increase in the money supply will

   (A) increase real GDP and the price level.
   (B) increase real GDP but not the price level.
   (C) increase the price level but not real GDP.
   (D) increase neither the price level nor real GDP.
   (E) increase the price level and employment.

7. Which of the following is not a financial
   intermediary in the U.S. economy?

   (A) The U.S. Mint
   (B) Commercial banks
   (C) Investment banks
   (D) Savings and loan associations
   (E) Credit unions

8. The nominal interest rate is 6 percent, and the
   inflation rate is 2 percent. What is the real interest rate?

   (A) −4 percent
   (B) 3 percent
   (C) 4 percent
   (D) 8 percent
   (E) 12 percent

9. If the real interest rate is above its equilibrium value, then there will be

   (A) an excess supply of loanable funds that pushes the real interest rate down.
   (B) an excess supply of loanable funds that pushes the real interest rate up.
   (C) a shortage of loanable funds that pushes the real interest rate down.
   (D) a shortage of loanable funds that pushes the real interest rate up.
   (E) a shortage of loanable funds that increases lending.

10. If the demand for loanable funds decreases, then the equilibrium real interest rate

    (A) rises but the equilibrium quantity of funds remains unchanged.
    (B) rises and the equilibrium quantity of funds increases.
    (C) rises and the equilibrium quantity of funds decreases.
    (D) falls and the equilibrium quantity of funds decreases.
    (E) falls and the equilibrium quantity of funds increases.

11. Imagine an economy that previously banned foreign investors now opens its doors to these lenders. We would expect to see the equilibrium real interest rate

    (A) rise and the equilibrium quantity of funds to decrease.
    (B) rise but the equilibrium quantity of funds to remain unchanged.
    (C) fall and the equilibrium quantity of funds to increase.
    (D) fall and the equilibrium quantity of funds to decrease.
    (E) rise and the equilibrium quantity of funds to increase.

12. Suppose our federal government needs to borrow more money than ever before. We would expect to see the equilibrium real interest rate

    (A) fall and the equilibrium quantity of funds to increase.
    (B) fall and the equilibrium quantity of funds to decrease.
    (C) rise and the equilibrium quantity of funds to decrease.
    (D) rise and the equilibrium quantity of funds to increase.
    (E) rise but the equilibrium quantity of funds to remain unchanged.

13. If foreigners decide to invest more in our economy than previously, then we would expect to see the real interest rate

    (A) fall and the equilibrium quantity of funds to increase.
    (B) fall and the equilibrium quantity of funds to decrease.
    (C) rise and the equilibrium quantity of funds to decrease.
    (D) rise and the equilibrium quantity of funds to increase.
    (E) rise but the equilibrium quantity of funds to remain unchanged.

14. Which of the following shifts the demand for money to the left?

    (A) An increase in the price level
    (B) An increase in the money supply
    (C) A decrease in the price level
    (D) A decrease in the money supply
    (E) An increase in the nominal interest rate

15. Which of the following shifts the supply of money to the left?

    (A) An increase in the price level
    (B) An increase in the money supply
    (C) A decrease in the price level
    (D) A decrease in the money supply
    (E) An increase in the nominal interest rate

Free-Response Review Questions

1. Use the equation of exchange to explain why a 10 percent increase in the money supply would lead to an almost proportional increase in the price level.

2. If the price level rises, will the supply or the demand for money be affected? Will it increase or decrease? Explain why.

3. Would a person demand more or less money when the nominal interest rate increases to significantly higher levels? Explain why.

Answer Explanations

1. **(D)** The equation of exchange is $M \times V = P \times Y$. The question gives three of these values, allowing P to found algebraically:

$$100 \times 3 = P \times 150$$
$$300 = P \times 150$$
$$\frac{300}{150} = P$$
$$P = 2$$

2. **(D)** The quantity theory of money posits a proportional relationship between the growth rate of the money supply and the inflation rate. Therefore, if the money supply decreases, then prices decrease.

3. **(B)** The quantity theory of money posits that a 5 percent increase in the money supply would increase the price level 5 percent and thereby affect nominal variables but not real variables. So nominal GDP would increase, but real GDP would be unaffected.

4. **(B)** The classical dichotomy is another name for the quantity theory of money. The theory indicates a proportional relationship between the growth rate of the money supply and the inflation rate.

5. **(A)** The classical dichotomy, which is the same thing as the quantity theory of money, concludes that only nominal variables are affected by a change in the money supply. Nominal GDP is the only nominal variable offered in the responses to this question.

6. **(C)** The classical dichotomy, which is the same thing as the quantity theory of money, concludes that only the price level, and therefore nominal variables, are affected by a change in the money supply. Therefore, real GDP is not affected by an increase in the money supply.

7. **(A)** Financial intermediaries shuttle money from savers to borrowers. U.S. Mints manufacture currency but do not transfer funds between savers and borrowers.

8. **(C)** This question is an application of Fisher's Hypothesis:

Nominal interest rate = real interest rate + inflation rate
6 percent   2 percent
Algebra yields 4 percent as the value of the real interest rate.

9. **(A)** Figure 15.2 indicates that when the real interest rate is above its equilibrium value, then there will be an excess supply of loanable funds that pushes the real interest rate down.

10. **(D)** Figure 15.4 shows that an increase in the demand for loanable funds increases the equilibrium real interest rate. So the answer in this question will be the opposite of that diagram.

11. **(C)** The supply of loanable funds increases when foreign investors are allowed to lend funds to the domestic market for loanable funds. The supply of loanable funds shifts to the right as in Figure 15.3. That figure indicates that the equilibrium real interest rate falls and the quantity of funds increases.

12. **(D)** When government borrowing increases, the demand for loanable funds increases, shifting the demand curve to the right as in Figure 15.4. That figure indicates that the equilibrium real interest rate rises and the quantity of funds borrowed and lent increases.

13. **(A)** The supply of loanable funds increases when foreign investors decide to lend more to the domestic market. The supply of loanable funds shifts to the right as in Figure 15.3. That figure indicates that the equilibrium real interest rate falls and the quantity of funds increases.

14. **(C)** A decrease in the price level results in people and firms needing less money in their wallets and checking accounts because the things they purchase do not cost as much. This is a decrease in the demand for money shifting the curve to the left.

15. **(D)** Only the Fed can change the supply of money. When the Fed decreases the money supply, the supply of money curve shifts to the left.

Free-Response Review Answers

1. The equation of exchange is true by definition. By assuming V and Y only change slowly over time, the equation mathematically stipulates that a 10 percent increase in the money supply results in a 10 percent increase in the price level approximately.

$$M \times \bar{V} = P \times \bar{Y} \quad \text{(The bars over the V and Y indicate they are rather stable.)}$$

   In these circumstances, the mathematics of the equation implies a 10 percent increase in M results in a 10 percent increase in P.

2. The supply of money can only be changed by the Fed. An increase in the price level results in an increase in the demand for money because people and firms need to have more money in their wallets and checking accounts to carry out their normal transactions.

3. A person would demand less money at higher nominal interest rates. This is because people are incentivized to pare down the amount they have in their wallets and checking accounts when that money can be used to buy the financial assets that are paying such high rates of interest.

16

Aggregate Supply and Aggregate Demand

Learning Objectives

In this chapter, you will learn:

- → Business cycles
- → Long-run aggregate supply
- → Short-run aggregate supply
- → Aggregate demand
- → Using the aggregate supply/aggregate demand model
- → Economic growth

Business Cycles

Every economy experiences ups and downs; good times and bad; recessions and revivals; expansions and contractions. Business cycles is another term for these economic fluctuations. Expansions are the periods of increasing economic activity. These last until the peak. Then comes the contraction or recessionary phase, and then the trough. A complete cycle goes from peak to peak or trough to trough.

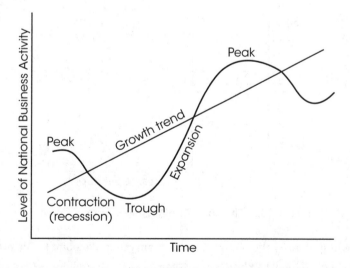

Figure 16.1 The Phases of the Business Cycle

Figure 16.1 is misleading because, although the ups and downs in economic activity are recurrent, they do not conform to a uniform schedule. The longest postwar recession in the United States lasted 18 months, the shortest just 2 months. The longest expansion was more than 10 years, while the shortest lasted only 12 months.

The fact that business cycles do not conform to a time schedule and differ in other respects, such as their severity, makes them extremely difficult to predict. Our task in this chapter, however, is not to predict when the next recession will occur but to explain *why* the economy moves in cycles.

We will build a replica, or model, of the economy and see if that model moves in cycles like the real economy. Our model should also display other well-known characteristics of capitalist economies. For instance, large increases in income tend to result in inflation. Does our model confirm this? Technological advances tend to increase output while putting downward pressure on prices. Does our model explain this? Inflation and unemployment tend to be inversely related—when one is up, the other is down—but not always. Does our model explain this tendency and is it flexible enough to allow for exceptions to the relationship?

TIP

The AS/AD model is the workhorse of macroeconomic analysis and is always prominently featured on the AP Macroeconomics exam.

The name of the model that addresses all of these questions is the *aggregate supply/aggregate demand (AS/AD) model*. The AS/AD model highlights the factors that determine output, income, employment, and prices in the economy. We begin with aggregate supply.

Long-Run Aggregate Supply

Aggregate supply is the amount of all goods and services brought to market by all domestic producers. It is the supply of everything by everyone. Aggregate supply is measured in dollars since simply counting items supplied doesn't make much sense. If total supply in the economy is 2 paper clips and 1 computer, it seems strange to say aggregate supply equals 3. An economy that produces 3 paper clips and 0 computers would have the same aggregate supply. Instead, we say aggregate supply equals $2,000.02, which is the market value of the 2 paper clips (1 cent each) and 1 computer ($2,000.00).

We want to graph the relationship between long-run aggregate supply (LRAS) and prices in the economy (Figure 16.2). The average price of products (price level) is measured on the vertical axis. Aggregate supply, measured in dollars, is on the horizontal axis.

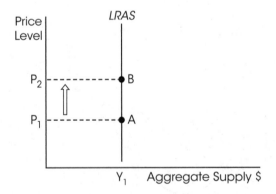

Figure 16.2 The Long-Run Aggregate Supply Curve

As the price level rises from P_1 to P_2, the economy moves from point A to point B. The price level is higher at point B, but the amount supplied by all producers is unchanged at Y_1. Only changes in resources or technology affect long-run aggregate supply. A change in prices does not affect long-run aggregate supply. A vertical LRAS reflects this fact.

In the long run, aggregate supply depends on only two factors: 1) the amount of resources and 2) the technology brought to bear on those resources. These are the two factors that shift LRAS.

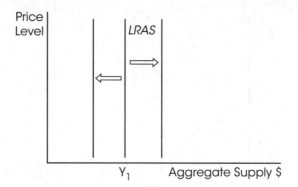

Figure 16.3 Shifts in the Long-Run Aggregate Supply Curve

LRAS is vertical because the amount supplied in the long run does not depend on the price level. Prices in the economy can be high or low; aggregate supply is going to be Y_1, an amount determined by the abundance of resources and the state of technology.

See Figure 16.3. An increase in resources or a technological advance shifts LRAS to the right. A reduction in resources or a decline in technological productivity shifts LRAS to the left.

Short-Run Aggregate Supply

The same two factors that shift LRAS shift short-run aggregate supply. However, in the short run, other things could affect the total supply of goods and services in the economy: 1) a change in the price level; 2) a change in the expected future price level; and 3) a change in the price of land, labor, or capital. Let's consider these three factors one at a time.

Suppose the Price Level Rises

If the price level rises, that means suppliers can get more for their finished products. Notice that we are assuming that the price of land, labor, and capital has not risen in tandem. If that were so, then producers would have no incentive to bring more product to market. Suppliers could get higher prices for their products, but their input costs have risen proportionally. Aggregate supply would be unaffected if the costs of production rose in tandem with the price level.

In the long run, that is exactly what happens: a change in the price level is eventually matched by a change in input costs. Therefore, a change in the price level does not affect aggregate supply in the long run. In the short run, it is possible to have a change in the price level that is not matched by a change in input costs.

Students often ask, "How long until the long run arrives"? It varies. In fact, the definition of "long run" in macroeconomics is "however long it takes for the economy to adjust to a change in the price level."

In the short run, a rise in the price level, *ceteris paribus*, causes an increase in aggregate supply. Graphically, this relationship translates into Figure 16.4.

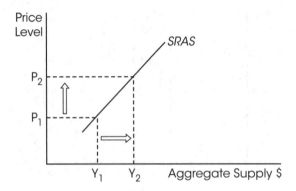

Figure 16.4 The Short-Run Aggregate Supply Curve

As the price level rises from P_1 to P_2, the amount supplied by all producers increases from Y_1 to Y_2. This is because suppliers are getting higher prices for their products but resource prices have not yet increased. Thus, the short-run aggregate supply curve (SRAS) is upward sloping to reflect this assumption (see Figure 16.4).

Suppose the Expected Future Price Level Rises

If prices are expected to be higher in the near future, then suppliers bring less to market right now. They would wait until prices rise, then bring their products to market. This results in a decrease in short-run aggregate supply. Nothing happens to long-run aggregate supply because resources or technology has not changed.

If we were to graph the relationship between the expected future price level and aggregate supply, it would be downward sloping. A downward-sloping line indicates a negative, or inverse, relationship: when expected future prices increase, aggregate supply decreases, and when expected future prices decrease, aggregate supply increases.

However, we want to graph short-run aggregate supply with the price level, not the expected price level, on the vertical axis. These are two separate things. We have already established an upward-sloping short-run aggregate supply curve when the price level is on the vertical axis. How can we show the effect of an increase in the expected future price level on this graph?

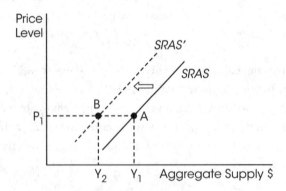

Figure 16.5 Shifts in the Short-Run Aggregate Supply Curve

See Figure 16.5. Starting at point A, if the expected future price level increases, then aggregate supply would decrease. However, the price level is unchanged at P_1. The only way to show this is by moving to a point like B.

In fact, the entire SRAS curve has shifted to the left with the increase in the expected future price level. Regardless of where we start, at point A, or at any other point on SRAS, now that prices are expected to be higher in the future, suppliers bring less to market.

This is a tip that will serve you well when working with the aggregate demand/aggregate supply model: if the factor listed on the vertical axis changes, then there is movement from one point to another along the line. The line shifts right or left when the factor causing the change is not listed on the vertical axis.

The case in point is an increase in the expected future prices. This will decrease short-run aggregate supply. Since the price level, not expected future prices, is listed on the vertical axis, the entire SRAS curve shifts leftward.

Suppose the Price of Land, Labor, or Capital Increases

Land, labor, and capital are the factors of production or inputs into the production process. Suppliers have incentive to cut back production when costs increase, *ceteris paribus*. Therefore, an increase in any of these prices reduces SRAS and the curve shifts leftward (see Figure 16.6).

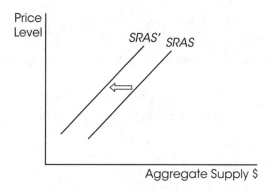

Figure 16.6 An Increase in Resource Prices Shifts SRAS Left

Summary of the Factors Affecting Aggregate Supply

In the long run, aggregate supply is only affected by the amount of resources and technology. An increase in either of these factors would shift LRAS rightward and a decrease would shift LRAS leftward (see Figure 16.7).

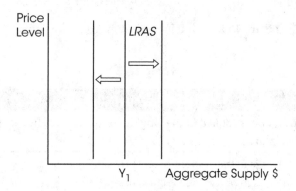

Figure 16.7 Shifts in the Long-Run Aggregate Supply Curve

LRAS is vertical because the amount supplied in the long run does not depend on the price level. Prices in the economy can be high or low; aggregate supply is going to be Y_1, an amount determined by the abundance of resources and the state of technology.

In the short run, aggregate supply is also affected by resources and technology but also by the price level, the expected future price level, and the prices of the factors of production. If the price level increases, then there will be an increase in the quantity supplied as shown by movement along the given SRAS curve (see Figure 16.8).

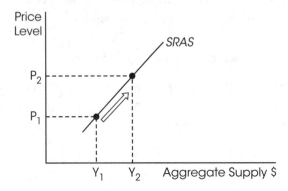

Figure 16.8 Movement Along the Short-Run Aggregate Supply Curve

If the change in SRAS is caused by any of the other four factors affecting it, then the entire curve shifts left or right. For example, if resource prices decreased, then SRAS would shift rightward (see Figure 16.9).

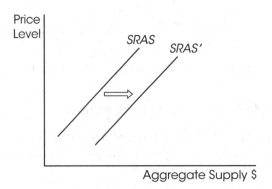

Figure 16.9 A Shift in Short-Run Aggregate Supply

Table 16.1

Long-Run Aggregate Supply	
Why is it vertical?	The amount supplied in the long run is not affected by the prices of final goods and services in the economy.
What can shift it?	■ A change in the amount of resources in the economy ■ Changes in production technology

Table 16.2

Short-Run Aggregate Supply	
Why is it upward sloping?	Suppliers have incentive to bring more to market if the price level rises because they can get more for their finished products while wages remain unchanged.
What can shift it?	■ A change in the amount of resources in the economy ■ Changes in production technology ■ Changes in expected future prices ■ Changes in the prices of land, labor, or capital

In order to make exam questions more challenging, a shift factor can be disguised. Instead of saying, "The economy obtains more resources…," the exam could say, "The labor force expands…." You have to realize that the labor force is a resource.

Aggregate Demand

Aggregate demand is the amount of goods and services demanded by households, businesses, governments, and foreigners. It is the demand for all final goods and services by everyone. It is measured in dollars.

Unlike aggregate supply, there is only one aggregate demand curve. Total demand in the economy is affected by so many things that it will be impossible to make an exhaustive list. However, the things that affect aggregate demand can be categorized.

Before getting to those categories, notice that aggregate demand will be affected by the price level in the economy. Consider this relationship graphically.

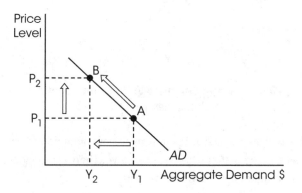

Figure 16.10 An Increase in the Price Level

In Figure 16.10, when the price level rises from P_1 to P_2, the dollar amount of aggregate demand declines from Y_1 to Y_2. There is movement up and along the aggregate demand curve from point A to point B.

Most people think that this is easily explained: when prices rise, demanders do not want or cannot afford as much. But this reasoning is wrong. When prices in general rise, this is inflation and inflation does not erode overall income in the economy. When the price level rises, most people and firms earn more income. Firms are getting more for their finished products, so why would they demand less? Profits are up, and those profits get passed on to the owners of the firm who live in households. So if households have more income, why would they demand less?

Foreigners, however, live in other nations and have not experienced the rise in prices and income. They would demand less since our goods have increased in price relative to theirs. So when the price level rises, one reason aggregate demand declines is because foreign demand falls. This is the foreign purchases effect.

Another reason aggregate demand is lower when the price level rises is because most forms of financial wealth are eroded. Consider a household that had saved $1 million for retirement. Now that prices have risen, that $1 million may not be enough to last throughout retirement. The household begins to save more and therefore spend less. Aggregate demand falls. This is the wealth effect.

The aggregate demand curve is downward sloping to show that the price level and total demand in the economy vary inversely. When the price level rises, aggregate demand falls and vice versa. However, the explanation for this inverse relationship is not that everyone can afford less when prices rise. Incomes rise in proportion to inflation. So why would less be demanded? The foreign purchases effect and the wealth effect.

Now let's turn our attention to factors aside from a change in the price level (and therefore a change in income) that can affect aggregate demand. Try to think of things that would affect household spending aside from prices and income. How about if households became more confident about their future job security or pay raises? They would spend more even though prices and income are unchanged.

To illustrate an uptick in consumer confidence on aggregate demand, shift the entire AD curve to the right (see Figure 16.11).

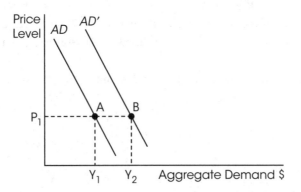

Figure 16.11 An Increase in Consumer Confidence
Shifts Aggregate Demand

This is because prices remained unchanged at P_1 while aggregate demand increased from Y_1 to Y_2. Indeed, the entire AD curve has shifted because no matter what the price level, there is more demand in the economy now that consumers have more confidence in their economic prospects.

Another factor that shifts aggregate demand is a change in taxes. A reduction in income taxes gives households more after-tax income, and that boosts their spending. If the tax reduction is aimed at businesses, then businesses spend more on plant and equipment.

Are there other factors aside from a cut in business taxes that would affect business spending? Another factor increasing aggregate demand is a change in expected future sales by firms. When businesses become more confident about their future sales, they start spending on plant and equipment in order to gear up right now.

An increase in the money supply usually lowers interest rates, and this stimulates firms to borrow and spend more on plant and equipment. Households also may be induced to borrow and spend more when the money supply is increased.

What could cause foreigners to spend more on our goods and services? What if they developed a taste for our products? Aggregate demand would shift rightward. What if our trade partners experience an economic expansion? They would purchase more of our products, and aggregate demand would increase.

Finally, local, state, and federal governments could increase spending for a variety of reasons. There is a lot of politics involved in these spending decisions, but regardless of the reason, an increase in government spending shifts aggregate demand rightward.

Why do all these factors shift aggregate demand as opposed to causing movement along the AD curve? Because they are not listed on the vertical axis of the graph.

Table 16.3

Aggregate Demand	
Why is it downward sloping?	Foreign purchases effect—foreigners demand less when domestic prices rise because their incomes have not risen in tandem; and domestic consumers prefer more imports since domestic prices are up. ■ Wealth effect—financial wealth is eroded when prices rise; this causes consumers to save more and spend less.
What can shift it?	■ Changes in consumer confidence ■ Changes in taxes ■ Changes in business confidence ■ Changes in the money supply ■ Changes in foreign demand due to preferences or income ■ Changes in government spending

Equilibrium

The short-run aggregate supply curve and the aggregate demand curve can be drawn on the same diagram. See Figure 16.12.

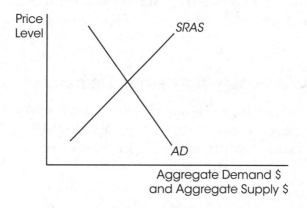

Figure 16.12 Aggregate Demand and Short-Run Aggregate Supply

Later we will add the long-run aggregate supply curve as well. For now, notice that the horizontal axis measures both aggregate supply and aggregate demand. These are both measured in dollars, as is GDP. Aggregate demand is total spending in the economy and is well approximated by GDP. Similarly, aggregate supply is total production in the economy and is well approximated by GDP. So we can relabel the horizontal axis as "real GDP." The price level, which can be measured with the GDP deflator, is on the vertical axis.

The economy will tend to operate where the two curves cross. This is known as the equilibrium point. See Figure 16.13.

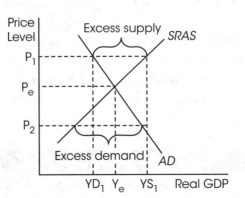

Figure 16.13 The Equilibrium Price Level (P_e) and Equilibrium Real GDP (Y_e)

If the economy is not operating at the equilibrium point, it will be shortly. Suppose the price level is not P_e but higher at P_1. At P_1 aggregate demand (YD_1) is less than short-run aggregate supply (YS_1). So there is an excess supply of goods and services. Producers will soon notice their inventories of finished goods piling up. The inventory accumulation induces suppliers to lower their prices. The excess supply will shrink but not disappear until the price level falls to P_e.

At P_e, there is no surplus or shortage of goods and services. We have a state of rest between opposing forces. Just the right amount is produced to satisfy demanders and suppliers. That amount is Y_e, the equilibrium quantity.

If the price level is below the equilibrium price level, there will be a shortage of goods and services. At P_2, aggregate demand is greater than aggregate supply. This excess demand causes inventories to dwindle. Suppliers soon realize that they can raise prices and still sell all they produce. Higher prices will reduce the excess demand, but it will not disappear entirely until the price level rises to P_e.

Once the economy achieves equilibrium, we know the price level (P_e) and the amount produced (Y_e). The economy is at rest in equilibrium, but don't expect P_e and Y_e to remain unchanged. Remember, there are many factors that can shift both SRAS and AD. When that occurs, the economy will have to adjust to a new equilibrium point.

Using the Aggregate Supply/Aggregate Demand Model

Now we can use the aggregate demand/aggregate supply model to explain business cycles and consider what causes them. Consider what happens when there is a significant decline in the foreign demand for a nation's products. This would occur if the foreign nations are experiencing a recession.

The aggregate demand curve shifts to the left (see Figure 16.14).

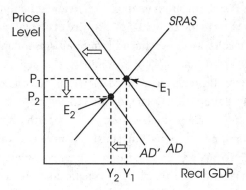

Figure 16.14 The Short-Run Effects of a Decrease in Aggregate Demand

The initial equilibrium point is E_1, where the price level is P_1 and real GDP is Y_1. The reduction of foreign demand in the economy shifts AD left. The new equilibrium point is E_2, where the price level is P_2 and real GDP is Y_2. The decline in foreign demand caused the price level and real GDP to fall.

The decline in real GDP implies three things: 1) production in the economy is lower; 2) income in the economy is lower because whenever anything is produced it generates an equal amount of income; and 3) there is more unemployment since less production means less demand for labor.

This example demonstrates the usefulness of the AD/AS model. If a nation's trading partners are in recession, then that will impact the domestic economy. Aggregate demand falls, and the recession is transmitted among trading partners. The model predicts falling prices, production, and income and an increase in unemployment.

Let's do another example. This time suppose the price of natural resources increases dramatically because speculators have bid on the price of oil, natural gas, and coal. Rising resource prices shift SRAS to the left, as shown in Figure 16.15.

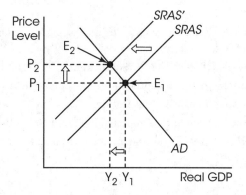

Figure 16.15 The Short-Run Effects of a Decrease in
Short-Run Aggregate Supply

Again, the model predicts a recession since real GDP decreases from Y_1 to Y_2. This time, however, the price level is expected to increase from P_1 to P_2. A significant increase in resource prices is expected to lower output and income while raising unemployment and the price level.

Stagflation

At E_2, the economy in Figure 16.15 is suffering from unemployment and inflation at the same time. The United States found itself in this exact situation in the early 1970s. The price of oil had risen sharply as oil-exporting nations restricted the supply. The result was a recession and simultaneous inflation. James Tobin, an economist at Yale, referred to the double trouble as "stagflation," and the name stuck. Stagflation is a recession accompanied by rising prices. It can only be caused by SRAS shifting leftward. However, quite a few things can cause this leftward shift. Review the section on aggregate supply in this chapter for a refresher.

In both these examples, the economy suffered recessions. We learned that a recession abroad or rising resource prices can potentially cause economic contractions. But a business cycle is a contraction followed by a trough and then an expansion rising toward the peak. Are the two economies we considered mired in recessions forever? Is there something that must occur to cause the expansion? To see the answers to these questions, we must include the long-run aggregate demand curve in our analysis.

Using the Complete Aggregate Supply/Aggregate Demand Model

An economy must be operating where all three curves intersect to be in full equilibrium, as in Figure 16.16.

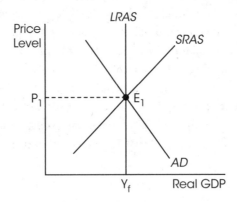

Figure 16.16 The Complete Aggregate Supply/Aggregate Demand Model

At E_1, the price level is P_1 and real GDP is Y_f. The "Y" stands for real GDP, and the "f" stands for full employment of resources. Since E_1 rests on the long-run aggregate supply curve, the economy is operating at full employment. It is akin to being on the production possibilities frontier.

Now consider a decrease in aggregate demand as depicted in Figure 16.17. This time suppose there is an income tax increase. This leaves households with less disposable income. Households reduce spending and AD shifts left.

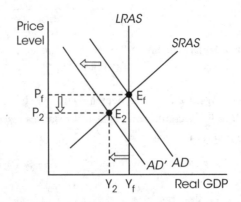

Figure 16.17 A Decrease in Aggregate Demand

The economy moves to E_2 and experiences a recession with output and income lower and unemployment higher. The price level has fallen to P_2. At Y_2 the economy is producing below its potential because it is to the left of Y_f.

E_2 is a short-run equilibrium since it does not lie on LRAS. Eventually, in the long run, the economy will move away from E_2. This is because whenever the economy is producing below its potential, as it is at E_2, there is unemployment and other unused resources. Some workers are willing to accept lower wages at this point. And owners of natural resources might accept lower prices for their commodities given that they are not selling as briskly as before the recession. Changes in the prices of land, labor, and capital are on our list of things that would shift SRAS. A decline in these prices shifts SRAS rightward as in Figure 16.18.

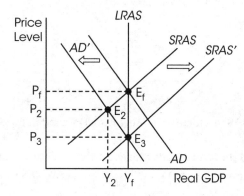

Figure 16.18 Long-Run Adjustment to a Recession

The economy ends up at E_3 where output is back to full potential at Y_f. Notice that the price level has fallen further to P_3. Let's review: Beginning at E_f the economy is doing just fine at full employment. Then income taxes are raised and this reduces AD, causing a recession. The economy is now operating at E_2. However, E_2 is only a short-run equilibrium. In the long run, resource prices fall because they are underutilized. Firms are willing to hire labor and buy resources at their lower prices, and this increases short-run aggregate supply. This results in SRAS shifting rightward.

In the long run, the economy returns to full-employment equilibrium. Notice that workers and the owners of other resources are not worse off even though they are getting less for their labor and other resources. The price of finished products has fallen to P_3, so they are no worse off than before the recession.

Also, notice that we have explained a full business cycle. A tax increase led to a recession, but eventually resource prices fell and SRAS shifted rightward. This rightward shift was the expansion as output increased from Y_2 back to Y_f.

Students always want to know how long it takes for the economy to return to full employment. The textbook answer is "in the long run." "How long is that?" It varies. It can take decades for resource prices to fall far enough to cause the expansion, or it can take months. The average recession in the postwar U.S. economy lasts nine months. But we shall see in the ensuing chapters that the U.S. economy was not left to self-adjust in any of those recessions. There are policies that can hurry the recovery along.

Before considering these recession remedies, let's tackle another example. In this case, let's begin at full-employment and then suppose there is an increase in business confidence. When businesses expect to be doing well in the near future, they immediately spend more on plant and equipment in order to gear up for higher sales volume. This shifts AD rightward, as in Figure 16.19.

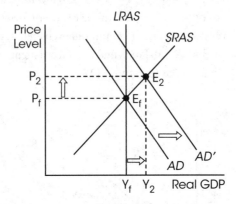

Figure 16.19 An Increase in Aggregate Demand in the Short Run

Now the economy is at E_2 in the short run, producing at Y_2. This amount is more than full-employment output, Y_f. The economy must be outside its production possibilities frontier. We know this is unsustainable, but now we can understand exactly why.

With more than full employment and resources strained beyond their potential, wages and resource prices rise. Firms must offer higher wages in order to induce workers to leave their current positions. Owners of other resources ask for higher prices as well. When wages and other resource prices rise, SRAS shifts left, as in Figure 16.20.

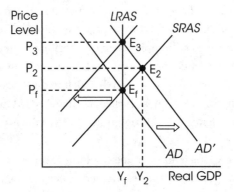

Figure 16.20 An Increase in Aggregate Demand in the Long Run

The economy ends up at E_3. Real GDP has fallen back to Y_f and the price level has risen to P_3. Workers and other resource owners got raises, but the price level increased proportionally so their real income is unchanged. Once again the macroeconomy has self-adjusted in the long run. This time an increase in resource prices was required to bring output back to Y_f.

Economic Growth

Consider what happens when an economy obtains more resources or experiences a technological enhancement. Either of these occurrences shifts both short- and long-run aggregate supply to the right, as in Figure 16.21.

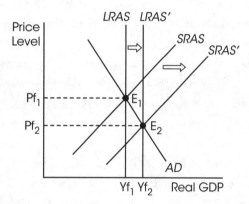

Figure 16.21 Economic Growth Is an Increase in Short- and
Long-Run Aggregate Supply

The results are good. The price level falls and real GDP increases. The production possibilities frontier has shifted outward since more resources are available or a better technology is being applied. Full-capacity real GDP has increased from Y_{f1} to Y_{f2} and the economy moves from long-run equilibrium E_1 directly to long-run equilibrium E_2. There is no intermediate short-run equilibrium point as in our previous examples.

Whenever the LRAS curve shifts, the SRAS shifts simultaneously. This is because only two things can shift LRAS: 1) a change in the amount of resources available in the macroeconomy and 2) change in production technology. Both of those factors shift SRAS as well.

If the economy obtains more resources or better technology, then full-capacity output increases. This is known as economic growth. An entire field of macroeconomics is devoted to studying economic growth. How can we grow the economy? Easy—obtain more resources or experience a technological advance that increases productivity. How can we do either of those things? Not so easy...

The U.S. government tries to promote economic growth by underwriting research and development and giving grants to universities to develop new technologies. To foster the development of new resources, the U.S. government subsidizes oil exploration and allows foreign workers into the country. Job training is an attempt to enhance labor—a critical resource. When labor becomes better trained and more effective, this is known as improving human capital.

Many growth theorists advocate saving. By saving instead of spending, more funds are available to be borrowed by firms and invested in new plant and equipment. This new plant and equipment is an expansion of resources and shifts SRAS and LRAS to the right.

SUMMARY

- No economy grows at a steady pace. Capitalist and centrally planned economies alike experience waves of economic activity know as business cycles. In this chapter we came to understand what causes economic fluctuations: anything that shifts short-run aggregate supply or aggregate demand. There are many factors that can impact these curves. That is to say there are many factors that cause business cycles.

- Suppose there is a decline in aggregate demand caused by a drop in consumer confidence. This results in the recessionary phase of the business cycle. In the next chapter we shall see that there are policies that can be applied to try to remedy the situation. But in this chapter, we saw that even if no policies are implemented, in the long-run resource prices fall, causing the short-run aggregate supply curve to shift rightward. This rightward shift increases real GDP and brings about the expansionary phase of the business cycle. Thus, the economy experiences these ebbs and flows of economic activity.

- This chapter also presented the concept of stagflation—inflation and a recession at the same time. Stagflation results whenever short-run aggregate supply or long-run aggregate supply shifts left.

- Economic growth is when the economy expands its productive capacity. We now understand that this is modeled by shifting short- and long-run aggregate supply to the right. Growth theorists study how to promote these shifts.

- The AD/AS model is prominently featured on every AP examination in Macroeconomics. It pays to learn to use the model with confidence. Study the factors that can shift each curve. Be able to show and explain how the economy self-adjusts from a short-run equilibrium that is to the left or right of long-run equilibrium.

Multiple-Choice Review Questions

1. A business cycle trough is immediately followed by the

   (A) nadir.
   (B) peak.
   (C) inflexion.
   (D) expansion.
   (E) contraction.

2. Recessions

   (A) are a thing of the past.
   (B) are very severe depressions.
   (C) are typically accompanied by job losses.
   (D) occur at regular intervals.
   (E) are marked by a sustained increase in output.

3. Which of the following would shift the long-run aggregate supply curve to the right?

   (A) Prices are expected to decrease in the near future.
   (B) Immigration increases the size of the labor force.
   (C) A fire wipes out much of the plant and equipment in the economy.
   (D) Prices are expected to increase in the near future.
   (E) New government regulations slow factory production.

4. Which of the following would shift the short-run aggregate supply curve to the right?

   (A) Prices are expected to increase in the near future.
   (B) New government regulations slow factory production.
   (C) A fire wipes out much of the plant and equipment in the economy.
   (D) Nominal wages decrease.
   (E) Nominal wages increase.

5. Which of the following would NOT shift the aggregate supply curve?

   (A) An increase in the price level
   (B) A decrease in the amount of resources in the economy
   (C) An increase in the amount of resources in the economy
   (D) An improvement in technology
   (E) A decrease in productivity

6. Which of the following would shift the aggregate demand curve to the left?

   (A) An increase in consumer confidence
   (B) Business firms reduce spending on plant and equipment
   (C) Foreigners develop a preference for our products
   (D) Government increases its level of spending
   (E) An increase in the money supply

7. Which of the following would NOT shift the aggregate demand curve?

   (A) A change in consumer confidence
   (B) A change in technology
   (C) A change in the money supply
   (D) A change in spending by state governments
   (E) A change in foreign tastes for our products

8. What will happen to the equilibrium price level and the equilibrium quantity of output if the aggregate demand curve shifts to the right? Assume an upward-sloping aggregate supply curve.

   (A) The equilibrium price level increases while the equilibrium quantity of output decreases.
   (B) The equilibrium price level decreases while the equilibrium quantity of output increases.
   (C) The equilibrium price level and quantity of output increase.
   (D) The equilibrium price level and quantity of output decrease.
   (E) The equilibrium price level increases while the equilibrium quantity of output remains unchanged.

9. What will happen to the equilibrium price level and the equilibrium quantity of output if consumer confidence increases? Assume an upward-sloping aggregate supply curve.

    (A) The equilibrium price level increases while the equilibrium quantity of output decreases.
    (B) The equilibrium price level decreases while the equilibrium quantity of output increases.
    (C) The equilibrium price level and quantity of output increase.
    (D) The equilibrium price level and quantity of output increase.
    (E) The equilibrium price level increases while the equilibrium quantity of output remains unchanged.

10. What will happen to the equilibrium price level and the equilibrium quantity of output if the aggregate demand curve shifts to the right? Assume a long-run aggregate supply curve.

    (A) The equilibrium price level increases while the equilibrium quantity of output decreases.
    (B) The equilibrium price level decreases while the equilibrium quantity of output increases.
    (C) The equilibrium price level and quantity of output increase.
    (D) The equilibrium price level remains unchanged while the equilibrium quantity of output increases.
    (E) The equilibrium price level increases while the equilibrium quantity of output remains unchanged.

11. What will happen to the equilibrium price level and the equilibrium quantity of output if the aggregate supply curve shifts to the left? Assume an upward-sloping aggregate supply curve.

    (A) The equilibrium price level increases while the equilibrium quantity of output decreases.
    (B) The equilibrium price level decreases while the equilibrium quantity of output increases.
    (C) The equilibrium price level and quantity of output increase.
    (D) The equilibrium price level and quantity of output decrease.
    (E) The equilibrium price level increases while the equilibrium quantity of output remains unchanged.

12. What will happen to the equilibrium price level and the equilibrium quantity of output if a major earthquake destroys much of the plant and equipment on the West Coast? Assume an upward-sloping aggregate supply curve.

    (A) The equilibrium price level increases while the equilibrium quantity of output decreases.
    (B) The equilibrium price level decreases while the equilibrium quantity of output increases.
    (C) The equilibrium price level and quantity of output increase.
    (D) The equilibrium price level and quantity of output decrease.
    (E) The equilibrium price level increases while the equilibrium quantity of output remains unchanged.

13. Stagflation occurs when

    (A) aggregate supply shifts left.
    (B) aggregate supply shifts right.
    (C) aggregate demand shifts left.
    (D) aggregate demand shifts right.
    (E) inflation slows down.

14. Which of the following will promote economic growth?

    (A) Laws limiting immigration
    (B) A decrease in the money supply
    (C) An increase in the money supply
    (D) Price controls that keep prices low
    (E) An increase in the supply of capital

15. Stagflation could be caused by

    (A) an improvement in consumer confidence.
    (B) a decline in consumer confidence.
    (C) an increase in resource prices.
    (D) a decrease in resource prices.
    (E) wages and salaries that are decreasing.

Free-Response Review Questions

1. Draw an aggregate supply/aggregate demand diagram. Label the axes of your diagram. Make the aggregate supply curve upward sloping. Show which curve shifts when foreigners suddenly develop a distaste for our products. What will happen to equilibrium output and the equilibrium price level in the short run?

2. Would you expect the same thing to happen to equilibrium output and the equilibrium price level in the long run? Redraw the aggregate supply/aggregate demand diagram using a long-run aggregate supply curve. Now what happens when foreigners develop a distaste for our products?

3. Explain why the long-run aggregate supply curve is drawn as a vertical line and the short-run aggregate supply curve is drawn upward sloping. Explain why the long-run effects of a change in foreign tastes are different from the short-run effects.

Answer Explanations

1. **(D)** See Figure 16.1 for the phases of the business cycle.

2. **(C)** This is the only correct response.

3. **(B)** Long-run aggregate supply shifts right when resources increase or technology advances. Labor is a resource, and immigration is increasing the amount available.

4. **(D)** When the price of resources decreases, short-run aggregate supply shifts to the right. Labor is a resource, and its price (nominal wages) is decreasing.

5. **(A)** A change in the price level would only cause movement along the short-run or long-run supply curve. Neither would shift.

6. **(B)** A reduction in spending, be it by businesses, government, consumers, or foreigners, shifts aggregate demand to the left.

7. **(B)** A change in technology shifts the long-run and the short-run aggregate supply curves, not aggregate demand. In fact, nothing that shifts aggregate supply shifts aggregate demand.

8. **(C)** The best way to answer questions like this is to use the AS/AD model. Shift the aggregate demand curve to the right as the question stipulates:

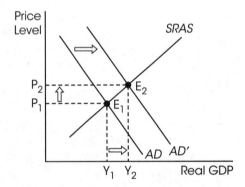

The equilibrium moves from E_1 to E_2. The price level is higher at E_2 and so is real GDP.

9. **(C)** When consumer confidence increases, the aggregate demand curve shifts to the right. Therefore, the situation is as depicted in the response to question 8 and the response is the same. The price level is higher at E_2 and so is real GDP.

10. **(E)** The best way to answer questions like this is to use the AS/AD model. Shift the aggregate demand curve to the right as the question stipulates.

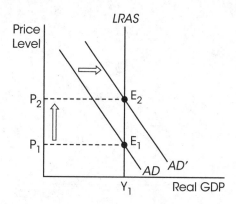

The equilibrium moves from E_1 to E_2. The price level is higher at E_2 but real GDP is unchanged at Y_1.

11. **(A)** The best way to answer questions like this is to use the AS/AD model. Shift the short-run aggregate supply curve to the left as the question stipulates.

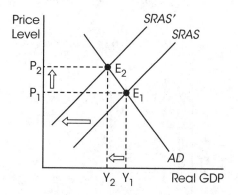

The equilibrium moves from E_1 to E_2. The price level is higher at E_2 and real GDP is lower.

12. **(A)** When a large portion of the economy's plant and equipment is destroyed, the short-run aggregate supply curve shifts to the left. Therefore, the situation is as depicted in the response to question 11 and the response is the same. The price level is higher at E_2 and real GDP, or output, is lower.

13. **(A)** Stagflation is when the price level rises and real GDP decreases. This can only occur when the aggregate supply curve shifts to the left.

14. **(E)** Economic growth is promoted when the economy gets more resources or experiences a technological advance. An increase in the supply of capital (plant and equipment) is an increase in an important set of resources.

15. **(C)** An increase in resource prices causes either aggregate supply curve to shift to the left. The result is a higher price level and less output, or real GDP. That is stagflation.

Free-Response Review Answers

1. The AS/AD model when foreigners develop a distaste for our products (with short-run aggregate supply curve) is shown.

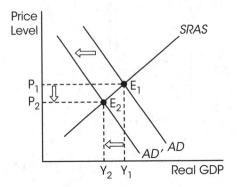

When foreigners develop a distaste for our products, the aggregate demand curve shifts to the left. This causes the equilibrium price level and the equilibrium quantity of output to fall.

2. The AS/AD model when foreigners develop a distaste for our products (with long-run aggregate supply curve) is shown.

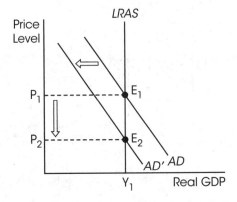

The long-run analysis indicates that the equilibrium price level will fall when foreigners develop a distaste for our products, but the equilibrium quantity of output will remain unchanged.

3. The long-run aggregate supply curve is drawn as a vertical line because aggregate supply is not affected by the price level in the long run. Only the amount of resources and the state of technology affect aggregate supply in the long run. In the short run, however, a decrease in the price level induces suppliers in the economy to bring less product to market. Therefore, when foreigners develop a distaste for our products, prices fall and this reduces the amount of product that suppliers are willing to bring to market. But in the long run, the change in foreign tastes has not affected the amount of resources or the state of technology, so the quantity of output remains unchanged.

17

Monetary Policy

Monetary Policy Defined

Monetary policy is changing the money supply and interest rates to promote maximum employment, stabilize prices, and promote economic growth. These are the three explicitly stated goals of the Fed. It is the Fed, and solely the Fed, that conducts monetary policy.

Only the Fed has the power to change the money supply and affect almost all interest rates in the U.S. macro-economy. The Fed reports to Congress about its intentions and past policies. But no branch of the U.S. government can dictate monetary policy. Not all central banks are as independent as the Fed.

Notice that changes in government spending, taxes, or other fiscal policies have no effect on the money supply. Consider an increase in government spending. The government gets the money from taxes or loans. No new money is created. The current money supply is used more intensely. The velocity of money increases.

The Fed has four tools to change the money supply and interest rates: 1) reserve requirements, 2) the discount rate, 3) open market operations, and 4) changing the interest rate on bank reserves. Not all of these tools are effective for monetary policy depending on the circumstances.

To promote maximum employment during a recession, the appropriate monetary policy is to increase the money supply and lower interest rates across the economy. To promote price stability during inflationary times, the appropriate monetary policy is to decrease the money supply and raise interest rates.

The Fed's goals of maximum employment and price stability are at odds with each other. To promote maximum employment, increase M1. However, this could very well cause inflation. To tame inflation, the Fed should decrease the money supply. But this could cause unemployment. Monetary policy is often a balancing act between these two contradictory goals.

The Fed's third goal, to promote economic growth, is achieved by stabilizing long-term interest rates at a moderate level. Interest rates that are stable and moderate promote borrowing and lending and that, in turn, promotes investment spending on all sorts of capital. The economy grows because it has more capital resources.

Expansionary monetary policy is increasing the money supply to promote maximum employment and remedy a recession. Contractionary monetary policy is decreasing the money supply to lower the price level and remedy inflation. During inflationary times, a decrease in the money supply is warranted. This increases nominal interest rates and therefore borrowing costs. There is less borrowing and spending, resulting in a decrease in aggregate demand.

Monetary Policy in Theory

An increase in the money supply promotes maximum employment and can remedy a recession. With more money in circulation, it is cheaper to borrow as reflected in lower interest rates. The increase in borrowing and spending increases aggregate demand.

Money supply ⬆ ⟹ Interest rates ⬇ ⟹ Borrowing & spending ⬆ ⟹ Aggregate demand ⬆

The AS/AD diagram below (Figure 17.1) represents an economy suffering from a recession.

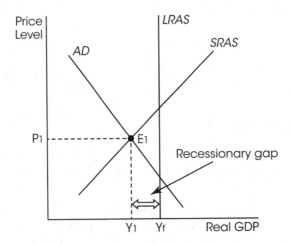

Figure 17.1 A Recessionary Gap

We know this because real GDP is at Y_1, which is less than full-employment real GDP, Y_f. The distance between Y_1 and Y_f is called the recessionary gap—the shortfall of real GDP from its full-employment potential. The economy is producing inside its production possibilities frontier.

Because the long-run aggregate supply curve does not cross E_1, it is a short-run equilibrium, and the economy will adjust so that all three curves cross in the long run. Specifically, the recession leaves many resources, including some labor, to be idle. Workers and resource owners lower their asking wages and prices, and this induces firms to increase output, shifting SRAS to the right, as in Figure 17.2.

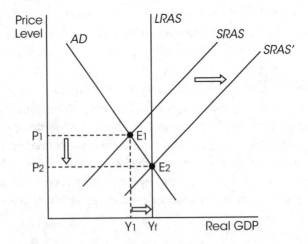

Figure 17.2 Long-Run Adjustment to a Recessionary Gap

The result is a long-run equilibrium at E$_2$. The price level has fallen to P$_2$ and the recession is over with output rising from Y$_1$ to Y$_f$. The only drawback of this scenario is that it could take a long time for resource prices and wages to fall. In addition, there may be policies in place, such as minimum wage laws and government price supports for some resources, that prohibit some wages and resource prices from falling.

Expansionary monetary policy can be applied during a recession rather than waiting for wages and input prices to fall in the long run. The Fed increases the money supply, which lowers interest rates. With more money in circulation, it can be borrowed at a lower rate. The lower interest rates stimulate borrowing and spending. This shifts AD to the right.

Figure 17.3 shows that this shift in AD closes the recessionary gap.

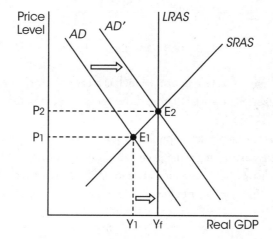

Figure 17.3 Expansionary Monetary Policy to Close a Recessionary Gap

Beginning at short-run equilibrium E$_1$, the economy is experiencing a recession. Output is at Y$_1$, which is to the left of Y$_f$. The increase in the money supply shifts AD rightward. The new long-run equilibrium is at E$_2$. Output is now Y$_f$ and the recession is over.

The price level increased from P$_1$ to P$_2$. This is not a problem in the long run because incomes will increase proportionally. However, the rise in the price level implies some amount of inflation in the short run and inflation has its costs.

The expansionary monetary policy closed the recessionary gap but caused a spate of inflation. The Fed will have to be careful in applying such policies because their mandate calls for them to promote full employment and price stability. Here those goals are at odds with each other. Expansionary monetary policy promotes full employment during a recession but causes inflation.

The following AS/AD diagram (Figure 17.4) represents an economy suffering from inflation.

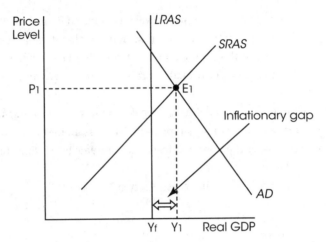

Figure 17.4 An Inflationary Gap

We know there is inflation because real GDP is at Y_1, which is greater than Y_f. The distance between Y_1 and Y_f is called the inflationary gap—the surfeit of real GDP from its full-employment potential. The economy is producing outside its production possibilities frontier.

Becasue E_1 is not on the long-run aggregate supply curve, it is a short-run equilibrium and the economy will adjust so that all three curves cross in the long run. Specifically, the high production level strains resources. Labor is working overtime, and resources are being depleted at a rapid rate. Workers and resource owners demand higher wages and prices, and this induces firms to lower production, shifting SRAS to the left, as in Figure 17.5.

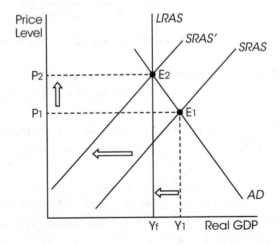

Figure 17.5 Long-Run Adjustment to an Inflationary Gap

The result is a long-run equilibrium at E_2. The price level has risen to P_2 and the inflationary gap is closed with output falling from Y_1 to Y_f. There is a major drawback to this scenario. The rising price level means more inflation and the Fed has a mandate to fight price instability.

Contractionary monetary policy can be applied during inflationary periods rather than suffer through further price increases in the long run. The Fed decreases the money supply, which raises interest rates. The higher rates discourage borrowing and spending. This shifts AD to the left.

Figure 17.6 shows that this shift in AD closes the inflationary gap.

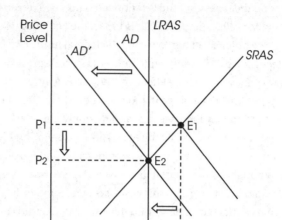

Figure 17.6 Contractionary Monetary Policy to Close an Inflationary Gap

Beginning at E_1, the economy is experiencing inflation in short-run equilibrium at E_1. Output is at Y_1, which is to the right of Y_f. The decrease in the money supply shifts AD leftward. The new long-run equilibrium is at E_2. Output is now Y_f and the price level falls to P_2. The inflationary gap is closed.

Monetary Policy in Practice

Monetary policy in practice is more complicated than it appears in theory. First, recessionary and inflationary gaps need to be detected. Then, the exact amount of the increase or decrease in the money supply must be determined. Finally, there is no guarantee the policy will be effective.

Economic data are only available with a lag. Even then, the data will be revised in the months and years ahead. Determining when the economy needs a monetary intervention is an art with science mixed in.

Once a gap is detected, the Fed determines the exact amount the money supply should be changed by focusing on interest rates. Remember, the change in the money supply affects the macroeconomy through interest rates. The Fed is well aware of this and keeps a close watch on one interest rate in particular: the *federal funds rate*. The federal funds rate is the interest rate charged when one bank loans funds to another for a short amount of time. This is not to be confused with the discount rate—the rate charged by the Fed when making a loan to a bank.

One bank can make a loan to another at whatever rate it can negotiate. However, the Fed keeps an eye on these loan agreements as they occur. If the Fed wants this interest rate to be at 2.0 percent and it sees that loans from one bank to another are occurring at 2.2 percent, then it increases the money supply. As we saw, this lowers the interest rate. The Fed will continue to pump money into the economy until there is enough so that a loan from one bank to another occurs at 2.0 percent interest, not 2.2 percent. Once the federal funds rate decreases, other rates usually follow suit.

In order to stimulate the economy, the Fed would increase the money supply, most likely through open market purchases, in order to lower the federal funds rate to the desired level. Targeting the federal funds rate in this manner determines exactly how much the money supply should be changed to close the recessionary or inflationary gap.

In 2007, coming into the financial crisis that spawned the Great Recession, the federal funds rate was 5.25 percent. In response to the crisis and the recession, the Fed flooded banks with reserves, enabling one bank to borrow short-term funds from another at 0.25 percent. That is to say, the Fed undertook an aggressive expansionary monetary policy in the face of the financial crisis, lowering the federal funds rate from 5.25 to 0.25 percent. This may have prevented the Great Recession from swelling into another Great Depression.

Despite this example, monetary policy may not be effective. The Fed can always change the federal funds rate to the desired level. However, it is uncertain if the change in interest rates will actually change borrowing and spending in the economy. For instance, the Fed may increase the money supply, thereby lowering the federal funds rate. But banks may not loan out the reserves pumped in by the Fed. And consumers and businesses may not want to take out loans during the recession. Aggregate demand does not increase, and the recessionary gap does not close.

Another reason monetary policy might be ineffectual in the face of a recession is a *liquidity trap*. This occurs when the federal funds rate is already close to zero. In this case, it is nearly impossible for the Fed to lower the federal funds rate any further. Some central banks have tried negative federal funds rates, but doing this raises a separate set of problems.

When banks are flush with reserves, two of the Fed's four tools of monetary control are largely ineffective. Suppose the Fed wants to decrease the monetary base and thereby increase interest rates at a time when banks have ample reserves. If required reserves are raised, nothing happens because banks already have more than enough reserves on hand to meet the higher reserve requirement. Indeed, the Fed gave up using this tool long ago. The Fed's reserve requirement is zero, and U.S. depository institutions currently hold as many reserves as their managers see fit. Since the U.S. banks currently hold plenty of reserves, changing this requirement would be ineffective.

When the banking system has plenty of reserves, the Fed can sell Treasury securities to banks with open market operations. This will draw bank reserves down, but it will not increase the federal funds rate since banks have ample reserves to buy Treasuries and continue making loans to other banks at low rates.

In this situation, the most effective tool for increasing interest rates in the economy is to increase the interest paid on bank reserves. The federal funds rate will increase because no bank will lend to another at a lower interest rate than that paid on bank reserves. If a bank wants to borrow funds from another, it must at least offer to pay more in interest than the lending bank is currently receiving on its idle reserves.

Increasing the discount rate will help in this situation because no bank will borrow from another if the funds could be borrowed from the Fed at a lower rate. A higher discount rate allows for a higher federal funds rate.

When the banking system is well capitalized and holds ample reserves, changing reserve requirements and open market operations are ineffective tools for monetary policy because the federal funds rate will not be changed. Banks will continue to lend to one another at the prevailing rate because they have plenty of reserves to do that and meet the new reserve requirement or buy Treasuries. In this circumstance, the only way to change the federal funds rate is to change the interest paid on bank reserves and to change the discount rate.

The interest paid on bank reserves serves as a floor for the federal funds rate. No bank will lend to another when more could be earned by holding the funds as reserves. The discount rate serves as a ceiling on the federal rate. No bank will borrow from another if the funds could be obtained from the Fed at a lower rate.

In a banking system with ample reserves, the federal funds rate lies between the interest paid on bank reserves and the discount rate. Increasing both these policy rates increases the federal funds rate. Other interest rates in the economy follow suit. The higher rates discourage borrowing and spending. Aggregate demand decreases, and inflationary pressures are reduced.

To lower the federal funds rate and conduct expansionary monetary policy when banks have ample reserves, the Fed would lower the interest rate it pays on bank reserves along with the discount rate.

The Phillips Curve

Bright students may have noticed another issue with monetary policy. Expansionary monetary policy to remedy a recession causes the price level to rise. That is inflation. And contractionary monetary policy to fight inflation causes real GDP to decrease and that means more unemployment.

The idea that inflation and unemployment move in opposite directions was first noticed by A. W. Phillips. Looking back over 100 years of British economic history, he discovered that when inflation was high, unemployment was low. When inflation was low, unemployment tended to be high. The inverse relationship between inflation and unemployment became known as the Phillips tradeoff.

Phillips graphed the relationship between inflation and unemployment. The results were similar to Figure 17.7. A high inflation rate, such as point A, is associated with a low unemployment rate. A low inflation rate, such as point B, is associated with a high unemployment rate.

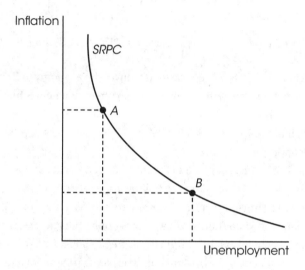

Figure 17.7 The Phillips Curve

Phillips published his findings in 1958, and his relationship has been looked for in many economies over various time periods. For instance, unemployment and inflation behaved according to this relationship in the United States in the 1960s, but the 1970s defied the Phillips tradeoff—both inflation and unemployment were high in the mid-1970s.

Economists are now able to explain why the Phillips relationship holds in some periods and not in others. Notice that when the aggregate demand curve shifts to the left, it results in the price level falling (lower inflation) and the quantity of output falling (higher unemployment). When the aggregate demand shifts to the right, just the opposite occurs—inflation rises and unemployment falls. All of this is in line with what Phillips discovered. This indicates that the aggregate demand curve must have been shifting about in the United States in the 1960s while the aggregate supply curve remained stable.

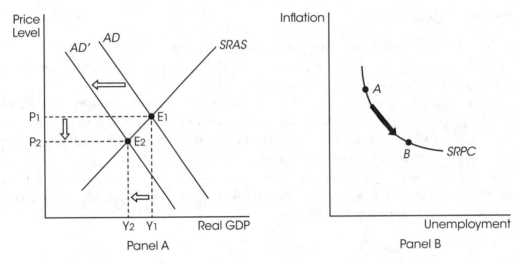

Figure 17.8 A Decrease in AD Causes Movement Down and Along the Phillips Curve

Beginning at E_1 in Panel A of Figure 17.8, a decrease in AD moves the economy to E_2 in the short run. Prices are lower at E_2, so inflation has decreased. Real GDP is lower at E_2, so unemployment is increased. Inflation is down and unemployment is up—that is the Phillips tradeoff.

Starting at point A on the Phillips curve in Panel B of Figure 17.8, a decrease in inflation and an increase in unemployment moves the economy to point B.

The Phillips relationship only prevails, as shown in Figure 17.8, if aggregate demand shifts left or right. If short-run aggregate supply shifts in either direction, then the Phillips tradeoff does not hold true. In fact, when the short-run aggregate supply curve shifts, the entire Phillips curve shifts in the opposite direction.

To see this consider what happens when short-run aggregate supply shifts right. Figure 17.9, Panel A, depicts this event for the short run. The initial equilibrium is E_1. Then the aggregate supply curve shifts right, and the new equilibrium is E_2. Prices are lower at E_2 (inflation is down), and output is higher (unemployment is down). This goes against the Phillips relationship. Both inflation and unemployment have decreased.

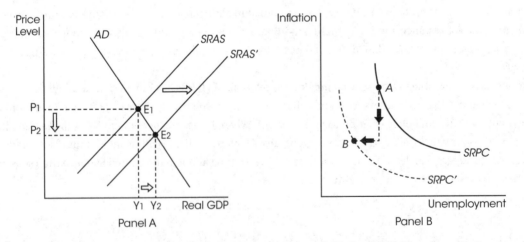

Figure 17.9 An Increase in Short-Run Aggregate Supply Shifts the Phillips Curve Left

In Panel B, start at point A on the solid Phillips curve. From Panel A we know inflation and unemployment both decreased. Moving down from point A to show the decrease in inflation and then left to show the decrease in unemployment, we end up at point B. Indeed, the whole Phillips curve has shifted to the left.

The Phillips tradeoff only holds in the short run. That's why the curve is labeled SRPC (short-run Phillips curve). Even then, the short-run aggregate supply curve must remain stable or the tradeoff breaks down. In the long run, it is doubtful that the Phillips tradeoff exists under any circumstances. Consider an increase in aggregate demand with a long-run aggregate supply curve as portrayed in Figure 17.10.

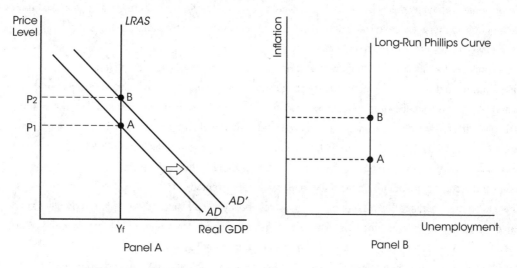

Figure 17.10 An Increase in Aggregate Demand in the Long Run

In Panel A, the increase in aggregate demand increases the price level to P_2. This means inflation is up. Real GDP, however, remains unchanged at Y_f, so unemployment is unchanged.

Panel B shows that the Phillips curve is a vertical line in the long run. Starting at point A, the increase in aggregate demand increases inflation but unemployment remains unchanged, moving the economy to a point such as B.

POINTS TO REMEMBER

If the aggregate demand curve shifts right, the economy slides up the Phillips curve.

If the aggregate demand curve shifts left, the economy slides down the Phillips curve.

If either aggregate supply curve shifts left, the Phillips curve shifts right.

If either aggregate supply curve shifts right, the Phillips curve shifts left.

The long-run Phillips curve is a vertical line.

SUMMARY

- The macroeconomy is plagued with business cycles. The booms and busts can be tamed, at least theoretically, with monetary policy—deliberate changes in the money supply to cure recessions or inflation. Expansionary monetary policy is the appropriate policy to remedy subpar GDP growth and unemployment. Contractionary monetary policy remedies an overheated economy and high inflation rates.

- Why do we suffer unemployment and inflation when we have monetary policy available? Because it has a downside. Lowering unemployment with expansionary monetary policy causes inflation, and lowering inflation with contractionary monetary policy causes unemployment. This is the classic Phillips tradeoff.

- In addition, monetary policy does not always work. If the Fed pursues an expansionary policy, the interest rate falls almost immediately. However, low interest rates do not always encourage borrowing and spending. Businesses may not want to borrow during a recession when the outlook is bleak. Why expand now? And banks are uncomfortable making loans to businesses or households during a recession. Times are tough and there is a greater likelihood that the loan will not be repaid.

- There is another instance when expansionary monetary policy will be ineffective—during a liquidity trap. A liquidity trap is when interest rates are near zero. If the Fed expands the money supply, interest rates cannot fall very far and so there is no increase in borrowing and spending.

- It is difficult to correctly time monetary policy. The Fed tries to anticipate where the economy will be in the near future and get ahead of the curve by changing the money supply before recessionary or inflationary gaps occur. Another concern is exactly how much to change the money supply. The Fed targets the federal funds rate, increasing or decreasing the money supply until that interest rate hits the desired level. The changes to the federal funds rate are usually gradual since adjustments can be made as more economic data become available.

- When the banking system has plenty of reserves to begin with, changing reserve requirements or open market operations will not affect the federal funds rate. In this situation, the Fed changes the interest rate paid on bank reserves along with the discount rate. Logically, the federal funds rate must lie between the interest rate paid on bank reserves and the discount rate.

Multiple-Choice Review Questions

1. In a banking system with limited reserves, a decrease in the supply of money

   (A) lowers interest rates, decreases borrowing, and thereby decreases aggregate demand.

   (B) raises interest rates, increases borrowing, and thereby increases aggregate demand.

   (C) raises interest rates, decreases borrowing, and thereby decreases aggregate demand.

   (D) lowers interest rates, increases borrowing, and thereby increases aggregate demand.

   (E) lowers interest rates, increases borrowing, and thereby decreases aggregate demand.

2. To reduce unemployment in the macroeconomy, the Fed could try

   (A) to decrease interest rates in the economy.

   (B) increasing the federal funds rate.

   (C) decreasing income taxes.

   (D) contractionary monetary policy.

   (E) decreasing aggregate demand.

3. To reduce inflation in the macroeconomy, the Fed could try

   (A) increasing the money supply.

   (B) increasing the federal funds rate.

   (C) increasing income taxes.

   (D) expansionary monetary policy.

   (E) increasing aggregate demand.

4. An effective contractionary monetary policy can

   (A) increase employment.

   (B) increase production.

   (C) close a recessionary gap.

   (D) decrease the price level.

   (E) increase the money supply.

5. In the short run an expansionary monetary policy will cause

   (A) an increase in real GDP.

   (B) an increase in interest rates.

   (C) a decrease in consumer spending and an increase in investment.

   (D) an increase in consumer spending and a decrease in investment.

   (E) a decrease in consumer spending and a decrease in investment.

6. A recessionary gap closes in the long run when wages and resource prices _____ , shifting _____ to the right.

   (A) fall; aggregate demand

   (B) rise; long-run aggregate supply

   (C) fall; long-run aggregate supply

   (D) rise; short-run aggregate supply

   (E) fall; short-run aggregate supply

7. In a liquidity trap, expansionary monetary policy will not work because

   (A) banks do not want to make loans with their excess reserves.

   (B) interest rates cannot fall much further.

   (C) there is no way to liquidate government bonds.

   (D) firms and households prefer to rid themselves of liquid assets.

   (E) the Fed does not have the means to buy government bonds.

8. If the economy is experiencing an inflationary gap, _____ monetary policy could be used to _____ aggregate demand and _____ the general price level.

   (A) expansionary; decrease; decrease

   (B) expansionary; increase; decrease

   (C) contractionary; increase; increase

   (D) contractionary; decrease; increase

   (E) contractionary; decrease; decrease

9. In order to fight inflation the Fed should

   (A) increase the money supply in order to increase the federal funds rate.

   (B) increase the money supply in order to decrease the federal funds rate.

   (C) decrease the money supply in order to increase the federal funds rate.

   (D) decrease the money supply in order to decrease the federal funds rate.

   (E) decrease the money supply in order to tighten up budgets.

10. If the Fed uses contractionary monetary policy, in the short run unemployment would

    (A) worsen, but inflation would come down.
    (B) improve, but inflation would worsen.
    (C) worsen as would inflation.
    (D) improve as would inflation.
    (E) improve while inflation remained unchanged.

11. If an economy is producing below its long-run potential, expansionary monetary policy would

    (A) increase output and prices.
    (B) decrease output and prices.
    (C) increase output and decrease prices.
    (D) decrease output and increase prices.
    (E) increase output and leave prices unchanged.

12. If an economy is producing above its long-run potential, an increase in interest rates would

    (A) increase output and prices.
    (B) decrease output and prices.
    (C) increase output and decrease prices.
    (D) decrease output and increase prices.
    (E) increase output and leave prices unchanged.

13. If the federal funds rate is above the Fed's target, the Fed should

    (A) buy bonds to increase the money supply.
    (B) buy bonds to decrease the money supply.
    (C) sell bonds to increase the money supply.
    (D) sell bonds to decrease the money supply.
    (E) raise the reserve requirement to decrease the money supply.

14. If the Fed conducts an effective contractionary monetary policy, then

    (A) the economy slides up the Phillips curve.
    (B) the economy slides down the Phillips curve.
    (C) the Phillips curve shifts right.
    (D) the Phillips curve shifts left.
    (E) the aggregate demand curve shifts right, but the Phillips curve is unaffected.

15. If the prices of resources increase, then

    (A) the economy slides up the Phillips curve.
    (B) the economy slides down the Phillips curve.
    (C) the Phillips curve shifts right.
    (D) the Phillips curve shifts left.
    (E) the aggregate demand curve shifts right, but the Phillips curve is unaffected.

Free-Response Review Questions

1. Use the aggregate supply/aggregate demand diagram to portray an economy suffering from a recessionary gap. Be sure to label all axes and curves. Do you recommend expansionary or contractionary monetary policy in this case? On the diagram, show which curve shifts which way because of the appropriate monetary policy.

2. Use the aggregate supply/aggregate demand diagram to portray an economy suffering from an inflationary gap. If nothing is done to address the gap, will resource prices rise or fall in the long run? On the diagram, show which curve shifts which way once resource prices change.

3. Draw a short-run Phillips curve, making sure to label the axes correctly. Mark a point labeled "A" on the Phillips curve that represents an economy with a high unemployment rate. Do you recommend expansionary or contractionary monetary policy in this case? On the diagram, indicate how point A will change if the appropriate monetary policy is effective.

Answer Explanations

1. **(C)** This is how a change in the money supply affects the macroeconomy. It changes interest rates, which in turn affects the amount of borrowing and spending. Higher interest rates discourage borrowing and spending and thereby reduce aggregate demand.

2. **(A)** Decreasing interest rates encourages borrowing and spending. This increase in aggregate demand induces employers to hire more workers and increase production.

3. **(B)** Increasing the federal funds rate is achieved by reducing the money supply. When the federal funds rate increases, other interest rates typically follow. Higher interest rates discourage borrowing and spending and thereby reduce aggregate demand. Firms lower prices in response to the increase in aggregate demand.

4. **(D)** Contractionary monetary policy is simply a decrease in the money supply. When it works, the price level decreases.

5. **(A)** Expansionary monetary policy is simply an increase in the money supply. When it works, real GDP increases.

6. **(E)** A recessionary gap will close in the long run with no monetary policy. Eventually the lack of demand for workers and other resources reduces their prices. This encourages producers to hire more employees and use more resources. More is produced, and the short-run aggregate supply curve shifts to the left. Long-run aggregate supply does not shift because new resources and workers were not added to the economy. The existing ones were used more fully.

7. **(B)** In a liquidity trap, interest rates in the economy are already very low. Therefore, they cannot be lowered much further in order to stimulate aggregate demand.

8. **(E)** Contractionary monetary policy is used to fight inflation. It works by reducing aggregate demand, which lowers prices in the economy.

9. **(C)** Contractionary monetary policy is a reduction in the money supply that raises interest rates in the economy. The Fed is especially focused on the federal funds rate when it conducts monetary policy.

10. **(B)** One drawback to contractionary monetary policy is that it will reduce employment. That is a cost of bringing down inflation.

11. **(A)** Expansionary monetary policy stimulates the economy. This means output, income, and employment will increase. Unfortunately, so will the price level.

12. **(B)** An inflationary gap occurs when an economy is producing above its long-run potential. An increase in interest rates is a contractionary monetary policy that will reduce output but also inflation.

13. **(A)** The Fed would increase the money supply in order to reduce the federal funds rate when it is above the target level. One way to increase the money supply is for the Fed to buy bonds in the secondary market.

14. **(B)** An effective contractionary monetary policy reduces inflation but causes unemployment in the short run. This means the economy will move to a point down and to the right on a given Phillips curve.

15. **(C)** An increase in the prices of resources shifts the short-run aggregate supply curve to the left. When this happens, the Phillips curve shifts to the right.

Free-Response Review Answers

1.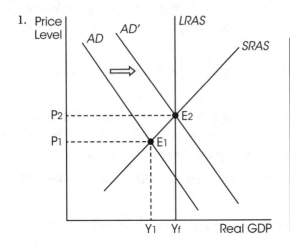

The recessionary gap is the distance between Y_1 and Y_f. Expansionary monetary policy shifts the aggregate demand curve to the right. This moves the economy from short-run equilibrium at E_1 to long-run equilibrium at E_2. At E_2 the recessionary gap is closed and the economy is producing at Y_f, the full-employment level of real GDP.

2.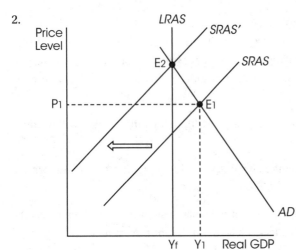

The inflationary gap is the distance between Y_f and Y_1. Y_1 is to the right of Y_f. This means resources are stressed and inflation is likely a problem. The overuse of resources raises their prices. Rising resource prices shift short-run aggregate supply to the left. The economy moves from E_1 to long-run equilibrium at E_2.

3.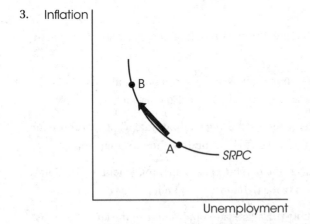

Point A represents high unemployment since it is toward the right on the horizontal axis. Expansionary monetary policy will lower the amount of unemployment but increase inflation. This moves the economy up the Phillips curve toward point B where unemployment is lower and inflation is higher.

18

Fiscal Policy

Learning Objectives

In this chapter, you will learn:

→ Fiscal policy defined
→ Fiscal policy in theory
→ Fiscal policy in practice
→ Crowding out
→ Government spending and tax multipliers
→ Automatic stabilizers
→ The national debt and deficits

Fiscal Policy Defined

Fiscal policy is changing the level of government spending or tax revenues to achieve economic stability. Congress and the President control the federal budget in the United States and are, therefore, the parties that conduct fiscal policy. The Employment Act of 1946 charged the government with the responsibility of maintaining employment opportunities for any American wanting to work. The United States is obligated to promote "maximum employment, production, and purchasing power."

Expansionary fiscal policy is increasing government spending and/or decreasing tax collections in order to stimulate the macroeconomy. When federal government expenditures exceed tax revenues, it is called deficit spending. The government borrows the money to finance the spending increase or the shortfall in tax collections.

Contractionary fiscal policy is decreasing government spending and/or increasing tax collections in order to cool off the economy and lower the price level. The federal government runs a surplus when tax revenues exceed government expenditures.

Fiscal Policy in Theory

Expansionary fiscal policy is appropriate to remedy a recession. The aggregate supply/aggregate demand diagram in Panel A of Figure 18.1 represents an economy producing below its potential, Y_f. Resources, including labor, are not fully employed. We know this because real GDP is at Y_1, which is less than Y_f. The distance between Y_1 and Y_f is called the recessionary gap—the shortfall of real GDP from its full-employment potential. The economy is producing inside its production possibilities frontier.

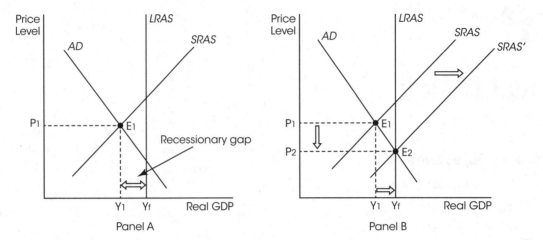

Figure 18.1 Long-Run Adjustment to a Recessionary Gap

The economy has the potential to close the recessionary gap in the long run without fiscal policy. Consider Panel B of Figure 18.1. The economy is operating at E_1 where the price level is P_1 and real GDP is Y_1. This is short-run equilibrium since all three curves (AD, SRAS, and LRAS) do not cross at E_1. To attain long-run equilibrium, wages and other resource prices must fall. This could very well occur since unemployed workers and idle resources put downward pressure on wages and other production costs during recessions. When resource prices fall, firms are encouraged to increase production since costs are lower. Supply increases, shifting short-run aggregate supply to the right as in Panel B of Figure 18.1. The price level falls to P_2 and real GDP increases to Y_f. The economy is producing at its potential. The recessionary gap is closed, and the economy is in long-run equilibrium at E_2.

One concern with allowing the economy to close the recessionary gap on its own is it could take a long time for wages and other resource prices to fall. Moreover, there could be policies in place, like minimum wage laws and government price supports for some resources, that prohibit some wages and resource prices from falling.

Expansionary fiscal policy can be applied during a recession rather than waiting for wages and input prices to fall in the long run. The federal government increases spending or reduces tax collections, which increases aggregate demand. An increase in government spending on highways, space exploration, national defense, or bowling balls has the same effect: an increase in aggregate demand.

If income taxes are cut, households are left with more funds in their budgets and they spend and save more. If corporate taxes are cut, then the owners of corporations have more income and, once again, spending increases.

Figure 18.2 shows that this increase in aggregate demand closes the recessionary gap.

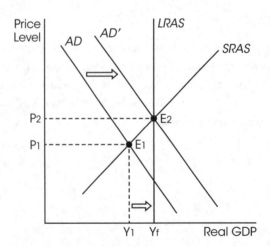

Figure 18.2 Expansionary Fiscal Policy to Close a Recessionary Gap

Beginning at E_1, the economy is experiencing a recession since output is at Y_1, which is to the left of Y_f. The tax cut shifts AD rightward. The new long-run equilibrium is at E_2. Output is now Y_f and the recession is over. If the expansionary fiscal policy is an increase in government spending rather than a tax cut, then aggregate demand increases as well. The diagram is exactly the same whether there is a tax cut or an increase in government spending.

The expansionary fiscal policy increased the price level from P_1 to P_2. This is not a problem in the long run because incomes will increase proportionally. However, the rise in the price level implies some amount of inflation in the short run and inflation has its costs.

The expansionary fiscal policy closed the recessionary gap but caused a spate of inflation. The government will have to be careful in applying such policies because inflation has negative economic consequences. Expansionary fiscal policy promotes full employment during a recession but causes inflation.

Another downside to expansionary fiscal policy is budget deficits. If there are no surplus funds to draw on, then the government's budget will be in negative territory. The government will have to borrow the funds to finance the expansionary fiscal policy. Either way, increasing spending or cutting taxes, the government will be spending more and taking in less revenue.

Contractionary fiscal policy is appropriate to remedy inflation. The aggregate supply/aggregate demand diagram in Panel A of Figure 18.3 represents an economy producing above its potential, Y_f. Resources, including labor, are more than fully employed. The unemployment rate is extremely low, and resources are stretched. We know this because real GDP is at Y_1, which is greater than Y_f. The distance between Y_1 and Y_f is called the inflationary gap—the surfeit of real GDP over its full-employment potential. The economy is producing outside its production possibilities frontier.

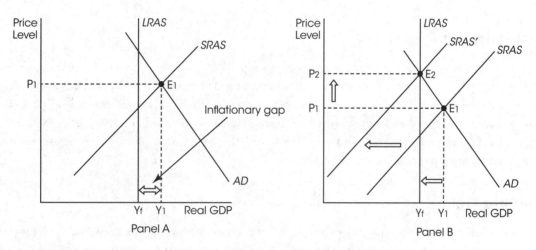

Figure 18.3 Long-Run Adjustment to an Inflationary Gap

In Panel B of Figure 18.3, E_1 is a short-run equilibrium and the economy will adjust so that all three curves cross in the long run. Specifically, the high production level strains resources. Workers and resource owners demand higher wages and prices, and this induces firms to let workers go and production falls, shifting SRAS to the left.

The result is a long-run equilibrium at E_2 in Panel B of Figure 18.3. The price level has risen to P_2 and the inflationary gap is closed with real GDP falling from Y_1 to Y_f. There is a major drawback to this scenario. The rising price level means more inflation, and the Fed has a mandate to fight price instability.

Contractionary fiscal policy can be applied during inflationary periods rather than suffer through further price increases in the long run. The government decreases spending and/or increases taxes. This decreases aggregate demand.

TIP

In macroeconomics, the long run is when the price level is given time to adjust to recessionary or inflationary gaps. It could be months or years.

Figure 18.4 shows that a leftward shift in AD closes the inflationary gap.

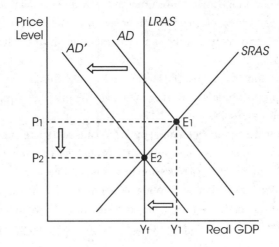

Figure 18.4 Contractionary Fiscal Policy to Close an Inflationary Gap

Beginning at E_1, the economy is experiencing inflation in short-run equilibrium at E_1 and output Y_1, which is to the right of Y_f. The decrease in government spending and/or the increase in taxes shifts AD to the left. The new long-run equilibrium is at E_2. Output is now Y_f and the price level falls to P_2. The inflationary gap is closed.

Contractionary fiscal policy closes inflationary gaps by reducing aggregate demand. Tax collections are up and/or government spending is down. Either way, the policy implies the government budget will tend toward a surplus.

Fiscal Policy in Practice

Fiscal policy in practice is more complicated than it appears in theory. First, recessionary and inflationary gaps need to be detected. Then, Congress and the executive branch need to agree on the details of the change in spending. If the policy is expansionary, then what government programs are to be expanded? Are new programs to be developed? Politicians want the spending to occur in their jurisdictions. If the expansionary fiscal policy involves a tax cut, then which taxes are to be reduced and by how much? These are vexing questions, and legislation must be enacted to initiate any fiscal policy.

Crowding Out

Once enacted, expansionary fiscal policy can be ineffectual because of crowding out. Crowding out is the increase in interest rates and subsequent decline in spending that occur when the government borrows money to finance a deficit.

To see how crowding out works, imagine an economy mired in a recessionary gap. Suppose the government implements the appropriate fiscal policy and runs a deficit. This means the government will need to borrow money. If the government borrows a large portion of the funds available for lending, then interest rates would rise.

To understand this, consider what would happen if you walked into a bank for a car loan just after the government had borrowed a good portion of the bank's loanable funds. They could give you the car loan but probably at a higher rate of interest than before. Now, you may decide that the monthly payments on the car loan would be too high. You do not buy the car and hundreds of people make decisions similar to yours. The demand for cars drops and autoworkers are laid off.

Crowding out can be shown on a diagram of the market for loanable funds. One of the largest demanders of loanable funds in the United States is the federal government. When the federal government deficit spends in order to stimulate the economy, the demand for loanable funds shifts right in Figure 18.5, Panel A. This results in a higher equilibrium real interest rate. The higher interest rate discourages borrowing and spending, especially for investment. The decrease in investment spending by businesses can offset the government's expansionary fiscal policy.

TIP

Recent AP exams have tested students' understanding of crowding out by asking questions concerning the market for loanable funds.

Diagrammatically, crowding out is reflected in an aggregate demand curve that shifts back to the left after a fiscal policy has just shifted it to the right. This is shown in Figure 18.5, Panel B. Originally the economy is in a recession at E₁. An expansionary fiscal policy is used to shift the aggregate demand curve to the right. The new equilibrium is E₂ and the recessionary gap is closed. However, interest rates rise because of the government borrowing associated with the fiscal policy. This is shown in the loanable funds market in Panel A. The demand for loanable funds shifts to the right. The new equilibrium interest rate is r₂. The higher rates of interest induce consumers and businesses to borrow and spend less than before. This decline in consumer and business spending shifts the aggregate demand curve back to its original position, and the economy returns to E₁ and the recession.

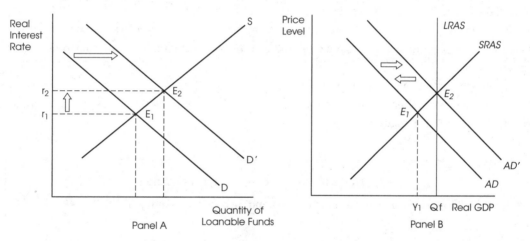

Figure 18.5 Crowding Out

This is how crowding out can nullify the beneficial effects of fiscal policy. Crowding out is not always an issue. Sometimes there are plenty of loanable funds available and the government can borrow and deficit spend without an adverse effect on fiscal policy. Other times, the government borrowing raises interest rates, which chokes off consumer and business spending. The declines in consumer and business spending offset the increase in government spending and fiscal policy is ineffective.

Government Spending and Tax Multipliers

Despite the problems with fiscal policy, it has the potential to be very effective. The reason is because any initial change in spending has ripple effects throughout the economy.

To understand how these ripples emanate you must first understand the marginal propensity to consume (MPC)—given an extra dollar, how much is spent. Young people generally have high MPCs. Given an extra dollar, little is saved. But when they get older, people begin to save more and may squirrel away money for a new car or retirement. Time is important in this analysis. Most people bequeath very little, or even negative amounts, in their estates. They spend all the dollars that came their way over their lifetimes.

Studies show the typical American spends 97 cents out of every extra dollar over the long run. Over a shorter time span, the typical American spends about 80 cents out of an extra dollar in a year. That implies Americans save 20 cents out of every extra dollar in the short run and 3 cents out of every extra dollar in the long run. This brings up another concept related to the MPC—the marginal propensity to save (MPS). If the MPC = 0.97, then the MPS = 0.03.

How does this concept create ripple effects? If the government increases its spending by $100, then that $100 becomes someone's income. Say the government buys $100 worth of gum. The gum manufacturer receives $100. Some of this is profit and is therefore the income of the owners of the gum company. Some goes to pay workers, and this is their wage income. Some goes to pay rent, utilities, and other services, and this becomes income for those people. You will remember that if $100 worth of gum is produced, then $100 worth of income is earned.

If the MPC = 0.8, then there will be another $80 in spending forthcoming. This is the first ripple. The government spent an extra $100, which created $100 more income in the economy. The people who receive this income increase spending by $80 and increase saving by $20.

If the $80 is spent on shoes, then the people involved with the manufacture and sale of shoes have an extra $80 of income. They will spend $64 (= $80 × 0.8) and save $16 (= $80 × 0.2). This is the second ripple. Wherever they spend the $64 dollars, it becomes someone's income and they in turn spend $51.20 . . .

An initial spending increase generates ripples of further spending that eventually fade out. If we add the initial $100 with all the ripple effects, we get a total increase in spending of $500.

How do we know total spending will increase $500? Because the initial increase in spending and the ripple effects are a declining geometric progression: $100, $80, $64, $51.20, . . . and there is a formula to calculate the sum of this progression.

First calculate the spending multiplier: $1/(1 - \text{MPC}) = 1/(1 - 0.8) = 1/0.2 = 5$. A spending multiplier of 5 means any initial change in spending will be magnified 5 times. So the initial $100 increase in government spending creates a $500 increase in total spending.

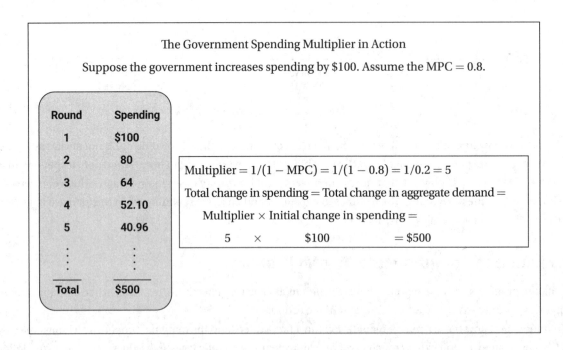

The Government Spending Multiplier in Action

Suppose the government increases spending by $100. Assume the MPC = 0.8.

Round	Spending
1	$100
2	80
3	64
4	52.10
5	40.96
⋮	⋮
Total	$500

Multiplier = $1/(1 - \text{MPC}) = 1/(1 - 0.8) = 1/0.2 = 5$

Total change in spending = Total change in aggregate demand =

Multiplier × Initial change in spending =

5   × $100   = $500

The spending multiplier works in reverse as well. If the government reduces spending by $200 and the spending multiplier equals 5, then total aggregate demand decreases by $1,000.

Say the government spends $200 less on drones. Then drone manufacturers have $200 less in income and they reduce their spending by $160. This is the first ripple. If the drone manufacturers reduced their spending on groceries, then people in the grocery industry have $160 less in income. Since the MPC = 0.8, these people cut their spending by $128. This is the second ripple. When all is said and done, the total change in aggregate demand is −$200 × 5 = −$1,000.

> **TIP**
> Recent AP exams have been calling the total change in spending the "total change in national income."

The spending multiplier can also be applied to a change in taxes, but there is a slight hitch. If the government lowers tax collections by $100, then households have an extra $100 to spend. Households, however, will only increase spending by $80 if the MPC is once again assumed to be 0.8. So the initial change in spending is an increase of $80 when the government cuts taxes by $100. Say the households spend the $80 on shoes. The $80 becomes the income of people in the shoe industry, who in turn spend $64. This is the first ripple.

When taxes are changed, the initial change in spending is the amount of change in tax revenue times the MPC. Then the spending multiplier is applied: $100 × 0.8 = $80. $80 × 5 = $400.

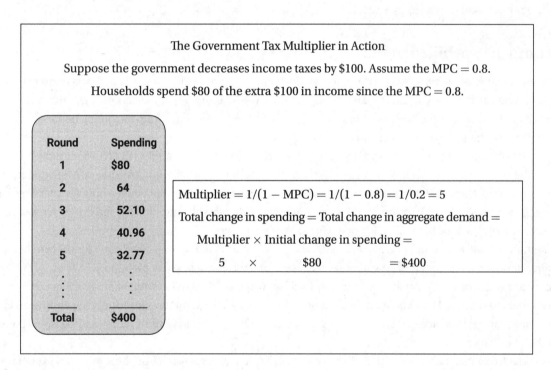

The tax change multiplier works in reverse as well. If the government increases taxes by $100 and the multiplier equals 5, then total aggregate demand decreases by $400:

$$-\$100 \times 0.8 = -\$80$$
Multiplier × Initial change in spending =
$$5 \quad \times \quad -\$80 \quad = -\$400$$

The Balanced-Budget Multiplier

The fact that a $100 change in government spending is slightly more effective than a $100 change in taxes creates an interesting situation. Suppose the government's budget was balanced with tax collections matching the amount of government spending. The government's budget would remain balanced if spending was increased by $100 and taxes were also increased by $100. This is a balanced-budget move.

Yet there would be a slight fiscal stimulus. Assuming an MPC of 0.75, the government spending multiplier is 4: $1/(1 - \text{MPC}) = 1/(1 - 0.75) = 1/0.25 = 4$. Because of the ripple effects, the increase in government spending of $100 boosts aggregate demand by $400: $100 \times 4 = \$400$.

But the tax increase of $100 only reduces aggregate demand by $300. The multiplier is still 4, but the initial decrease in spending is $75 when taxes are raised $100. $-\$75 \times 4 = -\$300$. The initial decrease in spending is $75 because, when $100 in extra income is taken away from consumers, they cut spending by $100 \times \text{MPC} = -\$100 \times 0.75 = -\$75$.

The end result is that an increase in government spending of any amount, matched by a tax increase of the same amount, creates an increase in aggregate demand of that same amount. Similarly, a decrease in government spending of any amount, matched by a tax decrease, creates a decrease in aggregate demand of that amount. These results hold regardless of the value of the MPC. That means the balanced-budget multiplier is equal to 1.

Knowledge of the balanced-budget case allows students to quickly do a problem like this: Suppose the government cuts spending $2,234 and reduces taxes by the same amount. Assume the MPC = 0.7865475. What is the total change in aggregate demand?

Answer: A decrease of $2,234: $-\$2,234 \times 1 = -\$2,234$.

Aggregate demand decreases by $2,234.

Automatic Stabilizers

Automatic, or built-in, stabilizers are government policies already in place that promote deficit spending during recessions and surplus budgets during expansions. In other words, automatic stabilizers promote the correct fiscal policies over the course of the business cycle. These policies prevent recessions from becoming depressions. They also help keep inflations from turning into hyperinflations.

Income taxes and antipoverty programs such as Temporary Aid to Needy Families (TANF) are examples of automatic stabilizers. Consider how income taxes are affected as the economy falls into a recession. More and more people become unemployed or make less income as the recession progresses. But when a household makes less income, it owes less in taxes. In other words, government tax revenues will automatically fall during a recession and this is exactly the type of fiscal policy called for to fight a recession.

Automatic stabilizers cannot prevent a recession because the drop in income is necessary for them to begin working. However, built-in stabilizers can prevent a recession from becoming a depression.

Let's consider how a program like TANF would work as an automatic stabilizer. Again, imagine an economy slipping into a recession. More and more households will qualify for TANF funds. Government spending on antipoverty programs automatically increases during a recession, and a boost in government spending is just the sort of fiscal policy that is required at that time.

Also notice that income taxes and TANF would work to prevent an expansion from becoming too exuberant. As the expansion continues, inflationary pressures build as households make more and more income. But more income means higher tax payments for households. Higher taxes are the appropriate fiscal policy to fight inflation.

In addition, fewer households will qualify for TANF funds as the economy expands. This means government spending on this program will be decreasing. Cuts in government spending are the appropriate fiscal policy to fight inflation.

Automatic stabilizers work to prevent business cycles from becoming too extreme in either direction. Many economists credit automatic stabilizers for the decreased amplitude of business cycles since World War II.

The National Debt and Deficits

A federal deficit occurs when government spending exceeds tax revenues. The government borrows the funds to deficit spend. Federal deficits are appropriate during recessionary times.

A federal surplus occurs when tax revenues exceed government spending. The surplus tax revenue could be used to pay back the funds borrowed during recessionary times. However, the U.S. government has run budget deficits almost every year since 1969. For four years, 1998–2001, there were surpluses, but this was followed by years of record-level deficits.

Table 18.1

Year	Deficit (−) or Surplus (+)
1970	− $2,842,000,000
1980	− $73,380,000,000
1990	− $221,036,000,000
2000	+ $236,241,000,000
2010	− $1,294,373,000,000
2020	− $3,132,439,000,000

These numbers are too large to be meaningful. It would take a person 17.5 days to count to a million if you counted a number a second and only stopped to sleep 8 hours a day. To count to $1.3 trillion, the deficit in 2010, it would take 62,329 years.

Source: U.S. Office of Management and Budget

The national debt is the amount the government now owes to all its creditors. It is the sum total of the federal government's borrowings over the years minus the amount that has been repaid. It is safe to say that when the U.S. government borrowed $984 billion dollars to cover the deficit in 2019, the national debt went up by about the same amount.

Table 18.2

Year	U.S. National Debt
1970	$377,484,000,000
1980	$894,744,000,000
1990	$3,198,461,000,000
2000	$5,698,931,000,000
2010	$13,390,438,000,000
2020	$26,098,561,000,000

Source: U.S. Office of Management and Budget

Every penny spent by the U.S. government comes out of a checking account called "the general account" at the Federal Reserve Bank in Washington D.C. When there is a deficit, that account is empty and the bills are piling up. The government must borrow the money to pay those bills. It does so by issuing Treasury securities. These are like an I.O.U. from Uncle Sam saying how much was loaned to the government, for how long, and at what rate of interest.

Most people do not want to see or hold the actual Treasury security. It is just an electronic entry in their accounts and in the accounts of the U.S. Treasury. If the loan is for a year or less, the security is called a Treasury bill; a loan of 1−5 years is called a Treasury note; and a loan of 6−30 years is a Treasury bond. But these are all Treasury securities.

Who loans money to the U.S. government in exchange for these promises to repay? Anyone and everyone: U.S. banks, U.S. citizens, U.S. businesses, foreign banks, foreign citizens, foreign businesses, foreign central banks, etc. Everyone clamors to loan money to Uncle Sam because he has never failed to repay in full, on time, and with interest.

A Treasury security is safer than having money in a bank. However, it only earns slightly more interest. The $3 trillion Uncle Sam needed to borrow in 2020 was done at an average interest rate of about 2 percent. With everyone wanting to loan him money, he does not have to pay much interest to get all he needs.

For many nations, a debt that is greater than GDP would be excessive. But for the United States, the economic prospects are better than anywhere else in the world. Even with such a large debt, lenders believe that Uncle Sam will come through.

There must be some problems associated with the U.S. debt and deficits. You may have heard the claim that "our grandchildren will be burdened by our overspending!" Maybe. Like previous generations, our grandchildren most likely will have the choice of borrowing more to pay off the obligations we pass onto them, or they could take it upon themselves to raise taxes, cut spending, and pay off the national debt.

The generation that came of age after World War II did exactly that. They denied themselves government services, paid relatively high taxes, and paid off the war debt. The generations since then have elected to borrow more to refinance the debt rather than be burdened.

344 AP MICROECONOMICS/MACROECONOMICS

"Crowding out will occur!" The government will borrow so much that there will be nothing left for households and businesses to borrow. Maybe. So far crowding out has not occurred in the U.S. since funds pour in from all over the world to be loaned to Uncle Sam. Also, the Fed could increase the money supply to lower interest rates should crowding out manifest itself.

"Foreigners will own us!" Definitely not a problem. Uncle Sam could simply refuse to repay the loans, what is known as sovereign default. Many countries have done this throughout history, e.g., Spain (1557), Denmark (1850), Argentina (2000), and Greece (2014). Do the foreigners get to come over and take national treasures and private property back to their countries? Do people have to work for the foreign countries? Nonsense. The only penalty is that the next time the nation goes to borrow money there will be higher interest rates.

Considering all this, a refusal to use deficit spending to remedy a recession based on the idea that future generations will be burdened, or crowding out, or xenophobia, is nonsense.

The one valid concern with the national deficit is that it leads to an increase in the national debt. The one valid concern with the national debt is that interest has to be paid on it each year. Those interest payments could have been used to fund new or existing government programs. The almost $345 billion in interest paid on the federal debt in 2020 could have been used to fund half the defense budget.

SUMMARY

- The macroeconomy is plagued with business cycles. The booms and busts can be tamed, at least theoretically, with fiscal policy—deliberate changes in government spending and/or taxes to cure recessions or inflation. Expansionary fiscal policy is the appropriate policy to remedy subpar GDP growth and unemployment. Contractionary fiscal policy remedies high inflation rates.

- Fiscal policy works by adjusting aggregate demand. During recessions, when resources are idle and unemployment is a concern, aggregate demand can be increased by increasing federal spending or reducing tax collections. During inflationary periods, aggregate demand can be decreased by reducing federal spending or increasing tax collections.

- It is critical that you are able to draw and manipulate the aggregate supply/aggregate demand model to portray fiscal policy. There is no way to pass the AP exam in Macroeconomics without that capacity.

- Other important issues that will merit at least a question or two on the exam are crowding out, tax and spending multipliers, automatic stabilizers, and the national debt and deficit. Straightforward definitions are rarely featured on the exam but being able to define a concept is halfway to understanding it. Try the practice questions below to see if you have a grip on all the important concepts surrounding fiscal policy.

- Another issue that sometimes finds its way onto the AP exam in Macroeconomics concerns nations that have a lot of foreign trade. Both monetary and fiscal policy are less effective in these nations because some of the impact gets spread overseas. Imagine an income tax reduction to stimulate an economy in a recession. Consumers receive a boost in disposable income from the tax cut, but a portion of their increased spending goes on foreign goods. Less of the impact is felt domestically, and some of the impact goes to their trading partners.

TIP

Be careful not to say that an increase in government spending increases the money supply. It does not. An increase in government spending increases aggregate demand, which, in turn, increases real GDP, income, and prices in the short run. But the money supply is unchanged.

Formulas

Marginal Propensity to Consume $= \dfrac{\text{Change in Spending}}{\text{Change in Income}}$

Multiplier $= 1/(1 - \text{MPC}) = 1/\text{MPS}$

Total Change in Aggregate Demand $=$ Multiplier $\times$ Initial Change in Spending

Multiple-Choice Review Questions

1. Fiscal policy is

    (A) increases in taxes to fight recessions.
    (B) decreases in taxes to fight inflations.
    (C) changes in government spending and taxes to fight recessions or inflations.
    (D) federal deficits.
    (E) federal surpluses.

2. A federal deficit occurs when

    (A) exports exceed imports.
    (B) imports exceed exports.
    (C) federal tax collections exceed spending.
    (D) federal spending exceeds federal tax revenues.
    (E) the federal government spends less than last year.

3. The appropriate fiscal policy to remedy a recession is

    (A) for the federal government to run a deficit.
    (B) for the federal government to run a surplus.
    (C) increased taxes and government spending.
    (D) decreased government spending and taxes.
    (E) increased taxes and reduced government spending.

4. The appropriate fiscal policy to remedy inflation is

    (A) for the federal government to run a deficit.
    (B) for the federal government to run a surplus.
    (C) increased taxes and government spending.
    (D) decreased government spending and taxes.
    (E) decreased taxes and increased government spending.

5. To close a recessionary gap

    (A) the aggregate demand curve should be shifted to the right.
    (B) the aggregate demand curve should be shifted to the left.
    (C) the aggregate supply curve should be shifted to the right.
    (D) the aggregate supply curve should be shifted to the left.
    (E) prices should be raised.

6. To close an inflationary gap

    (A) the aggregate demand curve should be shifted to the right.
    (B) the aggregate demand curve should be shifted to the left.
    (C) the aggregate supply curve should be shifted to the left.
    (D) government spending should be increased.
    (E) tax collections should be decreased.

7. One drawback of using fiscal policy to close a recessionary gap is that

    (A) unemployment will rise.
    (B) taxes will have to be raised.
    (C) the equilibrium price level will rise.
    (D) government spending on important programs will have to be cut.
    (E) equilibrium output will fall.

8. Suppose government spending decreases by $8 million and the MPC = 0.75. If there is a full multiplier effect, then this will cause aggregate demand to

    (A) increase by $8 million.
    (B) decrease by $8 million.
    (C) increase by $6 million.
    (D) decrease by $6 million.
    (E) decrease by $32 million.

9. Suppose the government decreases taxes by $8 million and the MPC = 0.75. If there is a full multiplier effect, then this will cause aggregate demand to

    (A) increase by $8 million.
    (B) decrease by $8 million.
    (C) increase by $6 million.
    (D) decrease by $6 million.
    (E) increase by $24 million.

10. Crowding out is when

    (A) fiscal policy outperforms monetary policy.
    (B) interest rates fall due to government borrowing.
    (C) government borrowing raises interest rates, causing cuts in business spending.
    (D) rising interest rates cause cuts in government spending.
    (E) falling interest rates cause cuts in government spending.

11. Automatic, or built-in, stabilizers cause government tax collections to _____ during recessions and _____ during expansions.

    (A) increase; increase
    (B) increase; decrease
    (C) remain unchanged; remain unchanged
    (D) decrease; decrease
    (E) decrease; increase

12. A simultaneous increase in government spending of $200 and an increase in income tax collections of $200 _____ aggregate demand by _____. Assume an MPC of 0.8.

    (A) does not affect; any amount
    (B) increases; $200
    (C) decreases; $200
    (D) increases; $160
    (E) increases; $1,000

13. Which of the following would cause unemployment and prices to rise?

    (A) A climate event that wipes out a portion of the economy's natural resources
    (B) An increase in the money supply
    (C) An increase in consumer confidence
    (D) An increase in taxes
    (E) A decrease in taxes

14. If government spending is reduced, then unemployment _____ and inflation _____.

    (A) increases; increases
    (B) increases; decreases
    (C) remains unchanged; remains unchanged
    (D) decreases; decreases
    (E) decreases; increases

15. An income tax cut may not affect the macroeconomy very much if

    (A) consumers spend a good portion of their tax reduction on domestic goods.
    (B) consumers spend a good portion of their tax reduction on foreign goods.
    (C) the tax cut is permanent.
    (D) consumers are optimistic about the economic future.
    (E) the Fed simultaneously increases the money supply.

Free-Response Review Questions

1. Draw an aggregate supply/aggregate demand diagram that portrays a recessionary gap.
   Be sure to label the axes of your diagram and the aggregate demand curve, the short-run aggregate supply curve, and the long-run aggregate supply curve.

2. Should government spending be increased or decreased to close a recessionary gap? Show how this change in government spending is reflected in the diagram drawn for question 1.

3. If the government does nothing in the face of a recessionary gap, would wages and resources prices be expected to increase or decrease in the long run? Explain. Which curve of the aggregate supply/aggregate demand model would shift which way once wages and resource prices changed?

Answer Explanations

1. **(C)** This is a straightforward definition of fiscal policy.

2. **(D)** This is a straightforward definition of federal deficit.

3. **(A)** During recessions, the appropriate fiscal policy is for the government to spend more or collect less in taxes. Either way, the federal budget is in negative territory.

4. **(B)** When inflation is a problem, the appropriate fiscal policy is for the government to spend less or collect more in taxes. Either way, the federal budget tends toward a surplus.

5. **(A)** Expansionary fiscal policy works by increasing aggregate demand.

6. **(B)** Contractionary fiscal policy works by decreasing aggregate demand.

7. **(C)** Expansionary fiscal policy works by increasing aggregate demand, but that causes prices to rise.

8. **(E)** First calculate the spending multiplier $= \frac{1}{1 - \text{MPC}} = \frac{1}{1 - 0.75} = \frac{1}{0.25} = 4$. This means any change in spending will be magnified 4 times. In this case, the change in spending is a decrease of $8 million: $4 \times -\$8$ million $= -\$32$ million. Aggregate demand has the potential to decrease by $32 million because of the initial $8 million decrease in government spending. Note that recent AP exams have used slightly different terminology, saying "national income" will decrease by $32 million rather than "aggregate demand."

9. **(E)** First calculate the spending multiplier $= \frac{1}{1 - \text{MPC}} = \frac{1}{1 - 0.75} = \frac{1}{0.25} = 4$. This means any change in spending will be magnified 4 times. In this case, the change is spending is not $8 million. If people get $8 million in extra income due to the tax cut, they increase spending by 75 percent of that due to the MPC. The $8 million tax break increases spending by $6 million $= \$8$ million $\times 0.75$. Finally, multiply the $6 million by 4 to get $24 million. Aggregate demand (or "national income" as recent AP exams have been wording it) increases by $24 million.

10. **(C)** This is a straightforward definition of crowding out.

11. **(E)** During recessions, income falls and the government automatically collects less in taxes since taxes are based on income. During expansions, incomes rise and the government automatically collects more in tax revenue for the same reason.

12. **(B)** This is a compound problem. The effects of the increase in government spending can be worked out, and separately the effects of the tax increase can be calculated. The two responses can then be combined to arrive at the final answer. However, clever students will notice this is a balanced-budget problem.

If the government's budget was balanced, it will remain balanced after the two changes in this problem. Government spending went up by $200, but so did tax collections. Since both spending and taxes increased, the final answer is an increase. Since both spending and taxes changed by $200, the final answer will be $200.

13. **(A)** It is called *stagflation* if both unemployment and the price level rise. Stagflation can only be caused by either or both aggregate supply curves shifting to the left. A destructive climate event would do just that.

14. **(B)** A reduction in government spending shifts the aggregate demand curve to the left. The new equilibrium will occur at lower real GDP, which implies more unemployment. The new equilibrium price level will be lower than initially.

15. **(B)** If the tax reduction is spent on foreign goods, then the expansive effects occur overseas.

Free-Response Review Answers

1.

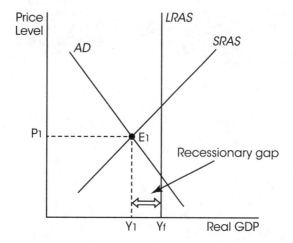

2. Government spending should be increased to close a recessionary gap. As illustrated:

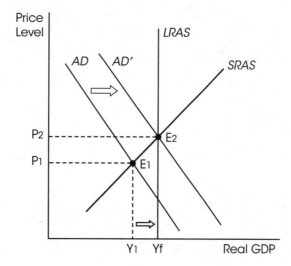

3. Wages and resource prices would decrease in a recession because there is less demand for labor and resources. Declining wages and resources prices shift the short-run aggregate supply curve to the left.

19

International Trade and Finance

Learning Objectives

In this chapter, you will learn:

→ The balance of trade
→ Trade restrictions
→ The balance of payments
→ Exchange rates
→ Monetary and fiscal policy in an open economy

The Balance of Trade

In 2021 the United States was the world's second largest exporting nation, selling $2.5 trillion worth of goods and services abroad. However, in that same year, the United States imported $3.4 trillion worth of goods and services. Isn't this a problem? Doesn't the United States owe its trading partners something in return? Wouldn't there be more jobs in the United States if imports were limited?

A nation's balance of trade is equal to its exports minus its imports. Earlier we called this figure net exports. For the United States in 2021, the balance of trade was negative $918 billion (= $2.5 trillion − $3.4 trillion). When the balance of trade is negative, it can be referred to as a *trade deficit*. The last time America had a trade surplus was 1975. Are these chronic trade deficits a problem, and what, if anything, can be done about them?

Trade deficits can indeed be symptomatic of underlying economic problems. For instance, if a nation's exports are of inferior quality or cost too much relative to the competition, then it may experience a trade deficit. Or a country might rely heavily on imports just to meet its subsistence needs while it has nothing to export. This dire situation would result in a trade deficit as well. Finally, a nation's currency may be overpriced for one reason or another. This would make it expensive for foreigners to buy their products. A trade deficit could be the result.

Incomes and the standard of living in the United States is greater than its trading partners. Many Americans are doing well and can afford the best of everything no matter where in the world it is produced. This swells America's imports. Unfortunately, many other places in the world are not doing as well. Those nations cannot afford to buy America's exports, and the trade balance of the United States falls into negative territory.

If this idea about the origin of our trade deficits is correct, then we should see smaller deficits, or even surpluses, when our economy is experiencing a recession. During the 1991–92 recession the trade deficit shrank to $30 billion. The last trade surplus in the United States was in 1975 on the tail end of a severe 16-month recession.

Trade Restrictions

Arguments for Trade Restrictions

Even if trade deficits spring from high living standards, they can still be problematic. When foreign textiles are imported, that means there is less demand for domestic textile workers. Imported textiles could mean unemployment for domestic textile workers.

Barriers to free trade across nations have been erected for a variety of reasons. One argument is to protect jobs from foreign competition. However, there is a steep price to pay for this protection. Everyone who buys textiles will be paying more for them because competition was thwarted. We know from our earlier analysis of comparative advantage that free trade enables the countries involved to consume more than under restricted trade.

Other reasons for trade restrictions include the infant industry argument, the diversity argument, and dumping. Infant industries are those that are just getting started. At this point they are in no condition to compete with foreign industries that have all the advantages of being well established. The argument is that these infant industries will be able to compete after they have developed. At that point, the trade restrictions could be dropped.

Another reason to protect an industry from foreign competition is for the sake of diversity. A nation should not rely too heavily on others. What if a war broke out? Do you think our enemies would continue to export to us? We need to encourage some industries despite their inefficiencies because diversity is healthy. Trade barriers can promote diversity.

Dumping is a technical term in international trade. It describes a situation where foreign producers are selling a product in the domestic market for less than it cost to produce it. The foreign firms would like to establish a foothold in our markets, so they are willing to absorb the loss. Domestic producers argue that prices will soon rise once the foreign firms have put them out of business. Trade barriers can be used to prevent dumping.

Table 19.1 lists major arguments for trade restrictions. Most economists think that the benefits of free trade outweigh all of these reasons for restricting the flow of goods and services between nations.

Table 19.1 Arguments for Trade Restrictions

- Promote domestic employment
- Infant industry argument
- Diversity of production
- Prevent dumping

Instituting Trade Restrictions

There are a variety of ways to discourage or prevent imports from coming into a country. Quotas, tariffs, and licensing requirements are the most common.

1. **AN IMPORT QUOTA IS A LIMIT ON THE AMOUNT OF A PRODUCT THAT CAN BE IMPORTED.**

   When the import quota is set at zero, domestic producers are completely protected from foreign competition. Figure 19.1 shows the effects of an import quota on the domestic market for rice.

   If free trade is allowed, then the price of rice will be P_1, the world price. If no trade in rice is allowed, then the price will be P_3, the domestic price in the absence of trade. If a quota allows in some rice, then the supply of rice curve will shift to the right by that amount. As shown, compared to free trade, the quota raises the domestic price of rice and less rice is consumed. In addition, it can be shown that consumer surplus is reduced by the quota as is total surplus.

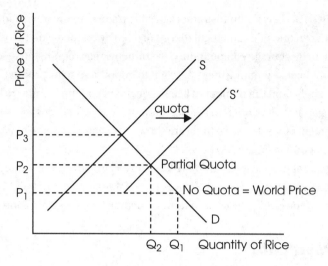

Figure 19.1 A Quota on Rice Imports

2. AN IMPORT TARIFF IS A TAX ON THE SPECIFIED IMPORTED PRODUCT. The tariff serves to raise the price of the imported product in the eyes of domestic consumers. This gives the edge to domestic producers. Figure 19.2 shows the effects of an import tariff.

> **Trade Restrictions**
> - Quotas
> - Tariffs
> - Licensing requirements

The price of rice would be P_1 except that the tariff raises it to P_2. The higher price causes a decrease in the quantity of rice demanded, and the amount actually bought and sold is now lower (Q_2). The tariff, like the quota, raises the domestic price of rice and lowers the amount bought and sold. These higher prices and reduced amounts of consumption are the costs of trade restrictions.

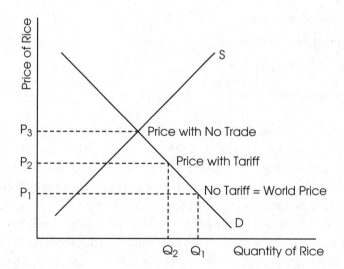

Figure 19.2 A Tariff on Imported Rice

3. **OTHER RESTRICTIONS.** Clever administrators can stifle trade in many ways aside from quotas and tariffs. Arcane rules and regulations are often developed with no other purpose in mind than to discourage competition. Governments may require businesspersons to obtain a license granting them the right to import a specific product. The government need only limit the number of licenses it grants and the amount to be imported by each license holder in order to restrict trade. The effects of licensing agreements and rules and regulations that stifle trade are shown in exactly the same manner as the import quota diagram in Figure 19.1.

TIP

Trade restrictions are bad for consumers because they raise prices and limit choices.

Economists are generally against any trade restrictions. Comparative advantage suggests that free trade allows nations to consume more goods and services than if trade was restricted. Moreover, the arguments for trade restrictions are dubious while the costs in terms of higher prices and less consumption are more definite.

The Balance of Payments

The balance of payments is composed of the current account and the capital and financial account. The current account is primarily net exports with some additional items. The capital and financial account measures investment dollars flowing into the United States minus investments by U.S. entities abroad. For 2021 the capital and financial account balance is positive, meaning more investment dollars flowed into the United States than flowed out in foreign-asset investments. Table 19.2 delineates the balance of payments for the United States in 2021.

Table 19.2 United States Balance of Payments in 2021 (Billions of $)

Current Account		−821.6
Net exports	−861.4	
Other Items	39.8	
Capital and Financial Account		821.6
Net Foreign Purchases of U.S Assets	824.0	
Net Financial Capital Transfers	−2.4	

Source: U.S. Bureau of Economic Analysis

The current account and the capital and financial account should sum to zero. This is an accounting necessity. When the current account is negative, as it was in 2021, this means that the U.S. has been spending more abroad than foreigners have been spending here. This excess spending abroad puts dollars in foreign hands.

The capital and financial account accounts for those dollars that were put in foreign hands. The capital and financial account for 2021 indicates that most of the dollars that wound up in foreign hands were used to buy assets in the United States. Had foreigners not wanted to use their dollars to buy investments in the United States, they could have just held on to them. Even so, that is an investment—an investment in U.S. currency.

The capital and financial account must be positive by the same magnitude that the current account is negative. This is because all the dollars that wind up overseas must be accounted for.

Exchange Rates

The exchange rate is the value of one country's currency in terms of another's. Exchange rates are determined, as we shall see, by supply and demand. Table 19.3 shows selected exchange rates.

Table 19.3 Selected Exchange Rates in 2021

One U.S. dollar equals:	
1.42	Australian dollars
0.81	British pound
1.28	Canadian dollars
7.02	Danish kroners
0.95	Euro
78.44	Indian rupees
135.17	Japanese yen
19.89	Mexican pesos
15.84	South African rands

Source: Federal Reserve Bank of New York

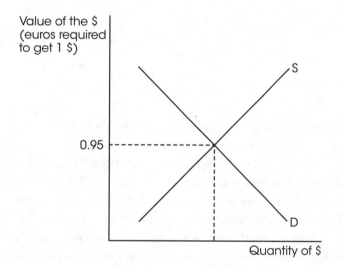

Figure 19.3

The demand for dollars in the foreign exchange market is not the same as the demand for money. The demand for money is how much the public wants to hold as currency and in checking accounts. The demand for dollars in the international exchange market is how many dollars are wanted in exchange for foreign currency, say euros. See Figure 19.3.

The demand for dollars in the foreign exchange market is downward sloping, which implies that the quantity of dollars demanded will be greater when its price in terms of the euro is lower. This makes sense: more European people and firms would want to acquire dollars if they could get a lot of them for each euro.

The supply curve for dollars reflects how many dollars are available in exchange for euros. It is upward sloping, which implies that the quantity of dollars supplied will be greater when the dollar price is higher. Again, this makes sense: more people and firms would be willing to part with their dollars if they could get more euros for each one.

The exchange rate between the dollar and the euro is changing constantly because the supply and the demand for dollars in terms of euros are shifting constantly. Let's consider the demand for dollars in the international marketplace first. There are basically two things that could cause the demand for dollars by foreigners to increase:

1. Foreigners want more American products
2. Foreigners want to invest more in America

If Europeans develop a taste for American bourbon, then they will have to acquire more dollars to get the bourbon. The demand for dollars increases, as in Figure 19.4:

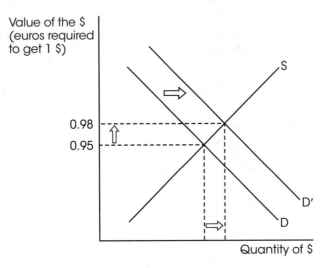

Figure 19.4

The result is a rise in the value of the dollar, in this case to 0.98 euros from 0.95 euros. When the value of the dollar increases as above, this is known as an "appreciation" of the dollar. Or looked at from the other side, the euro has "depreciated" vis-à-vis the dollar. Notice that the number of dollars traded on the international exchange has increased as well. On the horizontal axis, the quantity of dollars is now further to the right, or greater.

The second factor that could increase the demand for dollars is foreigners wanting to invest their money in America. If Europeans want to make more financial investments in America, then they will have to change their euros into dollars. That means offering up their euros and demanding more dollars on the international currency exchange. The diagram looks exactly the same as above as the demand for dollars increases and the dollar appreciates.

The exchange rate between the dollar and the euro is changing constantly because the supply and the demand for dollars in terms of euros are shifting constantly. Let's now consider the supply of dollars in the international marketplace. There are basically two things that could cause the supply of dollars to increase:

1. Americans want more foreign products
2. Americans want to invest more abroad

If Americans develop a taste for French wine, then Americans will have to acquire more euros to get the wine they want. The supply of dollars increases, as in Figure 19.5.

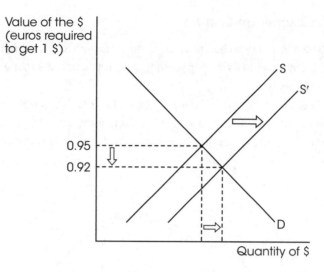

Figure 19.5

The result is a decline in the value of the dollar, in this case to 0.92 euros from 0.95 euros. When the value of the dollar decreases as above, it is known as a "depreciation" of the dollar. Or looked at from the other side, the euro has "appreciated" vis-à-vis the dollar. Notice that the number of dollars traded on the international exchange has increased as well. On the horizontal axis, the quantity of dollars is now further to the right, or greater.

The second factor that could increase the supply of dollars is Americans wanting to invest their money abroad. If Americans want to make more financial investments in Europe, then they will have to change their dollars into euros. That means offering up their dollars and supplying more dollars on the international currency exchange. The diagram looks exactly the same as above as the supply of dollars increases and the dollar depreciates.

Our analysis of exchange rate determination is somewhat superficial. It appears as if exchange rates only depend on how much foreigners want our products or how badly they want to invest in our economy versus how much Americans want foreign products or how badly Americans want to invest in foreign economies. This is correct.

However, many factors determine how much foreigners want our products. These factors include advertising, the U.S. price versus their price, taxes, and more. And a host of factors determines how badly foreigners want to invest in America: What is the U.S. rate of return on investment versus their home country? How stable is the political environment in the U.S.? What are the future prospects for investment returns in America versus the home country?

And let's not forget that the supply and the demand for a currency can be driven purely by speculation. People supply or demand currencies just because they think the exchange rate will be lower or higher in the future.

Table 19.4 Determinants of Exchange Rates

- Demand for a nation's exports (tastes)
- Relative interest rates
- Political stability
- Relative level of income
- Relative prices (theory of purchasing power parity)
- Speculation

Side-by-Side Foreign Exchange Graphs

At least two currencies will be affected by a change in any of the factors affecting foreign exchange rates: the currency under consideration and that of its trading partner or partners. In order to illustrate these effects, side-by-side exchange rate graphs may be used.

Consider a case where Americans suddenly develop a passion for India's exports. Looking at the market for rupees in Panel A of Figure 19.6, there is an increase in the demand for rupees. American importers need to obtain rupees in order to obtain the goods from India. The increase in the demand for rupees results in an appreciation of the rupee (R_1 to R_2) and an increase in the quantity of rupees traded (Q_1 to Q_2).

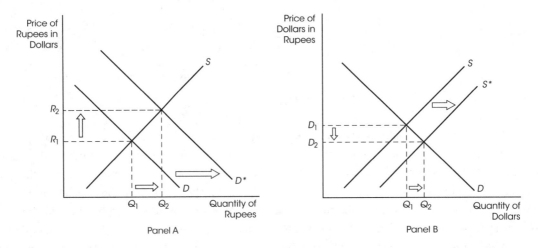

Figure 19.6

However, looking at the market for dollars in Panel B, there is an increase in the supply of dollars. American importers need to supply more dollars on the foreign exchange market in order to obtain the rupees they want.

Notice the difference between Panels A and B. Panel A shows the supply and demand for rupees, while Panel B shows the supply and demand for dollars.

The increase in the supply of dollars results in a depreciation of the dollar (D_1 to D_2) and an increase in the quantity of dollars traded (Q_1 to Q_2). Thus, we may conclude that when Americans increase their preference for Indian goods, the rupee will appreciate while the dollar depreciates.

Exchange Rate Regimes

Before the Great Depression, most of the large economies of the world were on a gold standard. Essentially, the gold standard kept exchange rates between countries fixed. Since the dollar was worth a certain amount of gold and the franc was worth a given amount of gold, the value of the dollar versus the franc would be established. If the value of the franc appreciated vis-à-vis the dollar, people could use their dollars to buy gold and then use that gold to buy francs and then use those francs to buy more dollars than they started with.

Arbitrage of this sort kept exchange rates between nations fixed, but the gold standard was not without flaws. If tastes changed and Americans clamored for French products, the exchange rate did not rise to choke off some of this foreign demand. In such a situation, the United States would develop a balance of payments deficit as French citizens and institutions piled up dollar holdings. Many historians and economists point to balance of payment crises caused by the gold standard as one of the central causes of the Great Depression.

Modern international exchange is no longer based on gold. The Bretton Woods regime replaced the fixed exchange rate system based on gold in 1944. In the Bretton Woods system, the dollar was as good as gold. Countries pegged the value of their currencies to the dollar, and the United States stood ready to trade any dollar holdings of foreign governments to gold at $35 an ounce. This system broke down in 1971 when the United States, running chronic trade deficits, could no longer support the $35 an ounce price of gold.

Managed Float

The current system for determining international exchange rates is referred to as a *managed float*. Supply and demand determine exchange rates between currencies as outlined above. But if exchange rates change in a manner deemed to be detrimental, nations will intervene. Intervention involves coordinated buying and selling of currencies in order to adjust their equilibrium values determined by supply and demand.

For example, because the United States runs chronic trade deficits, there is an abundant supply of dollars in international markets. This tends to depress the value of the dollar. A depreciated dollar would lower America's demand for foreign products. This would help with our chronic trade deficits, but it would hurt the countries that export to us. If governments decide to support the dollar, they would intervene by buying dollars. This results in the dollar appreciating in value.

A managed float allows supply and demand to determine exchange rates within a range of values. Once exchange rates exceed that range, governments use their currency holdings to intervene.

Monetary and Fiscal Policy in an Open Economy

Monetary and fiscal policy can be used to fight inflation or recession. However, our previous discussion of these policies ignored their effects on the exchange rate and the balance of trade. The impacts of monetary and fiscal policy in the context of an open economy are more complicated.

> **TIP**
>
> Monetary and fiscal policy are less effective when the economy is more open as opposed to closed to foreign trade.

An expansionary monetary policy still stimulates the economy in the short run by increasing the quantity of output and putting upward pressure on prices. This will worsen the balance of trade since the increase in output means an increase in income. Rising incomes tend to drive imports, worsening the balance of trade. And rising prices tend to discourage exports, again worsening the balance of trade.

Policy makers need to keep in mind the effects of monetary policy on imports and exports. In a closed economy, an increase in the money supply stimulates output and income in the short run. In an open economy, these effects will be dampened because imports will rise. That is to say, some of the stimulatory effect will be spent overseas, and exports will fall because of the inflation resulting from the increase in the money supply.

The effects of an expansionary fiscal policy are tempered in the same way in the context of an open economy. An increase in government spending and a reduction in taxes will increase output and income in the short run while putting upward pressure on prices. Higher levels of income tend to raise imports, while higher prices tend to discourage exports. This worsens the balance of trade and implies that the effects of the fiscal policy will not be as pronounced.

Also notice that monetary and fiscal polices will affect exchange rates because these policies alter incomes and prices. Remember that exchange rates are impacted by the relative level of income and the relative level of prices in a nation.

SUMMARY

- The United States has been importing more than it has been exporting since the mid-1970s. However, our trade deficits are more a symptom of how well off we are relative to our trading partners than a cause for alarm. Most economists agree that trade restrictions, such as import tariffs, quotas, and licensing agreements, are harmful. Free trade, where countries specialize according to the law of comparative advantage, benefits consumers in the countries involved.

- Nevertheless, most nations restrict trade in one way or another. The arguments for trade restrictions vary from promoting employment to preventing dumping. Infant industries and the benefits of a diverse manufacturing base are two more reasons put forward to justify trade restrictions. However valid the reason, economic analysis shows that the cost of restricting trade is higher prices to the consumer. In addition to this damage, there is another cost to trade restrictions. Since our trading partners will be exporting fewer goods and making less income, they will, in turn, purchase fewer of our exports. Domestic exporters are hurt by trade tariffs.

- A nation's balance of payments accounts for the funds that flow into and out of the country. If there is a deficit in the current account, there must be a corresponding surplus in the financial and capital accounts.

- The exchange rate is the price of one nation's currency in terms of another's. In today's world, exchange rates are determined by the supply and demand for a nation's currency—up to a point. Occasionally, nations will intervene in the market by supplying more or less of a particular currency or demanding more or less. Nations use their official reserves during these interventions in order to prop up or devalue a given currency. In other words, countries can adjust the position of the supply and demand curves for a currency, but only if they have the cooperation of the major trading nations. Without cooperation, no single nation has enough reserves to make much of an adjustment to the supply or demand curves of most currencies. This international monetary system, where supply and demand determine exchange rates with the occasional intervention by a consortium of trading partners, is known as a managed float.

- Exchange rates, therefore, are free to float about where supply and demand might take them—just so long as they don't go too far and trigger an intervention. Anything that can affect the supply or the demand for a nation's currency will affect its exchange rate. The demand for a nation's exports affects the demand for its currency, as do relative interest rates. Relative prices and income also affect exchange rates. And speculation can play a role. If market participants expect a particular currency to appreciate in the near future, they will try to buy as much as they can now. As we have seen, this increases the demand for the currency, which, in turn, causes it to appreciate, the fulfillment of a self-fulfilling prophecy.

- Exchange rates are affected when a country pursues monetary and fiscal policy because, in the short run, these policies affect income and prices. Moreover, the balance of trade will be affected by monetary and fiscal policy because imports and exports are impacted by changes in income and prices as well. The short-run effects of monetary and fiscal policy are not as pronounced in an open economy.

Formulas

Balance of Trade = Net Exports = Exports − Imports

Balance of Payments = Current Account + Capital and Financial Account

Multiple-Choice Review Questions

1. When a country has a balance of trade deficit

   (A) it must make up the difference by shipping gold to its creditors.
   (B) its exports exceed its imports.
   (C) its currency will appreciate.
   (D) corrective actions must be taken.
   (E) its imports exceed its exports.

2. If Americans suddenly develop a passion for India's exports, then the Indian rupee will _____ against the dollar and the American dollar will _____ against the rupee.

   (A) appreciate; hold steady
   (B) hold steady; depreciate
   (C) depreciate; appreciate
   (D) appreciate; depreciate
   (E) depreciate; hold steady

3. One strategy a corporation may use to gain market share in a foreign market is

   (A) raising the price of its product.
   (B) convincing its government to put an import tariff on the product.
   (C) convincing its government to place a quota on the product.
   (D) cornering.
   (E) dumping.

4. Tariffs and quotas on imports

   (A) result in higher domestic prices.
   (B) promote trade between nations.
   (C) do not necessarily affect domestic prices.
   (D) affect domestic prices: the former raises them while the latter lowers them.
   (E) are ways to fight inflation.

5. Tariffs and quotas on imports

   (A) result in lower domestic prices.
   (B) sometimes raise and sometimes lower the amount of the product sold domestically.
   (C) reduce the amount of the product sold domestically.
   (D) raise the amount of the product sold domestically.
   (E) do not affect domestic prices or quantities.

6. Suppose expansionary monetary policy raises national income and the price level in an economy. As a result, net exports _____. Therefore, the expansionary monetary policy is _____ effective than if the economy were closed.

   (A) increase; more
   (B) increase; less
   (C) decrease; less
   (D) decrease; more
   (E) hold steady; equally

7. If the value of the U.S. dollar depreciates, *ceteris paribus*, then U.S.

   (A) imports will increase.
   (B) unemployment will increase.
   (C) net exports will decrease.
   (D) exports will increase.
   (E) net exports will be unaffected.

8. If a country has a negative value on its current account, then it must

   (A) pay that amount to its trading partners.
   (B) have a positive value of equal magnitude on its capital and financial account.
   (C) depreciate its currency.
   (D) appreciate its currency.
   (E) send gold abroad.

9. With a managed float

   (A) countries occasionally intervene in foreign exchange markets.
   (B) countries never have to intervene in foreign exchange markets.
   (C) countries must constantly intervene to maintain the value of their currencies.
   (D) exchange rates are fixed.
   (E) each currency is worth a stated amount of gold.

10. Expansionary fiscal policy

   (A) increases unemployment in an open economy.
   (B) lowers the nominal interest rate, which results in currency appreciation.
   (C) is less effective in an open economy.
   (D) will not affect the nominal interest rate.
   (E) increases the nominal interest rate, which results in currency depreciation.

11. In the balance of payments, the trade balance

   (A) is ignored.
   (B) appears in the capital and financial account.
   (C) appears in the current account.
   (D) is included in the official reserves.
   (E) is counted as part of "net transfers."

12. If interest rates rise in the United States relative to other nations, then

   (A) the value of the dollar will tend to appreciate.
   (B) the value of the dollar will tend to depreciate.
   (C) exchange rates will be affected but not the value of the dollar.
   (D) the exchange rate will not be affected.
   (E) the balance of trade will tend toward a surplus.

13. If prices rise in the United States relative to other countries, then

   (A) the value of the dollar will tend to appreciate.
   (B) the value of the dollar will tend to depreciate.
   (C) exchange rates will be affected but not the value of the dollar.
   (D) the exchange rate will not be affected.
   (E) the balance of trade will tend toward a surplus.

14. If the demand for dollars rises while the supply of dollars falls, then the

   (A) dollar will appreciate.
   (B) dollar will depreciate.
   (C) exchange rates will be affected but not the value of the dollar.
   (D) exchange rate will not be affected.
   (E) balance of trade will tend toward a surplus.

15. If the demand for U.S. exports rises while U.S. tastes for foreign goods falls off, then

   (A) the value of the dollar will tend to appreciate.
   (B) the value of the dollar will tend to depreciate.
   (C) exchange rates will be affected but not the value of the dollar.
   (D) the exchange rate will not be affected.
   (E) the balance of trade will tend toward a deficit.

Free-Response Review Questions

1. Suppose two counties, Alpha and Beta, trade freely and allow investments to flow across their borders as well. Draw two graphs—one for the supply and demand for Alpha's currency and one for the supply and demand for Beta's currency. Be sure to label the axes of your graphs. Show how the value of each currency will be affected if the interest rate on investments in Alpha rises while the return on investments in Beta remains unchanged.

2. Given your response above, how will the imports and exports of each country be affected?

Answer Explanations

1. **(E)** The definition of a balance of trade deficit is imports exceed exports.

2. **(D)** When Americans demand more Indian exports, the demand for rupees increases. This appreciates the rupee. Looking at the supply and demand for dollars, the supply of dollars increases. This depreciates the dollar. Thus, the rupee appreciates and the dollar depreciates. See the side-by-side foreign exchange graphs in Figure 19.6.

3. **(E)** Dumping is selling a product abroad for less than it costs to produce the good. One reason to do this is to gain a foothold in the foreign market.

4. **(A)** The cost of trade restrictions is higher prices for domestic consumers.

5. **(C)** Trade restrictions raise prices, and higher prices decrease the quantity demanded for all but perfectly inelastic goods.

6. **(C)** When national income increases, so does the demand for foreign products. Imports increase. In addition, when the price level increases, the foreign demand for the nation's products decreases. Exports decrease. Both of these factors cause net exports to decrease. The boost to national income from expansionary monetary policy is weaker in an open economy because net exports decrease.

7. **(D)** A depreciation causes an increase in exports because the nation's goods are now less expensive to foreigners. To get the exported goods they want, foreigners have to pay less of their currency to obtain the depreciated currency.

8. **(B)** It is an accounting necessity. The capital and financial account must equal the current account but be of opposite sign.

9. **(A)** With a managed float, nations only occasionally intervene in the foreign exchange market.

10. **(C)** Expansionary fiscal policy is less effective when a nation has substantial imports and exports because some of the spending changes caused by the fiscal policy take place overseas.

11. **(C)** The trade balance is the main component of the current account.

12. **(A)** The high interest rates attract foreign investors. Foreigners need to acquire dollars to invest in the United States. This increases the demand for dollars, thereby appreciating the dollar.

13. **(B)** The demand for dollars decreases because foreigners do not need dollars since they do not want the high-priced American goods.

14. **(A)** The best way to handle questions like this is to use the foreign exchange diagram. Increase the demand for dollars by shifting the curve right, and decrease the supply by shifting the curve left. The equilibrium moves from E_1 to E_2 and the value of the dollar is higher at E_2.

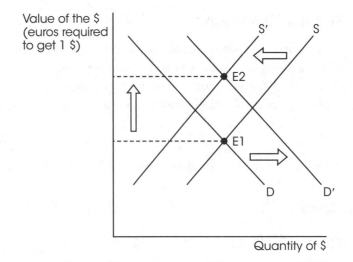

15. **(A)** This is the exact same question as above. When the demand for U.S. exports increases, the demand for U.S. dollars increases because foreigners need dollars to get the U.S. goods they want. When U.S. demand for foreign goods declines, the supply of dollars decreases. There is no need to supply dollars to obtain foreign currency because their goods are no longer desired. The diagram mapping these changes is exactly the same as for question 14.

Free-Response Review Answers

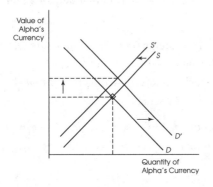

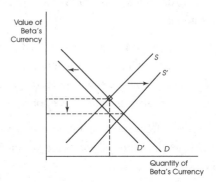

1. With higher returns in Alpha, the demand for Alpha's currency will rise. Foreigners will want to invest in Alpha and need its currency to do so. It also is possible that the supply of Alpha's currency will decline as more domestic investments are undertaken. These two shifts are shown in the figure on the left. Alpha's currency will appreciate in value.

   With higher returns in Alpha, the supply of Beta's currency will rise. It also is possible that the demand for Beta's currency will decline as more of Alpha's investors undertake domestic investments. These two shifts are shown in the figure on the right. Beta's currency will depreciate in value.

2. Since Alpha's currency is appreciating, Alpha's exports will fall and its imports will rise. Alpha's net exports will fall. Since Beta's currency is depreciating, Beta's exports will rise and its imports will fall. Beta's net exports will rise.

   These changes make sense. Alpha's current account is declining, but its capital and financial account is rising. Beta's current account is improving, but its mirror image, the capital and financial account, is worsening.

The Big 5 Graphs of Macroeconomics in Action

Knowing the Big 5 graphs of macroeconomics is one key to doing well on the AP exam. Here, each of the graphs is put into action. But before that, you should ask yourself, "Can I label both axes of the graph if they were not already?" "Can I label all the lines inside the axes?" If you answered "no" to either of these questions, then you have more prep work before exam time. If you can do all the labeling and follow the action in the boxes beside each graph, then you are primed to do well on the AP exam in Macroeconomics.

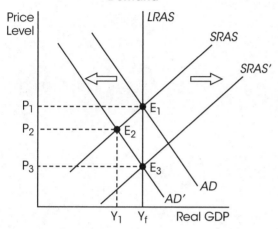

Aggregate Supply and Aggregate Demand

The economy is in equilibrium and at full employment at E_1. A decrease in aggregate demand shifts the AD curve to the left. The new short-run equilibrium is E_2. However, in the long run nominal wages and other resource prices will fall. This increases short-run aggregate supply, causing SRAS to shift to the right. The new equilibrium is at E_3. This is a long- and short-run equilibrium as all three curves cross here. The lesson: a decrease in AD can cause a recession in the short run, but it will not prevail in the long run.

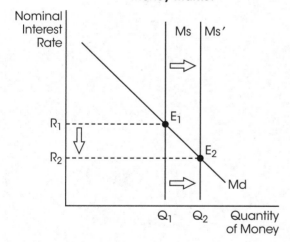

Money Market

Here the axes are the nominal interest rate and the quantity of money in circulation. An increase in the money supply moves the equilibrium from E_1 to E_2. This decreases the nominal interest rate and, of course, there is more money in circulation.

Loanable Funds Market

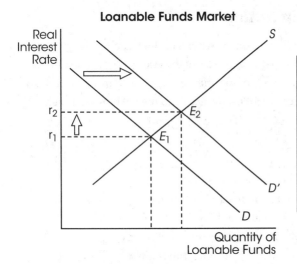

Notice the labels of the axes: real interest rate and quantity of loanable funds. An increase in the demand for loanable funds, say because consumers are confident, moves the equilibrium from E_1 to E_2. The real interest rate is higher, and the quantity of funds loaned and borrowed increases.

Foreign Exchange Market

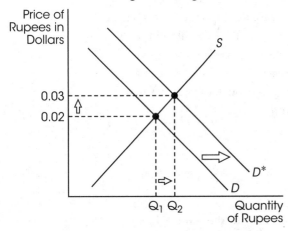

Phillips Curve

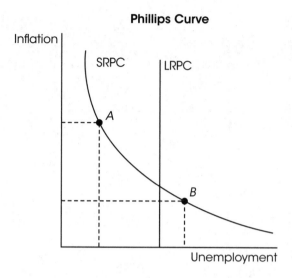

The Phillips curve has inflation on the vertical axis and unemployment on the horizontal axis. The economy slides down the short-run Phillips curve (SRPC) from point A to point B when aggregate demand decreases.

The decrease in aggregate demand causes unemployment to increase and the price level to fall. Starting at point A, an increase in unemployment and a reduction in inflation ends up at point B.

The long-run Phillips curve (LRPC) is vertical to indicate there is no relationship between inflation and unemployment in the long run.

Plus 1:

Production Possibilities Frontier

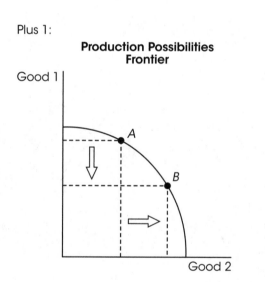

The production possibilities frontier shows amounts of two goods that the economy can produce using all of its resources fully and efficiently. At both points A and B, the economy is operating at its potential.

As the economy moves from point A to point B, it is producing more of Good 2 at the expense of Good 1.

ANSWER SHEET
Macroeconomics

MACRO PRACTICE TEST

Multiple-Choice Questions

1. Ⓐ Ⓑ Ⓒ Ⓓ Ⓔ 21. Ⓐ Ⓑ Ⓒ Ⓓ Ⓔ 41. Ⓐ Ⓑ Ⓒ Ⓓ Ⓔ
2. Ⓐ Ⓑ Ⓒ Ⓓ Ⓔ 22. Ⓐ Ⓑ Ⓒ Ⓓ Ⓔ 42. Ⓐ Ⓑ Ⓒ Ⓓ Ⓔ
3. Ⓐ Ⓑ Ⓒ Ⓓ Ⓔ 23. Ⓐ Ⓑ Ⓒ Ⓓ Ⓔ 43. Ⓐ Ⓑ Ⓒ Ⓓ Ⓔ
4. Ⓐ Ⓑ Ⓒ Ⓓ Ⓔ 24. Ⓐ Ⓑ Ⓒ Ⓓ Ⓔ 44. Ⓐ Ⓑ Ⓒ Ⓓ Ⓔ
5. Ⓐ Ⓑ Ⓒ Ⓓ Ⓔ 25. Ⓐ Ⓑ Ⓒ Ⓓ Ⓔ 45. Ⓐ Ⓑ Ⓒ Ⓓ Ⓔ
6. Ⓐ Ⓑ Ⓒ Ⓓ Ⓔ 26. Ⓐ Ⓑ Ⓒ Ⓓ Ⓔ 46. Ⓐ Ⓑ Ⓒ Ⓓ Ⓔ
7. Ⓐ Ⓑ Ⓒ Ⓓ Ⓔ 27. Ⓐ Ⓑ Ⓒ Ⓓ Ⓔ 47. Ⓐ Ⓑ Ⓒ Ⓓ Ⓔ
8. Ⓐ Ⓑ Ⓒ Ⓓ Ⓔ 28. Ⓐ Ⓑ Ⓒ Ⓓ Ⓔ 48. Ⓐ Ⓑ Ⓒ Ⓓ Ⓔ
9. Ⓐ Ⓑ Ⓒ Ⓓ Ⓔ 29. Ⓐ Ⓑ Ⓒ Ⓓ Ⓔ 49. Ⓐ Ⓑ Ⓒ Ⓓ Ⓔ
10. Ⓐ Ⓑ Ⓒ Ⓓ Ⓔ 30. Ⓐ Ⓑ Ⓒ Ⓓ Ⓔ 50. Ⓐ Ⓑ Ⓒ Ⓓ Ⓔ
11. Ⓐ Ⓑ Ⓒ Ⓓ Ⓔ 31. Ⓐ Ⓑ Ⓒ Ⓓ Ⓔ 51. Ⓐ Ⓑ Ⓒ Ⓓ Ⓔ
12. Ⓐ Ⓑ Ⓒ Ⓓ Ⓔ 32. Ⓐ Ⓑ Ⓒ Ⓓ Ⓔ 52. Ⓐ Ⓑ Ⓒ Ⓓ Ⓔ
13. Ⓐ Ⓑ Ⓒ Ⓓ Ⓔ 33. Ⓐ Ⓑ Ⓒ Ⓓ Ⓔ 53. Ⓐ Ⓑ Ⓒ Ⓓ Ⓔ
14. Ⓐ Ⓑ Ⓒ Ⓓ Ⓔ 34. Ⓐ Ⓑ Ⓒ Ⓓ Ⓔ 54. Ⓐ Ⓑ Ⓒ Ⓓ Ⓔ
15. Ⓐ Ⓑ Ⓒ Ⓓ Ⓔ 35. Ⓐ Ⓑ Ⓒ Ⓓ Ⓔ 55. Ⓐ Ⓑ Ⓒ Ⓓ Ⓔ
16. Ⓐ Ⓑ Ⓒ Ⓓ Ⓔ 36. Ⓐ Ⓑ Ⓒ Ⓓ Ⓔ 56. Ⓐ Ⓑ Ⓒ Ⓓ Ⓔ
17. Ⓐ Ⓑ Ⓒ Ⓓ Ⓔ 37. Ⓐ Ⓑ Ⓒ Ⓓ Ⓔ 57. Ⓐ Ⓑ Ⓒ Ⓓ Ⓔ
18. Ⓐ Ⓑ Ⓒ Ⓓ Ⓔ 38. Ⓐ Ⓑ Ⓒ Ⓓ Ⓔ 58. Ⓐ Ⓑ Ⓒ Ⓓ Ⓔ
19. Ⓐ Ⓑ Ⓒ Ⓓ Ⓔ 39. Ⓐ Ⓑ Ⓒ Ⓓ Ⓔ 59. Ⓐ Ⓑ Ⓒ Ⓓ Ⓔ
20. Ⓐ Ⓑ Ⓒ Ⓓ Ⓔ 40. Ⓐ Ⓑ Ⓒ Ⓓ Ⓔ 60. Ⓐ Ⓑ Ⓒ Ⓓ Ⓔ

Macroeconomics Practice Test

Two hours are allotted for this exam: 1 hour and 10 minutes for Section I, which consists of multiple-choice questions; and 50 minutes for Section II, which consists of three mandatory essay questions. You may use a four-function calculator.

Section I—Multiple-Choice Questions

TIME—1 HOUR AND 10 MINUTES

NUMBER OF QUESTIONS—60

PERCENT OF TOTAL GRADE—66$^2/_3$

DIRECTIONS: Each of the questions or incomplete statements below is followed by five suggested answers or completions. Select the one that is best in each case and then fill in the corresponding circle on the answer sheet.

Don't forget about the online test for extra practice for AP Macroeconomics.

1. Consider an economy at full employment equilibrium. In the long run an increase in the money supply results in

    (A) a proportional increase in the quantity of output.
    (B) stagflation.
    (C) an increase in the real rate of interest.
    (D) an economic expansion.
    (E) a proportional increase in the price level.

2. You buy 100 shares in XYZ Corporation on the Internet, and your broker charges you $29.95.

    (A) This will increase the investment component of GDP and therefore overall GDP.
    (B) This has no effect on GDP.
    (C) This will increase GDP by $29.95.
    (D) This will increase GDP by the cost of the shares minus $29.95.
    (E) This will increase GDP by the cost of the shares plus $29.95.

Use the following graph for question 3.

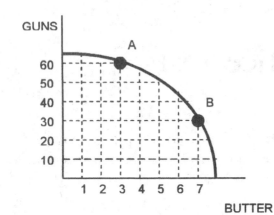

3. Given the graph above, the opportunity cost of 4 additional units of butter as the economy moves from A to B is

   (A) 7 units of butter.
   (B) 30 units of guns.
   (C) 60 units of guns.
   (D) unobtainable.
   (E) indeterminant.

4. In the short run, contractionary monetary policy causes aggregate demand to _____, output to _____, and the price level to _____.

	Aggregate Demand	Output	Price Level
(A)	Increase	Increase	Increase
(B)	Increase	Increase	Decrease
(C)	Decrease	Decrease	Increase
(D)	Decrease	Decrease	Decrease
(E)	Decrease	Increase	Increase

5. Assume bank reserves are limited and the reserve requirement is 5 percent. If the Fed sells $10 million worth of government securities in an open market operation, then the money supply can potentially

   (A) increase by $200 million.
   (B) decrease by $200 million.
   (C) increase by $50 million.
   (D) decrease by $50 million.
   (E) increase by $150 million.

6. Given the table below, which statement is true?

   Labor hours needed to produce a unit of:

Country	Wine	Cheese
France	40	80
Belgium	15	60

   (A) France has the absolute advantage in both products.
   (B) France should specialize in and export wine, while Belgium should specialize in and export cheese.
   (C) France has the comparative advantage in cheese.
   (D) France has the absolute advantage in cheese.
   (E) Belgium has the comparative advantage in both products.

Use the following graph for question 7.

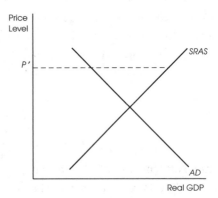

7. At P′ in the diagram above,

   (A) inventories will be unintentionally drawn down, and the price level will fall.
   (B) inventories will be unintentionally increased, and the price level will fall.
   (C) inventories will be unintentionally drawn down, and the price level will rise.
   (D) inventories will be unintentionally increased, and the price level will rise.
   (E) inventories will be unintentionally drawn down, but prices will not be affected.

8. Suppose taxes are cut in an economy that is in equilibrium at full employment. In the long run the tax cut will

    (A) raise real output and raise the price level.
    (B) lower real output and raise the price level.
    (C) raise real output and lower the price level.
    (D) lower real output and lower the price level.
    (E) raise the price level.

9. As a result of automatic stabilizers, during economic expansions government expenditures

    (A) and taxes fall.
    (B) and taxes rise.
    (C) rise and taxes fall.
    (D) fall and taxes rise.
    (E) remain stable.

Use the following graph for question 10.

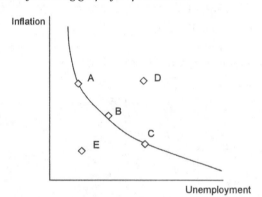

10. Consider the diagram above. In the short run, stagflation will move the economy from point B to

    (A) point A.
    (B) point A and then back to point B.
    (C) point C.
    (D) point D.
    (E) point E.

11. Which of the following shifts the production possibilities frontier outward?

    (A) A decrease in the price level
    (B) An increase in labor productivity
    (C) An increase in the money supply
    (D) A decrease in the unemployment rate
    (E) A decrease in the minimum wage

12. In the circular-flow diagram households send _____ to firms in return for _____.

    (A) resources; spending
    (B) spending; resources
    (C) resources; wages and profits
    (D) goods and services; wages
    (E) goods and services; spending

13. An Italian company opens a shoe factory in the U.S. The production from this shoe factory is included in

    (A) the Italian GDP.
    (B) the U.S. GDP.
    (C) both the Italian and U.S. GDP.
    (D) both the Italian and U.S. GDP split 50/50.
    (E) neither the Italian nor U.S. GDP.

14. Which of the following is NOT included in GDP?

    (A) Federal government purchases of goods and services
    (B) Imports
    (C) State and local government purchases of goods and services
    (D) Exports
    (E) The change in business inventories

15. In the short run, an increase in the price level reduces the quantity of goods and services demanded in the economy because

    I.   consumers' incomes cannot go as far now that prices have risen.

    II. foreigners buy less.

    III. higher prices result in higher interest rates, which reduce spending.

    (A) Only I is correct.
    (B) Only I and II are correct.
    (C) Only I and III are correct.
    (D) Only II and III are correct.
    (E) I, II, and III are correct.

16. Suppose real GDP increases. We can conclude without a doubt that

    (A) prices are higher.
    (B) there has been a technological advance.
    (C) production is higher.
    (D) prices and output are greater.
    (E) the price level is lower.

17. An appropriate fiscal policy to remedy a recession is to

    (A) increase government spending and taxes.
    (B) reduce government spending and taxes.
    (C) increase government spending and reduce taxes.
    (D) decrease government spending and increase taxes.
    (E) increase the money supply.

18. Which of the following would lead to a decrease in the money in a banking system with limited reserves?

    (A) The central bank lowers the discount rate.
    (B) The central bank sells government securities in the secondary market.
    (C) The federal government spends less money.
    (D) The central bank lowers reserve requirements.
    (E) The interest rate the central bank pays on bank reserves is decreased.

19. If interest rates rise relatively more in country A than in country B, then the value of country A's currency will

    (A) appreciate.
    (B) depreciate.
    (C) remain unchanged.
    (D) change indeterminately.
    (E) depreciate by the difference in interest rates.

20. If the marginal propensity to consume equals 0.75 and government spending increases by $100 million, then overall real GDP can be expected to

    (A) decrease by $133.33 million.
    (B) increase by $133.33 million.
    (C) decrease by $400 million.
    (D) increase by $400 million.
    (E) increase by $75 million.

21. Inflation

    (A) hurts creditors who do not anticipate it.
    (B) hurts creditors who anticipate it.
    (C) hurts debtors.
    (D) benefits debtors who do not anticipate it.
    (E) both A and D are correct.

22. Which of the following persons is (are) considered to be unemployed?

    I. Mary, who has quit her job to look for another

    II. John, who fulfilled his dream by retiring from work at age 45

    III. Diane, who works part-time but would like to work full-time

    (A) I only
    (B) II only
    (C) III only
    (D) I and III
    (E) II and III

Use the following graph for question 23.

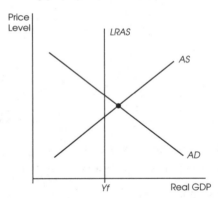

23. The economy depicted in the figure above is experiencing _____. In the absence of monetary or fiscal policy, the economy will eventually move to a point where the price level is _____.

    (A) a recession; higher
    (B) a recession; lower
    (C) extremely high production; higher
    (D) extremely high production; lower
    (E) extremely high production; unchanged

24. The population of country X is exactly the same as country Y, but country X produces twice as much output as country Y. We can conclude that

    (A) the people of country X are smarter than the people of country Y.
    (B) the people of country X enjoy a standard of living twice as much as country Y.
    (C) the people of country Y enjoy a standard of living twice as much as country X.
    (D) the people of country Y work twice as hard as the people of country X.
    (E) country X is bigger than country Y.

25. If the government of country Z increases spending by $12 million and raises tax collections by the same amount, then what will be the overall impact of these moves on real GDP in country Z?

    (A) Real GDP will increase by $6 million.
    (B) Real GDP will decrease by $6 million.
    (C) Real GDP will remain unchanged.
    (D) Real GDP will increase by $12 million.
    (E) Real GDP will decrease by $12 million.

26. Suppose you observe an economy where prices are falling and real GDP is rising. This may have been caused by

    (A) stagflation.
    (B) an advance in technology.
    (C) an increase in government spending.
    (D) a decrease in government spending.
    (E) a decrease in the money supply.

27. Which of the following would reduce economic growth?

    (A) A decline in investment
    (B) An increase in immigration from abroad
    (C) A technological advance
    (D) An increase in the labor force
    (E) An increase in the savings rate

28. Currency held by the public

    (A) is not part of the money supply, but currency held by banks is.
    (B) is part of M1 but not M2.
    (C) is part of the money supply, but currency held by banks is not.
    (D) and by banks is part of the money supply.
    (E) or banks is not part of the money supply since it is not included in M1.

29. The equation of exchange demonstrates the neutrality of money only if the

    (A) velocity of money supply and the quantity of output are constant.
    (B) money supply and its velocity are equal.
    (C) velocity of money supply equals the speed of transactions.
    (D) money supply and its velocity are inversely related.
    (E) money supply and the exchange rate are inversely related.

30. Economy X is an open economy. Economy Y is closed. Expansionary monetary policy is

    (A) more effective in X because the policy will increase net exports.
    (B) more effective in X because the policy will decrease net exports.
    (C) equally effective in X and Y.
    (D) less effective in X because the policy will increase net exports.
    (E) less effective in X because the policy will decrease net exports.

31. An increase in the price of forklifts imported into the United States from Belgium will

    (A) increase the consumer price index and the GDP deflator.
    (B) increase the consumer price index but not the GDP deflator.
    (C) increase the GDP deflator but not the consumer price index.
    (D) increase the GDP deflator and the producer price index.
    (E) have no effect on the consumer price index or the GDP deflator.

32. An increase in the demand for money in the economy could result from

    (A) a recession.
    (B) a higher price level.
    (C) higher interest rates.
    (D) expected future inflation.
    (E) a decrease in the supply of money.

33. The international value of the dollar will appreciate if

    (A) American income falls relative to the rest of the world.
    (B) American interest rates fall relative to interest rates in other countries.
    (C) American prices rise.
    (D) foreigners boycott American products.
    (E) speculators expect the value of the dollar to depreciate.

34. The impact of an open market operation will be diminished if

    (A) the public prefers to hold less cash.
    (B) the velocity of money falls.
    (C) depository institutions decide to hold more excess reserves.
    (D) the marginal propensity to consume falls.
    (E) the international value of the dollar falls.

35. An increase in the federal deficit may affect the demand for loanable funds and therefore the real interest rate and investment spending. Which of the following gives the correct direction of these effects?

	Demand for Loanable Funds	Real Interest Rate	Investment Spending
(A)	Increase	Increase	Increase
(B)	Decrease	Decrease	Decrease
(C)	Decrease	Decrease	Increase
(D)	Increase	Increase	Decrease
(E)	Increase	Decrease	Increase

36. If the inflation rate is expected to increase in the immediate future, then

    (A) consumers will begin saving more now.
    (B) the velocity of money will fall.
    (C) this will put upward pressure on the nominal interest rate.
    (D) this will put downward pressure on the real interest rate.
    (E) the international value of the dollar will rise.

37. If the economy is in disequilibrium where the price level is such that the aggregate quantity of products demanded exceeds the aggregate quantity of products supplied, then

    (A) prices will be driven upward to restore equilibrium.
    (B) supply will increase.
    (C) demand will decrease.
    (D) supply will decrease.
    (E) a recession is inevitable.

38. If 200 computers with a retail value of $100,000 are domestically produced in 2005 but not sold until 2006, then GDP in 2005 is

    (A) $100,000 higher because of the computers.
    (B) 200 higher because of the computers.
    (C) unaffected until 2006 when the computers are sold and the figure for GDP in 2005 is revised upward by $100,000.
    (D) higher by the wholesale value of the computers.
    (E) unaffected because the computers are counted in GDP for 2006.

39. Appropriate fiscal and monetary polices during the contractionary phase of the business cycle include

    (A) budget surpluses and higher discount rates.
    (B) tax reductions and open market purchases.
    (C) budget surpluses and lower discount rates.
    (D) increases in government spending and higher discount rates.
    (E) decreases in government spending and lower discount rates.

40. A change in government spending will have a greater short-run impact on real output when

    (A) the marginal propensity to consume is lower.
    (B) the velocity of money is lower.
    (C) the velocity of money is higher.
    (D) the marginal propensity to consume is larger.
    (E) interest rates rise.

41. Suppose a country produces only two goods, pizza and soda. Given the information in the table below, nominal GDP, real GDP, and the GDP deflator in 2005 are (assume 2004 is the base year):

Year	Pizza Production	Soda Production	Price of a Pizza	Price of a Soda
2004	8	20	$10	$1
2005	10	30	$17	$3

	Nominal GDP	Real GDP	GDP Deflator
(A)	800	400	200
(B)	130	260	50
(C)	260	130	200
(D)	260	196	133
(E)	800	400	400

42. If the economy experienced a decrease in real GDP and price level, this could best be explained by

    (A) a decline in labor productivity.
    (B) a technological advance.
    (C) a decline in investment.
    (D) an uptick in net exports.
    (E) a reduction in interest rates.

Use the following graph for question 43.

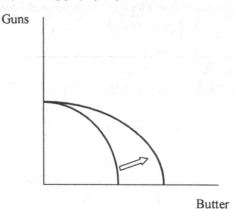

43. The shift depicted in the diagram above could have been caused by

    (A) better production methods in the gun industry.
    (B) an increase in the number of cows in the economy.
    (C) an increase in the number of workers in the economy.
    (D) a technological setback in the gun industry.
    (E) a reduction in farmland available due to pollution.

44. Suppose the real interest rate in a country rises. What can be expected to happen to the demand for this nation's currency and, therefore, the value of its currency and net exports?

	Demand for Currency	Value of Currency	Net Exports
(A)	Decrease	Appreciate	Decrease
(B)	Decrease	Depreciate	Decrease
(C)	Decrease	Depreciate	Increase
(D)	Increase	Appreciate	Increase
(E)	Increase	Appreciate	Decrease

45. In the short run, a decrease in aggregate demand will cause the price level to _____ and real GDP to _____.

    (A) decrease; decrease
    (B) decrease; increase
    (C) remain unchanged; decrease
    (D) increase; decrease
    (E) increase; increase

46. In the long run, an economy in recession can return to full employment once nominal wages _____ and the price level _____.

    (A) decrease; decreases
    (B) decrease; increases
    (C) increase; remains unchanged
    (D) increase; decreases
    (E) increase; increases

47. If the cost of the basket of goods and services the Bureau of Labor Statistics uses to calculate the consumer price index rises from $200 in the base period to $400 in the current period, then the consumer price index

    (A) equals 0.5 in the current period.
    (B) has risen 5 percent from the base to the current period.
    (C) equals 50 in the current period.
    (D) equals 200 in the current period.
    (E) has risen 200 percent.

48. Contractionary monetary policy implies which of the following about the discount rate, the nominal interest rate, and aggregate demand?

	Discount Rate	Nominal Interest Rate	Aggregate Demand
(A)	Decrease	Increase	Decrease
(B)	Increase	Increase	Decrease
(C)	Decrease	Decrease	Decrease
(D)	Increase	Increase	Increase
(E)	Increase	Decrease	Decrease

49. A decline in the demand for money could be the result of

    (A) higher prices.
    (B) more money placed in checking accounts.
    (C) higher returns on bonds.
    (D) fewer credit cards.
    (E) open market purchases by the central bank.

50. An important assumption underlying the idea that an increase in the money supply causes a proportional increase in the price level is that the

    (A) marginal propensity to consume is constant.
    (B) money supply is continuous.
    (C) exchange rate is fixed.
    (D) velocity of money is stable.
    (E) exchange rate is flexible.

51. Which of the following policies is most likely to bring about economic growth in the long run?

    (A) Imposing tariffs to protect domestic industries from foreign competition
    (B) Increasing taxes on savings
    (C) Increasing government spending
    (D) Increasing the money supply
    (E) Promoting improvements in the education of the population

52. An increase in the price level and a decrease in real GDP in the short run could be the result of

    (A) a decrease in aggregate supply.
    (B) a decrease in the money supply.
    (C) an increase in aggregate supply.
    (D) an increase in consumer confidence.
    (E) an increase in the money supply.

53. In 2021, the United States had a trade deficit. Therefore,

    (A) net exports were positive.
    (B) net foreign purchases of U.S. assets were positive.
    (C) America's government spent more than it took in.
    (D) the U.S. balance of trade was positive.
    (E) the government had to make payments to foreign countries of $600 billion.

54. GDP measures a country's level of

    I. production.

    II. stability.

    III. income.

    (A) I only
    (B) II only
    (C) III only
    (D) I and II
    (E) I and III

55. Which of the following lists contains only central bank actions that will decrease interest rates in a banking system that has limited reserves?

    (A) Raise the interest on bank reserves; lower the discount rate; sell bonds.
    (B) Raise the interest on bank reserves; lower the discount rate; buy bonds.
    (C) Raise the interest on bank reserves; raise the discount rate; sell bonds.
    (D) Lower the interest on bank reserves; lower the discount rate; sell bonds.
    (E) Lower the interest on bank reserves; lower the discount rate; buy bonds.

56. Which of the following lists contains only policies that will close an inflationary gap?

    (A) Increase the money supply; run a federal budget deficit.
    (B) Decrease the money supply; run a federal budget deficit.
    (C) Decrease the money supply; increase taxes; reduce government spending.
    (D) Increase the money supply; increase taxes; reduce government spending.
    (E) Decrease the money supply; decrease taxes; reduce government spending.

57. Suppose the exchange rates are 0.5 British pound per dollar, 10 Mexican pesos per dollar, and 100 Chinese yuan per dollar. Further suppose that a Big Mac costs 3 dollars in America, 2 pounds in England, 50 pesos in Mexico, and 200 yuan in China. In which country is a Big Mac most expensive?

    (A) America
    (B) England
    (C) Mexico
    (D) China
    (E) England and China are equally most expensive.

58. Potential GDP will fall, *ceteris paribus*, if

    (A) the unemployment rate rises.
    (B) the retirement age is lowered.
    (C) tariffs protecting domestic jobs are eliminated.
    (D) more immigration is allowed.
    (E) the minimum wage is raised.

59. If nominal GDP = $1,500 and real GDP = $1,000, then the GDP deflator equals

    (A) −$500.
    (B) 66.67.
    (C) 150.
    (D) 200.
    (E) $500.

60. Imagine someone who is not looking for work because he is embarrassed in the interview process when his inability to read is revealed. However, this person would take just about any job that was offered. According to the Bureau of Labor Statistics, this person is

    (A) in the labor force and unemployed.
    (B) in the labor force and employed.
    (C) not in the labor force.
    (D) not in the labor force but counted as unemployed.
    (E) not in the labor force but counted as employed.

Section II—Free-Response Questions

PLANNING TIME—10 MINUTES
WRITING TIME—50 MINUTES
PERCENT OF TOTAL GRADE—$33^{1}/_{3}$

> **DIRECTIONS:** You have 50 minutes to answer all three of the following questions. It is suggested that you spend approximately half your time on the first question and divide the remaining time equally between the next two questions. In answering the questions, you should emphasize the line of reasoning that generated your results; it is not enough to list the results of your analysis. Include correctly labeled diagrams, if useful or required, in explaining your answers. A correctly labeled diagram must have all axes and curves clearly labeled and must show directional changes.
>
> Students should consider doing a "sketch" (main points, quick graph, etc.) of the answer before actually answering the free-response questions. When you use graphs on the free-response questions, label the axes and make direct references to any symbols, e.g., MR, P, output, on the graphs when you respond to questions.

1. Country X is in short-run equilibrium at a level of output below full employment.

    (a) Draw a correctly labeled graph of aggregate demand, short-run aggregate supply, and long-run aggregate supply that depicts the situation in Country X.

    (b) Identify an appropriate fiscal policy to bring about full employment in Country X.

      (i) Show the effects of the fiscal policy on the graph from part (a). Be clear about which curve(s) is/are shifting which way.

      (ii) State how the fiscal policy affects output, the price level, and the level of employment.

    (c) Draw a correctly labeled graph of the money supply and money demand showing the equilibrium nominal interest rate.

      (i) Show the effects of the changes in the price level and output from (b) (ii) above on the graph of the money supply and money demand. Be clear about which curve(s) is/are shifting which way.

      (ii) Explain how the change in the equilibrium nominal interest rate will impact investment expenditures.

2. (a) Draw a correctly labeled diagram of the supply and the demand for the U.S. dollar vis-à-vis the euro. Be sure to label all curves and axes.

    (b) Now suppose U.S. consumers significantly increase their demand for European products.

    (i) Show the effects of the change in U.S. consumer tastes on the graph from part (a). Be clear about which curve(s) is/are shifting which way.

    (ii) State how the value of the dollar will be affected by the change in U.S. consumer tastes.

    (c) U.S. net exports decreased when U.S. consumers demanded more European products. State how U.S. net exports will be affected once the value of the dollar has changed.

    (d) Draw a correctly labeled diagram of the supply and the demand for the euro vis-à-vis the U.S. dollar. Be sure to label all curves and axes.

    (e) Now suppose U.S. consumers significantly increase their demand for European products.

    (i) Show the effects of the change in U.S. consumer tastes on the graph from part (d). Be clear about which curve(s) is/are shifting which way.

    (ii) State how the value of the euro will be affected by the change in U.S. consumer tastes.

    (f) European net exports increased when U.S. consumers demanded more European products. State how European net exports will be affected once the value of the euro has changed.

3. Describe how an open market purchase of $7 million by the Federal Reserve will affect the money supply. Assume bank reserves are limited.

    (a) Assuming a required reserve ratio of 5 percent, what is the maximum amount by which the money supply can change due to the open market operation?

    (b) How will your answer to (a) above change if banks decide to hold reserves over and above the required amount?

    (c) Suppose a large corporation makes the open market purchase of $7 million. Explain how the money supply will be affected in this case.

    (d) Suppose the banking system has ample reserves. Explain how the federal funds rate will be affected by the open market purchase.

Answer Explanations

Multiple-Choice Questions

1. **(E)** (Chapter 16) Aggregate demand shifts right with an increase in the money supply. This will result in a higher price level no matter which aggregate supply curve is used.

2. **(C)** (Chapter 12) Financial transactions are not counted in GDP, but brokerage services are counted.

3. **(B)** (Chapter 2) At point A the economy is producing 60 guns and 3 units of butter. At point B production is 30 guns and 7 units of butter. The 4 additional units of butter come at a cost of 30 guns.

4. **(D)** (Chapter 17) Contractionary monetary policy is a decrease in the money supply. This shifts aggregate demand to the left. A leftward shift in aggregate demand results in a lower level of output and a lower price level. This is seen in the aggregate demand/aggregate supply model.

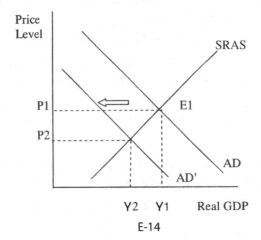

E-14

5. **(B)** (Chapter 14) If the reserve requirement is 5 percent, then the money multiplier is 20 ($= 1/0.05$). Bank reserves fall by $10 million because of the open market operation. The money supply falls by $200 million ($= \$10$ million $\times$ 20).

6. **(C)** (Chapter 2) Since Belgium can produce both wine and cheese with fewer labor hours than France, Belgium has the absolute advantage in both products. The opportunity cost of cheese in Belgium is $60/15 = 4$ wine; the opportunity cost of cheese in France is $80/40 = 2$ wine. France has the lower opportunity cost of producing cheese and therefore the comparative advantage in cheese production.

7. **(B)** (Chapter 16) Since AS > AD at P' inventories will unintentionally increase. In order to lower excess inventories, firms will be forced to lower prices, and the price level falls.

8. **(E)** (Chapter 18) The trick to answering this question correctly is to use a vertical aggregate supply curve. You know to do so because the question asks about the long run. The tax cut shifts AD right to AD'. This results in a higher price level (P_2) but the same level of output (Y_1).

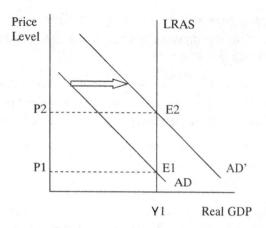

9. **(D)** (Chapter 18) During an economic expansion output, income, and employment increase. This results in fewer households qualifying for income maintenance programs such as food stamps and housing subsidies. Government expenditures fall, but tax collections rise because more income means more tax revenue for the government.

10. **(D)** (Chapter 17) Stagflation is inflation and recession (unemployment) at the same time. The only point shown with higher inflation and unemployment than B is point D. Indeed, stagflation causes the Phillips curve to shift right through a point such as D.

11. **(B)** (Chapter 2) Only changes in technology/productivity or changes in resource availability can shift the production possibilities frontier. Many students choose D here, but notice that a decrease in unemployment will move the economy onto the frontier from a point inside the frontier.

12. **(C)** (Chapter 2) Households own the resources (land, labor, capital) in the economy. They sell them to firms in exchange for wages and profits.

13. **(B)** (Chapter 12) It does not matter where the company has its headquarters. GDP counts production within a nation's borders.

14. **(B)** (Chapter 12) Consider the equation GDP = C + I + G + X. X is exports minus imports. So exports are included in GDP, but imports are subtracted out. G is federal, state, and local government purchases; I is business spending on plant and equipment plus the change in business inventories.

15. **(D)** (Chapter 16) When the price level rises, so does total income in the economy. Therefore, I is not correct. However, foreign incomes do not rise, so foreigners buy less of our products. II is correct. III is a statement of Fisher's Hypothesis and is also correct.

16. **(C)** (Chapter 12) When real GDP rises, it can only be due to more production. Price changes do not affect real GDP. Employment (and therefore unemployment) may or may not change with changes in real GDP.

17. **(C)** (Chapter 18) Increasing government spending and reducing taxes stimulate aggregate demand and fight recessions. Increasing the money supply does this as well, but that is monetary policy.

18. **(B)** (Chapter 14) When the central bank sells securities in the secondary market, it gets paid with checks drawn on bank accounts. Bank reserves fall and the money supply falls by a multiple of the decline in bank reserves.

19. **(A)** (Chapter 19) When interest rates rise in country A, people from country B will want to buy bonds there. People from country B will need to obtain the currency of country A in order to do this. The demand for country A's currency rises. This causes it to appreciate.

384 AP MICROECONOMICS/MACROECONOMICS

20. **(D)** (Chapter 18) If the marginal propensity to consume is 0.75, then the multiplier is 4 (= 1/(1 − 0.75)). The increase in government spending gets multiplied by 4 to determine the overall increase in spending and therefore real GDP. 4 × $100 million = $400 million.

21. **(E)** (Chapter 13) Inflation hurts lenders because they are repaid in dollars that are not worth as much. Some lenders, however, anticipate this and demand higher rates of interest when the loan is made. Borrowers, or debtors, do not mind inflation because they get to repay loans with dollars that are worth less.

22. **(A)** (Chapter 13) Mary is frictionally unemployed. Retired persons presumably are not looking for work, so they are not part of the labor force. People who work part-time are counted as employed even if they would like to work full-time.

23. **(C)** (Chapter 14) The economy is experiencing an extremely high production level since it is in short-run equilibrium to the right of potential, or long-run, real GDP. In the absence of government policies to correct the situation, the SRAS curve will shift to the left. Prices are expected to be higher in the future, and so aggregate supply decreases right now. The short-run aggregate supply curve shifts left until a new equilibrium is reached at potential, or long-run, aggregate supply.

24. **(B)** (Chapter 12) The standard of living depends on real GDP per capita. Country X has twice the output per person as country Y.

25. **(D)** (Chapter 18) This is a balanced-budget move—government spending is increasing and tax collections are increasing by the same amount. It is not necessary to know the MPC. In this situation the net impact on real GDP is a change equivalent to the change in government spending.

26. **(B)** (Chapter 16) A technological advance shifts the aggregate supply curve to the right.

27. **(A)** (Chapter 16) Less investment implies less plant and equipment in the future. That reduces economic growth, whereas choices B through E all enhance growth.

28. **(C)** (Chapter 14) Currency in the vaults of depository institutions is not counted as part of the money supply. However, if you withdraw $100 from your checking account, M1 is unaffected. When the money comes out of the bank's vault and goes into your pocket, that in itself raises the money supply by $100—but your checking account went down by $100 because of the withdrawal. It's a wash.

29. **(A)** (Chapter 15) The velocity of money supply and the quantity of output must be constant in the equation of exchange or else, by algebra, a change in the money supply will not have a proportional effect on output in the equation of exchange.

30. **(E)** (Chapter 19) The more open an economy, the less effective monetary policy will be. Consider an increase in the money supply. This will raise real GDP and prices in the short run. However, if the economy is open, then the increase in real GDP will boost incomes and therefore importation (which reduces real GDP somewhat), and the increase in prices will reduce exports (which also reduces real GDP somewhat).

31. **(E)** (Chapter 13) The consumer price index will not be affected by the increase in the price of the forklifts because forklifts are an industrial product, not a consumer product. The GDP deflator is not affected because import prices are ignored by the deflator.

32. **(B)** (Chapter 15) When prices rise, people and firms want more money in their wallets and checking accounts in order to conduct their transactions.

33. **(A)** (Chapter 19) If income in America falls relative to the rest of the world, then Americans' demand for imports will decrease. Therefore, the supply of dollars will decrease relative to the demand for dollars. In turn, the value of the dollar increases.

34. **(C)** (Chapter 14) If the central bank increases bank reserves but banks decide to simply hold onto the new reserves, then the money expansion process will be curtailed. The process depends on banks using their new reserves to make loans out or buy investments.

35. **(D)** (Chapter 18) The government must borrow to finance the federal deficit, and this raises the demand for loanable funds. The result will be an increase in the real interest rate and decrease in investment spending. This chain of events is known as crowding out.

36. **(C)** (Chapter 13) Fisher's Hypothesis states that the nominal interest rate equals the real interest rate plus expected inflation.

37. **(A)** (Chapter 16) If the price level in the economy is below the equilibrium price level, then the quantity of products demanded will exceed the quantity supplied. There will be a shortage, and shortages drive prices up.

38. **(A)** (Chapter 12) Products get counted in GDP in the period they are produced. If they are produced but not sold, then they are in inventory. The change in inventories is part of GDP. Inventory changes are included in investment.

39. **(B)** (Chapter 17) Reducing taxes is a stimulatory fiscal policy, and open market purchases are expansionary monetary policy.

40. **(D)** (Chapter 18) The multiplier is $1/(1 - \text{MPC})$. Therefore, the higher the MPC, the higher the multiplier. With a higher multiplier, changes in government spending will have more impact on real GDP.

41. **(C)** (Chapter 12)

Calculating GDP for 2005

Production	Price	Value
10 Pizzas	$17	$170
30 Sodas	$3	$90
	GDP =	$260

Calculating real GDP for 2005

Production	Price	Value
10 Pizzas	$10	$100
30 Sodas	$1	$30
	Real GDP =	$130

Calculating the GDP deflator for 2005

$$260/130 \times 100 = 200$$

42. **(C)** (Chapter 16) Aggregate demand must decrease for real GDP and the price level to fall. A decline in investment causes aggregate demand to decrease.

43. **(B)** (Chapter 16) Shifts such as these are the result of a technological advance or an increase in resources that benefit only one of the two industries. If the economy produced only guns, then an increase in the number of cows would not help increase production.

44. **(E)** (Chapter 19) Higher real interest rates attract foreign investors. These investors demand the nation's currency, which in turn appreciates its value. This makes domestic products more expensive to foreigners and foreign products less expensive to domestic citizens. Thus, net exports decrease.

45. **(A)** (Chapter 16) This can only be the result of aggregate demand shifting left—a lack of demand or spending.

46. **(A)** (Chapter 16) In the long run, a recession causes wages and prices to fall. The falling prices stimulate demand for products, while the falling wages stimulate demand for labor. This pickup in demand ends the recession and brings about full employment.

47. **(D)** (Chapter 13)

$$\text{CPI} = \frac{\text{Total Cost This Period}}{\text{Total Cost Base Period}} \times 100 = \frac{400}{200} \times 100 = 200$$

48. **(B)** (Chapter 17) Contractionary monetary policy means decreasing the money supply. The Fed would increase the discount rate, which results in a higher nominal interest rate. Higher interest rates discourage spending, which decreases aggregate demand.

49. **(C)** (Chapter 15) When the return on bonds and other assets rises, people and firms want to hold less money in their wallets and checking accounts and, instead, put the money into these assets with high returns.

50. **(D)** (Chapter 15) According to the equation of exchange, this would not be true if the velocity of money fluctuated.

51. **(E)** (Chapter 16) Economic growth is stimulated by investment in resources. Education enhances one of the most important resources in the economy—labor.

52. **(A)** (Chapter 16) This is stagflation, and it is caused by decreases in short-run and/or long-run aggregate supply. Declines in aggregate supply are the result of reduced resource availability or decreases in productivity.

53. **(B)** (Chapter 19) A trade deficit means a country's imports exceed its exports. In this case, a country is consuming more than it is producing.

54. **(E)** (Chapter 12) The income and expenditure approaches to calculating GDP highlight the fact that GDP measures not only production but income as well.

55. **(E)** (Chapter 17) The four tools at a central bank's disposal for decreasing interest rates are lowering reserve requirements, lowering the discount rate, buying bonds on the open market, and decreasing the interest rate paid on bank reserves.

56. **(C)** (Chapters 17 and 18) Aggregate demand needs to be decreased to close an inflationary gap. This can be accomplished with contractionary monetary policy (decreasing the money supply) or contractionary fiscal policy (increasing taxes or reducing government spending).

57. **(C)** (Chapter 19) One way to solve this problem is to put all the different prices in dollar terms:

Country	$ Price of a Big Mac
America	$3
England	2 pounds ÷ 0.5 = $4
Mexico	50 pesos ÷ 10 = $5
China	200 yuan ÷ 100 = $2

The Mexican Big Mac costs 50 pesos, which translates into $5. This is the most expensive Big Mac.

58. **(B)** (Chapter 19) Potential GDP is how much could be produced using all resources fully and efficiently. In order for potential GDP to fall, resources must become less available or inefficiencies must be introduced into the production process. Lowering the retirement age decreases the amount of labor available. This is different than an increase in the unemployment rate. When that happens, the labor is still available, only it is not being used.

59. **(C)** (Chapter 13) The GDP deflator equals (nominal GDP/real GDP) × 100. In this case, ($1,500/$1,000) × 100 = 150.

60. **(C)** (Chapter 13) People like this are neither employed nor unemployed according to the Bureau of Labor Statistics because they are not counted as part of the labor force. To be in the labor force, one must be actively seeking employment or employed.

Free-Response Questions

1. (a)

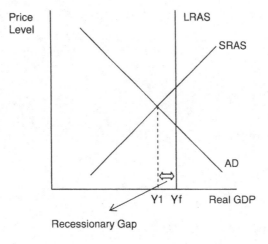

(b) A reduction in corporate taxes, a reduction in income taxes, or an increase in government spending are all appropriate. An increase in the federal deficit is also an acceptable response.

  (i) Aggregate demand shifts to the right.

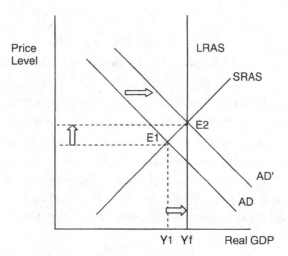

  (ii) This would cause the equilibrium price level and the equilibrium level of real GDP to increase. Since output is increasing, employment will increase as well.

(c)

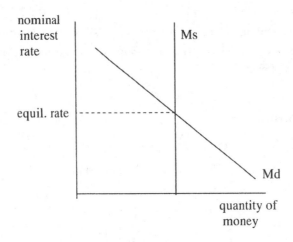

(i)

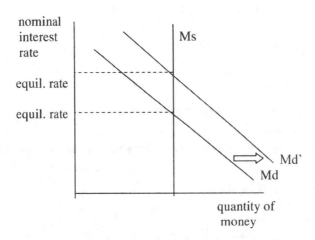

(ii) The increase in the equilibrium price level serves to increase the demand for money, as does the increase in the level of output. The increased demand for money, in turn, raises the nominal rate of interest. Finally, higher nominal interest rates decrease investment expenditures since plant and equipment expenditures are often financed with borrowed funds.

(iii) The increased nominal rate of interest will impact the economy in a variety of ways: (1) Higher interest rates will encourage saving and reduce consumption; (2) investment will fall; and (3) higher interest rates will increase the value of the dollar and thereby lower net exports. All in all, higher interest rates tend to reduce aggregate demand and thus reduce the impact of the initial tax cut. The tendency of interest rates to rise with expansionary fiscal policy and consequently reduce the fiscal thrust is called "crowding out."

2. (a)

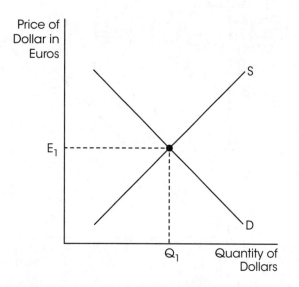

(b)

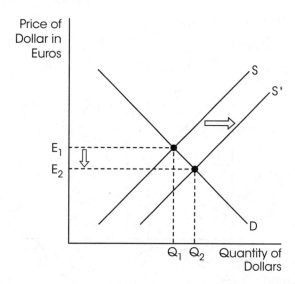

    (i)   The supply of dollars increases in the international currency market since U.S. consumers must supply dollars to obtain euros in order to get the European goods they demand.

    (ii) The dollar depreciates to E_2 from E_1.

(c) After the dollar loses value, European products will appear more expensive to Americans, so U.S. imports will decrease. U.S. products will appear less expensive to Europeans, so U.S. exports will increase. Net exports will increase, perhaps back to their original level before the change in U.S. consumer preferences.

(d)

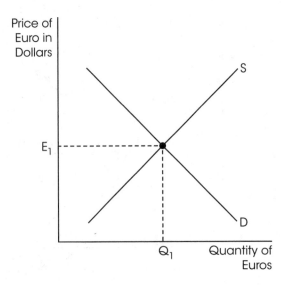

(e)

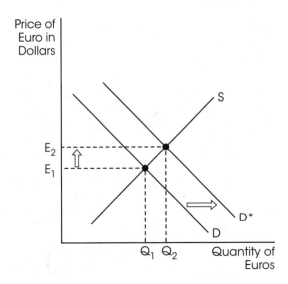

(i)   The demand for euros increases in the international currency market since U.S. consumers must acquire euros to obtain the European goods they demand.

(ii) The euro appreciates to E_2 from E_1.

(f)   After the euro gains value, European products will appear more expensive to Americans, so European exports will decrease. U.S. products will appear less expensive to Europeans, so European imports will increase. Net exports will decrease, perhaps back to their original level before the change in U.S. consumer preferences.

3. An open market purchase of $7 million by the Federal Reserve Bank will serve to increase the money supply by more than $7 million. The purchase itself puts $7 million in new reserves into the banking system. Banks then make loans or buy investments with these additional reserves. The loans and investments generate new deposits, which are additions to the money supply.

(a) When the reserve ratio is 5 percent, the money multiplier is 20 (= 1/0.05). This implies that any change in bank reserves could possibly be magnified 20 times. Therefore, the open market purchase of $7 million could lead to a $140 million (= $7 million × 20) increase in M1.

(b) The $140 million figure is based on the assumption that banks use their additional reserves as much as possible to make loans or buy investments. If banks hold reserves over and above the requirements, then the money expansion process will be diminished. The money supply will expand by less than $140 million if banks hold reserves above the required amount.

(c) The money supply is unaffected in this case. The corporation's bank account declines by $7 million while the seller's account rises by the same amount. No new reserves are added to the system, so the money supply does not change.

(d) An open market purchase increases the reserves of the banking system and the monetary base. However, when banks are flush with reserves, the open market purchase does not affect the federal funds rate since banks already have enough reserves. Giving them more reserves does not induce them to make loans, even to other banks, at lower rates.

Index